MAN, MYTH, and MONUMENT

Mycenaean excavations at the foot of the Acropolis in modern Athens come to a forced halt at the railroad tracks.

MAN, MYTH, and MONUMENT

by MARIANNE NICHOLS

WILLIAM MORROW AND COMPANY, INC.
NEW YORK
1975

DF
220
N 45

Grateful acknowledgment is made for permission to quote from the following:

Book III, lines 388-394 and 398-404, from *The Odyssey* by Homer; translated by Robert Fitzgerald. Copyright © 1961 by Robert Fitzgerald. Reprinted by permission of Doubleday & Company, Inc. Tabulations on pages 183-184 from *From the Silent Earth* by Joseph Alsop. Copyright © 1962, 1964 by Joseph Alsop. Reprinted by permission of Harper & Row, Publishers, Inc., and Martin Secker & Warburg Ltd. Pages 106-107 and 52-66 from *Greece Before Homer* by John Forsdyke, published by Max Parish, London. Reprinted by permission of MacDonald and Jane's Publishers. Volume 5, 11.5.3, pages 235-237, from *The Geography of Strabo*, translated by Horace Leonard Jones, 1923. Reprinted by permission of Harvard University Press. "The Libation Bearers," by Aeschylus, translated by Richmond Lattimore in *Aeschylus, the Complete Greek Tragedies,* Volume I, edited by David Grene and Richmond Lattimore. Copyright © 1942, 1953, 1956, 1960 by the University of Chicago. Reprinted by the University of Chicago Press. Pages 86 and 95-98 from "The Shaft Graves," in *Greece in the Bronze Age*, by Emily Vermeule. Copyright © 1964, 1972 by the University of Chicago. Reprinted by permission of the University of Chicago Press. Book XI, page 251, lines 633-636, of *The Iliad* by Homer, translated by Richmond Lattimore. Copyright © 1951 by the University of Chicago. Reprinted by permission of the University of Chicago Press. Page 82, lines 315 ff, from *The Voyage of Argo* by Apollonius of Rhodes, translated by E. V. Rieu, 2nd edition, 1971. Copyright © 1959, 1971 by E. V. Rieu. Reprinted by permission of Penguin Books Ltd. Book IX of *Guide to Greece* by Pausanias, Volume I, translated by Peter, S J (1971). Copyright © by Peter Levi, 1971. Reprinted by permission of Penguin Books Ltd. Pages 142-143 (IX: 103 ff) from *The Odyssey* by Homer, translated by E. V. Rieu, 1946. Copyright © 1946 by E. V. Rieu. Reprinted by permission of Penguin Books Ltd.

Illustration #42, "Mourning Women on a larnake at Tanagra," reproduced with special permission of the excavator, Theodore G. Spyropoulos.

Chronology of Crete and Thebes, found on pages 52-53, reprinted by permission of Schocken Books, Inc., and Sidgwick & Jackson Ltd., Publishers, from *Mead and Wine* by Jean Zafiropulo. Copyright © 1964 by Jean Zafiropulo; translation copyright © 1966 by Sidgwick & Jackson Ltd.

Printed in the United States of America.

1 2 3 4 5 79 78 77 76 75

Library of Congress Cataloging in Publication Data

Nichols, Marianne
  Man, myth, and monument.

  Bibliography: p.
  1. Classical antiquities. 2. Mythology, Classical.
  3. Excavations (Archaeology)—Greece, Modern.
  I. Title.
  DF220.N45   938   75-11971
  ISBN 0-688-02943-4

Book design by Helen Roberts

For Peter

Acknowledgments

It is a pleasure to be able to thank the many colleagues and friends who helped me with this book. I especially thank Professor Bluma Trell for supporting its original idea, and Professor Larissa Bonfante Warren for many hours of intelligent counseling. I am indebted to the Institute for Hellenic Studies at Athens for helpful and pleasant talks during my visit to Crete; to Professor Tzavella-Evjen for inviting me to her excavation at Lithares and offering many valuable comments about the settlement. One conversation with Mary Aiken Littauer about the early history of the horse was more enlightening than many printed studies on the subject. So, too, brief talks with Professors Edith Porada and Ellen Davis made hard-to-find scholarly materials readily available to me. Miss Rouli Tatki lightened my research tasks considerably, and Miss Adele Pilewicz rescued me from hours of typing. To all of them, to many others, and to my patient editor, John Willey, I am grateful.

Contents

Acknowledgments vii
I   From Myth to History 1
II The Rape of Europa: Migrations
    and Metamorphoses 13
III Cadmos Founds Thebes 32
IV Horsemen and Centaurs 59
V   The Age of Perseus 87
VI Theseus and the Mycenaeans at Knossos 118
VII Heracles, Vassal to Mycenae 146
VIII Agamemnon's World 174
IX Jason, Argonaut and Merchant Prince 206
X   The *Odyssey*, Folktale and Travelogue 248
XI Odysseus, The Last Mycenaean 280
    Appendix I Chronology 318
    Appendix II The Parian Chronicle 319
    Select Bibliography 325
    Index 331

List of Maps

MAPS DRAWN BY DYNO LOWENSTEIN

1. The Cadmeia at Thebes   43
2. The Mycenaean World   88-89
3. The Network of Mycenaean Drainage Canals and Tunnels at Lake Copais   211
4. Continental Trade Routes in the First and Second Millennia. Adapted from map in J. R. Bacon's *Voyage of the Argonauts*, by permission of Methuen & Co. Ltd.   223
5. The Black Sea area according to geographers of the Archaic Age and including names in the *Argonautica*   235
6. The Mediterranean World   250-251
7. The Ionian Islands   277

List of Illustrations

All photographs not otherwise credited are the property of the author. Drawings executed by Lisa Kayne.

Mycenaean excavations at the foot of the Acropolis in modern Athens   *frontispiece*

1. Table of phonetic values in Linear A and B. Adapted from artwork in *Mycenaeans and Minoans* by L. R. Palmer, 1963, with permission of Faber and Faber Ltd., Publishers.   7
2. Linear B tablet An 15 = 129 from Pylos. *Photo:* University of Cincinnati.   8
3. Europa and the Bull. *Photo:* Anderson-Art Reference Bureau.   15
4. "Town House" tiles from Knossos.   24
5. Leda and the Swan. Acropolis Museum at Athens.   29
6. Limestone sarcophagus, seventh century B.C. National Archaeological Museum, Athens.   39
7. Theban stirrup jar. Adapted from artwork in *Mycenaeans and Minoans* by L. R. Palmer, 1963, with permission of Faber and Faber Ltd., Publishers.   47
8. Babylonian cylinder seal. *Photo:* courtesy of Prof. Edith Porada.   49
9. A room in the settlement at Lithares.   62
10. Part of the settlement at Lerna.   65
11. Stele from Grave Circle A at Mycenae. *Photo:* Alison Frantz.   73
12. Heracles killing the centaur Nessos; detail on proto-Attic amphora. National Museum of Athens. *Photo:* Alinari.   75
13. Horse burial at Marathon. *Photo:* Tombazi.   78
14. Poseidon. National Archaeological Museum, Athens.   81
15. Poseidon's temple at Sounion.   82
16. The Gorgon Medusa with Pegasus. Syracuse National Museum. Reproduced with the permission of Gallimard.   98
17. Sketch restoration of Mycenae's Grave Circle. Reproduced with the permission of Princeton University Press.   100
18. Pelops and Hippodameia. Olympia Museum.   106
19. Gemstone from Mycenae.   112
20. The "Minoan" Vapheio Cup. *Photo:* Hirmer Fotoarchiv   116
21. Gemstone found at Mycenae.   117
22. Theseus discovers the weapons of Aegeus. *Photo:* Reproduced by the Trustees of the British Museum.   121
23. Theseus and companions; detail, François vase. Archaeological Museum, Florence. *Photo:* Hirmer Fotoarchiv.   122
24. Designs from Minoan pottery.   129
25. Bull Leapers fresco from Knossos. Herakleion Museum. *Photo:* Alison Frantz.   136
26. Bull leaper at Landés. *Photo:* courtesy of Prof. L. B. Warren.   138
27. Mosaic of Theseus in the Labyrinth. *Photo:* Kunsthistorisches Museum, Vienna.   140
28. Detail of Illustration 27.   140
29. Bull Fresco wall at Knossos.   142
30. Floor plan of domestic wing at Knossos.   144
31. Aerial view of Tiryns. *Photo:* Deutsches Archaeologisches Institut, Athens.   149
32. Heracles brings Cerberus to Eurystheus; the Caeretan hydria. Louvre. *Photo:* Alinari.   150
33. Ring from Tiryns. *Photo:* Hirmer Fotoarchiv.   153
34. The Lion Gate at Mycenae. *Photo:* Alison Frantz.   166
35. Reconstruction of the facade of the Treasury of Atreus. *Photo:* British Museum.   170

36. Detail drawing of the design in Illustration 35.   170

37. Aerial view of Mycenae. From George E. Mylonas, *Mycenae and the Mycenaean Age* (copyright © 1966 by Princeton University Press), Plate 8a. Reprinted by permission of Princeton University Press.   171

38. The Trojan Horse on Wheels. *Photo:* Deutsches Archaeologisches Institut, Athens.   178

39. The Argive principalities. Copyright © 1959 by The Regents of the University of California; reprinted by permission of the University of California Press.   181

40. The underground cistern at Mycenae. From George E. Mylonos, *Mycenae and the Mycenaean Age* (copyright © 1966 by Princeton University Press), Plate 39. Reprinted by permission of Princeton University Press.   186

41. Aegisthus stabbing Agamemnon. Drawn from a fifth-century vase painting.   187

42. Mourning women on a larnake at Tanagra.   188

43. Gold face mask. National Museum, Athens.   190

44. Hagia Triada sarcophagus. Herakleion Museum. *Photo:* Alison Frantz.   191

45. Amazon on horseback, Vatican Museum. *Photo:* Alinari.   237

46. Jason and the dragon of Colchis, Vatican Museum. *Photo*: Alinari.   239

47. Odysseus blinding the Cyclops. Detail of a painted vase at Eleusis. *Photo:* Deutsches Archaeologisches Institut, Athens.   262

48. Odysseus clinging to the belly of a sheep. Drawn from a fifth-century vase painting.   262

49. Horse frieze at Pylos. From *The Palace of Nestor at Pylos in Western Messenia,* ed. by Carl W. Blegen and Marion Rawson (copyright © 1966 by Princeton University Press), Vol. II—The Frescoes by Mabel L. Lang (copyright © 1969 by Princeton University Press. Published for the University of Cincinnati. Reprinted by permission of Princeton University Press and the University of Cincinnati.   285

50. Bathtub in the palace at Pylos. From *The Palace of Nestor at Pylos in Western Messenia,* by Carl W. Blegen and Marion Rawson (copyright © 1966 by Princeton University Press), Vol. I, part 2, Plate 139 (photographed by Alison Frantz), "Room 43: Larnax Set in Stuccoed Base. From Northeast. 1955." Published for the University of Cincinnati. Reprinted by permission of Princeton University and the University of Cincinnati.   286

51. Floor plan of the palace at Pylos. From *The Palace of Nestor at Pylos in Western Messenia,* by Carl W. Blegen and Marion Rawson (copyright © 1966 by Princeton University Press), Vol. I, part 1. Published for the University of Cincinnati. Reprinted by permission of Princeton University Press and the University of Cincinnati.   287

52. Linear B tablet from Knossos. Adapted from artwork in *Mycenaeans and Minoans* by L. R. Palmer, 1963, with permission of Faber and Faber Ltd., Publishers.   294

53. Athena. Acropolis Museum, Athens.   310

I

From Myth to History

No one today is likely to confuse Greek myth with Greek history. Although both are concerned with the intellectual heritage of the race, the distinction between them is sharp. A myth is essentially a story. Its characters may be divinities or demons, heroes or slaves; its plots may be beautiful or terrifying; but these are conceived of imaginatively, and fantasy may serve their truth. A history is essentially a record. Whereas men, their gods, and their devils enact its plots, these are conceived of from the facts about men's experience, and fantasy is usually indulged at the expense of truth. Mythmaking is an artistic endeavor to capture a common experience, or understanding, or idea, or activity in pictographs and symbols: its form is nonliterate and often irrational. Making history is an endeavor to capture the past in accounts that are expository and sequential: its form, taken to mean its discipline, is rational and written.

To the Greeks before the Classical Age, nevertheless, myth *was* history—the evidence of an ancient epoch, glorious in its heroes and splendid in its wealth. Myth to them had no connotation of unreality, as the adjective *mythical* has in modern English. If sometimes a myth's characters and events were difficult to understand, that was merely because its method of telling a story was unfamiliar and the key to the method had been lost. There was, moreover, no reason to believe that the life lived in those distant times should be recognizable in all its features, so it did not follow that what was different was untrue. Then, too, myths had been told and retold over hundreds of years, acquiring with each recital the shape of the storyteller's inspiration. When through the lapse of time an original meaning was forgotten, a new meaning was invented to satisfy contemporary curiosity. The habit of mind is familiar to us in changing interpretations of mythic art and poetry: explanations may vary with fashions in criticism, but the work of art keeps the myth itself alive.

So confident were the Greeks that a golden era had existed long before their own that chroniclers and logographers composed genealogies precisely in order to link mythic and real times, to join legendary men to known ones. In their attempts to make sense of the long period of obscurity between the seventh century B.C., in which many were composed, and a brilliantly envisioned Age of Heroes, such genealogies sometimes condensed the millennium between c. 650 B.C. to c. 1500 B.C. into a few centuries, or they expanded certain segments of that time to unconscionable lengths. Still, they were read as absolute chronologies and gave the Greeks an idea of their history as fundamental to them as the idea of the twelve tribes of Israel was to the Hebrews. Sometimes, counting backward by generations of twenty-five or thirty years each brought a known family's line to the end of the eighth century, when Greece had begun to awaken from the long cultural sleep that followed the Dorian invasions. Often folk memory could be called upon to establish the lineage of a recent king back to approximately that same point in time, the eighth century. At that gateway to the mysterious and illiterate Dark Ages, both memory and counting faltered, and therefore the one or two dates that had been fixed by the Greek oral tradition were called upon for aid. The fall of Troy after a ten-year-long siege was thought to have occurred in 1075 B.C. The quasi-mythical Dorian invasions that ushered in the Dark Ages were presumed to have come shortly thereafter. It followed, then, that the lives of the sons and grandsons of the Trojan War's heroes had spanned the lost years between Troy's fall and Greece's reawakening; and so these descendants of the great were enlisted into family trees proudly and surely. Just as frequently, the most famous Trojan kings, their fathers, and their grandfathers extended a genealogy backward before 1075 to a hypothetical founding of the dynasty. Since, finally, heroes themselves traced their descent from the gods and goddesses who once roamed the earth, to many a contemporary king's heroic ancestry was added the supreme luster of a divine origin. The wondrous events memorialized in myth, then, were closely associated with the decades both preceding and following the Trojan War. The upper limit of that marvelous era could not be imagined, although the Parian Chronicle, a list of mythical kings, placed it with amazing near-accuracy in the sixteenth century B.C. Accurate, too, in a similarly general way was the belief that Troy's fall in the eleventh century had marked the culmination of an historical age that was followed by internal wars, dislocations, and a civilization's collapse.

So strong was the will to unify present and past that the Greeks sometimes recreated their golden age on chance similarities between the names of men and countries, like Pelops and Peloponnesos, or on purely fortuitous interpretations of heroic exploits. At other times, they legitimized ancestral remembrances of immigrations and sieges, of travels and natural disasters, of forms of worship and of play, of building techniques and burial practices simply by incorporating references to these into often told heroic sagas. By the seventh century myth had become so realistic that the famous impostors Dares and Dictys could offer "eyewitness" accounts of the Trojan War with finely scaled portraits of some of its leading characters. Dares, a Phrygian, claimed to have been an observer on the Trojan side; Dictys called himself a companion of the Minoan warrior-king Idomeneus. On their firsthand authority, Helen, the beautiful wife of Menelaos kidnapped by Paris, "was as handsome as her fair brothers, simpleminded, charming, with very fine legs, a mole between her eyebrows, and a tiny mouth." The great lord Nestor, they said, "was tall, broad, fair, with a long hooked nose. . . ."

Interpolated detail made the tales not only more believable, it made them more international. To every place that a hero was said to have visited, a body of particularities was attached about custom, dress, language, and the like. Even after the first stirrings of rationalism and science between the fifth and the first centuries, the general authenticity of the Greek oral tradition could not be cast aside completely. A growing consciousness of their own national identity made the Greeks secure enough to assign countries of origin to other Mediterranean peoples on the basis of their resemblance to incidents, features, or men in myth. Plato, although skeptical about some divine mythology, considered the story of Deucalion's flood seriously enough to decide it was chiefly a Greek phenomenon. Aristotle, whose systems of logic and natural philosophy were unparalleled until the nineteenth century, said that Italus, the king of the Oenotrians (?),* lent his name to Italy. Alexandrian scholars related the beginnings of peoples everywhere to Greek saga: the Illyrians descended from a son of Polyphemus; the Colchians on the Black Sea from Egypt. A tree native to Egypt but called *persea* must have been brought there by Perseus.

Attempts like these to understand the common past of mankind were biased by an essentially Hellenocentric world view and flawed by a methodology that could not accommodate so grand an aim. Still, it was only long after the science of history came of age in the western world that myth became suspect, a blend of folktale and fancy dismissed by all but poets and painters as charming but fictitious. And it was a still longer time before anthropologists began to examine myths seriously for their vestiges of ancient cult and ritual, or for expressions of a people's awareness of themselves as a cultural entity. Psychologists began to read them as archetypal stories that evoked universal human responses; scholars of religion looked for theological systems. The gap between myth and history, opened by a spirit of objective inquiry, was widened further by the specialized investigations of ethnographers, demographers, philologists, and other scholars. Artists continued to find in myth a rich source of subject and theme, and myth came to be many things. But it was not history.

Then, just before the turn of this century, the archaeologist's spade in the hands of the gifted amateur Heinrich Schliemann converted the mythical city of Troy into a visible, measurable reality. Or, more accurately, into several realities; for as later excavations more scientific than Schliemann's proved, Troy had been not one but several cities. Each had been built on the remains of a previous one, the earliest dating to the fourth millennium, the latest to the first. This overwhelming discovery of a continuous civilization from the Neolithic or Stone Age to just before the dark Iron Age was only the first in a series that revolutionized the chronology of the Aegean. Within a few years, Sir Arthur Evans revealed that a

---

* Here, as in succeeding pages, the parenthetic question mark indicates an unsolved riddle.

splendid and complex culture had flourished at Knossos on Crete; Schliemann and then other archaeologists after him excavated still another important center at Mycenae on the Greek mainland. These three roughly contemporary sites seemed to suggest the geographical boundaries of hitherto unknown Aegean cultures. The terms Mycenaean and Minoan were coined to refer to their remains on the mainland and Crete respectively; those at Troy were for a time simply referred to as Trojan.

As other cities and towns were discovered, it became apparent that the precious metals of their time were copper and tin. Weapons, tools, art, and artefacts forged in bronze became characteristic features at a rapidly increasing number of sites dating to the same period. The most inclusive name for the entire period, the Bronze Age, came naturally then from its most typical physical remains rather than from its still uncertain geographical scope. Continuing study brought more specific information to the new chronology. Even before sophisticated (and still controversial) dating methods like carbon 14 came to be used, it was approximated that the bronze-using population had appeared in the Aegean sometime between the twentieth and the sixteenth centuries, had reached full expression of its powers by the thirteenth century, and then had disappeared in the eleventh. Still more pertinently, the material evidence of the Bronze Age on the mainland was dated largely to the second half of the second millennium—the very years that the ancient Greek chroniclers had peopled with mythic heroes.

Between 1900 and 1935, archaeology made more, and more technologically expert, studies of the Aegean's buried treasures. As a growing number of once legendary cities and monuments began to yield up their reality to the excavator's tools, it began to seem as though Schliemann's initial transmutation of the gold of myth into the bronze of actuality was being repeated regularly. And, since the homes of mythic heroes—Hector at Troy, Theseus at Knossos, Agamemnon at Mycenae—were being brought out of poetic obscurity into the scientists' study, many observers seized upon myth and the oral tradition as a potential record of Bronze Age history. Others remained skeptical of the likelihood that an oral tradition could have preserved reliable facts for over two millennia. They saw the newly found Mycenaean citadels as floating islands in a sea of attractive speculations. Buildings, art, and artefacts were, after all, only mute testimonies to a dead civilization about which there were more questions than answers. How were these cities organized? What was their relationship to one another? What sort of economy sustained them? Still more fundamental, what people inhabited these sites? What language did they speak, and why had they vanished? For although their tombs and palaces had been built on Greek lands, their kinship to the later Greeks was far from certain. Several Aegean races, like the Phoenicians and the Hittites, had built settlements outside their own immediate borders, had flowered, and had disappeared between the Neolithic and Dark ages. Anatolians and other Asiatics had migrated and colonized many Aegean outposts and islands; Cycladic peoples had crisscrossed their oceanic geography and had established villages dating to high antiquity. The identity of the builders and inhabitants on the mainland, on Crete, and at Troy therefore was highly conjectural.

A huge obstacle to interpreting Mycenaeans and Minoans was removed in 1952 by the work of the late English cryptographer Michael Ventris. By a fortuitous quirk of fate, Ventris, a fourteen-year-old student at the time, was present at the fiftieth-anniversary celebration in London of the founding of the British School of Archaeology at Athens and heard Sir Arthur Evans lecture on his excavations at Knossos. As Evans talked about his find of clay tablets written in a strange language that he had named Linear A, Ventris became fascinated by the mysterious tablets and vowed he would someday decipher them. Studies in architecture, and later his service as a navigator in the Royal Air Force during World War II, did nothing to dissuade him from that challenge. Over the years Ventris added to his already developed interest in ancient scripts a considerable knowledge of languages ancient and modern, carrying on a correspondence with experts in the field on abstruse linguistic puzzles even while maintaining a successful practice as an architect. In the late 1940's, when digs that had been interrupted by the war were resumed, more clay tablets were found on both Crete and the mainland. It became increasingly apparent that two different but related languages had been used by the mysterious tablet writers: a Linear A that had been limited to Crete, and a scripturally more sophisticated Linear B that appeared at both Knossos and mainland sites (see Illus. 1). By 1952 there were a sufficient number of Linear B samples to make a concerted study of the language possible. Ventris, in an effort that was hailed as the most consequential intellectual achievement of our age,

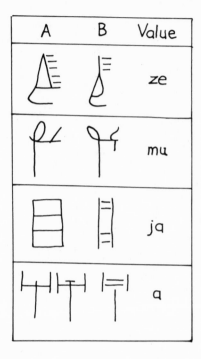

A	B	Value

1. Some characters in Linear A and B scripts closely resemble each other. The right-hand column gives Greek phonetic values.

deciphered Linear B and pronounced it to be Greek. The tablets were incontestable proof that the Mycenaeans were the ancestors of the later Greeks. Still more revolutionary, the Mycenaeans had been literate, unlike their immediate descendants in the tenth through the seventh centuries. Many clues to the workaday organization of some key Bronze Age sites are contained in the tablets' inventories of goods, population counts, and business transactions. Information about commercial relations between cities, social class structures, and the machinery of warfare is being pieced together from the ongoing and painstaking work of decoding. The combined evidence from the tablets, from monuments, and from art is making the Bronze Age more accessible than Schliemann could have dreamed possible. (See Illus. 2.)

Can one say, then, for more scientific reasons than those held by the early Greeks, that the gap between history and myth is closed? Hardly. The two terms are as distinct as ever, and it is, at the very least, etymological nonsense to equate them. It is, however, now possible to pose a more significant question: Is there some

2. A Linear B tablet from Pylos.

interrelatedness between myth, monument, and history? Many think yes.

Although their information is fragmented and inconclusive, both the tablets and the monuments have vindicated myth and the oral tradition in so many details that it is no longer possible to discount these as mere poetry. To isolate only one or two of the most striking examples: Some of the names of mythical gods are repeated on the Linear B tablets in contexts that make it clear that the gods were part of a living Mycenaean religion. The products of bronzesmiths and weapons makers are recorded on the tablets in such a way as to prove that Hector, Agamemnon, and other Homeric warriors carried some Mycenaean armor and equipment to Troy. As for the relation of monument to myth, the noted scholar of Greek religion Martin Nilsson observed as early as 1936 that, whereas most myths of other races are free-floating stories without time or place, Greek myths are very often localized, many of them centering on Mycenaean cities. Greek myths, therefore, must have existed in Mycenaean times, some as a Mycenaean heritage, others created by the Mycenaeans to describe, or to explain, or simply to recount their lives. Only a very few representations of myth have been found in Mycenaean arts, and there is no way of knowing what these representations may have meant to their makers. They are, nevertheless, extraordinary proofs that some mythic personalities known to us were also known to the Mycenaeans. In a beehive tomb at Dendra two plaques made of blue glass paste depict figures that have been identified as Europa and as Bellerophon with the Chimera. In a grave at Prosymna there are portrayals of some centaurs. It is the specialist's concern to distinguish between myths that the Mycenaeans inherited and myths that they created. More important to us are: 1) the high probability that both types contain kernels of reality, no matter how overembroidered with fictitious detail they may be; and 2) that both types ultimately found their way into the oral tradition that Hesiod and Homer preserved and passed down to us in its earliest surviving form.

What distortions the myths were subjected to during the eons of their transmission between the Bronze Age and Homer's is probably unknowable. Nor can one know all the transformations through which he put the material he received. Still, both the relation of Greek myths to the everyday lives of the Mycenaeans and their deliberate reworkings by Hesiod and Homer are probably responsible for their characteristic sensibleness and lucidity. Compared to the phantasmagorical nature of other mythologies, Greek myth seems to have been adulterated by logic. Its characters are either anthropomorphic or completely humanized rather than fabulous and dreamlike; its events and episodes more reasonable than extravagant. Zeus is a paternalistic ruler and a philandering husband; Hera is a vain mother and a jealous wife. Apollo and Athena plot military strategies and then do battle along with kings and foot soldiers. To get from place to place, Odysseus constructs a seaworthy raft according to sound principles of shipbuilding and navigates it by the stars. Nymphs and domestic servants alike spend their unmagical hours carding, spinning, and weaving. It is not always possible to distinguish between fact and fiction, or between poetic inventions and the surviving remains of Mycenaean lore. But it is probable that Greek myths as we know them have a more intimate connection to Bronze Age history than the simple definition of the terms myth and history would lead us to suppose. It is possible therefore for the twentieth century to put myth and Homer to new tests of historicity.

And it has been doing so. Correspondences between myth and archaeology are being made daily, especially since the ancillary disciplines of art, epigraphy, ethnography, and anthropology are being called upon to contribute to the growing picture of Mycenaean and Minoan society. Those correspondences are the subject of this book. In each chapter several facets of a myth or myth cycle and an accumulating body of evidence about Mycenaean life are made to shed light on one another. At the same time, chapters imitate the retrospective impulse of the ancient chroniclers by attempting to set myths in their Mycenaean environments. That is to say, the text retells briefly the Mycenaean event, or habit of mind, or ritual that generated a particular mythic expression. The book is therefore a *dis*continuous history of the Bronze Age from its birth in about 2200 B.C. to its decline sometime after 1100 B.C. Discontinuous for two reasons. The Bronze Age is old in time but new to us. There are whole periods in its span of over a thousand years and whole orders of information still shrouded in mystery. Secondly, some discontinuity inheres in the book's aim—*not* to be a history, but to present those segments of Mycenaean life to which a specific myth may point. Some myth cycles, like those of Cadmos or Agamemnon, do seem to be susceptible to approximate dating and therefore ask to be fit into a chronological sequence. The myths in Chapter II, for instance, seem to recall the migrations of peoples from the Near East to Crete and the mainland early in the Bronze Age. On the other hand, Odysseus' story, in the book's last chapter, seems to belong to the days when the end of the age is imminent. Assigning dates to other myths like Jason's is more an act of discrimination based on criteria like the type of myth it resembles or the kind of actuality it encapsulates. A story's political or economic implications may be isolated for attention in one chapter rather than another because these hint at solutions to particular historical problems in the period under discussion. Alternatively, several myths may speak to the same Mycenaean custom or ritual or aspect of social behavior and yet only one be singled out for notice. To compensate for these lapses from strict continuity, the text relies upon summaries of evolutionary changes in the general complexion of the Bronze Age. In addition, a modern Chronology is given in Appendix I.

The characteristics of this material—an amorphous body of oral tradition on the one hand and a variety of physical evidence on the other—mean that the most attractive of correspondences between them fall far short of proof. Even the most cautious judgments about the significance of archaeological finds are, almost by definition, hypotheses. Whereas a good deal about a single artefact may be provable, a theory derived from it is not. The provenance of certain clay pots found at Thebes, for example, is now known because the places of their manufacture could be traced by analysis of the elements in the clay's composition. How the pots got from those places to Thebes is a matter of educated guessing. And what may be said about the life of the peoples who carried the pottery is still more so. A related problem is that there is still no consensus on major physical evidences of the Bronze Age. Interpretations of huge palaces and tiny potsherds alike arouse passionate scholarly controversies that inhibit easy generalizations. At their most esoteric, such quarrels heap speculation upon conjecture in dizzying spirals that only the most expert can travel with confidence. For these reasons the book makes no attempt to prove one-to-one correlations between imprecise clues in mythology and the uncertain results of Bronze Age studies. Instead, the ambiguous content of myth and the most specific and accurate material evidences are simply placed side by side in order to suggest correlations between them. Astonishingly enough, the probability is very high that such correlations will eventually be proven "right."

For the sake of simplicity, technical terminology has been kept to a minimum. The term myth is used loosely to refer to the variety of folktale, story, legend, epic, and saga that comprise the oral tradition. Since several important and distinguished studies of Greek mythology fall outside the scope of this book, there was every reason to follow the precedent set by early Greeks themselves in avoiding any discrimination between the many types of narrative and poem that they embraced, happily, as *muthos*—a story or a plot. Only when analysis would have suffered have I made necessary distinctions. The term Mycenaean has been similarly used to refer to all the Bronze Age Greek peoples on the mainland, although that was inhabited by unique tribes with their own names, origins, and customs. Specifically, Mycenaean once applied only to the peoples who lived in and near Mycenae during the Late Helladic period. Now a Mycenaean may have been, in fact, a Minyan, a Pylian, or a Boeotian. Homer knows the Mycenaeans collectively as Achaeans, although he also refers to particular men by their tribal names.

More often than not, I have assumed that the names of ancient writers are familiar to the reader, so they appear in the text without preface or explanation. In addition, wherever possible, I have preferred a simple date—always B.C. unless otherwise stated—or a general reference to Early, Middle, or Late Bronze Age to the more cumbersome archaeological notations that divide periods into Early, Middle, and Late Helladic on the mainland and Early, Middle, and Late Minoan on Crete. The Chronology gives both formal and informal terms and, I hope, dispels any confusion. Finally, since there do exist a number of useful books about the Mycenaean and Minoan world (several are listed in the Bibliography), I have felt free to include new and interesting opinions on some of its aspects. So, for instance, Chapter V refers to a recent investigation into the evolution of kingship, rather than only to ideas about the nature and role of a Mycenaean king. And so, too, in Chapter VI a review of several theories about the circumstances of Knossos' fall seemed to be more timely than a synopsis of familiar knowledge about the site would have been.

Although three-quarters of a century have elapsed since Schliemann worked at Troy, and more than twenty years since Ventris deciphered Linear B, the Bronze Age is still in the throes of its re-creation. A wealth of new data is being added daily to the information yet to be sifted in the slow process of decision-making that precedes the conversion of research into history. We are in the delightful position of an audience at a dress rehearsal, seeing a play before the director has made the judicious cuts and additions that will determine the lines of the completed script. Having to choose between possible interpretations of evidence when each may turn out to be mistaken can be disappointing. But then, only if one sees history as absolute and given, rather than as mutable and discoverable.

II

The Rape of Europa:
Migrations and Metamorphoses

The story of Europa and the Bull is one part of a family saga which extends over several generations and many locales. Its content is political and geographical; its plot, like most of its characters, is symbolical; its actions highly specific and detailed. The myth cycle begins in Tyre, digresses to Crete, reaches an apex of complexity in Thebes, and ends in Illyria. Essentially, these several "chapters" are foundation myths, having to do with the origin and settlement of different cities and states by members of one dynasty, itself formed by an alliance of rulers.

The best-known version begins in the land of Canaan, where Agenor marries Telephassa. She bears him five sons and one daughter: Cadmos, Phoenix, Cilix, Thasus, Phineus, and Europa. Zeus falls in love with Europa and, in order to be near her, disguises himself as a snow-white bull among her father's herd of cattle. Walking along the seashore near the herd, Europa notices the beautiful animal and begins to play with him, putting flowers in his mouth and hanging garlands on his horns. As she overcomes her fear of the Bull, she climbs on his shoulders and lets him amble down to the water's edge, at which point he swims away with her on his back as she looks in terror at the receding shoreline. He swims as far as Crete and comes ashore near Gortyna. Then Zeus again disguises himself, this time as an eagle, and ravishes Europa in a willow thicket beside a spring—or, as one tradition has it, under an evergreen plane tree. Europa bears him three sons: Minos, Rhadamanthys, and Sarpedon, each of whom found cities and become the rulers of Knossos, Phaistos, and Mallia, respectively. (See Illus. 3.)

At first reading, this seems to be a simple tale—a pastoral idyll injected with the supernatural in the manner familiar to us from many of Zeus' love affairs. The god spies an appealing nymph in an Edenic setting. He kidnaps her and makes her his bride. When one tries to find the meaning of the myth, however, he discovers a rich complex of subject matter that belies the myth's surface simplicity. This is not because there are abstruse theoretical ideas hidden behind a mythic facade. Rather, a fairly large body of diverse material needs to be understood before we can see how certain of its details apply directly to the myth's significance. The wider the scope of our information, the better we are able to see the myth's ability to cite one or two particulars and through them call upon greater areas of knowledge. Part of the reason for this is germane to myth itself and to its mode of telling a story.

A myth does not announce its subject by topical sentences declaring, for instance, this tale is about the formation of a new Mycenaean dynasty. It neither generalizes from its own details nor does it make categorical distinctions between them. The burden of both these mental operations is on the hearer. Instead, it offers images of people, places, and things and says nothing about the relations among them. And then sometimes it puts these imaged people through actions that have little or no continuity. If one were to report an incident, using only a minimum number of nouns and verbs, avoiding all adjectives, adverbs, connectors, and transitions, and even ignoring the rules of syntax, he would have abrogated some of the power to narrate and nearly all of the power to describe. He would make no effort to transform isolated pictures into continuous narrative; he would be unconcerned with shades of difference between major and minor characters and actions. Such is myth's mode, one that has been called pictographic. Often a single male figure can symbolize a state; an epithet can indicate the degree of its power; and a single homely detail can be a reference to its economic or social or religious resources. Often in a phrase or two, the mythmaker evokes an entire early tradition or custom,

3. Europa and the Bull in limestone relief.

about which he himself may know nothing. Or, to take a further example of the method, naming a place and setting people in it can be a way of symbolizing a state's political identity and its relation to its neighbors. An action, too, can be symbolic or metaphoric, as is Zeus' rape of Europa. But stripped of its poetic significances, kidnapping Europa is simply a way of moving her from one place to another. To see in a myth all the meanings it may have had for the Greeks, and furthermore all the meanings it has for us, we must translate the pictures as though they were ideograms or symbols that expressed all their content in one abbreviated form.

For all these reasons several topics must be surveyed before we will be in a position to use them to interpret the myth proper. It will be helpful nevertheless if the Europa story is kept in mind

throughout the discussion that follows of genealogy, of the myth's
Mycenaean elements, of Cretan history, and of some aspects of the
Minoan-Mycenaean religion.

2

Genealogy is myth's strongest link with history. In trying to
reconstruct their past, the Greeks began in the present and counted
backward through all a family's known generations as far as
memory and traditions could go. When the last mortal man had
been counted, his descent was traced from a god. So it was when the
Greeks reckoned up the span of time known as the great Age of
Heroes, a period they saw as intervening between the historical
Iron Ages and the mythical Bronze Age, when gods and men
coexisted. But the Greek father of history, Herodotus, showed us
the way to read genealogies when he poked gentle fun at his
contemporary Hecataeus. Egyptian priests told him that Hecataeus
had boasted that his family, sixteen generations before, "went back
to a god." The priests, Herodotus said, showed their visitor statues
of noble fathers and sons who represented 345 successive generations, yet none of them had been gods or even demigods. Herodotus did not press his point. Modern historians do. They point out
that breaks in family traditions often signal breaks in folk memory.
Sixteen generations before Hecataeus there probably had been a
crisis in Greek history, a period of upheaval or migration, perhaps
recorded in an epic or other traditional oral form under the guise of
the founding of a new dynasty or the naming of a new state. Since
the founder was not related to the previous royal family, or had no
claim to power except his own military prowess, he claimed descent
from a divine ancestor.

When therefore a myth like the Europa one incorporates a
genealogy that leads back to a god, here Zeus, we are wise to
examine it as a sign that there has been a break in folk memory.
Immediately, then, our attention focuses on Minos, the first son of
this divine couple. Minos, who gives his name to the civilization on
Crete that Sir Arthur Evans revealed to the world, is a figure who
perfectly illustrates this genealogical principle. As though to prove
that there is a confused quasi-history at this point in the past,

several contradictory images have gathered around him. On one hand he is seen as an all-powerful ruler, beneficent enough to foster the gentle and sophisticated arts for which the Minoan culture is known. On the other hand he appears as forceful enough to exert maritime authority over all the Aegean seas, and enough of a tyrant to exact a tribute in human flesh yearly from the mainland. The probable explanation is that the Parian Chronicle, the most important of Greek genealogies (for these see Appendix II), lists two kings of Crete with the name of Minos. (And here we might digress to note that the name ought to be used much as the Egyptian word *pharaoh* is, to signify a "king" or "ruler" rather than an individual personage.) The first is the divine son of Zeus and Europa, who, again according to the Chronicle, ruled Crete in 1400.

Now in Crete there were three breaks in folk tradition when families were traced to a god. The first of these comes in 1400 when, Sir Arthur Evans claimed, the palace of Minos at Knossos was destroyed and the island economy collapsed. Although his chronology is now in dispute, the fact remains that the period from about 1450 to 1400 was one of upheaval and turmoil for Crete, since Mycenaean infiltration had begun by the middle fifteenth century and was followed by full occupation by the turn of the century. If there was a Minos, and if he was a ruler on Crete at that time, he was probably a usurper of power that had been vested in a Minoan line. Therefore what his semidivine ancestry tells us about him is that there was a gap in ancient genealogies. We thus have a vivid illustration of legend's habit to form when there is a break in historical continuity.

The second Minos seems to have descended from a different racial stock in a later Minoan period. As we have seen, an unflattering series of characteristics collected around his name. Homer knows him as the aged monarch Idomeneus, who sent a regiment to the Trojan War. But legend says that he is the grandson of the first Minos, thereby using genealogy to align two contrary Minoses. Too long a span of time is involved here, about two hundred years, for there to be any truth in the relationship of the two kings. Nevertheless we can see how dynastic and ethnic traditions have been reconciled by invoking a family tree. The second Minos, about whom nothing is known, is given respectable royal ancestry in the family of the supposedly original divine king.

3

When at the turn of the twentieth century Sir Arthur Evans
first excavated Knossos, he revealed a splendid civilization that he
promptly named Minoan after King Minos. History seemed to be
confirming legend, and with every turn of the archaeologist's spade
it looked as though the secrets of the origin of the Bronze Age
would be told. The palace and its related finds, then later in the
century the second palace at Phaistos, the villa at Hagia Triada,
town sites, cave sanctuaries, royal tombs, all seemed to prove that
this new European civilization had been the parent of a flourishing
Aegean culture in the second millennium. Had not the Greeks
themselves used the term Minoan to summon up the glories of their
Age of Heroes? Settlements and towns all over the Aegean were
presumed to have been founded by this Cretan civilization and so
were called Minoa. Sicily, where Daedalus was said to have found
refuge, became westernmost Minoa. From the viewpoint of myth
and tradition it seemed as though the entire quasi-historical period
was to be linked to the spread of Minoan culture. In our own time,
the capstone of the Minoan imperial edifice was thought to be the
Mycenaean mainland. It was supposed that so rich a civilization as
the Minoan must have been the decisive influence on the development of the more barbaric Mycenaean life.

We now know that links between the Minoan and Mycenaean
cultures were more complex than Evans surmised, that the differences between the two were as great as their similarities, and that
the newer Mycenaean culture eventually conquered (or occupied
in some other way) the older Minoan one. We would have had a
hint of this latter fact, however, even if archaeologists had not
presented it to us in painstaking detail. For many Greek myths
either have their origins in the Mycenaean past or incorporate
elements of story that reflect Mycenaean custom or habit. Only the
entirely different preoccupations of myth prevent us from seeing its
links to Mycenaean times more clearly. In the foregoing discussion
of genealogy, for example, it was implied that Minos was Mycenaean, although no such information is specified in the story. In a
similarly indirect fashion, the myth takes another opportunity to
insist on its Mycenaean origins, and that is in the appearance of

Zeus. Although the story purports to be about a Phoenician family, one of whose members comes to Crete to establish a Minoan dynasty, the agent of all this activity is the purely Greek sky god Zeus. The central event of the story, the rape of Europa, can be seen as a vivid metaphor for the usurpation of Minoan interests on both sides of the Aegean by a Greek claim. Once Zeus is seen as the symbol of Mycenaean power, the reason is clear why the actual rape takes place on Crete instead of in the Near East. In their early history the Mycenaeans had no direct dealings, either social or economic, with Phoenicia. But Crete, as we shall see, did. Therefore Near Eastern connections are subsumed in the myth's geography. Furthermore, it is on Minoan history that Mycenaeans are making a claim. Therefore Zeus' progeny are born on Crete to establish new dynasties under a figurative Mycenaean flag. Doubtless when they began to settle in Crete, around 1450, they brought their chief deity with them. A new set of myths must have been generated, among them one that tells of Zeus' birth on the island—mythology's way of establishing his worship among the Cretan peoples. In Crete, moreover, Zeus has attributes differing from those by which he is known on the mainland. Since Crete already had a young male god, Zagreus, authorities on Greek religion suppose that the Greek Zeus appropriated several of the earlier god's characteristics and that eventually the two cults fused.

The original cult of Zagreus was mystical. His worshiper felt the god to enter into his own being in a moment of ecstasy usually induced by orgiastic ritual. The culminating moment of the rite was often the eating of a newly slain animal, usually a bull, who was thought to embody the god. By partaking of the lifeblood and flesh of the deity's physical form, the worshiper believed himself to acquire the god's spirit and strength. On the other hand, what little is known about Zeus' worship shows it to be distinctly nonmystical in character. He is the anthropomorphic patriarch, more human than spiritual, more magical (in his control of the natural world and the weather) than philosophical, and always distanced from the affairs of men by the divine space and time of eternity. When animals figure in his worship, they are sacrificed to him, then cooked and eaten for simple nourishment. In Crete, however, Zeus has both these sets of characteristics. Inscriptions and hymns portray him as the leader of a mystery cult in whose service a young band of warrior youths, or kuretes, dance at his birthplace on Mount Dikte. The yearly reenactment of his birth resembles a ritual common to mystery and orgiastic cults and is thought to have been part of his ceremonies. This brief summary of differences between the two chief male gods does not pretend to explain the nature of male-god worship on Crete. It intends rather to draw attention to Zeus as foreign to indigenous Cretan cults and to indicate that his presence in the Europa story is the result of a fusion of Mycenaean and Minoan traditions. The political implications of his role can be made to say that Zeus' major function in the story is to make a Mycenaean claim on Minoan history.

4

When we look at the Europa myth from the perspective of its historical implications, a new set of considerations emerge. Just as mythical genealogy is the signal for a genuine concern with chronology, so mythical geography overlays a concern for what modern scholars would term ethnography, anthropology, or perhaps cultural history. The Europa tale, we notice, has several geographical settings; but we are at a loss to understand the reasons for them until we take into account several related oral traditions. One puts forward the idea that Cretans came to the island from somewhere in southwestern Anatolia. A quite different tradition holds that Europa was a native Cretan goddess. Both these ideas seem to fuse in the myth with still a third tradition that has each of Europa's brothers setting out in diverse directions from their Phoenician home to found new cities. If, as we have suggested, mythical geography is a key to history, a set of questions about this group of traditions arises: e.g., Are there true connections between Anatolia and Crete? And, if so, of what kind and duration? Although the queries are straightforward enough, the answers to them are anything but clear. We shall need to sift through a variety of evidence that begins with what is known about the origins of the Cretan peoples.

There is no evidence of an indigenous Neolithic culture developing out of a Paleolithic one on Crete. Anthropologists assume that the island was settled by people or peoples from elsewhere, perhaps from the coastal areas of Asia Minor, perhaps from Libya. The trip to Crete from Libya, directly northward, or from

Egypt, just north and east, was no more than a two-day sail. Nevertheless no one is certain about the origins of the earliest inhabitants. Skeletal remains show that at least three racial types mingled to form the nation. The majority of the population was of the Mediterranean type: a slender-boned people, of or below medium height, with dark hair and eyes, sallow complexions, and dolichocephalic or longheaded skulls. Early in the Bronze Age, in Early Minoan I and II, another racial element, an Armenoid and brachycephalic people, taller and generally bigger than the Mediterranean race, began to enter Crete. This type has been found in the Cyclades, in the mainland of Greece, and in Anatolia. After measurement of the relatively few skulls that have been found, it would seem that the Armenoid type were in the minority in Early Minoan I and II and they remained so in Middle and Late Minoan times. Their proportionate numbers, however, increased markedly in Middle Minoan, as did the numbers of a third, medium-skull type presumed to be a hybrid form produced by an intermingling of the two basic types. Although the samples on which these generalizations are based are very small, they nevertheless suggest the arrival of a new element in the population during Middle Minoan times. Where did it come from? Since the mainland was itself the goal of newcomers in the period (2000–1700), it is unlikely to have been the source of immigrants to Crete. The Cyclades also seem to have undergone a slight population increase, although they tended to remain trading places generally immune to large population shifts. That leaves Anatolia as the possible source of the broadheaded people; and here anthropology supports what cultural affinities and material remains have long suggested: that an Anatolian element which may have existed on Crete from Neolithic times increased in numbers and influence during the Middle Minoan period.

Unfortunately, the number of skeletons on which the anthropological predictions have been made are so small that they cannot be taken as conclusive. When, however, this physical evidence is placed alongside the accumulated weight of other examples of Anatolian influence, it seems clear that there was early and continuing contact between the Asiatic landmass and Crete. The difficult question yet unanswered is, What kinds of contact? Occasional trade? Ongoing commercial ties? Migration? All three? The mythmaker simply transports a personage whose semidivine offspring become glorious kings. Yet Europa and Zeus found a royal dynasty which purports to open a new era in Crete. We therefore ask, Does the myth encapsulate the remembrance of a migration from Asia Minor which changes the course of the island's development up to that point? Was there on Crete a break in historical continuity which permits of such speculation?

We have already seen that the Minoans were preceded on the island by a Neolithic culture of mixed racial origins. According to the carbon-14 method of dating, this culture developed slowly from 6000 to about 2600 B.C. with no major changes in its patterns of life in simple encampments or settlements. Gradually houses cease to be mere huts and become squared-off two- and three-room dwellings built on stone foundations with a proper hearth. Still more gradually customs of burial and pottery making change, but not in unpredictable fashion. Then suddenly, in the middle of the third millennium, a new and highly developed culture appears (see Chronology). It uses metals and builds palaces. Its social organization seems to be centralist and its economic wellbeing derives from seafaring. At a swift rate it evolves into a civilization that absorbs and reshapes the influences around it from Egypt and Cyprus, the Near East and the Cyclades. How do archaeologists explain this urban revolution? Some think that the old culture made a great leap forward as a result of new techniques, especially metalworking, and that this coincided with the influx of a small group of new peoples. Others claim that a new race from overseas brought with it the radical change, which owed little if anything to the older culture. On the basis of general characteristics, anthropological data, the particularities of toolmaking, works of art, and other features, the new race is shown to belong to the Mediterranean type that established kindred civilizations over the whole of the eastern Mediterranean. The origin of the branch that settled in Crete had links with both the Libyan and Anatolian regions; therefore it is possible that the migrants came from both areas at the same time, resulting in the formation of the mixed racial type combining Libyan and Armenoid characteristics.

Could this be the migration that the Europa myth seems to imply? If the founding of the first palaces and the concentration of power in the hands of kings are taken to be significant, the answer could be yes. To put it another way, we would then be saying that Anatolian invaders came to Crete bringing the new civilization with them. Any such statement, however, is filled with implicit controversy. One school of archaeologists believes the First Palace civilization to be a simple continuation of a pre-Palace period, and the new features to have evolved out of the old. Another school claims that there was a mass immigration of southeastern Anatolians called Luwians, a branch of Indo-Europeans. Its argument is based on linguistic evidence and a close resemblance between the palaces of Beycesultan in Anatolia and Knossos, Phaistos, and Mallia in Crete. In general, the linguistic similarity between the Luwian and Eteocretan languages rests on the endings of place names and other nouns that are not Greek and, so far as is known, not identifiable as any other non-Greek language. Words like *Knossos* and *Amnissos, Labyrinthos* and *Minos* are illustrations of this class of word which turns up all over Crete, the islands, and the mainland, too. If this pre-Greek language can be proven to be Luwian, it would follow that a sizable population carried the language from southwestern Anatolia to all of the places where these *-nthos* and *-ossos* names occur. Furthermore, a relation between the language and the yet undeciphered syllabic script Linear A, found later on Crete, would probably have to be demonstrated. At present there are not enough known points of resemblance between Cretans and Luwians to support the theory of a mass migration.

It seems to be more certain that economic and social developments during the First Palace period led to a growth of shipping and a strengthening of relations between Egypt, Anatolia, and the Aegean world, with Crete acting sometimes as a middleman in the commerce between Egypt and points east, and sometimes dealing with the East directly. One illustration of the attempt to work out the precise lines of this three-way contact relates to the fascinating puzzle of the origin of the Phaistos disk. In Early Minoan times, one or more languages were in use, none of which has been fully translated. One of these shows many affinities to Egyptian hieroglyphic and is presumed to be the precursor of the still mysterious Linear A. Another hieroglyphic language was used on the clay disk found at the palace of Phaistos. Evans regarded it as an import from Anatolia rather than a native work in a Cretan language. He and his followers argue from the fact that 1) no other example of this language has been found; and 2) several of the symbols are Asianic, such as a Lycian house on piles, a man with feathered headgear taken to be a Philistine or a Carian, and a woman with an un-Minoan costume.

Still another factor needs to be added to the complex of questions and answers about the kind and quantity of Minoan relations

with Anatolia and the Near East. Sometime around 1700, the Old
Palace civilization was utterly destroyed by an earthquake (or
earthquakes?) which devastated its centers at Knossos, Phaistos,
and Mallia. Thereafter, the segment of the island that faced the
eastern world and was presumed to be in close contact with it
declined. Its population dwindled and the center of power shifted
to the middle and western parts of Crete, which rebuilt their palaces
with still greater splendor than before. The buildings were designed
to new plans, more monumental and more labyrinthine than
before, with vast central and western courtyards, larger rooms,
majestic facades, and double and triple stories. Around each of the
palaces, town houses were clustered for the important officials of
the city. A group of faience tiles found at Knossos and dating from
this Second Palace period illustrates the urban quality of the
building (see Illus. 4). What looks like a remarkable coincidence is
that another increase of population occurs just at the start of this
Middle Minoan period, when new energies reach a peak of
productivity. As far as can be predicated on the evidence of anthropology, detailed earlier, this new population was largely Armenoid, that is, like that Anatolian one that came at the beginning
of Early Minoan I.

Along with the increase in building activity comes a corresponding increase in trade. Crete begins a direct trade with Syria of
oil and wine for copper. Vases, which may have been exported
empty, are plentiful in the Levant from the Middle Minoan period
onward and may have been retraded up and down the Asia Minor
continent. They have been found at sites as far apart as the Hittite

4. The "Town House" tiles from Knossos depicting building facades.

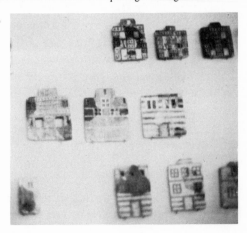

capital of Bogazkoy, Byblos, and Ugarit.* It may have been on one of these trading occasions that the Cretans learned the use of papyrus. They called it *byblos,* from which name the Greek term for "book" and the English word "Bible" were derived.

Evidence of trade in the reverse direction comes from an ossuary at Platanos, near Gortyna, where Europa landed. There a remarkable Babylonian cylinder seal was found with a design representing the goddess Ishtar praying to a male figure, the whole design of a type current in Hammurabi's reign (1792–1750). Its fresh condition proved it had not been in circulation long, and therefore it was valuable testimony that it had been transferred soon after its manufacture. At the same time, new cattle-raising techniques were imported from the Near East, and the importance of the bull god in Crete may well date to the extension of contact with the eastern countries of his origin.

The question that immediately comes to mind is, Could the makers of the Europa myth have had in mind a confused memory of the "founding" of this Second Palace society? For it was during this period that Minoan culture achieved its full flowering and began to exert its influence over the infant Mycenaean states. This would mean that there is a double layer of historical reference in the myth, one Minoan and one Mycenaean. The first and earliest would relate to the transfer of some features of the Anatolian civilization to Crete in Middle Minoan times, represented in the myth by Europa's journey. The second layer, fused in the narrative onto the first, would illustrate the Mycenaean occupation of Crete and subsequent appropriation of Minoan history, mentioned already in connection with the figure of Zeus. For the Mycenaean references, some dates are available. For the Minoan one, a date may be academic. The associations sketched out here between Crete and its Near Eastern neighbor were periodic and complex, beginning early in the formation of Minoan civilization and reaching a peak during its fullest flowering. There is one other group of considerations that bear on a possible date, and they have to do with the Cadmos portion of the story. Since Cadmos sets out in search of his sister, Europa, and since several details in his adventures do suggest a date, we may be in a better position to

* The remains of this ancient city, dating to the fifth millennium B.C., were discovered in 1931 on the site of the small modern Arab village of Ras Shamra, near Latakia.

hazard a suggestion about dating after the entire family saga has
been examined.

5

Perhaps none of the material and linguistic evidence of ties
between the Near East and Crete is as persuasive as the numberless
general resemblances between the Anatolian and Minoan cults of
the Great Mother. From earliest to late Roman times, Asia Minor
worshiped the Great Mother goddess who was Cybele in Phrygia,
Ishtar in Sumeria, Ashtoreth or Astarte in the Levant. She has her
counterpart on the Greek mainland in the earth goddess Demeter,
and in Crete in the great Nature Goddess with many names and
manifestations. As the lady with the snakes, her chthonic nature is
emphasized; as a huntress, she is Britomartis, the young virgin; as
the woman flanked by lions, she is the Mountain Mother; as the
female with doves, she is a celestial goddess. One of the many
emanations of the Minoan mother was Europa, originally named
Hellotis in Crete. In spite of her many impersonations (and for lack
of more definite knowledge), she is essentially one great goddess
whose principle extended to encompass all living things—animal,
plant, and human. Her worship centered in her representation of
the idea of fertility.

It is clear in the list of her configurations that the mother
goddess was not always revealed to her votaries as a mature
woman. She was also present in her potential form as a maiden who
promised later fruitfulness, and as an old woman whose fertile
years were past. In these three aspects she sometimes took on a
correspondence with the seasons of spring, summer, and fall and
also with the moon in its waxing, full, and waning phases. In most
myths the Great Mother is accompanied by a son or a young
consort who plays the male role in a fertility ritual. His importance
is limited to the annual performance of his function, after which he
suffers a ritual death. He thus comes to be associated with the death
of the crops in winter, when, in some versions of the basic myth, he
dwells in the underworld. Attis, the consort of Cybele; Tammuz,
the partner of Ishtar; and Adonis are all such figures.

Given the subsidiary role of the male god on Crete, the arrival of Zeus must have been fraught with difficulties. Everywhere he went he must have been confronted by the mother goddess and her worship, but he fared well in the competition because the Greeks were not exclusive about their religion. Instead, they paired him with full ceremony to one after another of the female deities in sacred marriages, just as they had done on the mainland when they married him to the earth mother Hera. The weather god, bringer of rain, became the fertilizing agent of the Mother Earth's womb, and the mother's maidens and consorts became their children, engendering new myths about their births from either or both parents. Although after their sacred union each deity retained much of his original nature, the female suffered a diminution for she now ruled jointly with the patriarch. This basic pattern of syncretism underlies the rape of Europa-Hellotis, a once powerful Cretan goddess who in the myth is reduced to the rank of a nymph.

Two quite different orders of complexity in the idea of the sacred marriage are taken for granted by this necessarily brief summary. One concerns the religious significance of the marriage as nature symbolism. To a settled agricultural or pastoral people, their religion, like their lives, is bound up with the fecundity of the earth. The most primitive religious idea in man's mind may have been the thought that to make the earth fruitful it must be impregnated, derived by analogy with human biological functioning. A sympathetic magic between men's acts and those of nature even precedes the conception of deity, for man guarantees nature's performance by his own, which then assumes a ritual and most sacred character. Ceremonies of various sorts, in which a union of Mother Earth and some fertilizing agent took place, must have played a role in the worship of Greeks and pre-Greeks alike, for their well-being depended upon the bounty of animal and vegetable life. This aspect of the sacred marriage is primary and distinct from the worship of the male god as a deity in his own right. Cult practices and rituals based on the principle of union are germane to an understanding of Europa's original nature, and to Zeus' manifestations as a baby and as a young man, in which roles he symbolizes the notion of fertility and growth.

The other implication of the sacred marriage is historical and represents a fusion of Great Mother worship with the idea of a supreme male deity, Zeus. The effect of Zeus' introduction was that whereas in the past the goddess was the unquestioned mistress who commanded the services of a youthful consort, the union now became a solemn marriage in which Zeus took the leading role. One could say that the god of the invading Greeks imposed himself as the dominant partner, a role he maintained without difficulty in the aristocratic societies of the mainland cities. Where he appropriated the function of the partner in the ancient fertility cults of the common people, as he did on Crete, there remained many traces of the earth mother's independent worship. For this reason, variations in local cult practices are countless, sometimes retaining features from earlier cults, sometimes adding new attributes to Zeus' already manifold ones.

At Gortyna, where tradition says Europa and the Bull first touched land, a coin series tells the story of their marriage in pictorial designs that include Minoan cult objects like sacred trees, birds, and bulls. Mythologically the coins are significant because Gortyna was once called Hellotis, and because the city has a tradition of Hellotis-Europa coins dating back to the fifth century A.D. Outside of Crete, the Hellotis-Europa motif recurs on coins from both Sidon and Tyre suggesting that these Phoenician cities in which the opening of the legend is set fostered a Europa tradition that excluded Zeus.

Just as Europa in the myth replaces or absorbs the earlier Cretan goddess Hellotis, so as we have seen Zeus displaces the young male god Zagreus. To judge from the remains of cult offerings and clay figurines at sanctuaries and shrines, there was no male god of the rank and importance of Zeus in Early Minoan times. The appearance therefore of male deities in pictorial art in Middle Minoan times gives an important indication that Zeus had already arrived on Crete by then and had established his influence. Very probably, the existence of Zagreus and the additional separate significance of bulls smoothed the way for the acceptance of the Greek sky god whose manifestation was the Bull. The idea that Zeus metamorphoses into an eagle at the moment when he rapes Europa is probably due to a confusion with cults of the moon goddess and Hellotis, in both of whose cults birds and sacred trees figure. Zeus as a bull, on the other hand, may be evidence that the myth of Zeus and Europa ultimately derives from a Phoenician myth of the bull god El and the mother goddess Asherat. El is ordinarily associated with the sun and Asherat with the moon, correspondences that sort well with the similar ones of Zeus and Europa. (See Illus. 5.)

This last suggestion, that there were Phoenician prototypes for

Zeus and Europa, adds a new dimension to our story. It is difficult, if not impossible, to be absolutely certain about the order in which elements come together in the formation of a completed myth. In a very general way, however, one can say that the primary elements in a myth of the Europa type are those with cult or ritual associations. These would form the basic core on which other dynastic or ethnic elements would be built up. The fact that El and Asherat, Zeus and Europa are parallel figures therefore probably means that the characteristics of the newer gods, their cults, and their myths were to some extent patterned on the older ones. This, of course, presupposes contacts between the two cultures which would set the stage for the borrowing to occur. Discovering the likeliest place and time of the borrowing would shed light on the very problem of how the final myth was formed.

Now there is evidence to suggest that Minoans made the acquaintance of the older myth in Middle Minoan times, when, as we have seen, interchange between the two cultures was at its height. At that period Ugarit was a vital center of Cretan trade. Several different languages were spoken at this international city, which supported an intermingling of Near Eastern and Aegean cultures, among them proto-Phoenician. There is thus a strong possibility that the city provided the opportunity for the fusion of the cult of

5. Leda and the Swan; a late version of the Europa-Eagle motif?

the bull god and mother goddess, El and Asherat, with the indigenous cult of Europa-Hellotis. Support for this idea comes from a related legend that the arrival in Greece of the Cadmeioi, Europa's family, coincides roughly with the expulsion of the Semitic Hyksos from Egypt by Ahmosis, c. 1580 B.C. To see how this is relevant we must turn back to the story line of the Europa myth.

The opening lines relate that Agenor, Europa's father, left Egypt as a young man to settle in the land of Canaan, where he married and produced a family. Since Agenor was not a native Egyptian, it is fair to assume either that he was a member of the Hyksos, or that he independently repeated their pattern of movement from Canaan to Egypt and back again. If either of these two possibilities is the case, the myth's addition of this bit of narrative could have occurred only when the dispersal of the Hyksos was an accomplished fact. In the light of several other factors, it could only have been added to the tale in Syria, for Crete was not directly concerned in Egypt's Semitic relations. Evans was sure that there were peaceful relations between Hyksos-ruled Egypt and Crete because of his discovery of an alabaster lid, inscribed with the name of the Hyksos pharaoh Kyan, found in a Middle Minoan stratum at Knossos. It is not likely, however, that the myth's allusion to Agenor and the Hyksos migration would have come to Crete from Egypt, since few correspondences exist between the legends of the two countries. Crete and Syria, on the other hand, do have parallel religious elements in their myths, and were in direct contact at Ugarit.

There are then two possible ways that this detail could have found its way into the myth. Either the Phoenicians, who are identified with the Cadmeioi by Herodotus and others, brought their cults directly to Crete and Greece from Syria, or the Minoans and Mycenaeans learned about the chief Semitic deities El and Baal in Syria and brought them home with them. On religious grounds, the second is more unlikely because history has shown that the discovery of one religious idea does not necessarily modify another. Usually it takes a prolonged contact of a sort afforded by occupations and settled living together for there to be an exchange of ritualistic personalities or a fusion of cults. If, however, the Cretans were exposed to the Phoenician cult and story in the course of their Syrian trade, and if this exposure was reinforced by the transport of both cult and story by the Near Easterners who settled in Crete, then there would be sufficient reason to assume that the adoption of Near Eastern forms for gods and myths represents more than a casual borrowing. The parallelism would speak for an order of contact between the two peoples as strong and as important as that between Minoans and Mycenaeans.

With this in mind we can look back at Zeus' introduction into the Europa story with renewed understanding. Before the Minoans could make him their own, as they did at Gortyna, for example, the Mycenaeans would have had to do more than trade with Crete over a long period of time. Steady exposure or even royal ukase would have had to be imposed on the daily practice of Great Mother worship for it to admit of new features. Given the conservative nature of Minoan religion, which changed little over centuries, it is more likely that the invading Mycenaeans, at the close of the Middle Minoan period, absorbed Minoan cults. Such a process would be consistent with what is known about the development of Greek religion and would represent a movement in the same direction, toward syncretism, that we have already seen in the idea of the sacred marriage.

To summarize, we may see the growth of the legend as follows: From Syria would have come the idea of a sacred marriage between a bull god and a mother goddess which eventually influenced the Cretan cult of the mother goddess Hellotis. From Syria, too, came the information about Agenor's identity with the fortunes of the Hyksos. Mycenaeans, creating a rationale for folk traditions about their early relations with the Minoans, identified the bull god with Zeus, who came to Crete with the first Mycenaean settlement there in Middle Minoan times. In Crete, Zeus metamorphosed into an eagle, and the willow tree became a prominent feature in the story because the earlier cults of both Hellotis and Zagreus involved sacred willow branches and bird epiphanies. Other Greek or Cretan traditions about the origins of the race in Anatolia contributed the three settings for the action of the saga in Phoenicia, Crete, and thirdly, as we shall see, on the mainland. Finally Minos, Rhadamanthys, and Sarpedon were legitimized as Mycenaeans by being made the semidivine children of Zeus and Europa, whose union symbolized the usurpation of Minoan power by Mycenaeans.

III

Cadmos Founds Thebes

There are repercussions in Tyre when Europa's kidnapping is discovered. Agenor commands his sons to search for their sister, so they set forth at once to comb the eastern Mediterranean. Myth memorializes their journeys by linking their names to the places visited. Phoenix travels west to Carthage, there giving his name to the Punics. After his father's death, he returns to Canaan, which is renamed Phoenicia in his honor. Cilix goes to the land of the Hypachaeans, thereafter called Cilicia. Phineus goes off to the Black Sea area and is much harassed by the Harpies. Thasus and his followers come to colonize the island named after him, Thasos, and remain to work its rich gold mines. Cadmos, however, sets sail with his mother, Telephassa. They first stop at Rhodes, where they dedicate a caldron to Athena; then they build a temple to Poseidon and initiate a priesthood to care for it. Next they land on Thera and build a similar temple. The Thracian land of the Edonians (?) receives them hospitably; and then the exhausted Telephassa dies. Cadmos and his companions, at a loss for a direction, decide to consult the Delphic oracle. To his surprise Cadmos is advised to give up the search for Europa. Instead, he is instructed to follow a cow wherever it may lead until the animal sinks down out of sheer weariness. At that place he is to build a city.

* * *

What the story lacks in action in this section it makes up for in fullness of detail, a fullness which implies both that the tale was told often and that its highly specific geographical information was important. The brothers' journeys west, north, and south from their homelands on the Asia Minor coast repeat the motif of Europa's own travel from Tyre. In capsule form the myth says that each brother conquers, settles, or colonizes a land that takes his name. Nothing is told about the peoples in Hypachae or on Thasos simply because it is not important to the mythographer. The history of Hypachaeans and Thasians, whatever it was, is now rewritten; their identities are re-created in terms of their new rulers. And, since almost by definition a hero's victory is also his tribe's, each brother also personifies the introduction of the tribe's new social or political customs.

The way the myth utilizes information and refashions it can be illustrated by the case of Phoenix' journey to Carthage. The Phoenicians, the "red-skinned men" to the Greeks, did establish trading posts in North Africa as early as the twelfth century. During the next three hundred years they founded new stations and regular colonies which were already prosperous when, in 814 B.C., Tyrian colonists settled a city they called Carthage. These were the facts which the early Greek mythographers knew. Then, late in the fifth century, there were a series of wars between the Greek colonies in Magna Graeca (southern Italy) and Carthage, and these may well have reinforced traditional images of the Phoenicians as aggressive and successful. There is therefore more than enough historical material on which the mythmaker could draw for his claim that the Phoenicians founded Carthage.

The travels of Europa's brothers probably ought to be read as indications of a dispersion of peoples from Asia Minor, just as Europa's own journey was read as a symbol of migrations. The directions they take fit the general pattern of successive migrations from east to west, and from the Anatolian coast to the islands and the mainland that occurred throughout the second millennium. Certainly Cadmos' journey, the only one to be treated in any detail, can be read in such fashion for both archaeology and the history of religion offer reasons for his choice of route. The tradition that sets Agenor's family at home in Lycia (later Cilicia) instead of Tyre does not make a great difference since these are nearby locations on the Anatolian coast (see Map 6). From the point of view of specific geography, however, the route that Cadmos took is inevitable if he started out from Lycia. Traveling due west, he first would have run straight into Rhodes, whatever his intentions.

In 1904 a Danish expedition to Rhodes discovered a whole catalog of "prehistoric" documents forged in ancient times belonging to the Rhodian Temple of Athena. Among them was a long inscription known as the Lindos Chronicle. Placed in the temple supposedly in the year 99 B.C., it listed gifts to Athena by legendary and historic persons. The third item on the list was a bronze caldron, "inscribed with Phoenician letters," from Cadmos. The chronicle was never taken to be anything but an ancient forgery. It is an excellent illustration, nevertheless, of the tenacity with which Rhodians held on to the legendary visit of Cadmos and Telephassa.

Although it is impossible to say categorically that archaeologists are led to the site of their discoveries by the clues given in legend, we cannot help but notice the coincidence between some of their finds and ideas maintained by folk custom. One such coincidence occurred in 1920, when a team of Italian archaeologists excavated at Ialysos, a major port on the easternmost tip of Rhodes. They found a settlement whose lowest levels reached back to the sixteenth century. Pottery at the site turned out to be Minoan in design, and so it was supposed that the settlement had been a halfway house on the trade route between Crete and the Levantine coast. This in itself was an important conclusion, for it had been assumed that Rhodes was well within the sphere of Mycenaean influence, a factor in the Aegean only after c. 1500. Then, in 1936, new evidence had to be fitted into the emerging picture. When the cemetery at Ialysos was excavated, a single tomb was found to contain a Hittite seal, an iron bracelet, an ivory comb, two cremations, and ten inhumations. In addition, a round stone block with geometric signs incised on it was discovered in the dromos, or antechamber, of the tomb. The stone seemed to represent some impulse to identify the dead through a primitive writing system.

Any one of these finds would have been dramatic confirmation that this part of the Aegean was being crisscrossed by new travelers and settlers. As more graves were found it became clear that cremation had been the chief form of burial. Since neither the Minoans nor the Mycenaeans adopted cremation until the early thirteenth or late twelfth century, theories about Rhodes' early affinities with both Aegean cultures were overturned. Cremation was, however, an Anatolian custom during the time that the cemetery was in use at Ialysos—from c. 1504 to 1380. It is now recognized that Ialysos was settled by peoples from the Near Eastern coast and that the traditional association of Cadmos with Rhodes is not at all fanciful. The close correspondence of tradition and archaeology is, in fact, still more startling when one realizes that the duration of the settlement is identical with the range of dates that have been theorized for the journeyings and foundings of new cities by Europa and the Cadmeioi.

The next leg of Cadmos' mythical journey is somewhat more difficult to understand. Thrace is in the far north, at the apex of the horseshoe curve formed by Anatolia and the mainland in the area of Macedonia and modern Bulgaria. Its coast shelters the island of Thasos, settled by Cadmos' brother. There seems to be no adequate reason why the mythmaker should have sent Cadmos to Thrace. Neither ocean currents nor sailing sense offer an obvious reason for this stopping place. The myth's information is meager: the Thracians are hospitable; Telephassa dies there. It is possible that the hospitable Thracians are distant kinfolk of the Cadmeioi, the precise relationship between them, if any, having been too blurred by time to be reconstructed. Such an assumption, however, is comprised of still other assumptions which end in a descending spiral of hypothesis too tenuous to pursue. It is also possible that in naming the northern reaches, the myth is simply saying, here is another point in the known world of the time. Certainly a Phoenician expedition to Thrace can be ruled out on factual as well as mythic grounds. So far as is known, Thrace was not attractive to Phoenician businessmen or settlers; and, had the myth wanted to allude to Phoenician explorations in the neighborhood, it would have expressed those allusions in the same unequivocal voice it used when referring to the "Phoenician" enterprises of the other brothers. That leaves the possibility that the Cadmeioi were not Phoenician at all, but Anatolians of another racial stock whose trade, travels, and migrations became associated with the traditions of the Phoenicians. If that were the case, any or all of the family could have originated on either side of the Aegean as Lycians or even as Mycenaeans. Their family history would then have been transposed to Phoenicia in order to satisfy certain other details of the Cadmos story, like the persistent idea that Cadmos brought Phoenician letters to Greece—a bit of information with many possible contexts.

If Cadmos came of either Mycenaean or western Anatolian stock, strains of which we have already shown to be related in the period of early migrations, then the myth's reference to Thracian hospitality would suggest that there were easy relations between the peoples living at Thrace's eastern and western borders. But this is pure conjecture, for little is known about Thrace before 1200 B.C. and nothing at all about her dealings with neighbors, either Anatolian or Mycenaean. Greece after all was not a nation—indeed, its borders are still in dispute—but a collection of tribes and principalities which consolidated slowly. Their origins were multiple and their unequal development was seeded by the many crisscrossings of races that must have occurred as the Aegean highway was traversed. Nor is there any attempt here to create a unity that did not exist. If anything can be learned from this segment of the Cadmos myth, it is that tradition does not minimize tribal distinctions; with one breath it emphasizes the particularity of tribal origins and with another, as we have seen in the case of Cretan history, it subsumes them in the totality of a later Greek experience.

2

To judge from the early chapters of his family's story, Cadmos is mute and dutiful, obeying his father, following his mother, venerating the gods. After Telephassa dies, Cadmos moves to the forefront of the legend and the legend itself changes key: it becomes more symbolical and folkloristic; he becomes more typically heroic, responding to oracular instructions and assuming the responsibilities of a leader. Once on Greek soil, Cadmos acquires from a local cowherd a cow with the mark of a moon on its flank. Obeying instructions from Athena, he follows the cow through the lush plains of Boeotia until it sinks to rest where the city of Thebes now stands. Then, in gratitude to his patron for showing him the place where he is to build his city, he erects an image to Athena, calling it by her Phoenician name, Onga. Next, warning his companions that the cow must be sacrificed to Athena without delay, he sends them to fetch lustral water from the Spring of Ares. He does not know that the spring (now called the Castalian Spring) is guarded by a great serpent, who kills most of Cadmos' men. He takes vengeance by crushing its head with a rock and proceeds with the sacrifice. Athena appears, praises him, and orders him to sow the serpent's teeth in the soil. He obeys and armed *spartoi* ("sown men") at once spring up, clashing their weapons together. Only five survive the brawling that immediately begins, and these offer Cadmos their services. Ares, however, demands reparation for the death of his serpent, so Cadmos is sentenced by a divine court to becomes Ares' bondman for "a great year." After eight (chronological) years in bondage, Athena secures for Cadmos the land of Boeotia. With the help of his five sown men, he builds the Theban acropolis, named the Cadmeia in his own honor.

A cow is not a very sensible animal, but this one does search out some of the best pasturage on the mainland. Literally, cows are an economic asset. Figuratively, this cow carries the mark of the moon goddess (we recall Europa's association with her and also Demeter's) and is also a sign from the gods that Cadmos has them—as well as history for a short time—on his side. The fact that the gods determine the site of the future city is the first of a series of features that make the Cadmos myth one of the true foundation types. Concerned with origins, such myths or myth fragments explain almost as much as they suggest. The racial background of Thebes' founder, its first noble family (Cadmos and Harmonia), the formation of Thebes' army (the *spartoi* rise from the soil in an autochthonous generation), all are proposed explicitly yet without reference to previous custom or future need. One might compare similar features in a myth about a colonizer who always has to justify imposition of his new rule on native inhabitants and so brings with him some mythic advantage like rare wealth, new weapons, or some magic token. The Theban tale, on the contrary, is based on the true reminiscences of a Mycenaean tribe who began a new city.

At least, they may have been Mycenaeans in spite of the myth's insistence that they are Phoenicians. About this kind of fact myth is not reliable. The chauvinist desire to make a Greek unity out of original ethnic diversity is always a strong influence on the shaping of a myth. When mythographers looked back on their past, they must have been tempted often to appropriate all sorts of heroic exploits by natives and foreigners alike and link them to folk memories of a new state's beginning, since the actual circumstances had been forgotten. Or Cadmos may have been remembered as being of Phoenician origins, but his achievement was to establish himself and his tribe on the Mycenaean mainland. In the retrospective view of the mythographer, he was not planting the Phoenician flag on new ground; he was revoking his former citizenship and declaring his new nationality. In fact, there are no Phoenician elements in the myth and for this reason alone one might say with perfect correctness that Cadmos the Phoenician was a Mycenaean.

Cadmos' battle with the serpent is a corroboration in supernatural terms of the myth's foundation theme. In a great many cosmological myths, a hero slays a sea serpent (or dragon or water snake) as the first step in his creation of a new world. In Near Eastern variants, most relevant because of Cadmos' heritage, the serpent seems to represent an idea of primordial chaos for he exists in a place uninhabitable by human beings. Before men can inhabit this place, its chaotic principle must be quelled. Sometimes the principle is symbolized by waters covering a land. These must recede before a "cosmos" on dry land can be established. Greek variations of this universal mythic theme usually separate the snake from the water symbolism. In the battle between hero and snake, the latter is not a symbol of chaos so much as a symbol of the primitive life-and-death cycle of the earth whose forces predate men and operate independently of them.

The first act of the young god Apollo, whom here we take to be a prototypical hero, is to draw his bow and wound the serpent Python that dwells on Mount Parnassos. Python complains to the oracle of Mother Earth, a sacred chasm at Delphi. But Apollo dares to follow him to the sanctuary, where with another arrow he kills the snake. Here the young god represents the triumph of the highest human (and therefore nearly divine) power over an elemental daemon, who is both terrible monster and, through his friendly association with Mother Earth, neutral genius. Audacity and the assertion of rationality are implied in the persistent use of weapons against which the oracle is no protection. The daemon, or spirit of both life and death, is conquered; the conqueror has declared his immunity to both the twin spirits; and thus the act is by definition heroic.

Cadmos' action against the serpent of Ares is in the same tradition. His brute strength is coupled with the good judgment to recognize that the dangerous serpent is his particular heroic trial. The Cadmos variant includes the water symbolism, for the snake is coiled near Ares' spring. The proximity of water and serpent suggests that the snake is to be regarded not only as the embodiment of Death, which must be conquered, but also as the *genius loci* of the place, which holds life-giving water. In some vase paintings on the theme, this association of the snake with fertility is emphasized by showing the snake entwined about the trunk of a flowering tree. The same association is hinted at in the myth of Apollo by the

6. Representations of an owl, a snake, and fruit-bearing branches on a seventh-century B.C. sarcophagus.

Python's request for protection from life-giving Mother Earth. All these cosmological snakes have twin aspects, one terrible, one benign. Together they reflect the potentialities to generate life and to threaten it. After Cadmos sows the serpent's teeth, they seed the life-giving earth, which produces a death-dealing army. (See Illus. 6.)

This very brief summary cannot do justice to the range of significances that attach to mythical battles between hero and serpent. There are, for instance, some echoes in the Cadmos story of a Near Eastern one that may be particularly relevant because of Cadmos' Near Eastern lineage. At the New Year, the Near Eastern myth says, there is a ritual combat between a divine hero and a dragon, a representative of the forces of evil. In their first encounter the heroic weather god is worsted by the dragon Illuyankas and calls on all the gods for aid. The goddess Inaras gives a banquet to which the dragon is invited. After he and his children have drunk to the bottom of every barrel, they cannot fit through the opening in the earth to their underground hole. The evil dragon is then bound with a rope and slain by the weather god, and the benign gods are thus triumphant for another year.

Slaying the serpent in this myth rids the universe of mysterious underworld evils and death much as killing Python does in Apollo's myth or killing Ares' serpent does in Cadmos' myth. In the Babylonian and Cadmean versions, the ritual murder has to be reenacted periodically—either at the New Year or at the close of a "great year," the eight chronological years of a king's reign. The element of repetition suggests a link to seasonal rituals that guarantee the earth's fertility, as well as to kingship rituals that test a ruler's ability to overcome forces of evil (or chaos, infertility, or more social ills) for another year. Cadmos in this sense is proving himself a good leader and future king by accepting the responsibility for his slaughter of Ares' serpent for the great year of servitude that the god later stipulates.

Years ago Jane Harrison, one of the early investigators into the history of Greek religion, suggested that Cadmos' killing of Ares' serpent was characteristic of an early misunderstanding that occurred in myths whenever heroes and snakes both had roles. She conjectured that the snake, because he was the symbol of life and fertility as well as of primeval terror, had been only *associated* with gods (and thereafter some heroes), not opposed to them. Perhaps the serpent's most ancient mythical attribute of immortality, earned by his natural habit of renewing his own life by shedding his skin, had something to do with the original association. The primitive practice of borrowing the characteristics of some revered form of animal life and raising it to a symbolic significance with which a man then identified represented another step in the evolution of associations between men and snakes. Early couplings of hero and snake, Harrison thought, had the character of man to totem rather than of conqueror to menacing danger. Because in crude depictions snake and man were placed side by side, they were wrongly interpreted to mean one killed the other. In some instances the error was perpetuated because of a superficial resemblance to hero-snake combats in other religions. Cadmos, who is a snake-slayer, is also a snake man and king of the snake tribe. This fact lies behind his metamorphosis into a snake at the close of his story, and it explains why the snake is the blazon of the *spartoi*, his sown men. At some time, the tribe probably took the lance as another mark of its affiliation. It is uncertain whether the twofold symbols of snake and lance owed to a fusion between two clans, but these gave rise to the *alternative* blazons of dragon and armed men. Several ancient writers, when referring to the *spartoi,* treat the lance as the sign of the earthborn men at Thebes. One goes so far as to say that the "lance is said to be imprinted on the Spartoi by their mother."

If we move back from these details to take an overview of the episode, we see that once again we are being reminded of Mycenaean features in Cadmos' story—this time by the presence of the gods Ares and Athena. That they are placed in opposition is a subtle refinement worthy of the best propaganda. For "manslaughtering Ares," as Homer calls him, is the god of war and senseless destruction. His characteristics adapt themselves well to the more ancient and symbolic level of the myth's victory over chaos. But the later Greeks were uneasy about Ares, and there seems to be little doubt that when they looked back to their Age of Heroes they denigrated him wherever they could. The Mycenaeans, nevertheless, were primarily warriors. They therefore reshaped the household goddess Athena to accommodate their warlike occupations. She kept her ancient role as mistress of the hearth and became in addition the protector of their citadels and the patroness of strategy and cleverness in warfare. Understandably, then, her advice to Cadmos to sow the serpent's teeth ultimately yields him an army of "five men" (tribes? families?) as fierce as the pre-Lucan serpent himself. Robert Graves suggests that Cadmos' great year of servitude to Ares may mean that the Cadmeans secured their claim on Boeotia by intervening successfully in a civil war among the native tribes. During the war the Cadmeans accepted the rule of the local king, whose reign was measured in eight-year periods. However that may be, Athena is finally triumphant and the mythical city is founded.

3

Has Cadmos' city ever been found? Ever since Schliemann's preliminary dig at Orchomenos, archaeologists have been producing evidence that Boeotia is the oldest area of Mycenaean settlement. As early as 1926 excavators published their discovery of a palace complex underneath the modern city of Thebes. It was immediately hailed as the Cadmea; but then the extensive work necessary to substantiate the claim was postponed indefinitely. A presumptive floor plan deduced from the uncovered rooms showed that the palace center lay immediately below the modern market-place. Short of reducing the city to rubble, nothing could be done. Then in 1963 the deep foundation for a new building was blasted and another corner of the palace was revealed. Archaeologists had found the most significant links between the mythical Cadmos and the ancient structure.

The results of the work at Thebes have been only briefly reported to date and the finds are yet to be assessed. It became apparent rather quickly, however, that there were two distinct palaces, both destroyed by violence. The newer building is different in orientation and plan from the older, and therefore suggests a break in the continuity of Theban royal occupancy. To substantiate the Cadmos myth cycle perfectly the old palace should turn out to be the Cadmea; the more recent one should then be the home of Oedipus and Jocasta, destroyed by civil war between their sons. Any attempt, however, to draw correspondences between oral traditions about Thebes or Cadmos has met with obstacles because there is still too wide a margin of possible dates for the buildings. So much time has elapsed since the day in 1907 when a trial excavation was begun, so drastically have archaeologists' methods changed, that certitude may never be possible. Because a clear system of strat-ification does not exist on the site, opinion based on the pottery styles dates the final destruction of Thebes at between 1375 and 1350. Greek tradition, on the other hand, would have it that members of the same generation that later fought at Troy first destroyed Thebes sometime between 1250 and 1200. Still a third suggestion, based on a collation of the available evidence, says that the destruction of the second palace took place no later than 1270 and that the House of Cadmos was destroyed thirty years earlier. The implications of this last opinion could mean either that the two palaces coexisted—a strange if not nonsensical idea—or that the second one was built and demolished within thirty years.

A partial solution to the problem came when a trial trench across the roadway from 14 Oedipus Street (see Map 1) uncovered a building with the same structural style and orientation as the Cadmea, which was therefore thought to have been erected at the same time. The large number of weapons and other bronzes found there gave rise to the speculation that the building had been an armory. Only when charred pieces of ivory wall moldings were discovered was the hypothesis about the building's function rejected, for it was suggested that so decorated a building was

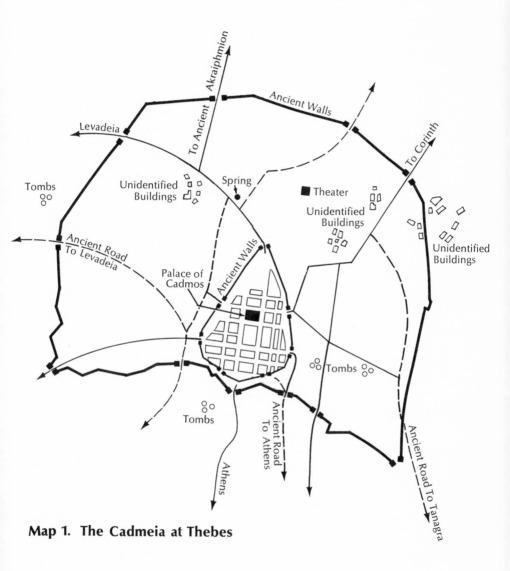

Map 1. The Cadmeia at Thebes

The House of Cadmos with its walls and seven gates lies beneath a section of the modern city. In the fourteenth century B.C. the city precincts were extended to the outermost circle of walls, including the tombs, theater, spring, and armory. The functions of the buildings shown in the upper right and upper left sectors have not yet been identified. Broken lines indicate ancient roadways.

probably a palace annex. Whether an armory or an annex mattered less to the value of the find than did the discovery that there were several different types of pottery in the building and that numerous repairs had been made on its floors. These indicated that the annex had been in use for a considerable period of time, probably after its parent house, the Cadmea, had fallen. Life thus went on after the palace collapsed.

Then another coincidence occurred. More excavation on the two palaces revealed two workshops for cutting semiprecious stones and making gold jewelry. It was so unlikely that two workshops with the same function should have existed simultaneously that very careful analyses of the remains were carried out. The results showed that the onyx in the House of Cadmos was of a different type from that at the New Palace. Moreover, at the New Palace, lapis lazuli was in plentiful supply whereas there was none at the House of Cadmos. This proved that the two could only have been in use sequentially and that the construction of the New Palace followed the destruction of the House of Cadmos.

Only one-half of the significance of any excavation derives from the buildings themselves. The remainder comes from the objects, art, and artefacts found in them. At Thebes the proportion is probably higher in favor of the small finds, for these included twenty-eight stirrup jars with inscriptions on their shoulders in a language that was then unfamiliar, and numerous inscribed clay tablets. At first the excavators, aware of the ancient tradition that Cadmos the Phoenician had brought writing to Greece, promptly named the script Cadmean. (This tradition probably arose in the eighth century, when the Greeks adopted the Phoenician alphabet. Naming the script helped to recall the early legend about a supposed Phoenician, Cadmos, who came to Greece, and so a link was forged between Cadmos and Thebes.) In still another room, fragments of a panel fresco turned up, showing a procession of women in pose and costume reminiscent of the ladies at Knossos. It was therefore speculated that the language used for the jar inscriptions was related to Sir Arthur Evans' Linear A.

To realize why the discovery of inscriptions—even unintelligible ones—is so overwhelmingly important, one needs to make an imaginative leap backward into a world without writing. No matter what contents the stirrup jars were meant to hold, no matter what the message of the tablets, in what language, their primary significance is that they carry writing. For all the attention necessarily given to pottery and other mute artefacts, they do not *testify* to the past. In that sense only written language is history. The distinction between Neolithic and "civilized" peoples is neither the quality of their clothing, nor of their hunting and farming equipment, nor the relative sophistication of their religious rituals. It is the written word. The challenge to decipher its form and content is always secondary to the fact that it exists.

In 1952 Michael Ventris made his brilliant contribution to studies of the ancient world by deciphering the language of the Theban inscriptions, Linear B. Some of his story has already been told in Chapter I; some of its results are referred to as they are relevant in other chapters. At Thebes there had been too small a number of tablets for the intricate and demanding labor of decoding to progress. It was necessary to compare the markings on hundreds of them, found at many sites, before analytical computations could be successful. And, although much of the content is still obscure, the presence of tablets tells more than the amazing enough story that Greece was literate. They also confirm what legends and the town remains imply: that Thebes must have wielded considerable power in order to require the extensive administrative arrangements recorded. Inventories of goods and peoples, foodstuffs, soldiery, furniture, weaponry, all manner of transactions presumably between the palace and individuals representing concerns larger than their own individual needs—all these details on just the few tablets that were found at Thebes imply that there was a need for elaborate government machinery. Historians have suggested the existence of subject territories in Boeotia owing tribute to Thebes, for Boeotia was a farm-rich province with only one other state, Orchomenos, as significant as Thebes—although probably at a much earlier date. Because place names change so dramatically there will always be doubt about the exact identity of the towns listed on the tablets. In legend, however, it is Argive cities that lose their sovereignty to Thebes. Polynices, the son of Oedipus, calls on six heroic Argive companions to march with him against his brother Eteocles, who refuses to relinquish the Theban throne when his term of office expires. All but one of the seven heroes fall before the city, and according to the terms usually exacted by victors, all but one city would have fallen under some sort of Theban jurisdiction. When the sons of the seven reach maturity in one generation, or about thirty years later, they avenge the deaths of their fathers by successfully taking the city. More will be said about the myth of the Seven against Thebes. It is important to note here that the picture of Thebes painted by tradition is strong and unequivocal. It withstands the combined might of seven cities and probably exacts reprisals stringent enough to motivate renewed wars. It is conceivable that a city strong enough to control the destinies of states relatively far off in Argos would have been capable of exerting command over smaller neighboring towns.

4

One question that arises in considering any Bronze Age city is, What was the source of its wealth and power? In the case of the mainland cities, the sheer exertion of arms must always have been the primary road to riches. Wars meant plunder first and new tax-paying subjects for as long as the city's strength lasted. Doubtless Thebes was no exception. But in Thebes the story told by the individual finds, rather than the monuments, has another theme. As a result of ongoing studies it would seem that Thebes was a center for international commerce. The palace rooms filled with ivory and other luxury goods and the workshops for lapis lazuli speak for foreign contacts. So, too, the pantries filled with plain crockery and the rooms where oil and wine were stored in large stirrup jars offer prosaic evidence of commercial success. In a dramatic fashion the stirrup jars with inscriptions, mentioned above, tell more of Thebes' mercantile story.

When the jars were found, in 1945, Linear B had not yet been deciphered. It turned out, however, that even after Linear B became accessible, the jars resisted decoding. Then a piece of philological detective work showed that the words on the jars recurred on some of the Knossos Linear B tablets, sometimes in similar groupings (see Illus. 7). The jars gave a personal name, a place name, and a personal name in the genitive case, or an adjective meaning "royal," as in the following example. *Ka-u-no* is the masculine proper name (perhaps the owner of the jar); *o-du-ru-wi-jo* transliterates the next symbol, which means a place in Crete; then *wa-na-ka-te-ro* is a word in the genitive case meaning "belonging to the king" *(wanax,* "king"). Since some of the names matched those on the Knossos tablets, and since the matching places on the tablets related to details of cattle they supplied, the supposition immediately obvious was that the jars told about some

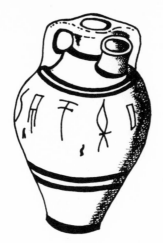

7. A Theban stirrup jar inscribed in Linear B.

commercial relations with Crete. Apparently, the jars contained special consignments of perfumed oil or unguents (information gathered from traces in the jars' interiors) presumably made at the place of the jars' origin. The sum of these conjectures showed that if the place of the jars' origin could be proved, other important pieces to the Theban archaeological puzzle might fall into place. Trade routes between cities would be known; as would something about the proliferation of Linear B script. Since Linear B was also found at Knossos, some light might be shed on the still controversial date of her fall. The proven origins of the jars would have a still wider complex of implications for the kind and duration of relations between Greece and Crete between 1400 and 1200.

In 1965 a study by spectroscopy of the clay used to make twenty-five of the jars was completed. Analysis was based on the 80 percent predictability of the presence of certain elements like calcium, chromium, nickel, and magnesium. By matching up clay samples from selected sites all over the Aegean, the investigators achieved surprising results. It was discovered that the jars were composed of clays from several different deposits, and thus it followed that they reached Thebes from different sources in the Peloponnesos, from Thebes itself, and not from Knossos but from eastern Crete. This last fact was extremely puzzling because one of the two source places in eastern Crete was destroyed in the first half of the fifteenth century, when Linear A script had not yet been superseded by Linear B. That the site, Zakro, had been important for trade had been conjectured from finds of raw ivory and copper ingots at its palace. But it seemed clear that either the date of the site's fall into disuse was wrong, or the clay analysis was wrong, until the analysts realized that both Zakro potters and others in the vicinity had been using the same nearby clay source and had continued to do so after the palace fell.

Commercial ties between eastern Crete and Thebes are fully proven by the stirrup jars. Although all of the jars are not necessarily contemporary, and although dating the Theban structures is still disputed, Crete was obviously still effective in the Aegean and Linear B was still in use late in the thirteenth century, well after the date that Sir Arthur Evans had given for the collapse of Knossos and all of Crete. It is possible that because of her close ties with Crete, Thebes was able to supplant the Minoans after their capitulation to the Mycenaeans and to take over her trading stations in Cyprus, Rhodes, and elsewhere. Evidence for this comes from another set of finds at Thebes, still unpublished, of a hoard of cylinder seals. In 1963 the team of Theban excavators announced their discovery of a treasure hoard in a basement room of the New Palace. In addition to jewelry of gold and glass paste, the cache contained a group of more than thirty-six cylinder seals of lapis lazuli and agate—all unmistakably Near Eastern. Designs and materials of Babylonian, Kassite, Mitannian, Syro-Hittite, and pre-Babylonian workmanship link the Cadmea to the Anatolian countries. Fourteen of the seals have cuneiform inscriptions; all bear the characteristically Near Eastern representations of gods, men, and monsters; and one gives the names and dates of a high official of the Kassite dynasty.

Anatolian scholars agree that the cylinders are the best of their kind and lament that no Babylonian collection is comparable. Until the seals are all published we can only speculate about their separate historical values. Early report says that some of the seals are of Mycenaean workmanship. Were these artisans brought from the east by Cadmos, as one scholar thinks? Or did Mycenaean craftsmen copy these imports in their own work—as is the case with some Minoan artefacts on Mycenaean soil? One flattened seal of onyx, for instance, shows a male figure being tossed by a bull. Perhaps it is a scene showing the capture of a bull; but it is tempting to link it with Minoan bull games. Another seal shows a procession of female worshipers bringing an animal offering to a deity. Considering the number and variety of female representations in Minoan and Mycenaean art, an analysis of this scene could be very illuminating indeed. A third seal, referring to the Kassite official, does give enough very specific information to remind us how valuable the study of the other seals will be. Its design is stylized, depicting a rain god, standing between two mountains, grasping in each hand a flow of water contained at its upper and lower limits by small round jars. The inscription identifies its owner as Kidin Marduk, son of Sculiman, high official of King Burnaburiash II of Babylon, who reigned between 1367 and 1346 B.C. Since the seal cannot be earlier than his reign or later than the destructions that buried it, an early-fourteenth-century date for the fall of the New Palace is ruled out. (See Illus. 8.)

When it was first discovered, Kidin Marduk's seal excited interest of still another sort because its design was thought to represent a god strangling enormous serpents with each hand. Since Theban coins minted in 394 B.C. show Heracles strangling two snakes, and since serpents are prominent features in the city's foundation myth, the seal design was quickly and wrongly interpreted as an early prototype for the Theban national emblem. The god could be Heracles, it was argued, dispatching Cadmos and Harmonia in their snake forms. One might read the symbolism as a triumph of later Mycenaeans over the original Theban dynasty. Whatever its mythic significance, the design illustrates the survival of Near Eastern iconographic motifs which were adopted in the Mycenaean Age and remained current through the Classical period.

As a group the seals ask more questions than they answer. What was the purpose of the hoard? Was it convertible into cash? In a system of barter or trade? Did it have religious value? If the workmanship did provide models for Mycenaean gem-cutters, shouldn't there be other, like seals buried in Mycenaean sites? An automatic assumption that gems are for those who can afford them

8. Babylonian cylinder seal found at Thebes. Cuneiform script identifies Kidin Marduk, the son of a Kassite high official.

implies a more splendid and diversified society than crude bronze weapons suggest. Yet, as becomes more apparent daily, this is the kind of contradiction that typifies the Bronze Age world—at once brutal and luxurious. The sealstones are unequivocal proof of the triangular relationship between the Anatolian coast, the mainland, and Crete—the same relationships that the entire Europa-Cadmos saga tells of. But whereas the myth is explicit about which characters moved in which directions, the sealstones as well as the stirrup jars and luxury goods leave unanswered questions about the places where the transfer of goods occurred. It is always possible, for instance, that the sealstones came from Anatolia to Thebes via Crete rather than by a direct route. Or that, as has already been suggested, the sealstones were collected by Thebans who had taken over a Minoan trading station on Cyprus or elsewhere. The other difficult task is to fix the dates within which these contacts rose, flourished, and declined, and then to collate those with the dates given in the tradition on one hand, and those arrived at for the monuments and artefacts on the other. To this task we turn next.

The seventh entry in the Parian Chronicle (Appendix II) reads as follows: "Since Cadmos son of Agenor came to Thebes . . . and built the Cadmeia, in the reign of Amphictyon at Athens, 1255 years = 1519." Here a very specific reference gives the turn of the sixteenth century as an upper limit for the arrival of Cadmos. Now we need to recall that, in the discussion of the growth of the Europa legend, the arrival of the Cadmeioi was shown to have some links with the expulsion of the Hyksos in 1580. Agenor, the father of Cadmos and Europa, either was one of the Hyksos or made the same journeys that they did to and from Canaan. Since the *idea* of the movement of peoples from the east to Crete and Greece could not have formed before an actual migration, the myth is referring to events in an earlier generation. Moreover, since sometimes generations are not reckoned literally as a span of thirty years, but metaphorically as sometime in a dynasty's past, the only necessary interpretation of Agenor's travels is that they preceded those of Europa and Cadmos. Therefore the date on the Parian Marble, 1512, agrees well with the only datable event in the sixteenth century thus far connected with the legend's development. The date is also in agreement with the archaeological discoveries at Rhodes. The settlement of Near Eastern peoples at Ialysos dates back to the sixteenth century, late in Middle Minoan times, when an influx of Anatolians occurred. The cemetery of Ialysos proved that the settlement was in use during the presumptive date of Cadmos' travels.

The next set of dates admits of some discrepancy. Mycenaeans arrived in Crete sometime in the middle of the fifteenth century, say 1450, when we have supposed that the Europa-and-Zeus element was introduced into the legend. Because the sequence of legendary events here is correct even when events themselves are misrepresented, Cadmos can only set out to search for his sister after she is kidnapped, even if the lapse of time be minutes. Thus 1450 could be the year of the legendary founding of Thebes, after one recalculates the Parian Marble for a correction of a few years in each of the generations counted. In fact, the total difference of sixty years is a phenomenally small discrepancy between tradition and approximated history. The next consideration is that neither the monuments nor the artefacts at Thebes have been dated earlier than 1400, and several scholars have wanted to date them later. Most of the effort of chronology, of course, is bent on fixing a date for the city's final collapse rather than for its foundation, since establishing the latter depends almost solely upon accurate scientific measurements. Now that the precision of uncalibrated carbon-14 dating has been challenged, differences of up to one hundred years can only be resolved by the introduction of fresh evidence.

One contemporary historian, using the uncalibrated carbon-14 dating method, devised a chronology as specific as that of the Parian Marble and more perfectly synchronized with the legend (see pages 52, 53). These results are gratifyingly neat but, from what little is provable about Crete, quite contradictory. The attempt, moreover, to treat the children of Zeus and Europa as literal rather than figurative descendants involves us in a bewildering variety of assumptions about gods and demigods. But probably the most grievous omission is the tradition for the founding of Thebes. Paradoxically, it is less possible now than it was in earlier years to discount tradition as a valuable record. So often it is as right as it is for the dating of the days of Theban power; as we shall see, it is also right about the date of her fall.

THEBES

1405 Knossos burned 1st time by the Achaeans

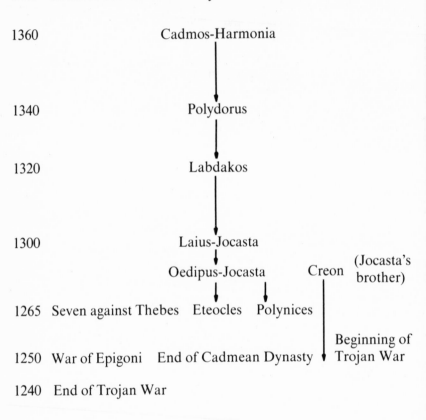

1360   Cadmos-Harmonia

1340   Polydorus

1320   Labdakos

1300   Laius-Jocasta
                          Oedipus-Jocasta   Creon   (Jocasta's
                                                         brother)

1265 Seven against Thebes   Eteocles   Polynices

                                                         Beginning of
1250 War of Epigoni   End of Cadmean Dynasty   Trojan War

1240 End of Trojan War

1180   Destruction of Pylos

1160   Destruction of Mycenae

1100   Knossos burned 2nd time

CRETE

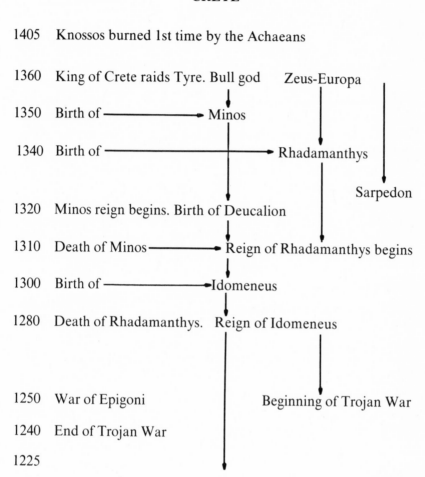

1405   Knossos burned 1st time by the Achaeans

1360   King of Crete raids Tyre. Bull god   Zeus-Europa

1350   Birth of ————————→ Minos

1340   Birth of ————————————→ Rhadamanthys

Sarpedon

1320   Minos reign begins. Birth of Deucalion

1310   Death of Minos ————————→ Reign of Rhadamanthys begins

1300   Birth of ————————————→Idomeneus

1280   Death of Rhadamanthys.   Reign of Idomeneus

1250   War of Epigoni   Beginning of Trojan War

1240   End of Trojan War

1225

1180   Destruction of Pylos

1160   Destruction of Mycenae

1100   Knossos burned 2nd time

5

At several junctures in this chapter it has been said that one important aim of the legend as a whole is to establish the Cadmeioi as Greek. Even the elements of folklore and the supernatural have been infused with this aim. Certainly it is clear in the treatment of the mystical signs given to Cadmos to found a city. It is clearer still in the closing segments of the saga, to which we turn now to show how the narrative machinery betrays its Mycenaean bias.

After Cadmos has made expiation to Ares for killing the serpent at the well, Athena persuades the god to give his daughter Harmonia in marriage to Cadmos. She is successful and there is a great wedding ceremony at which all the Olympians are the guests of honor. Twelve golden thrones are set up for them in Cadmos' house and they bring the mortals costly gifts. Cadmos is initiated into the Samothracian mysteries and Harmonia is taught the rites of the Great Mother. During the celebrations, Demeter assures the couple of a prosperous barley harvest by lying in a thrice-plowed field with Iasion. Pausanias says that in his time the Thebans still showed visitors the places where the Muses played the flute and sang for the occasion and where Apollo entertained on the lyre. In his old age Cadmos resigns the Theban throne, for unfavorable omens have persuaded Cadmos and Harmonia to emigrate. After a considerable amount of blood is spilled over the problem of succession by members of the clan, Cadmos and Harmonia succeed to the thrones of Illyria. There, where Cadmos builds the ancient city of Buthoe, their final serpent metamorphosis takes place. Cadmos is succeeded by Illyrius, the son of his old age.

First, accepting the givens of the entire tale, Cadmos is a foreigner, a Phoenician, or perhaps a Semite since his name has West Semitic affinities with words for "warrior." There is thus every reason why even without killing Ares' serpent Cadmos' person would have offended the Greek war god. Furthermore, Athena could not have been his patroness unless she had adopted him, and since this is her first appearance in the tale this seems to be the case. From what can be learned from other myths, Athena is the protectress of Mycenaean citadels and, by extension, of the Mycenaean warrior kings. She is at their sides throughout the siege of Troy just as she is with Odysseus through his perilous homecoming. One way to minimize Cadmos' Near Eastern heritage would be to place him under her patronage. It is, however, not enough to legitimize his past if he is to found a new state. Although modern historians are interested in his ties with his parent country, the national consciousness of the Greek mythmakers was concerned with establishing his Greekness. He is therefore married to the semidivine child of two more Olympians (albeit very suspect ones, for Aphrodite is probably a pre-Greek mother goddess) and feted by all twelve. The gift-giving at the wedding thus takes on the aspect of a kind of comic birthday party to celebrate Cadmos' adoption into the race. There is no question that his offspring will be Greek after both he and Harmonia have been initiated into Greek religious practices.

All this might suggest that the same sort of rationale is operating in the final actions of the tale, when Cadmos takes the throne in Illyria; that is, that a Mycenaean Greek claim is being extended over the far northern region. Although there is no way of knowing what may have been in the mind of the storyteller who fixed this episode onto the growing legend, it would be curious if he had a patriotic motive. For the Dorian tribes who invaded Greece and destroyed the centers of Mycenaean culture were probably of Illyrian stock. A loose grouping of Indo-European tribes, the Illyrians were a rude and barbarous people whose only contribution to the brilliant history of the Aegean civilizations was that they fought with iron instead of bronze weapons. There is therefore no reason that the real Thebans would have chosen Buthoe as a home. Interpretation of the myth should probably revert here to a religious level of meanings wherein the mythical hero does have reasons for emigrating. Illyria's rudeness is a fit atmosphere in which to retire into serpenthood, if we consider that the curse of Ares is still a potent force in the hero's life. His bloodguilt for the slaying of the serpent and the consequent plague on his family can only be assuaged by his exile from the city. So the royal couple leave Thebes.

6

All of the evidence about Thebes points to the fact that she was a great commercial power during the fourteenth and early part of the thirteenth centuries. During this period Thebes must have controlled most of Boeotia, whose fertile plains provided a variety of agricultural products that may have been sold to countries in the Near East. Her increasing wealth and status may have made rival Mycenaean states see her destruction as a necessity, for the personal histories of the late rulers of Thebes are as gruesome and sad as the city's late fortunes. The keynote is set by the reign of Pentheus, the grandson to whom Cadmos resigns his throne. The idealistic young man places himself in opposition to the god Dionysos and the celebration of his rites, earning as a consequence a horrible death at his mother's hands. Two Boeotians related to the royal family then rule as regents for the beautiful Antiope, too young to take the throne; but their jealous wives persecute the girl viciously, so they in turn are put to death by being tied to the limbs of a wild bull. The twin sons of Antiope, fathered by Zeus, give their energies to building the walls of Thebes and improving its relations with neighboring kingdoms. Yet one of them, Amphion, lives to see his seven sons and seven daughters killed by the arrows of Apollo and Artemis because their mother, Niobe, has foolishly boasted she was superior to the goddess Leto. The wife of the other twin is so envious of Niobe's many children that she tries to kill the eldest and accidentally succeeds only in killing her own son, asleep in the same room.

All this is as a preface to the following reigns of Laius and Jocasta, parents of the fated king Oedipus. The city is being plagued by the Sphinx, an Egyptian or Near Eastern monster who might well be a mythic expression of deteriorating relations Cadmos himself had established between those countries and Thebes. Laius consults the Delphic oracle about how to aid his city and there learns that he is destined to be killed by Oedipus, who afterward will marry Jocasta. In spite of extreme measures taken to prevent such a fate, first by the king and queen, who expose their infant son and leave him for dead, and then years later by Oedipus himself, the prophecy is ironically fulfilled. Oedipus, brought up from infancy by the king and queen of Corinth until he learns of the oracle and so leaves their house, meets with Laius on a crossroad and accidentally kills him. Traveling always away from Corinth, he next meets and overcomes the Sphinx, in the original myth probably by superior force, in Sophocles' drama by superior intellect. The grateful citizens of Thebes reward the young hero with the hand of the widowed queen Jocasta, and from their unknowingly incestuous union are born Antigone, Chrysothemis, Polynices, and Eteocles. After all the tragic circumstances have been revealed, Oedipus blinds himself and is exiled from the city; Jocasta takes her own life; and when the two princes come of age they rule Thebes jointly, each assuming full power in alternate years. The hazards to peace implicit in the nature of such an arrangement are quickly realized. When his term is completed, Eteocles refuses to relinquish the throne and expels his brother. Retaliation is swift and dramatic. Polynices seeks the aid of seven heroes and kings, each of whom agrees to lead an army against one of the seven gates of Thebes and lay siege to the city.

The story of the Seven against Thebes is one of the most celebrated in Greek mythology and is probably based on an historical conflict. Its mythological cause was the brothers' quarrel over succession; its real effect, ten years in the working out, was the ruin and sack of Thebes. In folk memory, the tale of the Seven and its sequel, the Epigoni, were second in fame only to the Trojan War. Why neighboring kings would defend Polynices' claim, we cannot know. If their gathering bears any resemblance to other great collective expeditions like the Voyage of the Argonauts or the more closely analogous Trojan War, Polynices would have had to pledge some portion of his gains to his supporters. Then, too, we do not know the extent of political allegiance a king could rely upon as a result of kinship obligations. Adrastus, the king of Argos who helped Polynices to enlist the heroes and their armies, was Polynices' father-in-law. Perhaps others of the Seven were related by marriage and family. In any case, the fact that the massed strength of the Seven was unable to take Thebes is an indication of the city's formidable power. Stories of individual heroes tell that the siege was bitter: Creon's son Menoicus kills himself in response to the declaration of the seer Tiresias that Thebes cannot be saved unless an unmarried *spartoi* voluntarily gives his one life for the many. The sacrifice does nothing to prevent many other deaths, among them those of Polynices and Eteocles, who kill each other in single combat—symbolically enough, *outside* the city's massive walls. The sons of the Seven are left a legacy to avenge their fathers, and so ten years later these Epigoni ("afterborn") wage a victorious war against Thebes and end its history.

In these last chapters of the Theban cycle, archaeological evidence and Greek tradition are reconciled. With the exception of the last, five kings stand in literal father-to-son relationship: Labdakos, Laius, Oedipus, Eteocles, Creon. If we were to assume that each king reigned for twenty or twenty-five years, this dynasty, the Labdakids, ruled for 100 to 125 years. Archaeology indicates that the life of the New Palace was of like duration and during that life

Thebes remained an active and important power in spite of the collapse of the House of Cadmos. On the evidence reviewed above of the gem-cutters' workshops, the final destruction of Thebes came in about 1250/1240. This implies the correctness of oral tradition: the generation of the Epigoni who fought at Troy first saw the fall of Thebes. Ultimately, accuracy about the tradition hinges on an absolute date for the Trojan War, a separate problem which will be reviewed in its place. In this context it needs to be noticed that the link between Troy and Theban tradition about the Epigoni is forged by the Catalog of Ships in Book II of the *Iliad*. Perhaps the most valuable section of the poem to the historian, it is a battle order listing among other facts the men and their commanders sent from Greece to make war on the Trojans. The list comprises a good deal of what is known about the geography of Greece in the thirteenth century and has been seen as a Baedeker of Bronze Age states and towns. Every town with a name sends a contingent of heroes. Yet Thebes, important as it doubtless had been, is merely mentioned along with a group of more than twenty Boeotian towns that all together sent 120 men in fifty ships. The only explanation possible is that the city was already in ruins. Whereas other Mycenaean centers fell before the invading Dorians at the end of the twelfth century, Thebes had exhausted itself in internecine quarrels a long time earlier. In spite of its place on the international scene in the thirteenth century, it played no role in the war that immortalized the Mycenaeans. As a result, its history was eclipsed by that of lesser cities, and only the dramatists referred to the once flourishing state as the home of the kings in Oedipus' line.

IV

Horsemen and Centaurs

Scholars still argue over the origin and identity of the pre-Greek inhabitants of Greece. The rough facts on which there is some consensus are drawn from an interpretation of archaeological sites on the mainland dating to pre-Classical times. These sites all show three successive levels of destruction, or interruptions, in the continuity of their inhabitance. After each interruption there are signs of profound cultural change: a different method of construction appears, or a new building design; there is a variation in the previous burial practice; or the introduction of a unique pottery shape. The last or third destruction level was caused by the upheaval that destroyed Mycenaean civilization. The fact that there are two earlier destruction levels implies that there must have been three separate occupations of Greece by peoples socially advanced enough to leave buildings. Of these, the Neolithic peoples came first, sometime between 6000 and 3000 B.C. They were succeeded by the metals-using people, probably from Anatolia, in about 3000 to 2500. And then the first wave of Greeks entered the mainland, in some cases assimilating the earlier cultures, in other cases destroying them, and ultimately imposing the characteristic buildings, habits, and usages which we come to know as distinctively Mycenaean. About the first two of these three groups of inhabitants an increasing amount of information has become available.

The life of Neolithic or Stone Age men was lived out in small settlements or villages whose chief concerns were the production of food. In the course of their history they learned to build outdoor ovens, a clear sign that they harvested grain and converted it to bread. Fossilized seeds and seed remains show that Neolithic farmers knew barley and wheat, millet and vetch; bones at the first destruction level are those of sheep and goats. They also knew the pig and the small bull, although these may not have been domesticated. The yield from hunting, fishing, and the cultivation of fruit trees supplemented their diet, while the associated activities motivated the development of skills and tools. From the first they had pottery, painted in designs that resemble those found on Balkan products and shaped in a variety of sizes, from large storage jars to miniature toys and votive figurines. It is from samples of the latter that we learn something about the nature of their religious practices. At site after site there turn up tiny squat female idols with exaggerated breasts and thighs that seem to tell of primitive fertility worship. The remainder of the evidence of Stone Age life is deduced from burial grounds and the rubble of buildings. They buried their dead in pits outside their houses, sometimes tumbling them in with older bones and sometimes crowding small children in together. If the skeletons that have been found are at all typical, they show that Neolithic man was fairly tall and had a long skull, fine features, and excellent teeth.

Buildings were small, rough affairs whose walls were constructed with a double row of medium-sized stones, loosely packed with pebble and earth. The whole was shaped like an elongated rectangle and the inside corners of the walls were often extended into the room to form benches. Roofing was probably made of a composite of dried mud and reeds. There was some variation in the pattern of Neolithic building. Houses in a settlement now in the process of being excavated at Lithares, a day's walk from Thebes, conform generally to the rectangular shape just described. Tiny benched rooms, sometimes no larger than five by four feet, open off an aisle one and a half feet wide to form rude shelters. In one of the Lithares houses, a collection of tiny bull figurines or idols was found in a room which may have had a religious function. To date these are the earliest indications that the bull may have played a role in the primitive forms of worship practiced by some late Stone Age people in Greece. (See Illus. 9.)

Not all Neolithic building conforms to the scale of the settlement at Lithares. The well-known fort at Dimini, dated c. 2650 B.C., is both larger and more extensive and is enclosed within a mazelike set of six concentric walls. The whole comprises an area of about ten thousand square yards, which in times of emergency contained all the village and its domestic animals. The construction of the walls suggests that the builders had a good deal of experience with sieges, for all but one of the gates are too narrow to permit two persons (invaders?) to enter abreast. The ground level outside the walls, moreover, is lower than that inside, where the defenders must have stood—at a distinct advantage over the hostile invader.

After taking into account the outer walls, the grouping of the buildings, and the altar located in the innermost protected area, one archaeologist has proposed that the whole plan suggests a centrality of control that we associate with one-man rule. Presumably, this kingship of some sort implies that the inhabitants at Dimini were less vulnerable to attack by foreigners than, say, were the loosely agglomerated buildings at a settlement like Lithares. Be that as it may, neither centralized government, if that is what it was, nor the ingenious design of the walls made Dimini proof against the second wave of inhabitants.

Just this brief summary is sufficient to suggest that toward its close, the Neolithic period was characterized by continual threats, most probably from neighboring tribes searching out fresh lands to put to the plow. Indeed, it was not until well after the Mycenaean period that farming techniques were advanced enough to divorce the quest for a high-yield crop from the need to settle new areas. But no one knows whether or not fortifications like those at Dimini are to be read as indications of tribal quarrels over land. Or, if so, whether that reason is more important than the ageless motives of plunder and pillage. The question hinges on the area's population growth as well as on patterns of social behavior, and about both of these there is more controversy than certainty. In fact, little can be said that is true for all of the Neolithic peoples in Greece since there are many local variations in their art, their buildings, and their language. Neither were they all of the same racial stock, although the consensus is that they originated in Anatolia. There, metal technology had utterly changed the social patterns that had existed from earlier agricultural times. Metallurgy resulted in the growth of

9. A small room in the settlement at Lithares. The worker, standing in the central corridor, provides an inadvertent reference to the scale of the building.

specialized trades, in an accumulation of personal wealth, and in the creation of impressive cities. These changes affected peripheral regions differently but no less than they did urban ones. Villages without metal and ones not trained to participate in its mining or shaping must nevertheless produce a surplus in order to buy new tools. Involvement in the new technology spurred the development of a commercial pattern of life utterly alien to the organization demanded by Neolithic farming. Concurrently, industry and architecture became more complicated and mobility increased among tribes with some knowledge of the new developments. Simultaneously with the social and economic revolution caused by the introduction of metals, Anatolia experienced a sharp increase in population, and it was apparently this which led directly to the colonization of the Greek coasts and many of the islands in a variety of movements.

By pinpointing the incidence of non-Greek place names away from the Asiatic landmass and nearby islands, the area of Anatolian settlement has been roughly mapped. It extended in an arc along the eastern mainland from Orchomenos through Attica into the Argolid and Arcadia (see Map 2). Other Anatolians settled central Lakonia and western Messenia, and perhaps the same group also invaded the westernmost Ionian islands. Crete received its contingent of Anatolians as probably did still unexplored areas in Macedonia and Thessaly. Ultimately the most conclusive proof that this second level of inhabitants was Anatolian is the linguistic phenomena already referred to in Chapter II. In addition to place names, there is a high incidence of non-Greek nouns for agriculture, plants, animals, birds, foods, and personal names that were absorbed into the Greek language. Most or many of these words end in *-nthos* or *-assos—kerasos* (cherry tree), *erebinthos* (pea), *kalaminthos* (mint), *alynthos* (wild fig). The origin of the words has been the occasion of more than one fruitless scholarly controversy. When the Greek-speaking tribes pushed their way into the mainland they either destroyed, subjugated, or assimilated the Anatolian population they found there. It has been regularly observed, however, that the language of a newcomer, who comprises the minority of a population, rarely is able to impose itself on or supplant the spoken language of the entrenched majority. Thus it has been argued that the evolved language we know as Greek must have been, at least in its essential forms, the language of the Neolithic and Early Helladic (Anatolian) folk already established on the mainland when the invaders came. The language the Greeks brought, whatever it was, could only have been absorbed into the matrix of the older one. The argument takes for its analogy the situation of English and French after the Norman invasions. Both were spoken for a while, with French remaining the language of the aristocratic invaders. Then some French was absorbed into the established tongue, Anglo-Saxon, which reemerged several hundred years later as Medieval English. The trouble with the analogy is that whereas only a minority of ruling-class Frenchmen ever landed and lived in England, the relative minority of Greeks remained on the land, bringing to it a higher level of technology—a point about which more will be said. Cultures do not supersede earlier ones in a downward direction; although a lower one may destroy a higher, wherever the two coexist the superior technology will prevail. This is what happened in Greece. The *-nthos/-assos* pre-Greek family of dialects may have survived for a while in all the localities where place names with these endings are clustered. Elsewhere it became a vestigial language, giving to later Greek a hint of what the earlier agricultural world was like.

While the Near East and Anatolia were consolidating changes effected by the metalworking revolution, to their north and west the first great age of Indo-European folk wanderings began. Why these movements occurred is another subject that has been interminably argued. Still, in the period between 2500 and 1900 B.C., one branch of the Indo-European family entered the Iranian plateau; another branch began the settlement of India; Hittites and Mitannians appeared in Asia Minor and Syria; a new people rebuilt Troy IV; and the Greek speakers entered Greece. With all these peoples came distinctive styles of wheel-made pottery, the apsidal house,* and the horse, the creature that was to revolutionize society in ways nearly as startling as had metal.

It is just possible that some of the stories that we classify as foundation myths date back to this moment in history—and several of these will deserve our attention below. But scholars in disciplines other than mythology also have tried to reconstruct the circumstances that might have existed when the Greek tribes arrived. One excellent such study has been in progress for some time now at the extraordinary site of Lerna (see Illus. 10), which experienced five thousand years of continuous habitation from Neolithic to Roman times. Lerna, like Dimini, was another city with circular walls, rebuilt several times. Lerna's walls, however, enclosed a small palace as mute testimony to the wealth it had amassed in the third millennium. Called the House of Tiles after the mass of terra-cotta and blue-green-schist roofing tiles which slid into the building when it burned and collapsed, it was a two-story building of relatively complex design. The fact that no smaller houses were built around it suggests that the occupants of the House of Tiles were the sole members of the town. Apparently farming (of leafy green peas, beans, and barley), hunting, and fishing were the basis of the town's economy; but its source of prosperity in this, the "Anatolian" period, remains mysterious. Cemeteries, always an important source of demographic information, have not been found and it is presumed they were dug some distance from the town. At about 2200 B.C., at the stratum designated as Lerna IV, the city obviously underwent an enormous change. Gray wheel-made pottery suddenly appears—earlier here, we might add, than elsewhere on the mainland. So do apsidal houses, the horse, and the skeletons of 234 men, women, and children, buried either intramurally or next to

---

* A four-walled rectangular structure with a hearth at one end. (See Illus. 10.)

their houses. The newcomer had arrived—three separate clans of Greeks each identifiable by minor variations in skull and bone measurements. The two largest clans, designated Northern and Western after their burial locations on the town grid, are of particular interest, for they show similarities in body build and skull size with northern Balkans and Anatolians. This latter fact has been called on to support theories that favor the Balkans as the immediate point of departure of the migrating Greek tribes. Thus far no agreement on the issue has been reached. There is, however, reason to suppose that the clans ultimately originated somewhere in the great Eurasian plain, for the Greeks, like the Aryans, Hittites, Mitannians, and others who migrated outward from the area, were horsemen.

Close study of the skeletons revealed the existence of six clans in all, four of whom may have comprised the original Anatolian population. Basing his deductions on dissimilarities between male and female bones, Dr. Lawrence Angel, Lerna's demographer, hypothesized that the Anatolian clans were matrilineal. On the basis of the same study, the Greek clans (Northern and Western) showed greater similarities between males and females, a physical phenomenon that is expected in patrilocal groupings. Dr. Angel's conclusions thus offer the earliest concrete evidence for the suppo-

10. The center of the settlement at Lerna. Remains of a circular "tower" date to the Neolithic period; other structures reflect continuous habitation down to the Early Helladic period of the House of Tiles.

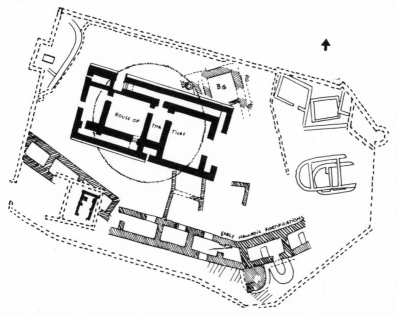

sition that the early Greeks, like the later ones, were patriarchal. He also showed that these clans were monogamous, each pair of parents bearing about five children of whom perhaps two survived to adulthood, and that a very high proportion of these people suffered from arthritis of the neck and abscessed teeth—two ills that probably were related. The more lethal disease they faced was malaria; it killed 10 percent of the population in each generation.

The heterogeneous group of six clans at Lerna, intermarrying, exchanging customs and religions, fostered a stronger hybrid individual than any one clan could produce. The still more important effects of the mixture of clans must have been cultural and social, for at Lerna, as at Troy, the Greeks did not destroy the material establishment of their host. In fact, even though body wounds appear on several skeletons, nothing supports a picture of the Greeks as warrior bands. Instead, both Northern and Western clans may have come originally as refugees to an area they knew through trade—a kind of advance party of their kinsmen yet to come.

Over a period of about six to ten generations new bands of invading Indo-European * kinsfolk kept appearing, forcing the pattern of daily life to respond to constant and rapid change. Whereas the original Anatolian clans were trading with areas of central Greece that had not yet met the newcomer, the hybrid clans set up trade contacts over a wider geographical area. The Southern and Marsh clan sectors, for instance, held Middle Minoan pottery of several styles and dates. There were also Cycladic pottery, probably from Melos, and many small finds of foreign tools and weapons, like riveted dagger blades and hammer-axes. These latter objects tell of continuing contact with Anatolia and the eastern Mediterranean. By the time the rest of Greece had been inundated with the new peoples, about 2000 B.C., the stratum labeled Lerna V begins. It reflects a continuing variety of house styles and the now regular custom of intramural cist and earth burials for all the population, styles probably learned from the Anatolian descendants. The overall picture, therefore, is of a mixed population choosing some customs and adapting others in a quiet process of mutual assimilation.

* The term refers to the family of languages spoken by these migrating tribes.

2

Although the picture of the origins of early Mycenaean society that emerges from an examination of Lerna seems generally coherent, it takes for granted three fundamental problems. One is related to the long process by which metallurgy develops. What precisely do we mean when we talk about a metals revolution? The most recent and original authority on this subject is Colin Renfrew. He theorizes that the Balkans were included among several areas in which inventions and discoveries about metals were taking place independently well before the techniques of alloying tin with copper to produce bronze were perfected. Harder and more malleable than copper, the development of bronze represented the single most important step in a series of innovations that ranged from trading to mining to smelting and casting. Too easily overlooked is the conservatism against innovations which new techniques always have to overcome: copper objects, for instance, were being made in Anatolia before 6000 B.C., yet apparently there was no further development in metallurgy for another two millennia. By bringing the new techniques with them, the Greek tribes had an advantage that local inventors trying to introduce the making of bronze objects would not have had. Certainly everyone in every place was not directly affected by the bronze revolution and the new industries it created. Gradually, however, the introduction of metals to replace stone and wooden tools and artefacts changed the economic face of the Greek mainland. For the duration of the Bronze Age, possession of metal weapons and tools remained a prerogative of the wealthy.

Another point that Lerna makes very clear to us is how over-generalized is our vision of the Greek-speaking tribes pushing down into Greece. Do we see individual clans moving independently over a period of decades, as in fact is proven to be the case at Lerna, or do we think of full-scale invasions, albeit in successive waves? About this there is something further to be borne in mind. Not much is known about the rate at which populations multiply under favorable circumstances, but it must be very great. The previous populations, the Anatolians, were entirely subjugated and in most cases destroyed, whereas within three centuries there were enough Greeks to settle and populate Mycenae, Tiryns, Iolcus, Troy, Orchomenos, Gla, Pylos, and so on. In 1600, the date that we have in mind when we cite these cities, the population of Greece was about three million. It is inconceivable that anything like that number of Greek-speaking tribes were invaders; nor by any dint of mathematical calculation can one assume that there were enough tribes to have multiplied to the extent of three million in just three hundred years. To take an example from other migrations which are better known, it is likely that a few long boats held all the ancestors of the population found on all of the combined Polynesian islands.

It is entirely possible that only fifteen thousand or so Greek speakers conquered the whole of Greece, which was very sparsely settled in any case. We can imagine them busy at making new lives for themselves in their new lands, introducing new social structures, adapting themselves to a new terrain, making contact with the Neolithic farmers. The resultant hybrid culture is the one we know of as the Aegean Bronze Age. But the Bronze Age did not come to all of Greece in uniform fashion. The northernmost region of Greece, Thessaly, retained for centuries its primitive culture. Geography cut it off from the influence of the advanced cultures of Egypt, Crete, and the Near East as well as from social and political developments to the south on the mainland. Long after Zeus had been established in his worship as the sky god, for example, the Thessalians continued to give special prominence to Poseidon in his aspect as ancient earth god and consort of Mother Earth. Some historians account for this tardy cultural development by the presence in Thessaly of an ethnic strain that differed from the races on the mainland, for its art shows affinities with the Neolithic arts of central Europe, southern Russia, Susa, and Turkestan. That and its subsequent isolation would account for the distinctive Neolithic character that the area retained. By about 1600 this self-contained culture gave way to a Bronze Age and to close connections with important cities to the south.

The third important point that arises is related to one of population and has to do with the superiority conferred upon the Greeks by their possession of horses. This last factor is so far-reaching in its implications that we will return to it below. Taking all three points together—the metals revolution, the size of the population, and the socioeconomic change brought about by the horse—we have the postulate that a few Greek-speaking tribes, equipped with better swords and the advantage of the horse, overcame a settled culture and established a Bronze Age in Greece.

It is impossible to overstress the impact of the horse. The changeover from purely agricultural pursuits to those of aristocratic warfare was massive and nearly instantaneous. The impact of horses on the imaginations of the Greek peoples themselves must have been equally overwhelming. For Greek myths are filled with horses. The animal appears as a manifestation of the gods, as a prize of battle, as a sign of wealth, as an aristocratic name for people and places, and as one of the most sacred of sacrificial animals. Legend even has it that Troy itself was founded by a horse. Common sense, rarely a useful criterion for understanding myth, says the legend is nonsense. It is interesting, nonetheless, to try to unravel the threads that lead outward from the legend, since they are interwoven (to keep the metaphor) with the famous city and the arrival of the Greeks.

When, in 1890, Schliemann first dug at a hill near Hissarlik in Anatolia, he discovered the home of Homer's Trojans. Though Schliemann was led to his work by an interest in mythology, he added nothing to the fanciful tale of the city's founding by a horse. When, in the twentieth century, the American archaeologist Carl Blegen dug at Troy, at the level called Troy VI dated to about 2000, neither was he persuaded to the animal identity of the city's founder. He did find, however, that a new group of people came to Hissarlik, bringing with them a distinctive wheel-made pottery, a new style of building with fortifications, and the horse. The pottery, Minyan ware, has been found only on the Greek mainland, on certain of the Aegean islands, and on two places on the Anatolian coast that were under the cultural influence of Troy from c. 2000 onward. The building style, superimposed on the foundations of the previous town, has the monumental walls and the projecting towers of the (four) gates that demonstrate the power and the assertiveness that are associated with the later Greek site of Mycenae. Indeed, like the citadel, Troy VI is a hill fortress and the center of a wealthy community. As for the horse, his bones were a unique and startling find. At no other site has there been found indisputable evidence of his existence and domestic use so early as the opening of the second millennium; and at none have the circumstances of his presence been so overwhelmingly associated with the people distinguished by their pottery, their building, and their houses as Greeks. There was no burning and destruction by the advance guard of the newcomers at Troy, and precisely how they assumed control is not clear. The changeover may have been peaceable, for the older populace seem to have been at a simpler, more agrarian cultural level. In any case, the early people left no trace of their life-style or culture from this time forward.

It is easy to read the multiple geological strata at Troy and see the break in cultural continuity caused by the coming of the Greeks because the site had been continuously occupied from the fourth millennium until its final destruction c. 1200. In addition, whereas mainland sites tended to be at subsistence levels of civilization when they were taken over by the horsemen, Troy was already a flourishing commercial center with accumulated wealth, possibly derived from a developed textile industry. Many objects, tentatively identified as spindle wheels, were found at the levels of Troy IV and V, and Schliemann's famous gold treasure is as likely to have been earned in the cloth industry as to have been acquired by piracy.

Associating horses with Greeks at Troy of course does not explain the city's legendary founding by a horse. It does, however, help to understand the "Greekness" of the horse, or, as James Joyce might have put it, the "horseness" of the Greeks. Where then did horse and Greek originate? For at Troy the evidence is incontrovertible that the two arrived together. So far as is known, the animal roamed wild in the central European plains from the sixth millennium, as the cave paintings at Lascaux and elsewhere are sufficient testimony. Later, by the third millennium, the place and number of bones suggest that he was being herded for riding (?) and hunted for food in northern Europe, in the steppes of southern Russia, and in Siberia. It is probably from the latter two areas that knowledge of the horse spread southward to the Iranian plateau. The tangled mountains of the Caucasus and of Anatolia blocked the north and south diffusion of men, animals, and technologies. Farther east, however, where no such barrier existed, there is a north–south archaeological trail of horse bones and teeth. Sites like Rana Ghundai in Baluchistan, which may have been camping grounds for nomads, suggest that these Iranian plateau peoples domesticated the animal.

A different clue to the horse's route south from the steppe area appears on a Mesopotamian tablet of the third millennium which mentions an animal called the "ass of the mountains." The phrase is rich in implied meanings: since the ass is known, the named creature is not an ass. It is nevertheless like the ass in some ways; and it comes from the hilly areas to the north of the flat Mesopotamian floodplains. This was probably the small European horse familiar to us from bas-reliefs. What is especially interesting about this poetic description is its reminder that equine animals like onagers and asses have to be carefully distinguished from the true horse whose remains were found at Troy.

How did the wild horse make this journey from north to south? The Indo-European steppe folk with whom the horse was originally associated were a semibarbarous people at a relatively primitive stage of culture. The Mesopotamian culture, on the other hand, was at its height: agriculture had been fully developed by a complex irrigation system of canals, and the crop yield was diversified by the products of several domesticated animals. In the north the horse was the hunter's transportation, and occasionally his source of food; in the south he became a draft animal, later associated with the light chariot. The transition from one to the other set of functions must have involved several intermediate steps. Indo-European nomads at scattered camping grounds may have been responsible for the animal's dispersion over the area.

Then somewhere in the grasslands between the European and Iranian plateaus, a pastoral people, familiar with the horse and perhaps racially akin to the Indo-Europeans, mingled with the many agricultural communities that had been settled in the area for centuries. The time for domestication to occur, and more time for the horselike "ass of the mountains" to become familiar to the Mesopotamian plains folk, may also have been the time in which several technologies fused. Somehow the combination of horse, rawhide reins, and crude four-spoke wheels resulted in the invention of the fast, maneuverable light chariot. Apparently the idea of hitching horselike onagers (wild asses) to four-wheeled vehicles was familiar in Sumerian times. Such wagons were slow and cumbersome and useful mainly for hauling and carrying. Clay reproductions of similar wagons also have been found at religious sites in Crete and Anatolia. Their presence among votive offerings suggests that wagons were part of religious processions, perhaps used to cart sacrificial animals and other offerings. In any case, the horse and his vehicle, the spoked, dual-wheel chariot, was of a new order of technology which has not been documented earlier than 1700 B.C.

By that point in time, about four hundred years after the arrival of the horsemen in Troy, there is clear evidence that the animal was a strategic weapon in warfare. New Indo-European

tribes in Anatolia, the Hittites, Kassites, and Mitannians, equipped
with horse, chariot, and bow, emerged as powerful threats to the
floodland Mesopotamians in the interior. Their arrivals on the
Anatolian coast probably were interspersed from c. 2100 to c. 1700,
so that it took these horsemen merely four hundred years to establish their ascendancy over the superior culture of the ancient
Babylonians. Their advent changed the political history of the
continent.

It is largely through our knowledge of these Indo-Europeans
on the Anatolian coast that we learn about their kinsmen, the
mainland Greeks, during the period before 1500. Hittites, Mitannians, and Greeks are all warrior aristocrats whose most important
possession is the horse. It is significant that the earliest example of
Greek representative art is a war chariot on a grave stele at
Mycenae, c. 1650. (See Illus. 11.)

Taking into account the geographical as well as the cultural
uniqueness of Troy VI, one historian guessed that Trojans acquired
their wealth by specializing in the breeding and export of horses.
Some weight is added to his speculation by the fact that in the old
formulaic poetry of the epic singers, Ilios (Troy) was called "city of
good horses" and the Trojans themselves "horse tamers." Eventually *hippios* came to be an epithet for many Achaeans, especially
in Homer, and there is reason to believe that Greeks learned the
arts of breeding and management from their Anatolian kinsmen.
The horse that was imported into the Anatolian plains was the
descendant of the western-steppe breed—a small, spirited animal
with fine legs and head, his posture emphasized by an elegantly set
tail—in all, very like the animal in the relief on the Mycenaean stele
already referred to. He needed time and training to acclimatize and
then to be brought into condition for pulling the chariot. The
process took several months and is described in detail in the famous
Mitannian *Book of Kikkuli,* clay tablets now at the Hittite capital of
Bogazkoy. First the animal was kept to severe fasting and phy-
sicking; then gradually muscle tone was built up by just as severely
regulated food intake and exercises, which were increased in rigor
by stages. Whether Troy did commercialize on its natural product
by breeding is speculation. The Mitannian manual proves that that
tribe did excel in training, and that the more powerful Hittites
turned to them for that specialty. By 1600 the Achaean Greeks on
the mainland may have been visiting the Hittite court to learn the
fine points of horsemanship, for eventually they also earned the
epithet "horse tamers."

11. Limestone stele from Grave Circle A at Mycenae showing a warrior in a chariot. The earliest monumental art in Greece.

Although they have been presented together in this brief summary, it must be emphasized that the horse and chariot did not arrive in Greece simultaneously. The all-important evidence of chariots and chariot gear is three or more centuries behind the evidence of the animal. It is likely that migrating Anatolians with women and children would have prized the strategic mobility of a pack animal—especially since the only equipment needed by primitive riders was rudimentary, a rope or rawhide. It is even plausible on those grounds to see the invaders with elementary cavalry rather than chariotry, although the small size of their ponies needs to be considered. Since, moreover, carts and draft animals were already known in Mesopotamia, the invention of the spoked wheel may have taken place there and even have preceded the entry of horse tamers. The latter point, however, is relatively minor, since an invention without function is no invention at all.

3

Horse, chariot, and Troy, too, deserve fuller stories than is permitted by the point made here—that wherever we find early Greeks there are horses playing an important role. When we attempt to change the focus of investigation, however, and look first at stories about horses and then at provable data about them, the ground is obviously more speculative. One approach to his ubiquity in the Greek oral tradition is that since the horse's appearance in the Aegean coincides with that of the Greeks, tales about him are likely to be among the oldest in the tradition. Several myths involving horses, furthermore, seem to crystallize a kind of primitive Greek ethnography—the Greeks' early consciousness of themselves as a distinctive people.

It is to this class of myth that tales about the centaur belong. The centaur is a composite of man and horse whose very looks suggest a blurred image of horse and rider (see Illus. 12.) He has the head and torso of a man; the body, legs, tail, and hooves of the horse. This duality in his appearance is consistent with a duality between his animal or natural attributes and his human or acculturated ones. Never are both sets of characteristics combined in one centaur myth; instead, stories and centaurs alike tend to fall into two groups. The first group lives beyond the northern limits of the cultivated mainland, in the mountains around the Thessalian plains, long a setting for tales of uncivilized deeds. These centaurs are wild, anarchic figures, likely to bring chaos into settled living habits. They eat raw meat, are tricky and arbitrary, and go mad on just the fumes of wine. When the centaur Pholus is compelled by the laws of hospitality to broach a jar of wine for Heracles, his kin catch the scent of the wine and run amok. Nessos, another centaur who figures in Heracles' adventures, combines diabolism with lechery. He offers to help the hero's wife, Deianeira, ford a stream; he then attempts to rape her on the opposite shore and loses his life to the hero's quick arrow. But not before inventing a potion for Deianeria, out of a mixture of his spilled seed and his blood, that is supposed to prevent its user from philandering. The jealous wife dips Heracles' shirt into this concoction with the horrible result that the cloth sticks to his burning skin and eventually prompts him to suicide.

Rape and bloodshed recur as elements in the myth of the

12. Heracles killing the centaur Nessos.

Battle between the Lapiths and Centaurs. The latter crash into the wedding of the Lapith king Peirithous to Hippodameia and try to kidnap the bride and rape the other women. Their fighting tactics are crude—they hurl boulders and tree trunks—and their behavior on the whole is uncontrollable and fierce.

Best known of all the centaurs is Cheiron, who personifies the contradiction of all these natural or horselike qualities. He is gentle, law-abiding, and wise; skilled in the arts of the bow and the lyre; a healer, a prophet, and the famous teacher of famous heroes. He has none of the passions of his wild kinsmen, and so far as one can judge by omission, he was never a young centaur! From the first, he is respected for his age, sagacity, and mastery of all the useful arts, and in the sum of his accomplishments he represents the extreme of

acculturation. Herein lies a further contradiction. Why should a
half-man, half-horse symbolize the epitome of culture? Why not a
hero or a god? Part of the answer lies in the awesomeness of nature
which gives primitive animism its force. A turbulent sky is an angry
god; the oak tree has prophetic power; the flight of birds evokes the
wisdom of a spirit world. The wild faces of nature are neither
controllable nor understandable to a prescientific mentality. They
are therefore invested with human (or superhuman) attributes. It is
in such a context that one must imagine the appearance of the
strange and novel creature called horse to the Neolithic peoples
already settled in Greece. To them, his descent from the far uncivilized north of Thessaly, his speed and fierceness, the strength he
shared with the newcomer himself—all would have combined in the
image of natural chaos that was later implied by one type of
centaur.

Some myths incorporate the fearfulness that would have been
experienced by peoples unaccustomed to the horse. There is, for
example, the tale of Diomedes, king of Bistones of Thrace—again, a
far north region—who fed his famous steeds on strangers. Heracles'
seventh labor is to stop this cruel custom, to civilize Diomedes.
Instead, the hero throws Diomedes to his own monsters (called
Dreadful and Bright Eye!), thus adding retribution to the tale's
elements of projected xenophobia and cannibalism. A folklorist
might see in the tale a shadow of the steppe peoples' custom of
living on mare's milk during a raid; or perhaps there is a reflection
here of the still earlier use of the animal for food. In any case, the
frightening aspect of the animal would not have been emphasized
by the peoples who lived with him, but by those who saw him as
foreign and potentially dangerous.

The tribes who knew the horse must have provided the initial
impulse for the incorporation of the centaur's benign aspects into
his overall characteristics. Economics doubtless played a large role
in shaping his attitude to the animal, for he was highly valuable
both living and dead. Alive, he was both swift transportation in
times of peace and a battle machine in war. He was a sacrifice to the
gods and, on those same occasions, a feast for men. Every part of
his body, moreover, was used in folk medicine—a fact which suggests the origins of the "good" centaurs' reputations as healers.
Babylonians who venerated the stars may also have known of the
horse's medicinal properties, for they saw the constellation Sagittarius, the healer god, as a horse. Even Nessos, the wild centaur,

knows how to prepare magical potions from his blood and seed. There is no evidence that a man in the Bronze Age paid for the robbery or death of a horse with his life. The Nessos story may nevertheless incorporate a confused reminiscence of some payment made to the owner of a killed horse. After Deianeira dips Heracles' shirt into the dead centaur's "love potion," the shirt clings to the hero's back as a vividly symbolic representation of his bloodguilt until he makes reparation.

4

The step from real values to symbolic ones is mysterious, and when the horse made it cannot be known. As centaur, the horse is partially anthropomorphic; as the object of worship he moves still further along the route to abstraction. Sometime early in the second millennium he became a god; for etymology and archaeology prove that horse cults existed in the northern regions. Their crude form and their occasional association with human sacrifice are proof of their high antiquity. Diomedes, just mentioned above, undergoes a metamorphosis in late Greek legends, becoming a courageous companion to Achilles. Originally his associations are to the barbaric horsemen in Thrace, for vestiges of those ties remain in his cult rituals. White horses were sacrificed to him as far west as the Adriatic coast and as far south as Cyprus. His own name is non-Greek, but his adoption by the Greeks is hinted at in the name of his wife Euippa, "beautiful mare." There is reason to believe that horse cults retained a good deal of their primitive force in Thrace long after they had become diluted by other ritual practices in central Greece.

At Marathon a double horse burial was discovered at the outer end, or dromos, of a chamber tomb. The animals are laid out symmetrically, facing each other, their legs overlapping in an attitude at once tender and strong. The position is one repeated on several Mycenaean seal masterpieces depicting two animals (see Illus. 13). The tomb, which had no trace of harness or carriage, is dated c. 1900, and is the only site of so elaborate a burial. Many tumuli in Thrace, however, suggest the presence of other burials under simple mounds. Hard evidence for cult practice comes from burials in Marathon, Argos, and Nauplia, at which sites horses were sacrificed. The excavator, Professor J. Caskey, reported that at Lerna most of the skeleton of a horse lay on a gravel pavement. The bones were in disorder in conjunction with the fragments of about thirty-seven drinking cups. He did not interpret the remains, which he said "provoked speculation." Other specialists connect this burial and others like it with the human burials in the same tomb and have deduced the existence of a cult practice which involved toasting the dead and then discarding the cup from which the toast was drunk.

In Crete, where the horse is a late introduction of the fifteenth century, one such burial was found in the tholos tomb of a priestess (?) at Arkanes, near Knossos. The horse, about six years old, had been cut up anatomically, head severed from neck, legs from body, and the latter broken at the spine. The parts were heaped up to the right of the tomb's entrance so as to take up as little room as possible. By analogy with other animal sacrifices, it seems probable that the horse was bled first in a ceremony of propitiation to the chthonic earth powers who demanded atonement or purification through blood offerings. When Homer's Nestor entertains Odysseus' young son, Telemachus, he sacrifices a bull in his honor. The animal is bled into vessels reserved for the purpose, and then the blood is poured in a libation to the earth deities before the carcass is cut up and cooked. The vocabulary of the sacrifice seems to indicate that the process of sacrifice is associated with the butchering of a beast for food. Since at Arkanes there was no positive evidence of a meal having been made, the archaeologists have also suggested that dismemberment of the horse may have been associated with

13. The horse team burial at Marathon.

the idea of destroying the dead person's treasured belongings so that they could not be used again by the living.

In fact, the cut-up horse at Arkanes has not been satisfactorily explained except by analogy to other Greek and Indo-European horse sacrifices. According to James Frazer, sun worshipers dedicated their horses to the deity in one of two ways: the land-locked Spartans conducted a ceremony on a mountaintop; the Rhodesians tossed his parts into the sea, which nightly "caught" the sun's chariot at twilight. Frazer also described a Vedic ritual marriage enacted annually between horse and queen. After symbolically lying with the queen, the animal was dismembered and buried, thus guaranteeing the land's fertility for another year.

Several rituals involving horses seem to skirt the very edge of mythological speculation, for countless horse stories incorporate elements that probably relate to Indo-European fertility practices. According to Homer, when Helen's suitors cast lots for her hand in marriage, her father, Tyndareos, made them swear on the parts of a severed horse that no matter who was chosen they would defend her and her choice against future wrong. Their oaths were then "bound," as magic terms it, by the burial of the pieces. The association of the ceremony and the forthcoming marriage, however, suggests that the story may be superimposed on an old fertility ritual, for Homeric myth probably refers to the thirteenth and twelfth centuries. By then there is abundant evidence of both horse sacrifice and horse cult in Crete, on the mainland, and most of all in Cyprus. Bones of horses are regularly found on the surface of tombs where they were slaughtered, sometimes with other animals, in a funerary rite of some sort. Propitiatory sacrifices of horses also play a role in Greek myths. When Jason greets the shipwrecked sons of Phrixus (son of the sun god) at the temple to Ares, they all together offer a sober thanksgiving sacrifice on the altar where Antiope, the Amazon queen, once sacrificed horses. It is not clear whether horses are chosen to placate the war god, Ares, because they are war engines, or whether the horse here represents the sacrificial choice of the sun worshipers.

Certainly Ares is not uniformly associated with the horse. Poseidon, however, is the figure whose connection with the horse is ubiquitous and complex. When the Greeks came they brought with them a one-word religion: Zeus, whose name is an etymological equivalent of the word *dios*, or God. That is as much as can be said unequivocally. So far as can be guessed, Zeus' large family—a jealous wife, quarrelsome children, and various amours over whom he held paternal sway—he found in the Aegean waiting for him. Yet it is not Zeus, who reigns over earth and sea, but Poseidon his brother who is associated with the horse. Zeus' symbolical equivalent is the bull, the animal that also represents the sky god of Near Eastern religions. Since Near Easterners were in contact with the Aegean in the Neolithic period, they may have brought the bull—or at least his image—to Greece long before Zeus arrived and expropriated it. The tiny bull idols at the late Neolithic site of Lithares have already been mentioned.

With Poseidon the case is probably reversed. His ancient Greek characteristics are those associating the horse with him as a sea god and probably derive from the period after the Hellenes had left the northern Balkans and established their lives around the Aegean. It is unlikely that landlocked tribes would either have had a sea god or would have assigned so distinguished a position as lord of the seas to a brother of Zeus. Perhaps he held a position similar to that of his underworld brother Hades, who was also associated with horses. But how to sort out Poseidon's connections with both sea and horse is not at all clear. Poseidon's constant epithet is *hippios,* "god of horses," and he himself takes on the shape of a horse in more than one tale. In Arcadia the story is told of how he meets Demeter, goddess of the earth and definitely a pre-Greek deity. The mother is pursued by Poseidon while she is searching the wilds for her daughter, Persephone, who has been abducted by Hades. To escape Poseidon she turns herself into a mare; he responds by taking the form of a stallion and captures her. Both god and goddess are worshiped in equine shape in several parts of Greece, perhaps as fertility figures. Out of their union is born Arion, the wonderful horse whose name means "very swift." The violent lover also counts among his children the winged horse Pegasus. And in still other stories he is credited with having invented the horse with a strike of his trident. (See Illus. 14.)

To these connections with horse are to be added the many proper names that have the root *hippios* in them, for on the authority of philologists they are all Greek: Melanippe, the general of the horsewomen Amazons; Hippolyte, the Amazon queen; Hippolytus, her son by Theseus killed by horses; Hippodameia, whose hand was won through a horse race. Horse, then, is not a coincidental image of the god; the horsemen must have come to Greece bringing a god shaped in their image. A freshwater god doubtless would

14. Poseidon as he was envisaged in the Classical period.

have been a more appropriate consort for the earth mother Demeter than a sea god, and perhaps this aspect of Poseidon's nature was lost by the time the late versions of the Demeter story were composed. For Poseidon is also lord of fresh water. Many springs are supposed to have had their origin in a strike of his trident and many of their names contain the suggestion—Aganippe, Hippe, Keats's "blushful" Hippokrene. Since springs issue from the earth and since he is husband of earth, it is likely that the horse god was a chthonic or earth force—he is also known for his threatening earthquakes—before the famous division of the world's domain by the three brothers Zeus, Poseidon, and Hades into sky, sea, and underworld.

Poseidon in his manifestations as the horse, the sea, father earth, and rushing spring was worshiped through Classical times with processions, songs, and offerings. His magnificent temple still stands at Sounion (See Illus. 15) on the rocky promontory south of Athens. The exact form his worship took, however, is the sheerest speculation, for often when such information is retrievable at all, it has been reshaped and deformed by the influences of later religious ideas. If animism was a force in early Greek religion, it is not especially apparent in Poseidon myths. Veneration of the god has furthermore to be distinguished from horse cults, although, as has been already implied, there are several possible connections between the two. We know that Poseidon was important to the Mycenaean Greeks, for he is mentioned by name on a Linear B tablet, dated c. 1200, unearthed at Pylos. Sometimes, however, there are clues as to the nature and form of religious practice in analogies. Demeter's mysteries, for instance, secret though they were, apparently changed little between Homer's time in 800 B.C. and Roman days, when they were depicted on frescoes at Pompeii in the second century A.D. Demeter, we remember, is associated with horses through her consort, Poseidon. In several versions of a discontinuous myth about the formation of Demeter's lesser mysteries, she, Poseidon, the centaurs, as well as the hero Heracles all have roles. The story tells us little about religious practices and that only indirectly. It is interesting to us, however, as an example of the way in which the horse goes off stage center, so to speak, waiting in the wings to appear again at the tale's conclusion in a new symbolical guise.

On his way to Mount Erymanthus to capture a wild boar and

15. Poseidon's temple at Sounion.

thus complete his fourth labor, Heracles stops with the "good" centaur Pholus. The centaur entertains him hospitably but is fearful to broach the communal wine jar lest the "wild" centaurs grow unruly. They nevertheless smell the strong wine, become angry when it is denied them, and, armed with great rocks, tree trunks, firebrands, and other weapons, attack Pholus' cave. Heracles defends himself while Pholus hides in terror; several centaurs run off in various directions, some being received at Eleusis by Poseidon, who hides them in the mountains. Others are killed, among them Heracles' old friend and teacher, Cheiron, who is struck by an accidental arrow. And because all his skill at medicines is unavailing to relieve his agony (he cannot die because he is immortal) he begs Zeus to take his life. Zeus accedes to Cheiron's wishes and then sets his image among the stars as the Centaur. (Some claim that the Centaur constellation is in honor of Pholus.) Sometime later, before undertaking his last and most difficult labor for Eurystheus, to bring the dog Cerberus up from Tartarus, Heracles goes to Eleusis, where he asks to take part in the mysteries. Eumolpus, the founder of the great mysteries, is loath to admit the murderer of the centaurs, but is persuaded to purify the hero as a preparation for initiation. Demeter, the Eleusinian goddess, is moved by the hero's wish to venerate her and founds the lesser mysteries in his honor. Eumolpus then initiates the hero into these secret rites.

One other episode in this sequence of events deserves to be mentioned before we turn to an interpretation. At one point during the subsequent performance of the labor and his sojourn in Tartarus, Heracles carries the underworld king, Hades, on his back while the ruler is bearing a large cornucopia filled with fresh fruits. This fact, along with others we will turn to in a moment, led the anthropologist Georges Dumézil to conclude that the descent into Hades must have taken place at the end of the natural year: that is, just before Persephone, Demeter's daughter and Hades' bride, is to make her reappearance on earth, bringing with her the spring growing season. Numerous myths that touch on Demeter's mysteries confirm that these are celebrated twice: the greater are held at the autumn equinox at the onset of winter, and the lesser mysteries at the spring equinox, when the sun is in the sign of the Ram. Of the two festivals, the spring one is distinguished by its joyousness and license among the celebrants, an appropriate attitude to both the promise of spring and its corresponding religious significance—the return of fertility to Mother Earth. Given these circumstances, it is probable that the mythic events in Heracles' career—the descent to Hades and the founding of the lesser mysteries—have come down to us in reverse order. The idea of the hero's journey to Hades to bring back hell's dog is probably based on the more ancient vegetation myth of Hades' rape of Persephone, in which Hermes is sent to the underworld to retrieve her after her prescribed sojourn of six months has elapsed. The solemn mystery or fertility ritual could only have been founded in celebration of the fact that the messenger god had performed his task of carrying spring to the upperworld.

Turning next to the seemingly minor role of the centaurs in this cycle of myths, Dumézil asks why it is important that Heracles be cleansed of the death of the centaurs, since the hero is famous for having killed numberless men with only accolades for reprisal. And why should the purification of the centaurs' murder be linked to the founding of Demeter's lesser mysteries? In answer, a good many small and isolated facts have to be borne in mind. First, the centaurs in the Pholus episode are linked to Eleusis, where they seek refuge from Heracles' arrows. Next, their semidivine natures need to be recalled: as horsemen they inspire some of the awe of the magical animal and are associated with the god of magical horses, Poseidon. And, finally, one needs to keep in mind the great antiquity of the Demeter fertility rites that existed long before the mysteries of Eleusis formalized them and long before the horsemen arrived in Greece. Horsemen and Poseidon, too, were new celebrants of those rites for Demeter's religion. These, like other rites of ancient Great Mother religions, were adopted by the newcomers in a manner characteristic of the Greek ability to embrace prevailing customs without giving up their own. The centaurs, then, could only have evolved out of some aspect of the fertility religion at a point in time when the Greeks were participating in the rites.

Examining a great number of other end-of-winter festivals in the Indo-European tradition, Dumézil found that most if not all were typified by a carnival atmosphere in which men paraded as demons, or in animal skins, or in costumes meant to mimic the natural world. Many of the festivities also involved carrying away a figure who represented death and winter, one corresponding to Hades' symbolic role in the mysteries. And, of course, at some juncture in the celebration, there was an offering made to the goddess of grain, or fruit, or other product of the earth's fertility.

Often these were heaped up in baskets or stuffed into cornucopias in varying shapes, to present forcibly an image of abundance. In spite of an atmosphere of riot and merrymaking, such ceremonies had a sacred character to which animals would have added a discordant element. It was probably for that reason that images of animals were preferred to the creature itself. At certain festivals in central Europe the head of a horse was fashioned out of straw and mounted on a long pole which was then ridden by the celebrant. This hobbyhorse, Dumézil surmised, was responsible for the introduction of the centaur to Eleusis, where an imitation of nature and natural processes was the aim of the ritual. His unspoken assumption, in this study at least, was that the centaur was born out of the image presented by such a man and straw horse together. He drew additional support for his argument from the image in Heracles' twelfth labor of the hero carrying the king of Hades piggyback while the latter bears a large cornucopia. This composite image is very likely to have been displaced out of festival tradition; Hades with a cornucopia is consistent with the attribution to him of great wealth kept stored in his underworld kingdom. But this, too, is an elaboration of the ancient vegetation myth notion that all the world's goods are hoarded beneath the earth in winter, awaiting their release in spring. It acquired additional significance in the age of metals which had to be extracted through hard labor from under the earth's surface.

Whether the centaur originated as a carnival costume come to life or, as we speculated earlier in this chapter, he was a conceptualization of the invading Greek horse and rider is, of course, not provable. Nor is there any reason that hypotheses need be limited to these two. Representations in art are varied enough to allow for interpretations by art historians and other scholars that are all equally valid. There is, for instance, a proto-Corinthian (Attic?) vase painting depicting a centaur, taking part in a sacred scene, who is unambiguously and totally human. To his loins, however, is attached the hindquarters of a horse, and on his head he wears part of a horse's head. Such representations would lead one to see centaurs as no less human than satyrs, those men transformed by their costume of goat ears, horns, tails, etc., into ecstatic followers of the god Dionysus.

5

At the start of this chapter, two pre-Greek levels of habitation were identified on the mainland. The horsemen added a third level which began at about 2000 and ended with the fall of the Mycenaean empire. Not all of that period can be called Mycenaean. For the first three centuries, archaeological remains are like those at Lerna, in that they record only the first tentative signs of Mycenaean life patterns that were soon to dominate first the mainland and then most of the Aegean basin. It is not until 1650 B.C., the age of shaft graves, that the Greeks evolved to a level of acculturation wholly identifiable as Mycenaean. That is to say, the shaft graves at Mycenae are still the earliest records of a fully developed Bronze Age. An introduction to the image that myth gives of that period is the concern of the following chapter.

V

The Age of Perseus

Mycenae is the city famous in legend that gave its name to a civilization. When the intrepid Schliemann first excavated there in 1876 he thought he had found the home of the great hero Agamemnon. Now the term Mycenaean is applied to so wide a spectrum of geographical, economic, social, and religious data that it has outgrown its direct relation to the palace and citadel that Schliemann found. It is, therefore, impossible to catch more than a glimpse of Mycenaean civilization by reading myths associated only with the city itself. For centuries Mycenaeans were evolving into a characteristic culture as a result of the random growth of differing communities, isolated from each other by geographic as well as racial and temporal barriers. These individual principalities maintained many of their own traditions until the close of the Bronze Age and in many cases generated their own myths and folk-tales. In order, then, to capture some idea of the rich variety of people and custom that contributed to Mycenaean life in the seventeenth through the fifteenth centuries, the two very different myths of Perseus and Pelops have been included in this chapter.

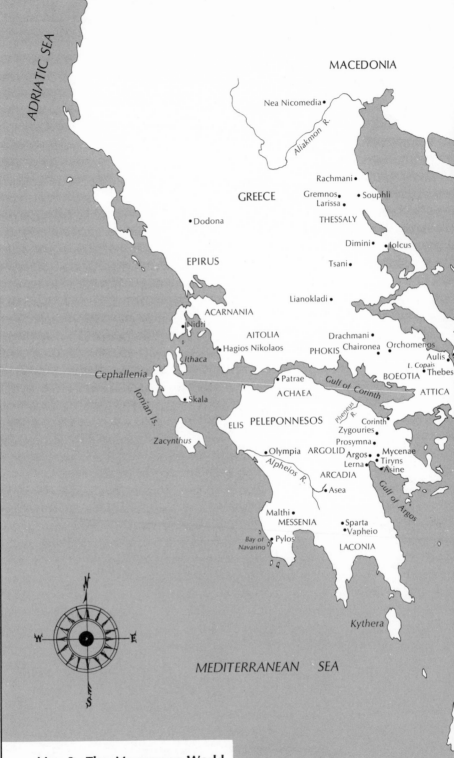

ADRIATIC SEA

MACEDONIA

Nea Nicomedia •

Aliakmon R.

Rachmani •

GREECE   Gremnos •   • Souphli
                Larissa •

• Dodona   THESSALY

                        Dimini •   • Iolcus

EPIRUS   Tsani •

                Lianokladi •

ACARNANIA

• Nidri

        AITOLIA   Drachmani •
• Hagios Nikolaos   PHOKIS Chaironea   • Orchomenos
Ithaca   Aulis •
                                        L. Copais   • Thebes
Cephallenia   • Patrae   Gulf of Corinth   BOEOTIA
                    ACHAEA   ATTICA
Ionian Is.
        • Skala   Pheneus R.
                ELIS PELEPONNESOS   • Corinth
Zacynthus   Zygouries •
                                     Prosymna •
                • Olympia ARGOLID Argos • • Mycenae
                                    Lerna • • Tiryns
                        Alpheios R.   • Asine
                        ARCADIA
                            • Asea   Gulf of Argos

                Malthi •
                MESSENIA   • Sparta
        Bay of   • Vapheio
        Navarino • Pylos   LACONIA

                                    Kythera

N
W   E
S

MEDITERRANEAN   SEA

Map 2. The Mycenaean World

2

Mycenae may have had a life as an unwalled village for centuries before its shaft graves were built. A king or chieftain of the early period, when populations must still have been small, ruled over a town not much bigger than a hamlet. The king's house would have been situated at the hilltop and within its walls he, his household, and perhaps some of his officials would have lived. A wall or stockade of some sort would have surrounded the house; the rest of the settlement would have consisted of rude huts for the commoners and stables for the horses, meandering some way down the hillside. In times of danger, nobles, commoners, and animals, too, would have crowded within the wooden walls, for the massive fortifications we associate with the Bronze Age were not built until the king and his goods had grown valuable enough to protect. If the megaron plan of building was in use here from the start, as it was in early Troy and Lerna, the main hall of the king's house would have been the center of the town's life. From here, when he was not fighting or at sea, he would direct the activities connected with the surrounding lands and preside over the legendary feasts. They would have been far from grand, however, in this early period, for there was little difference in the economic status of upper and lower classes. The warriors, who composed the remainder of the nobility, would have been overseeing if not actually tending the herds and flocks in times of peace; the noblewomen supervising the housework and weaving, assisted by the slaves brought back from raids. To the commoners fell the more menial tasks of hauling fuel, plowing, drawing water, and the like, performed with fairly primitive tools. At this social level, also, Greeks were nearly indistinguishable from the former population who had survived the incursions of the newcomers and had intermarried with them.

Nothing survives of this early town, possibly because its walls and buildings were constructed in perishable wood. Indeed, there are no remains of houses of any kind at Mycenae predating the monumental Citadel, built in several successive phases in the thirteenth century. As evidence of the Bronze Age before that time, there are graves and there are legends. Since Schliemann started out on his excavation of Mycenae curious about whether myth could be vindicated, it seems especially appropriate to turn first to a summary of Mycenae's legendary kings before we look at its archaeological history.

Mycenae's building is attributed to Perseus, son of Zeus and of Danae, daughter of the king of Argos. (We recall the habit of myth to refer ancestry to a god whenever there is a break in folk memory.) Pausanias explains how the site was chosen and how it received its name. According to him, the cap, *mykes*, of Perseus' scabbard fell off while he was traveling and he regarded this as a sign to found a city on the spot where it fell. Then Pausanias adds, "I have also heard that being thirsty, he chanced to take up a mushroom *(mykes)* and that, water flowing from under it, he drank and being pleased, he gave the place the name of Mycenae." A fine spring a short distance east of the Citadel known as the Perseia was pointed out in Pausanias' time as the one revealed by the plucking of the mushroom. Today the spring is a perennial of considerable volume about three hundred yards east of the hill on which Mycenae stands. It supplies water to the modern village of Charvati, about one mile down at the edge of the plain. Pausanias says nothing about the site's dominant position over the Argive plain giving it control over the mountain passes leading north, east, and west. But whatever prompted the choice of the site and gave it its name, Perseus was venerated as the founder up to Pausanias' time.

The dynasty established by Perseus was the earliest known to tradition. Apollodorus says that Perseus had five sons and a daughter by Andromeda. He does not record, however, how many of these descendants ruled over Mycenae and for how long. The best-known association of the Perseid dynasty with Mycenae occurs in the tales surrounding Eurystheus, Perseus' grandson, the king for whom Heracles performed his labors. Apparently, when Eurystheus was killed, there was no suitable Perseid available to rule, and therefore the way was left open for a descendant of Pelops, namely Atreus, to assume the throne. Tradition has it that this change of dynasties was peaceful, but the Atreus myth, much to the contrary, is filled with blood. And confusion. The genealogy of the Pelopids seems to have been worked and reworked so often that it is impossible to tell early tradition from late propaganda. Homer says that Pelops gave his scepter to Atreus, Atreus at his death gave it to Thyestes, and then Thyestes to Agamemnon. After him, Orestes and his son came onstage briefly before Mycenae and her kings disappeared into the Dorian age. Homer's version implies an amicable succession from father to son. In other versions of the Pelopids' story, Atreus and Thyestes are quarreling brothers, and the brothers Menelaos and Agamemnon are the sons of either a brother or a son of Atreus. To complicate the lineage further, two members of the family have tribal names, probably eponyms of the Thyestai and Orestai, barbarous Illyrians who lived in historical times. Pelops itself is a tribal name, but since no such tribe was known the name may have been invented to account for the name of the Peloponnesos. According to professional genealogists, Pelops' sons and daughters were legion, for their function was to transfer the glory of the Achaean nobility to the Dorian states.

The story that the bare king lists tell is of the development of Mycenae from a single city into the most powerful state on the mainland. In the days of the Perseid dynasty, the rulers of Mycenae also controlled the Argolid and the cities of Argos, Tiryns, and Midea. The city's power increased during Eurystheus' reign, when the exploits of Heracles brought new wealth to his sovereign. The growth and stature of Mycenae then reached its zenith in the days of the last Pelopids, for in the *Iliad* we find that Mycenae dominated the entire southern section of Greece: the Argolid as far as Corinth, the northeastern corner of the Peloponessos, many islands, and seven cities in an area far to the southwest of Mycenae which Agamemnon promised to give to Achilles if he would return to battle. One may also infer from the *Iliad* that Mycenae's dominion extended over the seas, for its contribution to the Trojan expedition is one hundred ships, the largest of any allied contingent. In addition, Agamemnon was able to lend sixty galleys to the Arcadians, a landlocked people who did not possess ships.

Homer and the dramatist Aeschylus are the sources for somewhat contradictory stories of the last days of the Pelopids, when Orestes takes revenge upon his mother Clytemestra and her paramour Aegisthus for their murder of Agamemnon on his return from Troy. Thereafter, Orestes ruled for a short time, was succeeded by his son Tisamenos, and both of their reigns are bound up with the collapse of Mycenae under the impact of the Heracleidae, the sons of Heracles, who are identified in legend with the Dorian invaders. When the Citadel was burned and looted, Mycenae was eliminated from its position of importance, and its power and prestige passed on to the city of Argos. Although some life apparently continued at the site for centuries after that destruction, legend does not record its fortunes. A contingent of eighty Mycenaeans joined the Greek forces at the famous battle of Thermopylae; Mycenaeans also played a small role in the direction of affairs connected with Nemean Games; and inscriptions and coins tell that in the third century B.C. the walls of the city were rehabilitated and some houses rebuilt as part of the establishment of a small township by the people of Argos. But no mention of the place by any of the ancient authors is enlivened by memories of individual men, royal or otherwise, and no distinctions accrue to the city's name.

Schliemann was armed with some or all of this tradition when he dug his first trench at Mycenae in 1876. His work initiated a series of investigations in archaeology, philology, art, history, and religion that continues with unabated enthusiasm to this day. No one could identify the peoples or assess the strange rich art that he uncovered in the six shaft graves now known as Grave Circle A. Knossos was still a mound of earth; early Greek chronology was an undifferentiated assortment of prehistoric legend. Schliemann's excitement is still almost palpable in the hurried notes made on excavating Grave V. Below a layer of pebbles at a depth of twenty-five feet he found:

> ... at a distance of three hundred feet from each other, the remains of three human bodies. ... on every one of the three bodies I found five diadems of thin gold plate ... a number of small knives of obsidian, many fragments of a large silver vase with a mouth of copper, which is thickly plated with gold and splendidly ornamented with intaglio work; unfortunately it suffered too much from the funeral fire to be photographed. ... the most remarkable wheel-made terracottas found in this tomb represent the lower parts of birds in black colour on a light yellow dead ground ... also a most ancient wheel-made vase, presenting on a light yellow dead ground a beautiful and fantastic ornament of plants ... in a very dark red colour.

The elements that made the shaft graves significant to historians are all here: multiple burials, the number of weapons, the mass of thin gold, the metals on vases and weapons, pottery decorated with birds and plants (now known to be imitations or imports from the Cyclades and Crete, respectively). When he dug Grave IV, one of the richest in the Circle, his confidence in the importance of his find was increased. An inventory of its four hundred entries shows why. There were gold crowns and diadems; swords and sword pommels of ivory, gold, alabaster, and wood; knives; "razors"; vases of gold, silver, bronze, alabaster, faience, and clay; there were rings and necklaces of gold, silver, and ivory; ornaments of gold from the funeral clothes of the five people buried in the tomb; a crystal-and-faience gaming board probably brought from Knossos; the famous gold Cup of Nestor with hawks on the struts; the equally well-known Silver Siege Rhyton; a bronze caldron incised with a

sign in Minoan script; ostrich eggs from Nubia (sent through Egypt
and Crete); lapis lazuli from Mesopotamia; alabaster and faience
from Crete; raw ivory from Syria; amber from Prussia. The gems
and swords in the collection were decorated with scenes of battle
and stag hunts, with lions and panthers and griffins in attitudes of
the hunt or the chase. The richness of these extraordinarily crafted
funeral gifts can be gleaned from a mere list. Schliemann was sure
he had found the tomb of the greatest of epic kings, Agamemnon.

From the viewpoint of present-day science, Schliemann was
unfortunately wrong. But he was not wholly wrong. Pottery dating
places Grave Circle A in Middle Helladic times, 1580–1500, before
Mycenae reached its fullest development. There is good reason to
believe, however, that the subsequently discovered Citadel with its
palace, Lion Gate, tholoi, and chamber tombs, its independent
houses on and near the fortified walls, its cluster of small dwellings outside them—in short, the entire complex including the
shaft graves—was standing when Agamemnon ruled. The wealth
of his society, its sophisticated technology, its combination of
monumental architecture and crude minor arts, its spectacular em-
pirical energy and middle-class mercantilism, its experimental
adaptation of ideas from older cultures of Crete and the Near
East and yet independent development into the most formidable
Aegean power, all began with the tale of the earlier shaft graves of
Circle B, discovered in 1951, and with the earliest hero king. If
there is any correspondence between myth and history at Mycenae, there should be clues to it in Perseus' story. It will be useful,
therefore, to examine it more closely here, and then return to Mycenae in a later chapter to see what other relations there may be
between the fortunes of the fully developed city and its best-
known mythic kings.

3

Perseus' road to the throne of Mycenae begins with the rule of
his grandfather, Abas, king over Argolis. Like the Cadmos myth
cycle, this cycle has Near Eastern roots, for Abas is a direct descendant of Danaus, the leader of the Danaan tribe that seems to
have connections with both the Cilicians in Anatolia and the Hyksos in Egypt. Abas bequeaths his kingdom to twin sons, Proetus and

Acrisius, bidding them to rule alternately and thus exacerbating their lifelong quarrelsomeness. As might be foretold, Acrisius refuses to relinquish the throne at the end of his term and Proetus has to engage an army to support his claim. Neither brother gains advantage in the ensuing war, and therefore the two agree to divide the kingdom between them: Acrisius takes Argos and its environs. According to Homer, Apollodorus, and Pausanias, too, Proetus' share is Tiryns, the Heraeum (now part of Mycenae), Midea, and the coast of Argolis. Seven gigantic Cyclopes who earn their living as masons accompany Proetus to Tiryns and build its massive walls.

Acrisius, meanwhile, is concerned that he has no male heirs, only a daughter, Danae. Told by an oracle that he will have no sons and that his grandson will kill him, he imprisons Danae in a well-guarded subterranean thalamus. Despite these precautions, Zeus visits the maiden as a shower of gold and she bears him the hero Perseus. Acrisius, disbelieving that the god is the child's father, fearing the oracle, and suspecting his brother of renewing a previous intimacy with Danae, locks her and the infant in a wooden casket and casts it into the sea. There follow a series of folktale adventures in the lives of mother and child omitted here for the sake of brevity. The best-known are Perseus' famous battle with the Gorgon Medusa, and his rescue of the "Ethiopian" maiden Andromeda and subsequent marriage to her before he returns to the neighborhood of the Argolid. His homecoming is dramatic. In the course of some funeral games for a nearby king, Perseus accidentally kills Acrisius with a discus. Shame drives him out of Acrisius' kingdom of Argos to Tiryns where Proetus has been succeeded by his son. Perseus persuades the boy to exchange kingdoms with him and then reigns over Tiryns. Eventually he reclaims the other two parts—Midea and the coast of Argolis—of the original kingdom. Sometime later, the hero fortifies Midea and founds Mycenae.

Already, at the very beginning of this Mycenaean cycle of myth, the groundwork is laid for a view of Mycenae as a considerable territory extending from the coastline inland as far as Midea and including Tiryns (see Map 2). If the myth's geography has any validity, it will obviate the need to guess about the growth of the city-state, for it would seem that Mycenae's founding was a direct result of the family's claims in the surrounding countryside. One particular is noteworthy, and that is that Tiryns and Mycenae were named as sister cities under the rule of one king here at the beginning of the cycle. Another related detail made clear here is that the Cyclopes built Tiryns a generation before they lent their skills to building the Citadel of Mycenae. Apart from these points, and the one made earlier about Danaus' probable association with the Near East, about which more will be said, the genealogies are of no value. As Martin Nilsson noticed long ago, they were probably invented in order to fit Perseus into the common pseudo-historical scheme. His own connection to Mycenae is so firm, however, that it must be based upon an ancient tradition which later mythographers went to great lengths to maintain. Apparently there was a Perseus cult at Mycenae in the Archaic Age, for an inscription in archaic letters referring to it was found between the Lion Gate and the "tomb of Clytemestra." Its message speaks of officials connected to the cult, so venerated that the Argives felt honor-bound to continue it after the destruction of Mycenae. All this would tend to prove that the myth of the founding of the city by Perseus was formed in the Mycenaean period and perhaps even then joined with the tale of the folk hero who was cast adrift in an ark and grew up to slay the Gorgon Medusa.

At least one of the myth's folkloristic details may have been added sometime after the Mycenaean Age, and that is the episode of Danae sealed up in the subterranean thalamus where Zeus found her. From its description the dungeon has been recognized as a beehive tomb, and any story incorporating such a detail could only have been invented after the tomb's original use had been forgotten. Other details seem to be products of folkloristic thinking in the Mycenaean Age itself and add support to the probability that the major part of the myth is Mycenaean. The name of Perseus' mother, Danae, for instance, signifies only "Danaan maiden," just as Danaus means "Danaan man." Danaoi is a tribal name, as indicated above, and seems to be Mycenaean, for it is recognized in Egyptian inscriptions from the times of Akhnaton and Rameses III and was obsolete in Homer's day. Consequently, a name like "Danaan maiden" can have been assigned to the mother of Perseus only in Mycenaean times, when, therefore, the birth story was created. Acrisius was introduced later and made the father of Danae so that Perseus' genealogy could be attached to Argos, the historical capital of Argolis.

A similar indication that the folktale has been interwoven with Mycenaean elements is the prominence of the single eye in the episode of the Gorgon Medusa. Perseus, tricked by a lie, offers to help one of his mother's suitors by obtaining Medusa's head for him. The Gorgon (probably a development of an apotropaic charm *) has serpents for hair, huge teeth, a protruding tongue, and altogether so ugly a visage that all who look on her are petrified with fright. She is not, however, easy to find. Her whereabouts are known only to her three sisters, the Graeae, who have a single tooth and eye among them. As the eye is being passed from one to the other, Perseus snatches it and so forces them to tell their secret. He then finds the Medusa and, guiding his arm by her reflection on his shield so he will not be turned to stone by her glance, he cuts off her head—Perseus' name means "the cutter." (See Illus. 16.)

The richness of this symbolism has intrigued many writers, Sartre among them. There is a ready association between eyes and the faculty of perception, and a more profound association to the psychological power of "looks that kill." Of course, neither of these ideas is peculiar to Mycenaean myths. They are nonetheless reminders that references to eyes persist in a group of words that etymologically predate the major Greek dialects. These words all contain the suffix *-ops.* There are round-eyed Cyclopes; the bar-barians Cecrops *(kerkops, kekrops)* who "see with their tails"; the Almopians, literally "salt" or "briny eyes"; the Dryopians, oak-eyed because their totem was an oak; and many others. The suffix is explained by the linguist Giuliano Bonfante as a Greek adoption from the Illyrian language, and its lexical connection with eyes as a late one—late, that is, in terms of the development of Greek from its Indo-European parent language. Might the definition have gained currency in the second millennium? All this attention to eyes as the creatures' most distinctive feature may be no more than linguistic coincidence. In this context it is nonetheless curious that Perseus' most precious gift from the gods is his cap of invisibility.

Several other details in the story, like Andromeda's "Ethiopian" parentage, and like Perseus' pause at Chemmis in Egypt for a rest after the Medusa episode, lead to the supposition that this mythical prince was a world traveler, familiar especially with the seats of more ancient cultures. And these indications, in turn, ask that Perseus' link through his mother with the Near Eastern Danaoi be reexamined in a new light. Herodotus made much of the connection between Danae and a Libyan invasion of Argos by the Danaans. There is not a bit of evidence for a triangular association of Near Easterners, Libyans, and Argives of the sort he describes. As so often happens, however, he was right in an essential and

---

* A frightful token, mask, or object used to ward off evil spirits.

16. Medusa carrying her son by Poseidon, the winged horse Pegasus.

wrong in the details. There were eastern princes visiting the mainland. The tradition of the Hyksos in Egypt, however, and his certainty that Greek religion was heavily Egyptian in its origins, led
him to invent plausible-sounding circumstances that often ob-
scured the value of his contributions. The Hyksos kings who
brought trouble to Egypt c. 1565 can only be associated with the
Danaoi by the loosest of racial ties: the Hyksos were Semitic and
the Danaoi (members of the tribe of Dan) *may* have been Semitic.
The conditional tense is necessary here because there is only linguistic evidence of this which is not universally accepted. And the
Libyans, whether led by or armed by Danaans, never invaded
Argos. There is every reason to doubt that either the Egyptians or
the Hyksos took the barbarian Mycenaeans seriously enough in the
sixteenth century to stage an invasion. The shaft-grave art which
relates to Egypt, as we shall see, is in the style of the Eighteenth
Dynasty, after the Hyksos had gone. The reverse, however, is very
likely: that a contingent of Argives invaded Libya, or at least an
area that can be roughly identified as Libya. When there the Argives might have met Semites as well as other men of the Near East.

It is not at all fanciful to assume that the early Mycenaean princes visited Ethiopia on both hostile and friendly terms at various times. For there seems to have been a Greek colony at Chemmis at the end of the second millennium B.C., where, as Robert Graves points out, Perseus was identified with the Egyptian god Chem. Confused as they doubtless are about the order and sequence of the links between Greeks, Near Easterners, and Egyptians, both the Perseus myth and Herodotus' reports are vindicated by the contents of the shaft graves. Even the very earliest Grave Circle B, dated to 1650, tells of the mainland's first turnings toward the south and east as sources of continuing vitality.

4

The origin of the shaft-grave idea has never been determined. Some scholars think that the new style developed naturally out of older cist graves at a time when tribal consciousness made a multiple vault desirable. New wealth would have inspired more gift-giving, they think, and a corresponding amplification of funeral rites. They point to the presence of several cists among the shaft graves of Circle B as an indication of transition rather than innovation. Other scholars emphasize the differences from older customs: the wooden roofing of the shafts, their greater depth, the carved stelae, the profusion of costly gifts, multiple skeletons. These are departures from tradition, they claim, that show affinities to burial customs of Anatolia and the northern hills. Kings and chiefs were buried in this style in Alaca in the third millennium; Bulgarians used gold funeral masks one thousand years later. If burial modes are evolutionary, progress must be slow, for there is no change in the constructions, styles, or techniques during the century between Grave Circles A and B. On the contrary, since some graves in Circle B are contemporary with those in A, it is clear that for a time both circles were used concurrently. The late Prof. Spyridon Marinatos suggested that the simultaneous use of two circles indicates two branches in the royal family at Mycenae, each having its own circle. He referred to the Atreus and Thyestes myth recorded in the *Iliad* as preserving such a tradition. Atreus is not succeeded by his son Agamemnon, but by his brother, Thyestes, after whose death Agamemnon becomes king. (See Illus. 17.)

The meticulous records of George Mylonas' excavation of Circle B show their construction. A rectangular pit was dug to a depth of about three and one-half meters and walled with small stones or bricks. Pebbles were laid on the floor before a body was lowered into the shaft on a rope sling. When the dead man's costume had been trimmed and his weapons, jewels, and foodstuffs laid beside him, logs were laid across the inner walls. A final covering of branches held together by a clay mixture completed the structure, which was then filled in to ground level with earth. If the grave was to be ornamented by a stele, it was pushed into place last. Sometime before that last step occurred, a funeral meal of meat and wine was eaten and the bones and broken cups thrown into the shaft.

Funerals must have been expensive and laborious. Each time another family member died, the entire building process was reversed and the older body and its gifts unceremoniously swept aside to make room for the new. The practice lends credence to the supposition that there was no belief in the sanctity of the body and perhaps none in immortality. The dead were buried with the honors befitting their lives, not venerated as cult figures after their deaths. But about this complex issue of Mycenaean beliefs more will be said at the appropriate place.

17. Mycenae; sketch restoration of the Grave Circle.

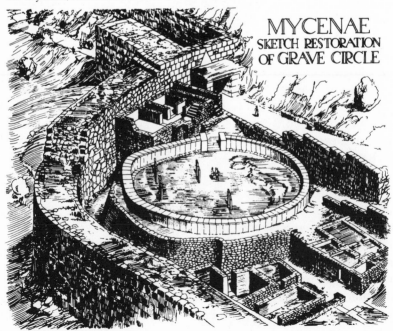

The chief difference between the two grave circles was in the luxury of their contents. Circle B was generally poorer than Schliemann's Circle and is a good indication that Mycenaean sources of wealth increased in the century between these graves and the newer ones in Circle A. There was less gold, fewer gems, and only one electrum * funeral mask; a greater number of the cups and vessels for foodstuffs were made of clay. Still, several daggers had ivory handles, proof of contact with Syria; and one male skull had three neat holes in it made during a trepanning operation, which, so it is thought, the Egyptians were the first to perfect. The single exception to the poverty of Circle B was Grave Rho, a much later tomb of the tholos type that for some reason was built inside an older, rock-cut shaft. This fifteenth-century tomb, although robbed in antiquity, is a testament to Mycenaean borrowings from the Near East, since its Canaanite design is typical of ones for the Semitic city at the same time. Clearly the Mycenaeans were visiting the East and imitating styles which caught their fancy. In all the shaft graves there was a marked difference in the wealth of royalty and subjects—a reminder that the Perseus myth, like most, does not concern itself with the lives of the commonalty. Whereas a male skeleton in one shaft of Circle B had no gifts of even the meanest sort, a child's skeleton in Circle A was almost entirely covered with a head-and-body mask made of thin hammered gold. Imitations of the child's toys were suspended from either arm: a rattle (?) and a set of scales. The child's skeleton was unique, since most of the graves in both circles belonged to mighty warriors. Their bodies were massive as well as tall, according to Dr. Lawrence Angel of the Smithsonian Institution, "since both the vertebrae and the thickness of all long bone shafts are extra large." At least three skeletons in Circle B were 6 feet tall, and they averaged 5 feet 7 inches in height, much taller than Middle Bronze Age commoners. One skeleton in Grave Sigma had two greenish polished stones under its lower right rib that Dr. Angel identified as "gallstones, suggesting a rich and perhaps truly 'Homeric hero' diet." George Mylonas in his account of the grave contents added, "the man suffered also from arthritis."

From the variety and profusion of styles in metalworking and precious stones and decorative objects, the grave contents take on an international character, consistent with the diversity of settings in the myths. It seems clear, however, that the Mycenaeans were in

* A light gold alloy of gold and silver.

an experimental stage of relations with foreign neighbors. Their trading—if trading it was—was sporadic and opportunistic rather than habitual and mercantile. These luxuries were occasional and portable, representing gifts purchased or exchanged as much for their newness as for their value as tangible, visible wealth. Nothing indicates that the exquisite rock-crystal bowl with the head of a swan (Grave Omicron, Circle B), perhaps the single most impressive work of art from the graves, was lived with as an object of beauty in daily life. On the contrary, it was a unique trophy or prize that points to the contrast between the simple dwellings and probably crude household furnishings even kings lived with and the splendid furnishings with which they died. Had the heaps of gold and silver been the measure of a widely based prosperity, there is likely to have been greater consistency in the amounts and kinds of treasure and in the styles of art in any one period; and possibly, too, a more finished architectural skill in the construction of the graves themselves. In analyzing the mixture of styles in metalwork (Cretan, Anatolian, later Scythian) found on three drinking cups from a single grave, the historian Emily Vermeule says:

> These stylistic incongruities drawn together in the Shaft Graves into a single artistic repertory may be tentatively explained in three ways. The inharmonious pieces may be really imported from different foreign areas; or different styles may have become attached to different subjects, as powerful curved Minoan modeling for bulls but flat stark carving for un-Minoan lions; or the princes of Mycenae had passed through several overseas districts bringing back models, ideas, and craftsmen (or alien princesses with prejudices and craftsmen in their retinue) who continued to work at Mycenae for a generation or two, each in his traditional way, until a genuine Mycenaean style gradually evolved.

To a lesser extent, eclecticism is also characteristic of the art of the grave stelae—the limestone slabs that represent the only monumental art of the period. Most of the designs incorporate the ornamental running spirals that come to be typical in later Mycenaean sculpture, frieze, and fresco, and the scenes depicted are also characteristic of later periods: war, chariot racing, hunting, and animal combats. The work is crudely executed and lacking in fine detail, but the compositions seem to have had both Egyptian and Near Eastern models. Their primary interest, of course, is not aesthetic but historical, for they confirm that Mycenaean society was militaristic, even in the solemn funeral entertainments staged at the death of a king, a scene that one stele represents. Male figures carry weapons and animals are in postures of attack or gallop, as they are when shown on other works of art. A fragment of a painted vase shows tall warriors wearing kilted tunics in combat. They carry long spears and figure-eight shields. (See Illus. 11.)

A more perfect and still provocative work from the graves is the well-known Silver Siege Rhyton. This drinking vase, found in incomplete fragment, illustrates a city at war. The hilltop citadel, much like that at Mycenae, is pictured in its complete landscape with a coastal plain separating it from the sea. Women waving their arms (in terror?) stand on the terraced edges of the city or lean from windows. Soldiers and civilians crowd each other on the hillside; near the water, archers tense as they draw their bows. On a lower section, usually seen as the sea, a long boat with several men in plumed helmets or caps is approaching a promontory on the other side of which lie scattered several bodies, either swimming or heaving themselves up on the rocks. The whole of this complex scene is often claimed to be a genuine historical relief, the only one in Aegean art. Are the plumed seamen Near Easterners? Others see it as a generalized expression of battle images that are repeated regularly in mainland art of the frescoes.

Warfare in this early Mycenaean period was occupational and carried on more often against neighbors than foreign enemies. It is an era of trained soldiers, perhaps serving as mercenaries, always searching out new bases of power nearby and abroad. One wonders then about the nature of their first contacts with the peaceful Minoans, for while the Mycenaeans in this period were experiencing the excitement of their transition from tribal to international life, the Minoans were recovering from a severe earthquake that ushered in the beginning of the last palace age. Whereas there is only occasional and fragmented evidence of contact between the two powers in the time of the earlier shaft graves (Circle B), there is strong Minoan influence in the later graves of Circle A, in which imported vases appear. With few exceptions the contents of graves are Mycenaean copies of foreign styles. Did the disturbance in Crete with the accompanying outlay of energy on their domestic affairs give Mycenaean sailors the foothold they needed in order to succeed, by 1400, in monopolizing Knossos? No answers are so precise as the questions. After Evans had excavated Knossos in the 1900's a resemblance between certain objects in the shaft graves and the art of Knossos was eagerly seized upon as evidence that

Crete had colonized the mainland. In addition to the vase painting styles that Mycenaean workmen copied, there were the emblems of hammered gold leaf that pictured bulls' heads with curving horns, double axes, horns of consecration, triple shrines topped with horns of consecration and birds, marine creatures like the favorite octopus and bell-skirted goddesses—all eminently characteristic of Minoan palace art and religious life.

Since the middle of the twentieth century we have asked instead, When did the mainland begin to infiltrate the older culture? In the seventeenth and sixteenth centuries B.C. Mycenaeans were too busy absorbing and learning from the accomplishments of their neighbors for the idea of infiltration to be tenable. The flow of peoples, goods, ideas, styles in living and in arts was obviously inward rather than outward and Crete was only one source, albeit the most important one, of that flow. Legends with their references to many tribes in Greece calling themselves by different titles and speaking different languages tell of this centripetal motion. Many foreign princes came to Greece to establish new kingdoms: Danaus the Egyptian was only one. Many mainland princes, too, were raised from their ordinariness by the expenditure of energy and adventurousness that the shaft-grave period generated. They, too, were the new people whose innovations were decisive in transforming Greece from an agrarian to an imperial nation. In mythical expressions, such men are the heroes, like Perseus, whose brief genealogies originate with divinities; it is as though myth is saying, "Mycenaean history begins here." It is nevertheless wrong to infer that all the independent principalities in Greece at the time were living out Mycenae's experiences as shaft-grave builders, soldiers, and seafarers. Some emerged from Middle Helladic obscurity to Late Helladic prominence with no intermediate steps in between. Suddenly population increased, Minoan forms swamped the experimental art styles, building techniques became uniform, mercantilism flourished, and, as we shall see, a new era announced itself. Until that happened, different localities came to their discoveries independently, undergoing periods of internecine wars as well as periods of arrest and consolidation. A good example of the point is made by some of the highlights of the Pelops myth, which begins with the arrival on the mainland of an eastern prince.

5

As though, for instance, mythmakers were aware of the scholarly puzzles about the sources of Mycenaean society, differing versions of the legend of Pelops present him either as an immigrant prince from Asia Minor or as a native of Argos. The variations hinge on the whereabouts of the kingdom of Tantalus, Pelops' father. Pausanias, so often referred to as arbiter whenever variants of legend need to be reconciled, claims that the tomb of Tantalus was on Mount Sipylus, therefore Tantalus, unlike his son, never left Asia Minor. According to Hyginus, the name of Tantalus, "son of Zeus," occurs in the list of the most ancient kings of Argos on the mainland. The discrepancy in the two versions of the story may never be cleared up, but it demonstrates how often a confusion in legend is paralleled by a controversy over the corresponding historical fact—here over the extent to which the early Mycenaean chiefs were foreigners who came to Greece and "founded" new principalities. Earlier chapters showed that contacts between the Greek mainland and the Aegean coast of Asia Minor were so recurrent a feature throughout Greek history that it is often impossible to tell which particular contact is being called upon to fill a gap in folk memory. It is to be remembered also that breaks in tradition are often reflected in myth by the claim of descent from a god, here "Tantalus, son of Zeus." It would seem then that the Pelops myth derives from a period when there was a break in historical continuity.

Pelops' origin is one provocative detail among several in the remainder of the legend. For reasons never made clear, Pelops leaves his father's kingdom for Greece, taking with him a great many followers and fabulous treasures. After casting about for a new home and a royal bride, he decides to sue for the hand of Hippodameia, the daughter of King Oenomaus, who rules over Pisa and Elis in the northwestern segment of the mainland. There are, however, enormous difficulties to surmount before Pelops can win her hand. Whether because the king has an incestuous passion for his own daughter, as some sources hint, or because an oracle has warned him that he will be killed by his son-in-law, Oenomaus has devised a way of preventing the girl from marrying. Each of her suitors is compelled to a chariot race with the king along a course from Pisa to the Isthmus of Corinth. The loser forfeits his life; the winner takes Hippodameia. Although the suitor is always given a head start, Oenomaus has been the victor in eleven such contests with suitors whose heads decorate the palace walls. Conditions, however, are always in his favor: his charioteer is Myrtilus, son of the fleet-footed messenger god, Hermes; his horses are divine twins given him by Poseidon; and he possesses a magic spear. In addition, Hippodameia is always made to ride beside each suitor and distract him from his task. (See Illus. 18.)

Hippodameia, attracted to Pelops from their first meeting and determined to save his life, enlists the aid of Myrtilus, who is desperately in love with her. She promises him her favors and half her kingdom if he will substitute wax for the linchpins of the axles on Oenomaus' chariot. Oenomaus is therefore killed and Pelops wins his bride. The couple flees, taking the charioteer with them. When en route Myrtilus attempts to claim his reward by violating Hippodameia, Pelops kills him and throws him into the sea. Sometime later, after he is purged of his bloodguilt, Pelops returns to conquer the kingdom, renamed Peloponnesos after him. Myrtilus' dying curse, however, remains to haunt the couple and their many children, of which Atreus and Thyestes are the best known. In the light of the significance of the horse and chariot to this story, it is interesting to notice that four others of Pelops' children have horse names: the argonaut Hippaleus, Hippasus, Archippe, and Hippothoe, who is abducted by Poseidon.

The only attribute of Oenomaus whose effect we see is his tyranny, and that is explained away in most versions of the story as either the operation of passion or the fear of an oracle. About passion one can scarcely make historical assumptions—incest is properly the (fascinating) concern of psychological and anthropological interpreters of mythopoeic thinking. As for myth's atti-

18. Pelops and Hippodameia led by the charioteer Myrtilus.

tude to oracles, they are seen either as mystical expressions of a god's will or as rationalizations of some inward promptings, yet neither view comes near an explanation of their ubiquity in myth. Often they seem to be warnings of a future disaster which the hearer goes to every length to avoid, only to meet it, nevertheless, at an unexpected turning. The oracle foretells a man's *moira,* or destiny, which nothing can prevent. Greek dramatists, we know, exaggerated this element in myth, making it the hinge on which ironies swing. Oenomaus has in common with most tyrants an inability to see the preparations of his own downfall, no matter whether the agent is seen as the treachery of his love-sick charioteer or more indirectly as the inevitable retribution for his many crimes of blood. It is the privilege (and handicap) of princes to be blind.

Pelops himself became a symbol in Greek mythology of the luxury of the East, brought with him in the form of treasures, a style of living, and a huge entourage to establish that style in the new land. Compared to the brutality and primitivism of Oenomaus, implied by his passion for his daughter and his torture and murder of her suitors, Pelops seems to have brought civilization to Pisa and Elis. These regions are located in the northwest corner of the Peloponnesos, where the establishment of the new Greeks is recorded archaeologically by the destruction of the previous Anatolian society. If all the characters in the parts of the myth had historicity, Oenomaus would be the original Greek invader who subjugated and then ruled the population with the help of his horse technology; and Pelops would represent the foreigner who came later, adopted what was best in the early Greek culture he found, and then enriched it with older customs of the East. To historians who take the position that the East was the Greek source of wealth and high technology, this pattern in the myths will have added meaning. A struggle between an eastern immigrant and a mainlander for control of a principality probably did take place several times in Mycenaean history. Certainly several foundation myths repeat this pattern: the Cadmos story in Chapters II and III is only one example; the myth of the Danaans is another.

The central event in the Pelops story, however, is not the institution of a new state, nor does it have the usual foundation-myth trappings of divine instructions or signs guiding the hero to a new land. All the elements of the story instead hinge on the horse race, a pastime that seems to be connected specifically with Indo-Europeans. We have its modern counterpart in car racing, a sport that in modern times is still associated with the western world. Even the use of the chariot in this myth as a vehicle is related to what we actually know about the uses of the chariot in Greek times. Each vehicle had its charioteer and it would seem that most were broad enough to hold two persons. In the story they are a suitor with Hippodameia at his side; or alternatively, the charioteer, who holds the reins and therefore stands in front, and the warrior, here the king, whose hands are busy holding the spear in ready position to thrust as soon as the circumstances are right. Since Oenomaus' racecourse was situated in a corridor that ran from Pisa to Corinth, in the district of present-day Olympia, there would seem to be a connection between the mythic race and the Olympic Games, especially the events in the Hippodrome. Sorting out the precise connection, however, involves one immediately in conflicting traditions about the history of Olympia, the home of Zeus and, before that, the original site of the ancient Pythian oracle.

During the ninth and eighth centuries, the period from which most of the information about Olympia is derived, Elis and Pisa shared control over the festivals for Zeus that took place at Olympia, and it was in that same period that the Olympic Games were instituted. Pisan and Elean traditions agree that the Games had existed in pre-Dorian times, but their regular celebration had been interrupted by the wars and general unrest that characterized the end of the Heroic Age. Officials of the Games in the ninth century were therefore eager for legends and other sources of authority about the past that would exalt the festival by giving it a glorious origin. Jealous of the fact that Pisa was the abode of the Olympian father of the gods, and the headquarters of the Olympian religion for the Greek world, Eleans invented, manipulated, and exaggerated legendary material that proclaimed Heracles as the founder of the Games. The hero was supposed to have celebrated the Games near the tomb of Pelops, using the spoils of his war with Augeias. He furthermore marked out the Altis, named the hill of Kronos, brought to Olympia the sacred olive tree, and established the laws that the judge of the Games administered. All of this justified the usurpation by Elean officials of control of the Sanctuary, and they ousted Pisans from their functions.

Pindar, our earliest authority on the Games, tells the story of Pelops in his first Olympic ode, but he does not connect him with the founding of the Games and does not regard the chariot race as the prototype of the Olympic race. Pausanias also refers to the origin of the Heraclean games, adding, however, that Pelops increased the splendor of the festival and enumerating five other celebrations of the Games under the presidency of other heroes. Pausanias says that his information was given him by the antiquarians of Elis, those same officials whose object was to exalt the antiquity of the festival and to justify the claims of Elis. Fortunately, the Pisan tradition, which still exists in fragments, was included by Phlegon of Tralles in his history, compiled during the reign of Hadrian. According to his account, Peisos (the eponymous hero of the Pisans), Pelops, and Heracles, in that order, were the first to establish the panegyris and the Olympic contest. Then, for some reason, the festival was neglected until after a period of civil wars throughout the Peloponnesos, when the king of Pisa, as a means of restoring the people to unity, decided to revive the ancient practice of the Games. He and two other leaders consulted the Delphic oracle and were told to proclaim a truce to those states wishing to take part in the festival. The Peloponnesians remained indifferent and were visited by a pestilence. Consulted again, the oracle announced that the pestilence was the work of Zeus' wrath at the neglect of his festival. It further spelled out that Peisos had first established the worship of Zeus; that Pelops had then appointed a feast and prizes for the death of Oenomaus; and then Heracles, son of Amphitryon, instituted a feast and games after the decease of his uncle Pelops. It was not until the oracle had been consulted several more times that the details of participation in the Games and their management, decisions about prizes for victors, the role of the symbolic olive tree, and the like were all worked out and accepted as a result of the oracle's authority. Phlegon's account is clearly a reconciliation of the Elean and Pisan traditions and is interesting for its strategy of referring to the Delphic oracle as a final authority. It is also interesting as the only Greek statement of the theory that the Olympic Games originated in Oenomaus' funeral rites.

Various ancient authorities emphasize different aspects of the two rival traditions. Pausanias, for instance, describes in some detail the bronze statue of Hippodameia standing at one turn of the Hippodrome, holding a ribbon with which to decorate Pelops for his victory. Yet he makes no precise connection between Pelops' legend and the founding of the Olympian Games. Strabo discounts the importance of Zeus' festival entirely, claiming that Olympia owed its prestige to its famous oracle. Recent finds at Olympia have most often been attributed to Hellenistic and Roman periods, when either the Elean or Pisan tradition was accepted—and consequently confused—so long as it carried with it some detail that exalted the antiquity of the Olympian festival. This craving for the authority of the past is well illustrated by some inscriptions on a bronze discus discovered at Olympia. The discus was dedicated by a Corinthian athlete, Publius Asklepiades, and bears on one of its sides the date Ol. 255 (i.e., A.D. 241). On the reverse, however, is inscribed the name of Alytarches Flavius Scribonianus, a "kinsman of senators and consulars," and the extraordinary date Ol. 456. When translated the date implies that the founding of the Games took place in 1580 B.C. Here is one of those fictions which unwittingly may hold a kernel of truth. There were no Romans in Olympia in the sixteenth century B.C.—or anywhere else for that matter. But the choice of the sixteenth-century date corresponds remarkably well to the educated guesses so often made by otherwise fanciful chronologists inventing Greek history from legendary traditions. By the sixteenth century eastern immigrants were visiting the mainland and perhaps some, like Pelops, did stay and establish themselves in the new expanding Mycenaean culture. Archaeology has not yet confirmed or denied any specifically eastern remains at Olympia. It has, however, recently uncovered to the west of the Metroon six prehistoric houses. The find tends to substantiate the traditional claim that Olympia had been a sacred area since earliest antiquity and might even have been used for games in the period of Oenomaus' reign.

Olympia has changed little since the time of Pausanias, our ultimate authority for the place. Not a city but a sacred precinct, Olympia was occupied by temples, dwellings for priests and other officials of the Games, and other buildings associated with them. The most important building in the precinct is the Temple of Zeus. It is one of the largest on the Peloponnesos, built from the spoils of Pisa after the city was sacked in 470 B.C. One of the pediments, the east pediment, is a sculpture group in Parian marble of the preparations for the chariot race between Pelops and Oenomaus (see Illus. 18). From what can be discerned from the remains of the sculpture, there were four horses on each team. Unfortunately, not a vestige of either chariot has been found; but marks of chariot attachments can be seen on the horses. In the center of the composition is the figure of Zeus. To the left stand Oenomaus and his wife, to the right Pelops and Hippodameia. Zeus, invisible to the contestants, looks toward Pelops, perhaps in token of his goodwill. On each side of the women are the four-horse chariots, that of Pelops attended by a boy, and behind the team of Pelops is his charioteer, Myrtilus.

A little to the south of the temple is a grove containing a small eminence and an altar to Pelops, the principal Olympian hero. The whole is enclosed within a pentagonal wall. According to Pausanias, there was once a pit nearby in which the contestants in the Games sacrificed a black ram to Pelops to ensure their victory even before they sacrificed to great Zeus. The black color of the animal, and the fact that the sacrifice was performed in a pit or trench instead of on an altar, indicated that Pelops was worshiped as a hero, not as a god. (See Illus. 19.)

The actual tomb of Pelops that Pindar mentions was probably a mound within the precinct. It is said that once a year all the boys of the Peloponnesos lashed themselves on the grave of Pelops till blood streamed down their backs. The blood was collected and offered as a libation to the departed hero. Pausanias adds another story in which miraculous virtues were ascribed to the hero's bones, much in the same way that miracles are attributed to the relics of saints in Catholic countries. When the Trojan War was dragging on, the prophets announced that Greeks would not capture the city until they brought Heracles' bow and a bone of Pelops to Troy. So they sent Philoktetes to fetch the hero's shoulder blade from Pisa. Unfortunately, his ship was wrecked by a storm off the coast of Euboea, and it was not until many years later, after the fall of Troy, that a fisherman hauled up the bone in his net. The bone had many other adventures before an Elean and his descendants were made perpetual guardians of the relic.

6

There is just a hint in the Pelops story of the multiple roles played by a tribal chieftain. Even at the relatively crude level of social organization that the myth reflects, a chief would have more power and authority to indulge himself in overtly aggressive behavior than would his followers. But how far his authority extended and what specifically we mean by authority are far from clear. Recently, investigation has shed some light on the possible evolution of kings from chiefs of simple agrarian organizations. The essential feature of chiefdom society is its social hierarchy, in which status is dictated largely by birth. Those males most closely related to the chief enjoy the highest position, and power descends with relationship through the male line. Often the chiefdom is divided

19. Gemstone found at Mycenae depicting an animal sacrifice.

into subgroups, each with its own chief, who traces his descent from one of the sons of the ancestral founder. The chief has economic as well as social functions. He officiates at religious ceremonies, and he leads in time of war, both occasions when several or all of the subgroups act in concert, all yet owing allegiance to the one chief. Economically, his office functions as a redistribution center. The dues or gifts of produce he receives are allocated to his people on some equitable basis, which in turn makes specialization possible. Farmers, for example, contribute their surplus to their local chief, who distributes some to his community and passes some on to the greater chief. The farmer then receives an allotment of the fisherman's surplus, which has been distributed in like fashion. Locally available resources are thus exploited and craft specialization is encouraged so that a level of diversified culture is achieved which a single family or clan could not achieve. Individual communities, much like each other, are thus socially and economically linked in a larger unit in which different members have different roles. The supreme chief can only accumulate a surplus large enough to be termed wealth if and when productivity and efficiency have reached a high point, or when the related phenomenon, population increase, has occurred so that larger individual communities have come about.

What parts of the Aegean world were most heavily populated and which unexploited in early Mycenaean times? What was the average (or large, or small) size of a village? What percentage of the populace lived in individual farmsteads? What percentage of that land was under cultivation? The answers to these and like questions would be essential to a full understanding of the transition from chiefdom to monarchical society. Unfortunately, doubts and sureties have equal weight in this matter of a relation between early chiefdom and later monarchical social structures. At the outset, each invading Greek tribe may have had its own royalty which settled, prospered, and established a family seat. Or all may have been members of one large tribe that looked up to one royal kinsman. By analogy to other Indo-European peoples, say the Hittites, kings may have been chosen by election, the candidates being drawn from the adult males of the royal family. For this early period and even after the time of the first shaft graves at Mycenae (1650), all answers to questions about the political organization are heavily hypothetical.

Conjectures about later Bronze Age social and political structures have a better chance of accuracy since they are based on interpretations of Linear B tablets, on archaeology, and on Homer together. Still, hardest of all to know is exactly what is meant by kingship. Homer gives us a picture of many kings and of one king with a higher status than the others. Since archaeology has shown that Mycenae was richer and stronger than other cities, it is likely that it was occupied by the high king. The geography of Greece, however, makes it difficult if not impossible for any one ruler to have absolute control over the whole of the mainland and still less over the islands and colonies. Mountains create natural barriers which divide the country into separate regions, and it is all too probable that each of these regions represented a principality. Since overland travel was and is to this day difficult, the probable lanes of communication were by sea. Command of the sea, therefore, must have been an important factor in determining which minor king or tribal chief became high king.

The implication here is that Mycenae had a powerful fleet, but proof of this is not yet forthcoming. The extremely full records on the Linear B tablets from Nestor's palace at Pylos, although dated to the end of the Mycenaean empire, testify to a social structure that was strictly hierarchical. The functions of the various office holders in the hierarchy, however, are not always clear. At the head was the *wanax*, or king. Since this title is also applied to the gods, one may infer that the king was regarded as in some way sacred. He probably performed as priest at religious occasions and other festivals; and this function, along with the ambiguity of the title, may be partly responsible for the insistence with which myth associates gods with kings, usually as semidivine relatives. Second to the king was the *lawagetas*, or leader of the host. He alone, besides the king, had his own landholding, or *temenos*, and his own household. Next in a descending order of importance and authority was the landholder, or *te-re-ta*. Certain of his duties might have been connected with religious holidays because in Classical times *tereta* was also a

religious title. At the base of this pyramidal structure were the
Followers, or *hequetai*. The actual status of the Followers is uncertain, although it seems that they stood close to the person of the
king, perhaps as dukes did to the sovereign in the Medieval period.
Certainly they were important in the military sphere. Again according to the tablets, chariots apparently were at their disposal and
it has been theorized that they acted as intelligence officers able to
communicate information rapidly to royal headquarters.

Each one of the Followers was attached to an *ao-ka*, very
probably a military unit of some sort. In the context that the word
appears in on the tablets, the *ao-ka* is referred to as "guarding the
coastal areas." Our lack of clarity about the precise operation of
this hierarchical structure is made even more unclear because of
our lack of information about the function of the king. It seems
indisputable that he was a war leader and about that we will have
more to say. For example, on the tablets that refer to land tenure,
the word *basileus*, "king," occurs frequently. In Homer there is no
apparent distinction between *wanax* and *basileus*. On the tablets,
however, the *basileus* seems to occupy a comparatively low place in
the social scale. It is difficult not to imagine that some of the lands
were not held in the king's name, since some of the lands were held
in gods' names. Perhaps one might simply suppose that the tenure
system was both communal and private. And, although the king
held his paramount place as war leader, one source of his authority
must have derived from his role as chief landlord, for the Greek
tradition is embarrassingly rich in its references to quarrels over
succession. Since lands along with metals and tributes were a
primary source of royal wealth, and the acquisitive instinct was no
less strong in the Bronze Age, kingship was a material as well as
symbolic prize.

7

In the chronology followed thus far, 1500 B.C. was still the
early period of Mycenaean development: after the shaft graves but
before the "empire," when the mainland states were beginning to
regularize their trade routes abroad as well as their traditions at
home. From this date until after the fall of Knossos, the appearance
of tholos tombs scattered over the countryside indicates that there

was a new turn in the spirit of enterprise that characterized the sixteenth century. Tholoi or chamber tombs were not an advance over shaft graves. For a time the two types were in use concurrently. Tholoi continued to be built until the end of the Mycenaean era and—the important point—did not develop out of shaft graves or Middle Helladic cist graves. They appeared suddenly,` fully developed, and therefore one tends to think of them as historically later than the shaft graves. Certainly their construction was more elaborate and more monumental—indeed, they are the earliest monuments in Greece. The tombs are cavelike graves cut horizon- tally into the slope of a hillside and composed of two parts: a dromos, or horizontal passageway, with a gently inclined floor left open to the sky, and at right angles to it a chamber hewn out of the living rock in a variety of shapes and sizes. Sometimes niches are cut into the chamber walls to hold the bodies of the dead; at other times pits are dug into the floor. All of the chamber tombs were designed for multiple burials and, as in the shaft graves, the bones and gifts of a previous tenant were often swept aside along the walls or placed in side chambers and niches to make room for a new interment.

In 1888 the archaeologist Chrestos Tsountas excavated a tomb of this type on top of a high hill at Vapheio, in the province of Lakonia. Much of it had collapsed and robbers had sifted through the contents. They had overlooked an underground pit that was fully paved and covered with stones containing the skeleton and gifts, intact, of a Vapheio prince. To Bronze Age historians he is well-known for his remarkably Minoan tastes and style: he was surrounded by heaps of gems and rings, over seventy amethyst beads on his chest, perfume vases, a mirror, and an earpick. In contrast with these delicate accouterments was his assortment of sword, knives, daggers, hunting spears, and axes, some packed in a wooden chest at the head of the pit. Some of his gifts were of Mycenaean bronze and stone; others, however, were more inter- national: an alabaster vase and ax of Syrian design, probably adapted by the Egyptians; amber beads from the Baltic; the first piece of iron known on the mainland and probably originating in Anatolia; and an exquisite gold-plated dagger inlaid with silver and niello figures of swimming men. At either hand were the renowned Cretan gold-and-silver Vapheio Cups, depicting scenes of netting and mating bulls (see Illus. 20).*

* Prof. Ellen N. Davis has recently shown that one cup may have been Minoan, the other Mycenaean. (*Art Bulletin*, Dec. 1974.)

The Vapheio prince could be an archaeological illustration of the myth, recounted above, about the foreign newcomer in Greece, for he seems to have been the true-to-life easternized Mycenaean. In his personal life he was something of an aristocratic aesthete; at the same time, one feels safe in saying, he was a successful warrior, for could the rough Mycenaeans have tolerated a leader who was not? And thirdly, he—or someone close to him—had been energetic enough to make a commercial enterprise out of occasional trading ventures. The assortment of gifts repeats the eclectic tastes of other shaft-grave princes, reinforcing the evidence that there was wealth enough to gratify such tastes. The high increase in the Minoan style of both the prince himself and his magnificent cups suggests, moreover, that the Spartan hill town of Vapheio was the terminus for a trade route from Crete. Several towns in the Lakonia area seem to have grown from rude Middle Helladic settlements into commercially active centers, for their tholoi show similar traces of Cretan imports and imitations. Lakonian red marble turns up in Knossos, at the other end of the trade route, as does the flecked green porphyry that the Cretans used in vase making. Horses, unknown in Crete until this period, may also have been offered in the exchange. One tiny gemstone shows a ship with a horse (?) standing on its deck, the earliest representation of the animal in Crete dating to this period. Goods probably traveled along the "good" sea-lane past Kythera, coming to port at the harbor of present-day Kalamata.

The still unsettled question is whether Cretan artisans were also imported. Workmanship on the Vapheio gems, for instance, is so markedly superior to that on the shaft-grave gems that some

20. The "Minoan" Vapheio cup.

historians doubt that Mycenaean craftsmen could have produced them. The short hair and kilts on a pair of hunters shown on one gem suggest, for example, that a Cretan artist was producing a work commissioned by his short-haired (therefore Mycenaean) patron. On another gem the theme is Mycenaean, the background and technique are not: a hunter duels with a boar in a Minoan-style landscape. The Vapheio treasure shows that Minoan styles had outpaced all other foreign ones in their influence on mainland art and that Minoan techniques were being mastered by native craftsmen. Some of the well-executed gems were certainly made by Mycenaean craftsmen, for their themes had no Cretan prototype. The Minoan goddess, it seems, had established herself on the mainland as firmly as had marine iconography, and both now were recurrent designs. Chariots and animals in racing postures which also appear were part of the original Mycenaean repertory. (See Illus. 21.)

In short, what began in the shaft-grave art as experimentation continued in the tholos art as polished adaptation, and the progress in excellence of workmanship is significant for what it says about the change in the relationship between Minoan and Mycenaean cultures. Whereas earlier forays into Crete can be described as fortuitous adventures, at this point one can speak of an association between the two areas, stabilized by its basis on continuing exchanges. Significantly, Mycenaeans profited more from the association since their technology, art, housing, dress and religion all became more sophisticated as they became more Cretanized. The result for Mycenae was a new combination of mainland energy and island civility. Crete, already overdeveloped in the opinion of some commentators, had less to gain and every reason to be watchful of the mainland's confidence.

21. Gemstone. The figure's beard and costume reflect a mixture of Mycenaean and Minoan styles.

VI

Theseus and the Mycenaeans at Knossos

The myth of Theseus has been linked to Knossos ever since Sir Arthur Evans began excavating there in 1899. He named the culture he found Minoan, after Minos, the legendary ruler of Crete. It was Evans, too, who described the palace of Knossos as "labyrinthine" in plan, recalling the mythic underground labyrinth that the great artificer Daedalus had constructed for the part-bull, part-man son of Pasiphae. Although Evans did no more than suggest, in this indirect fashion, a connection between the Theseus myth and his finds, since then scholars and laymen alike have taken for granted a closer correspondence between myth and history than modern archaeology has been able to prove. The labyrinth and the Minotaur have become almost synonymous with Knossos. And of Theseus' many adventures, none has achieved the canonical status of his visit to Crete.

It is true that there are a good many clear parallels between geographical locales specified in the myth and those uncovered by the continuing excavations. The harbor where Theseus' ship is supposed to have put in, Amnissos, was indeed discovered to have been the port for Knossos. The many-storied palace itself was found to be as complex as a small city and splendid enough to have been the seat of a great seafaring empire. Athens, too, known only when Evans was at work as a state dating from the Archaic Age, has been recognized as an important Mycenaean center. The discovery of these and other particular places makes it tempting to explain away portions of the story that do not fit discovered fact either with suppositions about inevitable distortions in the myth over its long life, or with arguments that the "proper" concerns of myth differ from those of history. Indeed, both arguments have been used elsewhere in this book. One reason they are less persuasive in this case is that the Theseus myth has less specificity than, say, Homer yet contains easily as much fable. The other reason is that, in spite of the fact that excavation at Knossos has passed its seventy-fifth birthday, interpreters of the data have not yet reached a consensus. New theories about the final days of Crete's history raise new questions about whether its end came in 1400, as Evans proposed, or in 1200, well after the island was under Greek dominion. In terms of the Theseus myth, these questions might be: Was the Minos in this tale Cretan or Greek? If he was Greek, would not the colonial kingdom have been familiar to the Athenians and their prince Theseus in some of its features? The myth makes Theseus an utter foreigner; yet Crete had been a parent culture to the Mycenaeans since at least the seventeenth century. Alternatively, if Minos was Cretan, at what period was he visiting Athens and in a position to demand its "tribute"? And how is it that the story implies Crete's decline as a result of Theseus' exploits? Before sifting through queries like these and choosing among hypothetical answers, the tale of Theseus' Cretan adventures must be told. The controversial historical data will then be summarized and examined as evidence for a link between story and fact.

2

Theseus, like most heroes, has a mysterious origin and a fabulous adolescence. Earthshaker Poseidon has visited Theseus' mother in Troezen on the night of the child's conception, so his paternity is always in doubt. Since mother and child live in seclusion, when Theseus comes of age he has to identify himself to his mortal father, King Aegeus of Athens, by retrieving a sword and some sandals that the king has left hidden under a huge rock. Many youthful exploits help him to develop the ingenuity, wit, and strength that enable him eventually to secure the tokens and prove himself the son of a king. In a moment when valor is called for, Theseus is able to move the huge stone, seize the weapon, and use it as befits a hero. Thereafter, the record of his achievements is nearly as long and easily as folkloristic as that of Heracles. He triumphs over the monsters Prokrustes and Kerkyon, overcomes unruly centaurs, and quells the bull of Marathon. When king of Athens he is victorious over invading Amazons, and throughout his career he is a lover and husband to several goddesses. None of his adventures, either before or after he earns his recognition, is so brilliant as the one in Crete. (See Illus. 22 and 23.)

The prelude to Theseus' visit begins in the days when the Cretan fleet plies the Aegean at will. Minos' young son Androgeus stops at Athens for a time and takes first prize in some athletic competitions. Immediately thereafter he is killed by jealous Athenians, and so King Minos begins a war in revenge. He captures nearby Megara and successfully begs Zeus to bring famine and pestilence to the Athenians. Frightened and exhausted after a long siege, the Athenians accede to oracular advice to give Minos the brutal tribute his peace treaty demands: seven boys and seven maids to be sent to Crete annually as food for the Minotaur. For several years before Theseus comes of age and arrives in Athens, the tribute is dutifully and sorrowfully paid. Then the young prince comes to the city and the situation changes. When next the Cretan galleys appear to collect their due, Theseus, much to his father's grief, volunteers to take the place of one of the boys. The young hero thinks he has had a sign from Poseidon that the god will protect him. Once on Crete, Theseus wins the love of Minos' daughter Ariadne, who coaches him in the secrets of the labyrinth. It may be she who tells Theseus that once, long ago, her mother, Pasiphae, conceived a passion for a white bull sacred to Poseidon. The queen confessed her unnatural passion for the bull to Daedalus, and the great inventor fashioned for her a wooden cow into which she might creep and so satisfy her lust. The resultant progeny was a monstrous half-man, half-bull; for him, the Minotaur, Daedalus also constructed a labyrinth from which no one emerged alive.

When it is Theseus' turn to confront the Minotaur—and variants disagree as to whether they meet in public or in private—Ariadne gives the hero a golden thread to unravel as he makes his way into the labyrinth so he may have a guide to the way out. Theseus executes his maneuver with success, killing the monster

22. Theseus discovers the weapons of Aegeus.

and returning with its head to Minos. As he does so, his patron Poseidon sends a great earthquake that destroys the palace and its inhabitants, allowing only Theseus and Ariadne to escape unharmed. There then follows an episode that has given many artists the materials for a tragic romance. The couple make their way to the island of Naxos, where the fickle Theseus abandons his brideto-be and continues his travels toward Athens alone. Eventually he comes in sight of the city and causes his father more sorrow by forgetting his promise to change the color of his ship's sails as a sign that he is still alive. Aegeus, seeing the ship's black sails, assumes his son has perished and leaps from a parapet to his death. The Athenians welcome Theseus as their new king and liberator from bondage to Crete.

In its wedding of Greek and Cretan elements, the myth is reminiscent of the Europa-Cadmos myth. The names of some of the characters indicate that the tale deals with divine and semidivine beings. Aegeus' name was a cult title for Poseidon, a hint at a resolution of Theseus' double paternity. His mother, Aithra, either is a goddess or is named for one. Pasiphae, "all-shining," is the name of a goddess worshiped in Lakonia, although the name itself does not seem to be Greek. Ariadne, under the title of Aphrodite Ariadne, had non-Greek votaries on Cyprus. Possibly, therefore, both women should be associated with the Cretan and Asiatic Great Mother religion. In addition, the adventures of Ariadne after she leaves Knossos form a confused secondary myth. She and Theseus are blown by storms to Cyprus, where she dies in childbirth. Her tomb is still shown to visitors of Amathus, and Cypriots apparently continue to celebrate her festival on the second of September. Some versions of her myth say that she does not remain alone on Naxos for long. Shortly after Theseus' callous departure, the god Dionysus finds her, loves her, and marries her. Still other versions, however, record that far from marrying her, the god is responsible for her death—Dionysus loves her *before* Theseus wins her; therefore, as a punishment for scorning him, he causes her death. Even the term Minotaur may be more than linguistic fancy, for there are a few half-man, half-bull representations in Minoan art. In the opinion of commentators on the ritual content of myths, the Minotaur is the remembrance of a cult ceremony in which the Cretan priest-king donned the mask of a bull. Annually (or once every eight years?) the king defended his crown against new claimants by engaging in a symbolic combat, during which he wore an elaborate representation of the sacred animal. The memory of that solemn event, it is believed, was encapsulated in the Theseus myth.

The major aspects of the myth, on the other hand, strike one as characteristically Mycenaean rather than Cretan. First, there is the obvious heroic bias that presents an Athenian youth as triumphant over the mysterious power of the ancient culture. Although it is not specifically said, it is clearly implied that Crete's authority over Athens was broken and her naval supremacy had come to an end. The inference is that the Theseus myth memorializes the period of

23. Theseus and his companions, homeward bound, arriving at Delos.

transition from Cretan to Mycenaean control of the island. The myth, nevertheless, does not go on to say that as a result of Theseus' victory Athens assumed rule over Crete. It merely adds, and this only in some variants, that the labyrinth was destroyed by earthquake. In fact, the Earthshaker can be seen as the hidden director of all the events. It was Poseidon who sent the beautiful bull from the sea with whom Pasiphae fell in love; it was Poseidon (in an episode not detailed above) who earned Theseus his welcome on Crete by helping him to retrieve a ring tossed into the sea by the Cretans when the young prince first stepped out on their shores. And lastly, it was Poseidon who devastated the Cretan palace with one of his earthquakes. All this emphasis on the mainland's chief god suggests that the Greeks were remembering a turn in historical events as the handiwork of a god. Or, if Poseidon entered the myth at the start of its invention in the Mycenaean period, his presence may be a grateful acknowledgment that military superiority over the Cretans might not have won the day without the god's favor. Either way, it is significant that Poseidon and not Zeus is the champion of the mainlanders in this myth. Zeus, after all, had his birthplace and home on Crete, whereas Poseidon was doubtless the most important deity to the mainlanders.

Details like these also tend to prove the Theseus myth's Mycenaean rather than Cretan origin or, more accurately, the Mycenaean origin of these portions of the myth. For like most heroic myths, this one is a complex blending of elements arising for various reasons out of different times and places. In the Archaic period, the Cretan expedition seems to have been known only in a few isolated references. By the Classical period, Theseus' story was widely known and fully represented in art and sculpture. Many elements grew onto the spare Mycenaean tale, for lyric and dramatic poets elaborated both Theseus' youth and his maturity. By then, too, Theseus had become the national hero of Athens. In the age of the birth of democracy, he became the first democrat and a guardian of equal rights for rich and poor. He was also credited with the abolition of local governments in Attica and the reorganization of the country along centralist lines under Athens. In keeping with this charismatic tradition, he was, moreover, supposed to have risen from the dead to invigorate Athenian resistance to the Persian invaders at the battle of Marathon. Popular imagination was captured so thoroughly by Theseus that the age of Pericles found him a useful instrument of propaganda, and there are many documented instances when his name was so used.

Was there a real Theseus living in the remote Bronze Age of his myth's origin?

3

In the first half of the one hundred years between 1500 and 1400, the inflow of Minoan styles to the mainland increased rapidly. All the objects and artefacts, pottery and jewelry that characterized the shaft graves and the tholos tombs continued to be imported, along with other products of Crete's Second Palace age. It was not long, however, before the Mycenaeans were incorporating Cretan elements into their own developing styles, so that by 1400 there was a distinctively Mycenaean style referred to by archaeologists and art historians describing buildings, dress, vases, cult objects, and the like. Not all Cretan influence was merely to enrich the quality of life. The Mycenaeans were quick to see the possibilities of copying Cretan wares and then exporting them to mature markets like Egypt. The seeds of experimentation sown when Mycenae began to imitate Crete flowered into an active exploitation of the island's expertise. An attraction to the polished art of Cretan vase making, for instance, proceeded by stages from an import of them, to reproduction of them, to the manufacture and aggressive sale of them to Crete's own outlets, and then to eventual replacement of the island country as supplier. This pattern, etched into historical record by deposits of pottery and artefacts, also describes the changing position of the Mycenaeans in the political fortunes of the Aegean. An essentially centripetal force reverses itself and becomes centrifugal: the import of styles, goods, and peoples from Crete and the Near East during the sixteenth century so nourished the mainland that by the fifteenth century it was extending (or exporting) itself outward into these same areas. By about 1400, Evans' date for Knossos' fall, Mycenae was ready and strong enough to step into a prominent position among the Aegean powers.

The turnabout, rapid in terms of historical time, was nevertheless gradual when measured by life-spans. For two generations, while the Mycenaeans were finding their own modes in architecture, setting up their own workshops for pottery, and increasing their output of bronze weaponry, their main concern was directed toward establishing the limits of local kingdoms and making arrangements to attract foreign wealth to them. The contents of tholos tombs in the period reflect the varying success each kingdom achieved and suggest the geographical areas toward which each king expended his energies. Westerners were trading along the Adriatic and around Sicily for amber, liparite, and obsidian, while the central and eastern mainlanders turned more steadily toward Crete and the Aegean islands. And even when the growing strength of these individual kingdoms was stabilized by their ability to rely upon a continuing trade resource, there was no one precise moment when it is accurate to speak of them as making an economic about-face—when, in popular terms, they suddenly became an affluent empire. (In fact, so far as we can tell, the mainland was never anything but a group of kingdoms whose boundaries changed regularly right up to the close of the Mycenaean Age. The use of the terms "Mycenaean" and "empire" is simply a matter of convenience.) Furthermore, both Cretan and Mycenaean ships were calling at the same ports in Egypt and the Levant throughout the sixteenth century. According to some scholars, the causes for Mycenaean ascendancy by 1400 lay very largely in her relationship with Crete before then. As they read the archaeological evidence, during the fifteenth century Crete's ancient markets in the East began to decline. Hittites, Mitannians, and Syrians were jockeying for power on the Anatolian mainland and long-established trading ports repeatedly changed hands or shrank away. Crete therefore began to research the potentialities of new trading centers and new independent colonies in the Aegean islands. Little Trianda on Rhodes, Phylakopi on Melos, and the island of Keos, off Attica, all received Cretan settlers. Eight other new ports were named Minoa and date to this phase of Cretan history. At the same time, the mainlanders were happily imitating their teacher, settling their old foothold on Miletos, and exploring other islands in the eastern and western seas. The two civilizations followed a policy of peaceful commercial coexistence, and the older one continued to lead the younger to long-known foreign markets.

By the fourteenth century Mycenaeans were firmly entrenched as either settlers, traders, or colonists on Cyprus, Rhodes, and several of the smaller Aegean islands in the north; they had depots at several points on the coastline of Anatolia, and "owned" a quarter of the city of Ugarit. The latter international city became their gateway to the eastern interior, the final destination of camel caravans laden with spices, perfumes, precious stones, and gold.

Copper filtered steadily into Mycenaean hands from Cyprus, and their settlement of Enkomi flourished.

Of all their emigrations, none was so fruitful as the settlement of Crete. At about 1450, the friendly neighbors were in the closest of relationships: ships regularly passed between Knossos, Mycenae, and Pylos, sometimes island-hopping through Kythera, Melos, and Aegina (see Map 2). It was a natural transition for the Mycenaeans to make—from merchant-visitor, to guest-friend, to settler; nor did the Cretans have any cause to be wary of mainland infiltration. Crete was at the pinnacle of her success. Her artistry was the admiration of the Mediterranean; her palace architecture was subtle and fully developed; her men were thoroughly trained athletes and sailors; her authority on the seas had no rival. Her pupil culture to the north could not have chosen a riper moment at which to sit at her feet, to gain extensive knowledge of Aegean commerce and domestic technology and luxury. Mycenaeans perhaps reciprocated with horses, manpower, and fresh energy. When the first soldiers or seamen came to Knossos to live, the town was already known to them. By the time the city suffered its destruction, Greeks had been intimates of Crete for two generations and so could assume the reins of power without interruption to the island's interior functioning or foreign trade.

This picture of Crete at the height of its development, of the Mycenaeans' eager pupilage, and of noncompetition between the two civilizations derives from an interpretation that is not acceptable to all scholars. One reason for objecting to it is that it prepares the way for a natural accident, rather than a sociological or political one, to be the cause for the fall of Knossos. Evans' idea, first proposed decades ago, that Crete suffered a devastating earthquake which leveled part of Knossos and many of the large palace complexes, has new support from investigators into the eruption of the volcano Santorini on the island of Thera. Sometime late in Late Minoan I A (around 1500), a violent eruption buried the town of Akrotiri on Thera's south coast, sixty miles from Crete. Although archaeological connections have not yet been made clear, some scholars believe that Crete may have suffered mildly from the eruption. A later eruption, in about 1450, did apparently cause a catastrophic ashfall and tidal waves that shocked Crete economically and politically. Some opinion has gone so far as to make Santorini's second eruption responsible for the destruction of the palaces on Crete. They dismiss the difference of fifty years between this date and Evans' as not archaeologically significant. To others the theory does not recommend itself. Only the towns of Gournia and Mallia are sufficiently low in altitude to have been subject to tidal waves. Secondly, volcanic eruptions, no matter how cataclysmic, tend to be localized; therefore the probability of extensive earth tremors as far away as Crete is small. It is at this moment, nevertheless, that Mycenaean adventurers (or seamen, soldiers, or settlers) seem to have moved into Knossos, perhaps to exploit the chaotic situation. Shortly thereafter, the Mycenaeans organized a proper settlement and, profiting from Crete's weakened condition, took over the administration of the island. The eastern segment of Crete had suffered little or not at all, and continued to participate in active trade with the Anatolian and Levantine coastal ports. Refugees from damaged palaces and towns may have fled eastward, for it would seem that the population in that part of the island remained Cretan rather than Greek, or a hybrid of Cretan and Greek. Tablets found at the unharmed palace of Zakro, at the eastern tip, show that Linear A, the Cretan script, remained in use there long after the Greeks had introduced their own Linear B script to Knossos.

An equally important objection to the peaceful-coexistence theory has been made by several important archaeologists. They think it significant that the mainland Greeks competed with and then surpassed the Cretans in their commerce with Egypt. Mycenaean pottery outnumbered Cretan pottery at various Egyptian sites by 5 to 1. Mycenaean colonies like Enkomi on Cyprus were prospering, while Cretan outposts on Rhodes and Trianda were in decline and quickly being deserted. In other words, opponents of the view that Mycenaeans and Minoans were friendly claim that Greek power was increasing while that of Crete, abroad if not at home, was clearly decreasing. Not all of Crete's overseas links (or trading posts or colonies, whichever may be the accurate term) necessarily eroded at once. Lately it has been found that the island of Kea (ancient Keos), where legend remembers a raid by "Minos," continued to be maintained by Minoans until close to 1400, a later date than that at which some of the other Minoan outposts are thought to have been abandoned. A curious feature of Kea is that the ancient site is fortified *only* on the side where there was danger of a raid from the mainland. The image here projected of the mainlanders as threatening, or potentially so, refers to the very point on which these two interpretations diverge. At some yet-to-be-determined date, one group of critics argue, the mainlanders invaded Crete and a Greek Minos ruled at Knossos. At another undetermined date thereafter, palace records began to be kept in Greek Linear B. Was Crete at the height of its powers, or was the Minoan civilization in decline?

A few years ago a psychologist analyzed the Minoan pottery designs in the Early, Middle, and Late Minoan periods (see Appendix I) and concluded that Crete went "not with a bang but a simper." The premises underlying his study were that societies at their peak comprise a large percentage of "high achievers" in their population—people demonstrating what he called an N factor. Such people in contemporary society all tend to draw, even doodle, in a distinctive way: with many single unattached lines rather than connected or overlaid ones; they tend to fill a page rather than leave blanks; their designs include many S-shaped and diagonal lines; and they tend to draw fewer continuously wavy or multiwave lines than do low achievers. When works of art from ancient Egypt and Classical Greece were examined for these characteristics, there seemed to emerge a correlation between the presence of these design elements and the affluence and power of the society as a whole. Crete's pottery has a careful and well-established chronology in which typical designs are linked to particular periods. A further investigation of Cretan art like that completed for Egyptian art therefore proceeded within a schema that was historically acceptable. The results can be seen in Illustration 24: the highest level of N factor designs occur in Early Minoan III, the period preceding the great flowering of Minoan art and culture. Thereafter, the N factor declines steadily, reaching its nadir in Late Minoan (about 1400?). The lowering of the N factor after 1600 could have been exacerbated by a general culture shock following the earthquake in 1650. Crete is thought to have recovered completely, since new palaces were built to plans that were larger and more complex than ever before. Yet analysis by this method of the art in the Second Palace period shows, on the contrary, that energy and output gradually deteriorated. Whether art historians would accept such evidence is debatable. Insights into history's enigmas offered by scholars in other disciplines are nevertheless interesting and valuable—especially when they add new facets to established information. The N factor theory undermines the supposition that Crete was flourishing on the day its final ruin came.

Whether relations between the two powers were friendly and Crete was destroyed by earthquake before mainlanders assumed control of the island, or whether relations were competitive and Crete was subjugated by one or more raids from the mainland,

24. Designs in columns left to right are taken from Early, Middle, and Late Minoan pottery respectively.

neither view answers direct questions about the Knossos drama and when it was staged. Precisely how did Mycenaeans gain control of Crete? How long did they maintain it? What caused the fire at Knossos that baked the Linear B tablets? Did Crete become a backwater after 1400? If so, how does one interpret the archaeological record of Mycenaean houses and artefacts lasting to 1200? Homer, so often vindicated by archaeology, gives us a picture of Crete's king Idomeneus as near to Agamemnon in importance during the Trojan War. His realm is described as including "a hundred cities," among them Knossos, Phaistos, and Gortyna, and "many peoples": Achaeans, Dorians, Kydonians, Eteo-Cretans, and Pelasgians. Recently, a scheme that takes all of these riddles into account was proposed by Professor C. W. Blegen and has been championed by Professor L. R. Palmer. Their theory sees the mainlanders as aggressors in Crete; its crucial difference, however, is that it dates the Knossos destruction to 1200 rather than to 1400 after Sir Arthur Evans. The Blegen-Palmer position is based on the assumption that Evans, although a prodigious worker, was not a modern archaeologist with stratigraphic training. Knossos was one of the most stratigraphically complex sites ever known, with improvements, repairs, damages from earthquake and fire, extensions, reconstructions, and alterations, spread over hundreds of years. Evans misread the evidence of the strata and therefore wrongly dated the collapse of the complex. Palmer further thinks that solid proof of Evans' miscalculation lies in the daybooks of the excavation kept by Evans' assistant, Duncan Mackenzie. An outline of the Blegen-Palmer scheme follows.

> I Up to c. 1450 the Minoans continue to control Crete, and the mainland grows in strength and power, challenging Minoan supremacy in overseas trade.

II Sometime between 1450 and 1400 Knossos is conquered by
a raid from the mainland and comes under rule of a
Greek Minos, who administers from the palace of
Knossos.

III The new Greek kingdom prospers for about two hundred
years. Archives are now kept in Linear B script. Perhaps
as late as 1300, the famous throne room at Knossos is
reconstructed after the plan for the hall of state in a
mainland palace. (Evans had admitted that the throne
room was a reconstruction.)

IV Soon after the ruin of Pylos in 1200 the Dorians invade
Crete. Knossos is burned and the Greek kingdom on
Crete is destroyed.

This revised view of what happened at Knossos has gained
more and more currency among modern archaeologists. The fact
that Cretan ports were rebuilt at around 1400 suggests conquest by
a maritime invader. The scheme, moreover, not only justifies
Homer, but it has the advantage of explaining away the riddle of
the Linear B tablets at Knossos. If Knossos was first destroyed by
earthquake and then taken over by Greek mainlanders, why were
Linear B tablets cooked in the destructive blaze? Or, if the mainlanders arrived and set up an administrative machinery (using
Linear B script) only to see it entirely destroyed by earthquake
within a few brief years, why do the Knossos tablets resemble so
closely those at Pylos? Professor Blegen has commented on the
striking similarity between the tablet archives at Pylos and Knossos: "based on epigraphical and other [evidence] as well as on the
nature of their contents ... one can hardly avoid reaching the
conclusion that the documents are more or less nearly contemporary products of a homogeneous society. Certainly they do not
exhibit obvious criteria pointing to a chronological range of 200 to
250 years." His judgment isolates the difficulty in supposing that
the Knossos tablets can have been baked in 1400 and those at Pylos
in 1200. Although in some writing systems there are few criteria for
measuring chronological differences of two hundred years, Greek
letters and script styles seem to have been in a state of almost
continuous evolution, and therefore some differences between the
styles of the documents at the two sites seem to be predictable.

The evidence other than epigraphical that Professor Blegen

refers to in the lines quoted is a great number of inscribed stirrup jars found on the mainland which Evans himself dated to the period following the destruction of Knossos. These jars bear place names which recur only in the Knossos tablets and, still more strikingly, the places form a coherent geographical cluster. Such a pattern of facts suggests that there was a viable export-import relationship between the mainland and Crete in Late Minoan III, well after the time that the island was supposed to have been cut off from world commerce. Taken as a whole, then, the Blegen-Palmer scheme and the evidence supporting it make a strong argument against Evans' chronology. It has the further advantage of including Crete in the network of events that caused the final collapse of the entire Aegean.

4

Armed with the foregoing information, we can now attempt to place the myth in one of three historical contexts. For the sake of clarity they are labeled A, B, and C.

A. The fleets of Minos had been visiting the Attic coast ever since the seventeenth century, when Cretan products found their way into Mycenae's shaft graves. At that date their supremacy of the seas can be taken as a certainty. Secondly, there seems to have been one or more earthquakes in the middle of the century which may have given rise to some myths or myth elements. Several Cretan palaces, including Knossos, suffered from the quakes and it is probable that the economy of the country was interrupted. But not for long; reconstruction was rapid, complete, and more grand than before, ushering in the Second Palace period. Finally, a quarrel of some sort between Athens and Knossos may have occurred, but it is difficult to envision because of the unequal statuses of the two cities. Whereas Knossos was the seat of a rich civilization, there is no archaeological evidence to show that Athens existed *as a city* in the seventeenth century. Excavation on the Acropolis has turned up a Neolithic house and some potsherds, a fact which indicates that the hill was continuously inhabited from Neolithic to sub-Mycenaean times. But there are many gaps in the archaeological data. Many fine pots of the Late Helladic I period were found in the cemetery in the present Agora, proving that the myth of Cecrops building a settlement there in 1581 has truth in it. In the same cemetery a handsome marine-style vase also was found, suggesting that there may have been direct contact between Crete and Athens by the sixteenth century. Synchronization is off, nevertheless, by about one hundred years.

B. The next period when historical conditions seem to fit some of the elements of the myth is the mid-fifteenth century. Then once again Cretan ships plied the Aegean, but their naval supremacy was no longer undisputed, as we have seen. Athens was perhaps a rude cluster of hovels, but nevertheless a town which might have been obliged to supply Knossos with slaves or other resources that were expressed in the myth as victims for the Minotaur. Meanwhile, Mycenaean strength was clearly growing, and therefore an abrupt reversal of the Knossos-Athens power balance is conceivable. Nothing in the myth indicates that the Athenians considered refusing to comply with Crete's demand; on the contrary, the most that the young hero can do to help his countrymen is to go along with them. Yet once in Crete he becomes the instrument of change: the Minotaur is killed, and by implication the rule of the Cretan Minos is overthrown. These circumstances could be a symbolic expression of the Greek invasion of Crete in 1450. Moreover, the earthquake on Thera in this same period just might have affected Crete. If this date is assigned to the myth, the relative foreignness of Crete to the Athenians—the original impetus for introducing the labyrinth into the story—gains added significance. At first, Ariadne has to lead Theseus through the labyrinth; that is, metaphorically, to teach him the ways of Knossos. The prince assimilates the lesson and carries it back to the mainland with him. For it is well after 1450 that the fresco painters at Tiryns, for example, portray women in Minoan styles of dress, proceeding around the walls in Minoan fashion. The argument from fresco art is, of course, peripheral, since styles and designs may have made their way back and forth anytime after the Greek invasion.

The obstacles to reconciling the myth with this date refer to Evans' position that Knossos, and thus the Minoan "empire," fell in 1400. The myth does not say that Crete became a backwater after Theseus left; neither does it say that Crete was left thriving. The point is left moot. Homer is the only ancient source who paints Crete as prosperous in the twelfth century, and it has already been shown that modern scholars are less and less willing to dismiss him as a spinner of fairy tales. To give his evidence equal value with scientific theory, however, still does not get us over every hurdle to dating the myth, since story elements that correspond to historical events in the earlier period do not correspond to those in the later one. A final summary will, it is hoped, illustrate.

C. From the Blegen-Palmer scheme outlined above: King Minos was a Greek overlord on Crete. Sometime after 1400 and close to 1300, Knossos was still a power to be reckoned with while Athens was now recognizable as a town. (The Citadel was built in 1300.) The two cities might have been rivals for any number of reasons without involving other cities or principalities in their contention. It seems anomalous, however, to think in terms of Cretan supremacy on the seas. As for the cultural context of the myth, the island had maintained its individuality in life-style, art, and religion. There was probably intermarriage between main-landers and islanders—therefore some additional point to the love affair between Ariadne and Theseus—and a free two-way flow of trade and techniques. (In this context we recall that the throne room of Knossos was reconstructed on the plan of a main-land hall of state.) Poseidon's role in the myth is somewhat dimin-ished by this proposed historical summary, for there were no recorded earthquakes in the thirteenth or twelfth century. He re-mains the patron of Theseus and was important to the Athenians, as the magnificent temple to him at Sounion proves. For unde-termined reasons, expressed in the myth as a combat between Theseus and the Minotaur, the Athenians were released from their tribute obligation to the elder city and both continued to flourish. Theseus returns to Athens and rules for a time. According to the *Iliad,* a successor of his leads the Athenian contingent to the Tro-jan War while Idomeneus, the son of Minos (the same Minos?), leads the Cretan fleet.

Homeric references place the myth late in the Bronze Age, about fifty to seventy years before Troy's war, for Idomeneus is supposedly a contemporary of Odysseus' father.

> One of the great islands of the world
> in midsea, in the winedark sea, is Krete:
> spacious and rich and populous, with ninety
> cities and a mingling of tongues.
> Akhaians there are found, along with Kretan
> hillmen of the old stock, and Kydonians,
> Dorians in three blood-lines, Pelasgians—
> and one among their ninety towns is Knossos.
> Here lived King Minos whom great Zeus received
> every ninth month in private council—Minos,

the father of my father, Deukalion.
Two sons Deukalion had: Idomeneus,
who went to join the
Atreidai before Troy
in the beaked ships of war; and then myself,
Aithon by name—a stripling next my brother.
(Odyssey, Book XIX, author's italics)

Even if one ignored purely genealogical data, because it tends to be both factitious and overly specific, a late-thirteenth-century date recommends itself on other mythological grounds. Apollodorus and Pausanias report that when Theseus first encounters his father Aegeus in Athens, the city is in a state of disorder. Fifty sons of Pallas, Aegeus' nephews, are baiting the old king in hopes of winning his throne for themselves. When Theseus is acknowledged to be Aegeus' son and heir, the sons of Pallas rise up against him. The young hero is nevertheless equal to them in force and routs their attack. Now quarrels over succession are commonplace in legend and probably reflect a true state of affairs throughout the Mycenaean Age. It is also true, however, that domestic upheavals are an especially prominent feature in the legends of the heroes associated with the period immediately before, during, and after the Trojan War. There will be occasion to look at some of these again in later chapters. Here it needs to be noticed that a legend speaks of local troubles, and that other factors in the legend suggest the time is the late thirteenth century—the very moment that the first waves of invaders probably entered Greece.

One other bit of mythological "evidence" is pertinent and that is the Parian Chronicle (see Appendix II). Entries 18 through 21 say that Aegeus was king over Athens from 1307 to 1259, a very long reign. After him Theseus ruled the city through the year 1256, when "the Amazons invaded Attica." However little one may credit this identification of mysterious invaders, and however skeptical one may be about the methodology of the chroniclers, the mid-thirteenth-century date for Theseus and for a new political structure in Athens are interesting confirmations of both Homer's dating and the Blegen-Palmer reconstruction of events. The theme, too, of local warfares fits the atmosphere of hostility that seems to have pervaded the thirteenth century. These are strong reasons to date the Theseus story to the late Bronze Age rather than to the Middle. Yet again, some threads are left loose, for the major theme of the myth, the cause of the rivalry between Athens and Knossos and its resolution, is unreconciled to the chronological information now available. So it is, then, that despite the great number of circumstantial parallels between fact and story, an airtight case for an exact correspondence between them cannot be made.

5

The quest for the true historicity of the Theseus myth continues to depend upon the true history of Knossos. Once the myth is removed from problematic theories about dating, however, it is easier to see that its core is neither the quarrel between cities nor the historical significance of tribute. The center of the myth is the encounter between the hero and the Minotaur. Their meeting has inspired countless works of art and literature since antiquity and there is no sign that the subject has lost any of its fascination. Artists as contemporary as Picasso and as surrealistic as Magritte continue to see in the Minotaur a symbol of unconscious impulses and psychic realities. The ritual school of anthropologists, on the other hand, insists on cult significances. It has interpreted the meeting between prince and monster as the vestige of an ancient ritual combat between a masked king and a contender for his throne. The famous bull-jumper fresco at Knossos and other works of Minoan art suggest very forcibly, however, that the combat between Theseus and the Minotaur was in fact based on a spectacular Cretan competition in which young athletes "danced" with a special bull. The sequence of events leading up to the dance began with the capture of a bull in nearby fields by a team of young boys and girls. Perhaps a decoy cow was used; or perhaps the bull was snared in a net, as depicted by the Vapheio Cup. Either way, leading the bull back to the palace may have been a ceremony in itself—as perhaps the "Sacred Grove" fresco from Knossos indicates.

The danger and excitement of the spectacle must have brought crowds of onlookers from everywhere. Initially the bull dance probably had a religious context, for bulls in Crete—and they are ubiquitous—are very often portrayed in the sacred contexts of shrines and cult practices. Eventually, however, social aspects of the occasion must have begun to predominate. The frescoes' gay audience of jeweled men and richly attired women vividly captures the spirit of high festivity these events seem to have generated.

While courtiers and ladies gossiped and showed off their finery, the team of dancers, or acrobats, readied themselves for their meeting with the bull. Girls and boys stripped to a functional costume of close-fitting boots and a loincloth drawn tight at the waist. Their hair was knotted in back, their wrists bound with colorful protective straps, and their necks circled with favorite jewels. Many months of training and exercise had been spent in preparation for this life-or-death act. In the arena each acrobat met the bull alone. Poised and taut, he awaited the precise moment of the bull's charge; then, throwing himself forward, he swept between the bull's curving horns and thrust himself upward as the bull flung himself to toss. The combined motion sent the lithe body of the acrobat over the bull's head in a somersault; he touched once on the bull's back and jumped off behind into the steadying hand of a "catcher" near the bull's tail. A great many young performers doubtless failed to execute the astonishing feat successfully, and their fate may be imagined only too clearly. The Theseus legend is certain that the youthful tribute will never be heard from again, and in this is probably accurate. Indeed, were it not for the many Minoan figurines, sculptures, and paintings showing various stages of the bull leap in progress, one might wonder it was ever accomplished at all (see Illus. 25).

The Mycenaeans were such ready pupils of other Minoan customs and beliefs one wonders why they did not also import the bull games. Or, if they did, they left us no archaeological evidence like open courtyards or theatral areas that would encourage us to speculate upon the likelihood. Perhaps the rough pragmatic life that is characterized by the style of most mainland citadels holds

25. Bull Leapers fresco from Knossos.

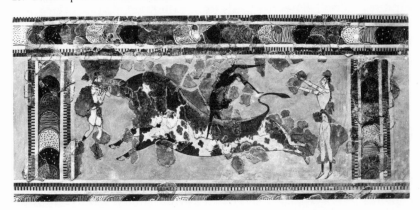

the answer. The existence of rigidly trained bull handlers, trainers, and acrobats implies that a fair number of the "middle class" on Crete were engaged in a variety of occupations unrelated to commerce, agriculture, or warfare, and that there also was an appreciative, leisured aristocracy willing to support a diversity of art forms. There are, nonetheless, some bull-jumper drawings on larnakes, or sepulchral chests, found at Tanagra that might someday shed light on Mycenaean familiarity with or attitudes toward the game. Since the larnakes are still being studied, they cannot be referred to here with any authority. It could be that, like some of the stirrup jars at the Cadmeia (see Chapter III), they were imports from Crete; or perhaps they were souvenirs of a rich merchant's visit to the island. Larnakes are rare enough on the mainland, and fully painted ones still more so. These may one day turn out to be critical evidence of the bull games' diffusion. Right now their illustrations are among the earliest examples of mythological subjects in art.

The spirit of the Minoan bull dance still lives in the Landés district of southern France, just across the Pyrenees from Spain. Between May and October there are regular performances of a "bullfight" in which the bull is a cow, the matador is an acrobat (called an *écarteur),* and the climactic moment is not a kill but a fantastic leap or *saut* over the charging animal. The French is unlike the Cretan version in that nobody actually touches the beast, who is somewhat inhibited in her movements by rope tied to her horns. The object of the sport instead is to provoke the cow and then avoid her charges by swaying movements, by vaults from side to side, and by a spectacular repertoire of great leaps. There is one in which the feet are tied together; there is a leap in which the arms are spread and the body flies horizontally over the length of the cow's body; and there is a forward flip in which the man is in midair while the animal passes beneath him. Also unlike the Cretan acrobats, those at Landés are skilled professionals competing for prize money. Although the feats are hazardous, the *écarteurs* almost always survive to fight another season. The similarities to the Minoan spectacle are nevertheless obvious and offer conclusive proof that with training and good luck the daring leaps could have been executed. (See Illus. 26.)

There are several explanations why all versions of the myth insist on locating Theseus' meeting with the bull in a labyrinth. Literally, the word means "house of the double ax," a reference to the weapon used in Cretan ritual animal sacrifice. In high antiquity,

26. Contemporary bull leaper performing at Landés.

the double ax became the chief symbol of Cretan religion, and it was a ubiquitous motif in every form of Cretan art. If the Mycenaean axes found on the mainland are a fair representation of their Cretan models, a huge bronze axhead with a span of about four feet was set on a wooden pole of about six and one-half feet in length. Those now in the Archaeological Museum in Athens are so unwieldy that it is difficult to imagine their being handled by a single, slight Minoan priest. In sharp contrast to the originals, tiny double axes of the most delicate gold leaf served as grave gifts and votive offerings. Hundreds of such miniatures were found in a house at Nirou Hani, a settlement on the road between Mallia and Knossos. Their large quantity suggests this was a factory and confirms the importance of cult practices to Cretan life. It is not surprising then to find that the island's most imposing building is named for the cult symbol.

Nevertheless, it is not the derivation of the term *labyrinth* that the myth calls upon but its direct meaning. Bewildered young victims are supposed to have wandered blindly in a maze that Theseus mastered only with Ariadne's help. Compared to any of the greatest palaces on the mainland, Knossos is immense and immensely complicated. Corridors, stairways, terraces, courtyards, halls, rooms, alcoves sometimes five stories high ramble in several directions over ten thousand square meters. A visitor today is challenged by the complexity; one from the mainland during the Bronze Age, when most houses were simple two-room structures with a porch, must have been baffled and terrified. He might well have forgotten the simple meaning of the term *labyrinth* and remembered instead his doubts and confusion. It is also conceivable that these grew each time his travel tale was retold, until eventually experience took precedence over formal learning and the House of the Double Ax lost its original definition. Perhaps, too, the myth of Daedalus was created to account for the labyrinth's construction. Who but a superhuman could have conceived of such a design? And for what devious purpose other than to hide a monster? (See Illus. 27 and 28.)

Recently it has been argued that the bull leaping could not have taken place in the central courtyard of Knossos, as Evans supposed, but must instead have been held in the theatral open area at the north palace entrance. The difficulty of herding a wild bull through the intricate network of halls, rooms, and passageways, which would have had to be traversed before reaching the court, would have been impracticable if not impossible. The area at the north side of the palace, on the other hand, has a long walled roadway about fifteen feet wide leading up to the main palace level. Wild bulls could have been maneuvered through the area in total safety, and there is ample space for the large crowd of spectators. Identifying the theatral area is one of the many points at which archaeology and tradition differ. According to the myth, and to countless illustrations, the Minotaur was to be found at the center of the labyrinth—generally understood to mean in the central court of the palace. While works of art cannot be conclusive evidence, the balustrades and palisades depicted in the Knossos frescoes do seem to be permanent structural features of a spectator area, rather than grandstands or collapsible awnings that might have been assembled and dismantled easily in the outer roadway. The balconies and windows around the central courts of Knossos, Phaistos, and Mallia also would have made ideal box seats for the aristocratic audience. One curious sealstone depicting the bull dance may be a significant clue to the puzzle. It depicts the bull in the act of placing his forequarters on a square stone or pillar that is decorated with diamonds drawn in diagonal lines. On the north side of the central court at Phaistos is a stone niche painted with just such diagonals. The sealstone and the niche have the only instances of diamond designs in all of Cretan art and therefore may offer a context for the debate about the location of the court. (See Illus. 29.)

Another argument for locating the bull game in the central court is purely analogical, based on the fact that palaces all over Crete are characterized by the same or similar architectural features. One in the little town of Gournia contains a small room off its

27. Theseus and the Minotaur at the center of the Labyrinth. A Roman floor mosaic at Salzburg, second century A.D.

28. Enlarged detail of Illustration 27.

court paved with blocks of stone. In one particularly large block a strange hole runs obliquely through the entire thickness. It has reminded several scholars of the tables or platforms, depicted on gemstones and sarcophaguses, on which bulls were trussed for sacrifice (see Illus. 19). Their blood probably was conveyed through the hole into a ritual vessel, just as the gemstone design shows. Near the platform in Gournia are remains of a portico that has been identified as a shrine, similar to ones at Phaistos and Mallia. Early in the excavation of Gournia, a pair of limestone horns were found next to the portico, apparently displaced from their original position atop. The presence of the shrine, the sacrificial table, and the sacral horns, all near the central court, gives rise to the probability that they all played a role in a ritual sacrifice attendant to the bull game.

6

An archaeological question like this interests us because of its bearing on the bull dance. To archaeologists it is another one of many concerning the design and building of Knossos that they despair of ever solving. Evans' reconstruction of the ruins, they are convinced, was overhasty. Not enough time had elapsed between excavation and restoration for the scientific community to study the find and reach a consensus on its significance. Faced with a completed edifice, an interpretation, and a seventy-five-year accumulation of research based on Evans' conclusions, new investigators have had the formidable task of disproving Evans before being free to present a new coherent theory.

To a great extent, the positive identification of rooms at other Cretan palaces has been the most fruitful source of new information. An example has already been made of the analogy between the central courts at Gournia, Phaistos, and Knossos. The newly excavated palace at Zakro on the eastern tip of the island offers even more promising comparisons since its inhabitants seem to have fled before its destruction, leaving most of its contents in place. Here, for instance, a kitchen area on the ground floor has been identified by cooking pots still standing on the hearth and a quantity of animal bones in one of the room's corners. On the second story, a large room with columns has been tentatively des-

ignated as a banquet hall, suggesting the same identification for
similar areas at Gournia and Mallia. Only Zakro's residential
quarters, however, closely resemble a similarly placed series of
rooms at Knossos. The labels on the floor plan (see Illus. 30) are one
scholar's opinion; many others think them optimistic.

A few years ago, to take an extreme case in point, Evans' very
identification of Knossos as a palace was called into doubt. A
petrologist named Hans Georg Wunderlich published a paper dis-
missing Evans' interpretation of the ruins as based on false
premises. Generations of archaeologists, he said, had been building
up a picture of a Minoan civilization that was luxurious, worldly,
and elegant because they accepted Evans' classification of the
famous ruins as palaces. Far from containing the residence of kings
and the administrative centers of storage governments, Knossos,
Wunderlich believed, like Phaistos, Mallia, and the Hagia Triada,
was the site of "cult buildings of complicated design for the worship
and burial of the dead." Were he not highly reputed in his own
discipline, and familiar with the scientific method, his attack on the
archaeological establishment might easily be discredited. As it is,
however, even if his conclusion is rejected, his doubts are pertinent
enough to have caused heated debate. Why, he asked, was there a
sacrificial altar in the king's room? Why were huge pithoi containing seventy-five thousand liters of olive oil placed in very small
subsidiary chambers? If the oil was to supply the royal household,
would not some of it have been kept handy in more convenient
vessels? Why for that matter were there no kitchens near the living
quarters? Why were there children's graves under the paving stones
of the floor? Given the fact that the principal building material was

29. A segment of the original Bull Fresco
wall at Knossos. Beneath, the passageway
along which bulls might have been led to
the central court.

a form of gypsum, the remains, he thought, were too amazingly well preserved. Gypsum is so soft and so porous that a few years' worth of footfalls—not to mention weathering—would have worn grooves in the flooring. (Today the floors in the areas open to tourists have been replaced with concrete.) The material is easily permeated by water and therefore, Wunderlich pointed out, particularly unsuitable for the floors in the queen's bathroom and the lustral areas. There were, moreover, no water pipes under these rooms, and it is hard to conceive of the Minoans constructing bathing places without a water supply.

Evans was persuaded that the room next to the queen's living room was a bath because it contained a clay tub with a drainage hole at its base. Perhaps his identification would have differed had he known that many similar clay chests—all with drainage holes— were to be found on Crete in locations that make their burial function clear. The most famous and best preserved of these, the Hagia Triada Sarcophagus (see illustration on page 191), is decorated on all sides with scenes of funerary custom that absolutely confirm it was meant to hold the body of an important person. It is true that in its general shape and size the sarcophagus at Knossos does resemble clay chests that probably were used as bathtubs. One found at Pylos, for instance, was distinguished from sarcophaguses chiefly by its painted design of swimming fish all around the chest's *inside* surfaces. Moreover, the same word in Greek, *larnax,* may refer to either a tub or a sarcophagus, so that sometimes an unqualified use of the term can be ambiguous. There will be an occasion to glance at one such instance in Chapter VIII.

But the point is relatively minor and does little to answer Professor Wunderlich's avalanche of queries and observations. All of these relate to what he saw as a fundamental lack of evidence that Knossos was ever lived in. His own theory provided answers always simple and sometimes startling. Many large pithoi, held to be containers for oil, wine, and legumes, were, he said, vessels for burying the dead. And indeed, pithoi with human remains have been found in other Bronze Age burial areas. Their large opening at the top, as broad as a man's shoulders, and breadth at the bottom were meant to distinguish them from oil containers, Wunderlich claimed. A peculiarity of Knossos and other Minoan palaces, for instance, was their complete absence of fortifications or defense works. It had been assumed either that the Minoans were utterly pacific or that their formidable power was its own deterrent against attack. Wunderlich simply asked, Who would ever dream of sur-

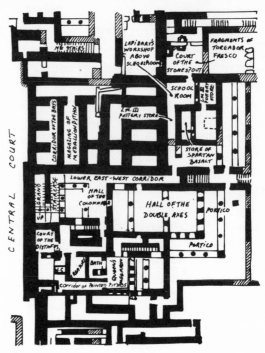

30. Floor plan of the domestic wing at Knossos.

rounding a cemetery or palace of the dead with defense works? Finally, his theory might explain why no later settlements ever rose out of the ruins of the historical site. In contrast to other Bronze Age palaces, Knossos for centuries remained abandoned to the mystery of its past.

The great stumbling block of Wunderlich's theory seems to be that if all the Minoan palaces are to be perceived as shadowy imitations of the real world, filled with delicate copies and fragile reminders of life, what happened to the sturdy originals? Where did the Minoans live? Could an extravagant gypsum world of cult survive thousands of years and a solid world of everyday disappear without a trace?

Wunderlich's theory is presented here not as an alternative to expert archaeological opinion, but as an illustration of the fact that after three-quarters of a century of scrutiny, Knossos and the Minoan world still tease the scientific imagination. In fact, architects think there are a sufficient number of building remains on the island to show that in Middle Minoan III standards of construction were higher than they were at any earlier time. Entire walls were constructed of soft stone blocks; doorjambs were made of wood and set onto bases of gypsum or other stone. The popularity of gypsum was due to its local availability and its easy susceptibility to cutting with a bronze saw. It was therefore readily used for indoor floorings and as lining for the walls of important rooms in grand houses. Areas like courtyards and unroofed atria were floored in limestone so that exposure to rainwater was not a hazard. Specific queries like Wunderlich's about building techniques and materials have in fact been both anticipated and answered by architects and archaeologists. The more important challenge about Crete is to Evans' chronology for it began a controversy that will generate close debate for years. Evocative though the world of the Theseus myth may be, it cannot solve problems of that nature and magnitude. It can only continue to do what myth does best: to suggest.

VII

Heracles, Vassal to Mycenae

If legend and archaeology could be made to correspond precisely, the Mycenaean kings Eurystheus and Atreus should have ruled during the fifteenth century, immediately following the reigns of the Perseids and the foreign princes. The subject matter of the myths dealing with these two kings, however, indicates that there is a gap in the chronological sequence of Mycenaean rulers between the fifteenth and the turn of the thirteenth centuries. What happened in the intervening two centuries may never be known. Mycenae must have been growing steadily in wealth, strength, and influence, for certainly its power over neighboring principalities on the mainland is often a source of mythical expression. Even Perseus' founding of Mycenae was referred to in traditional accounts as merely a further development of the Argolid area which was already under his family's dominion. Acrisius and Proetus, Perseus' mortal grandfathers, controlled Tiryns, Midea, Dendra, and Argos to the coast before Mycenae was added to the dynasty's lands.

How the city acquired sovereignty over the Argolid during the fifteenth century, if that is in fact what occurred, or how Mycenae's further acquisitions on the mainland were made and held is sheer guesswork. Raids are likely to have been a factor. Contingent upon them, the payment of tribute is likely to have been an important source of revenue. Whether lands were ceded as a form of tribute is uncertain, for there does not seem to be a word in Linear B to cover that sort of exchange. Possibly the debtor city or area was considered to be a dependency of the creditor city, and their relationship might have had a specific system of political obligations and rewards attached to it. The picture of chiefdom society sketched out in Chapter V may be instructive here, for the hierarchical structure of the chiefdom system corresponds in a general way to the picture of political organization one gets from several legends in which one city pays tribute to another.

One such tale in which Heracles has a role indicates that tribute was the consequence of an extraordinary event. A blood feud begins when the king of the Minyans is fatally wounded by the charioteer of the king of Thebes. The Minyan prince wages a successful campaign against the Thebans and then compromises by making the Thebans pay him tribute. As Minyan messengers are en route to collect the tribute, they fall in with Heracles, returning from a lion hunt on Mount Kithairon. The hero cuts off the noses and ears of the messengers, hangs them around their necks, and tells them they may take those to the king by way of tribute. The Minyan prince naturally retaliates at once and attacks Thebes. But Heracles, armed by Athena and backed by the Theban army, routs the Minyans and makes them pay double tribute to the Thebans in future. Here, the tribute owed by the Thebans to the Minyans is the "reparations clause" in their peace treaty. Heracles' bold defense of the Thebans then reverses the balance of power so that double tribute is now owed to the stronger city.

One cannot tell from this bare episode what form the tribute took, how systematic it was, or how long it was to continue. The implication is that tribute is the due of the strong from the weak. Legends of this type also make tribute the result of some offense against the code of hospitality, or of some criminal act; it is the brutally simple form of retribution for some aggressive action. In short, legends of this type do not lend themselves to a view of a social structure built on a regularized scheme of interdependencies like those in the chiefdom societies. Instead, they suggest a form of power politics in which small cities were at the mercy of greater ones, at least to the extent that geography and the physical environment allowed. If there was some reciprocity implied in the connection between the cities and kings, it was too subtle to have found its way into these rough stories.

If this were all that legend had to say about how cities were

related, we would have to conclude it was a poor source of information. There is nonetheless a richly suggestive series of myths
about Heracles which does feed speculation about the possible
kinds of ties between greater and lesser kings. The circumstances of
the hero's twelve labors tend to support the idea that at least
Mycenae had an ongoing relationship with other cities which resembled that between kings and vassal lords in Medieval Europe.

There seems to be agreement among mythographers that Heracles is a king in his own right over the citadel of Tiryns, as well as a
vassal of Eurystheus, the king of Mycenae. There is disagreement,
however, over the reason for his labors. Some say that after the hero
has been purified of bloodguilt for slaughtering his wife and children in a fit of madness, he visits the Delphic oracle to ask of it what
next he may do to expiate his crimes. The oracle directs him to
become a servant of Eurystheus for twelve years, which he does,
and the labors are performed at the king's bidding. In Euripides'
version of the hero's biography, Heracles' madness comes on him
after the labors are completed, and thus the original motive for the
labors, to be cleansed of bloodguilt, is ruled out. Here the confusion
over the correct sequence of events is typical of difficulties with
chronology throughout the hero's biography. They are the result of
the vast accumulation of Heracles legends from many sources and
over many historical periods. (See Illus. 31.)

Since we cannot accept the reliability of any one version over
the other about the reasons for the labors, we have only the labors
themselves from which to draw conclusions. Over the years they
have acquired something like a canonical order. The first six of
them are tasks set in the Peloponnesos, the last six range over the
limits of the known Mediterranean world (Crete, Thrace, the Black
Sea) and proceed to settings in the "far westernmost regions" of the
unknown and the "other" worlds. In the first six he triumphs over
nature: killing a lion and a hydra; trapping a wild boar, pursuing a
hind; clearing a bird sanctuary and then the stables of Augeias. The
other exploits oppose him to equally formidable opponents:
flesh-eating wild horses, Amazons, monstrous giants, and finally
the three-headed dog of Hades, Cerberus.

The mythic facade in the labors is perfectly maintained:
supernatural settings, aids from divinities, and feats of prodigious
skill combine to illustrate the single theme of the hero's indomita-
ble nature. Against all odds and single-handedly, the hero battles
against creatures too hideous to believe in and too horrible for the
Mycenaean king to want to see. When Heracles drags himself

31. Tiryns, aerial view.

before his lord in proof of a task accomplished, the fearful monarch cowers deep inside a bronze jar, exposing only the top of his head to both hero and trophy (see Illus. 32). Eurystheus, terrified at the sight of Heracles' first captive, the Nemean lion, has the bronze jar built under the earth, from whence he issues orders to the hero via Zeus.

If Heracles had brought Eurystheus a metals surplus, or some luxury goods, or the loot from a subjugated city, our task of finding the historical truth about their relationship would be simplified. Conversely, had Eurystheus declared bounty on lions or giants, then, too, there would be some evidence of an exchange of services and rewards. Instead, Heracles' works for the king seem to be without immediate purpose and it is because of this that they acquire their similarity to acts of fealty in courtly poetry. In fact, the scarcity of information in the myth framing the twelve labors leaves us free to analogize in other directions and see the labors as the equivalent of the knight's military service to his lord, rendered at the lord's will. Or, as some investigators have hypothesized, we are equally free to assume that the conquests over various phenomena

32. Heracles leads Cerberus to Eurystheus, who cowers in a large jar.

in the northeast Peloponnesos each represent attempts to annex the particular locality named. Still another possibility is that the hero is fulfilling the functions of a peace officer in the regions neighboring Mycenae over which the city exercised some rights of sovereignty. When all speculation is equally valid, none earns total credibility. What little consensus there is leans heavily on 1) Homer's picture in the *Iliad* of Agamemnon as "king over kings"; and 2) the fact that Tiryns, Heracles' citadel, is so near Mycenae that it could not have been entirely independent of the latter city without reducing its power severely. Still more important, had the rulers of the different towns been completely independent, Mycenae would have been cut off from the sea. Since tradition is consistent in naming Mycenae the principal power and archaeology corroborates Mycenae's importance, it is safe to see the king of Mycenae as the suzerain and the prince of Tiryns as his vassal.

2

Although Heracles myths continued to form all through the Archaic Age, Heracles' origins in the Mycenaean world are proven by his association with the site of Tiryns. Schliemann discovered the site in the late summer of 1876 and continued to dig there until 1885, accumulating evidence that the huge "herculean" walls of Tiryns were of Late Helladic date. In the 1930's, more scientific German archaeologists renewed work on the site and distinguished far older levels of habitation, the earliest footed on bedrock and proving that the site had been occupied since Neolithic times. The most singular remains excavated by the German team was a massive round building 286 feet in circumference underlying the center of the later palace. Calculations showed that if its height matched its diameter, the structure was over eighty-six feet high, a size that compared with the great nuraghi in Sardinia. The much older tower at Tiryns was destroyed by fire c. 1900 B.C. and therefore may be the unique evidence in Greece of the invasion of the Greek-speaking peoples. It is unique also in being the first monumental building on Greek soil.

The construction of Tiryns, produced in three phases, is equally impressive as the most monumental fortification known from the Mycenaean Age. The 250 years covered by these three phases—from the early fourteenth century to shortly after 1250—represent the full development and height of the Mycenaean culture, as we shall see. Technical competence and architectural skill in the manipulation of space, the floor plan of the palace, the central megaron with its altar and painted floor, the decor in dolphin and octopus patterns, the hunting and procession frescoes—all are comparable to the great structures at Mycenae, Orchomenos, and Pylos. Many details of its design, like the lighting by clerestories or the art of the frescoes, show the influence of Minoan style. Perhaps Heracles' sojourns in Crete (on the trail of the Marathon bull?) are to be read as evidence of the close and complex relations between the two empires, relations from which the Mycenaeans learned a good deal about the arts of living. There is, for instance, a gold ring made sometime between 1450 and 1350 which depicts fantastic theriomorphic * daemons bringing offerings to a seated

---

* Theriomorphic = conceived of in animal form.

goddess. The ring was part of a tomb robber's hoard from Tiryns and was buried and lost in the early Iron Age. It illustrates the difference between cult practices described in Homer and actual ones like that on the gemstone resembling Minoan cult. (See Illus. 33.)

Tiryns is of unique interest to mythologists because it possessed the only known Mycenaean painting of a mythical subject. Hunters and dogs are depicted chasing a boar while ladies drive in a chariot to witness the capture. If this is not an actual representation of the myth of the Calydonian boar hunt, it is probably the myth's human prototype. Only the remains of two houses, a fortification wall, and a few shards have been found at Calydon so there is some doubt about its importance as a Mycenaean center. There is no doubt, however, that the story of the boar hunt was extremely well-known. Like the saga of the Argonauts, the story attracted to itself a long list of heroes who lived in the generation preceding the Trojan War.

The king and queen of Calydon, the story goes, neglect to pay due honor to the goddess Artemis. To punish them, she sends a huge boar to ravage the land. Meleager, the king's son, calls upon the greatest of the heroes to help him hunt and capture the beast. Among those who come to Calydon are Theseus, Amphiaraus, Nestor, Peleus, Peirithous, and Jason. (Here the storyteller would flatter his audience by adding the name of a local hero or favorite son.) Atalanta the huntress also comes, and it is she who wounds the boar before Meleager kills it. Struck by her beauty, the young prince gives Atalanta the boar's head and hide as trophies of the hunt, thereby angering the queen's brothers. They attack the maiden, only to be killed themselves by Meleager. (Does the story hint at kinship relations common to matriarchal societies?) To avenge her brothers' deaths, the queen burns a magical firebrand on which Meleager's life depends. He dies, and then she, remorseful, commits suicide.

Tiryns, like Athens and Mycenae, had a water system whose sophistication bears out the Mycenaean reputation for having predicted almost every hydraulic achievement of Classical times. Wells outside the citadel and drains within it were dug through considerable depths of rock. In the late days of the empire, when the town lived under constant threat of attack by the Dorians, ingenious underground fountains were designed. Water was tapped from the hills a considerable distance away, conducted into the town in aqueducts that ran nearly thirty meters beneath the

33. Signet ring from Tiryns showing demons bringing gifts to a seated goddess.

fortress, and stored safely in deep rock basins inside the city walls. Within the citadel the water passages were corbeled tunnels with sloping stepped roofs and yellow-clay floors. The reservoirs were hollowed out of the natural rock, where pure springwater still seeps.

Respect for Mycenaean engineering is spiked by particular curiosity where Tiryns is concerned because of Heracles' mythic reputation as an hydraulics expert. In order to clear the stables of Augeias of the filth which was causing a pestilence in the land, Heracles is said to have cut through the foundation wall of the building and diverted the stream Alpheios (or in some versions two rivers, Alpheios and Peneios) through the stables. For this, his sixth labor, Heracles was offered payment by Augeias of some of his lands in Elis, the only labor to which any reward is attached. Were Mycenaeans called upon to perform feats of engineering for neighboring kingdoms and were they paid for their skills as artisans would be? Myth does not remember a middle class in the Heroic Age. All the wonderful remains of the Mycenaean civilization that the Archaic and Classical Greeks found were attributed to gods, giants, and monsters. The Cyclopes, for example, are supposed to have built the walls of Tiryns and the great fortifications of Mycenae's Citadel, although Pausanias does not believe it. In many cases the skill itself was lost for centuries. It would not be surprising, therefore, if the evidence of vast constructions like reservoirs, cisterns, dams, and canals, or the memory of them, took on the trappings of fairy tale, becoming associated on one hand with the wonderful deeds of heroes and on the other with one or another event in the history of a particular local area. Thus, according to the sixth labor, some especially difficult building enterprise involving waterpower may have been undertaken along the River Alpheios at the behest of the Eleans. The traditional association of Heracles with feats of daring, the evidence of the hydraulic work at Tiryns, and the well-attested hostility of the Eleans to Heracles are three possible reasons why the impossible (and unpleasant) task of clearing the stables was attributed to him.

The Alpheios has a mythic life of its own. The river is famous in legend as the final metamorphosis of the huntsman Alpheios, who fell in love with the wood nymph Arethusa and pursued her to Syracuse, where she, unwilling to marry, transformed herself into a water spring. The river, therefore, is said to cross the sea in order to mingle its waters with those of the spring. Herodotus says the tale is nonsense; Ovid immortalized it in his lovely verses. From a more mundane perspective, certainly neither Heracles nor any team of engineers ever diverted the entirety of the Alpheios. It is the largest and most important river in Greece, rising in the springs of Arcadia, enlarged with the waters of seven tributaries on its most famous stretch as it crosses through Olympia, and emptying into the sea on the west coast. One observer comments that even in the dry season of August, the Alpheios at Olympia is the strongest river in Europe. But it is not at all unlikely that some stretches of the river, which Pausanias says was "delightful to Zeus," were utilized by the inhabitants of the many villages it passes through even in Mycenaean times. At the junction of the Kladeos River and the Alpheios, in the Elean sector of Olympia, there was once a Mycenaean settlement. It has not been completely excavated, since part of it extends beneath the sacred area, so there is no way of knowing what, if anything, may have been constructed along the riverbanks. Because of possible depredations by spring floods to the scarce arable land in the rocky Peloponnesos, it is probable that some defenses against overflowing were a necessity.

There is another perspective from which to see that the story of the stables of Augeias may well be a confused memory of hydraulic construction, *not* at Elis, and not involving the Alpheios River, but at Tiryns and involving three mountain streams. The location at Tiryns would explain why Heracles is the hero of the tale. In the Late Helladic period the Mycenaeans of Tiryns built a massive barrier or dam just below the confluence of three streams. The large stream created by the merging cut a deep channel as it flowed west toward Tiryns and littered a wide area on either side with soil and gravel. Mycenaean engineers therefore used the accumulated debris to form the earthwork portion of the dam, which was secured from erosion on both sides by Cyclopean masonry. A more challenging problem remained in that the westward flow of the parent stream placed Tiryns and the nearby agrarian fields in danger of periodic flooding. To allow the stream to follow the land's natural gradient would, moreover, have threatened a necropolis east of the city with deposits of gravel and sand and water. The angle of the eastern wall of the dam embankment was therefore deliberately designed to curve in order to divert the stream to the south-southwest.

These two principal engineering concerns—deflecting the stream and controlling silt and gravel deposits—seem to be echoed in both King Augeias' dilemma and Heracles' solution to it. In the myth, an accumulation of unwelcome debris needs to be flushed out and a stream is diverted in order to do so. Mythologists and students of Mycenaean history may feel a little smug at the belated discovery by the Food and Agriculture Organization of the United Nations that the main problems in regard to control and utilization of water in Greece are a) flood control, b) erosion and silt control, c) drainage, and d) river regulation. The Bronze Age world also faced these obstacles and overcame them in sophisticated ways. A geophysical study published in spring, 1974, indicates that the soil composition, the precipitation pattern, the volume of water in rivers, and the drainage systems in the Mycenaean era differed little from those in present-day Greece. More reason, then, to be confident that the myth records a real event.

3

Perhaps because so many of his qualities are so thoroughly human—his brutality, his enormous appetites of every kind, his deceitfulness—Heracles has received more attention than all the remaining Greek heroes together. Yet in spite of his humanity, one sees in the Heracles episodes a quality of genuinely mythical invention. Like Pelops, Perseus, Jason, and Cadmos, Heracles' power depends upon his association with simple events of a fantastical and imaginative nature, rather than with those semirealistic epical events engaged in by Homeric heroes that stimulate more historical responses. This combination of the mundane and the mythical is apparent in interpretative responses to the labors, which have been pored over, rationalized, idealized, psychologized, and subjected to the inspiration of genius and ingenuity. As we have seen in the case of the labor for Augeias, the first six, perhaps because of their specificity, seem to encourage scrutiny by the prosaic eye of common sense—an antimythical posture. The second six, on the contrary, resist demythification and lead to a heightened appreciation of the way in which myth probes the spiritual sensibilities of a people. The following brief examinations of several of the labors will serve to illustrate the point. For the first of these we turn back to the theme introduced in the discussion of the labor for Augeias.

Recently the Dutch writer Jan Schoo suggested that all the labors located in the Peloponnesos are engineering feats involving waterpower. Schoo noticed that the figures of speech used to describe an animal's capture apply equally well to the process of damming and rerouting water routes. A river, like a wild animal, is *tamed;* water is *caught* in a basin; streams are *harnessed* and *bridled* so that they do not *run wild.* He concluded that several of the live animals that Heracles had to overcome in various places were actually waterways of some sort that were causing trouble to local farmers.

To illustrate, for his second labor Heracles is sent out to battle the many-headed hydra of Lerna. The creature is represented as having anywhere from five to one hundred heads; as soon as one is cut off another grows in its place. Armed with this information, Heracles proceeds as follows: as he cuts off one head, Iolas, his helper, cauterizes the stump with a firebrand and prevents new growth. Together they thus triumph over the monster. According to Hesiod, the hydra is the offspring of Typhon, the overwhelming storm wind, and Echidna, who was part woman and part snake. The name *hydra* simply means "water snake" and is closely related to the Greek word for water, *hydor.* (Our English words *hydrant, hydrogen,* and *hydrofoil* are derived from the Greek root.) This creature's dwelling place was the swamps of Lerna. A watery element thus is already present in the name of the monster and its habitat. Now geography shows that Lerna is very dry country with few permanent rivers but with seasonal appearance of fresh springs which make their way a short distance down the mountains, across the extremely narrow coastline, to the sea. In early spring the entire area is subject to floods that in ancient times were controlled by canalization, remnants of which were still visible to travelers in the nineteenth century. What Heracles probably encountered, Schoo thought, was a many-headed stream which resisted damming by sprouting subsidiary streams whenever the main one was stopped. Heracles, here representing a mythologized labor force, or team of engineers, drove fire-hardened poles into the ground wherever the stream threatened to overflow, thus forming the foundation for a stone wall which was then built along the stream's sides. In the myth this last act is represented as the burying of each of the hydra's heads under a stone.

As has already been shown, the Mycenaeans are known to have been excellent engineers. A huge complex of canals and drainage holes at Lake Copais complete with a system of walls, roads, and fortresses for its manpower has been studied and documented as evidence of their skill. (It is referred to in more detail in Chapter IX.) The dam at Tiryns is another proof of their technical proficiency. Just these two types of engineering construction also imply a breadth of scientific understanding, for the differing needs of each area could not be filled by only one learned technique reapplied at new locales. Each new purpose required a new kind of construction: canals for drainage or for irrigation; dams to create lakes or harness energy; conduits to maintain a city's supply of water or to release its excess. There is therefore good reason to suppose that a variety of hydraulic projects were undertaken in areas where the terrain had to be made suitable for agriculture, or where villages were threatened by flooding. Pausanias, in fact, takes for granted these spectacular building feats and reports another one attributed to Heracles with neither awe nor admiration.

> A mile from Orchomenos is a shrine of Herakles with a statue of no great size. Here are the sources of the Black River which runs like the others into the Kephisian Lake. The lake always covers the larger part of the Orchomenian territory: in the winter season when the south wind blows its worst, the water advances even further over the countryside. The Thebans say Herakles turned the river Kephisos into the Orchomenian plain: it once ran below the mountain into the sea, until Herakles broke open the chasm in the mountains. But Homer knew it was a true lake, not made by Herakles, and writes of a place "leaning on the Kephisian lake. . . ." Anyway, it is hardly likely the Orchomenians would not have discovered the chasm, broken down Herakles' construction, and restored the ancient course of the river. They had plenty of money right down to the Trojan War.

Pausanias' comments here and elsewhere in his observations about Boeotia collect references to another legend which tells how

Heracles, in his war with the Minyans, uses huge stones to block up a natural chasm through which the river flows into the sea. His plan is to flood the plain and make it useless to the Minyan cavalry. After his victory, he removes the obstacles to the underground river routes and the river returns to its old bed. Frazer's commentary on Pausanias confirms that the legend probably shows that the *katabothrae* or chasms on the northeast side of the Copaic basin usually sufficed to receive and discharge all the waters of the lake; occasionally they were blocked and the adjoining plain consequently became a marsh. Natural causes such as earthquakes or landslips may have been responsible for the blocking of the chasms—for which causes the agency of Heracles may be a mythical expression. It is also possible that the blocking of the chasms was the work of enemies who took this effectual means of damaging their rivals. Ernest Curtius, traveling in Greece in 1892, observed that one of the principal chasms through which the water of the lake escaped, the *katabothra* of Varia, was blocked with great masses of fallen rocks. In addition, one of the most important of the ancient canals made by the Minyans (see Chapter IX) leads directly to the mouth of this particular chasm.

These observations shed light on the possible meaning of Heracles' fifth labor, set in the same geographical neighborhood. According to the myth, he rids the area around the swampy Lake Stymphalia of "man-eating" pestilential birds "by making a great noise with a [bronze?] rattle." Jan Schoo, to whom we referred earlier, suggested that the "birds" were the unhealthy damps and fog rising from the marshes. His idea may be right since a demographic study at Lerna showed that the early Mycenaean population suffered from malaria. The evil malarial air very likely bred mosquitoes, creatures who would account for the legendary "sharp feathers" of these "man-eating birds." The lake, like that into which the Kephisos River fed, was characterized by poor drainage. Water leached out of the limestone chasms, which had to be kept free of obstructions lest the lake dam up and become rank in the summer season. Heracles' feat was perhaps to clear a channel into one of these caves or chasms; the resultant waterfall would have made a thunderous noise, or "rattle." Keeping the cave free of debris would then be the equivalent of producing a noise, a sign that all was well. No water flow, conversely, would have meant an absence of noise.

The same natural phenomenon at Pheneus nearby was observed and commented upon first by Pausanias. In antiquity, as now, the limestone plain was either a fertile valley or a beautiful lake, depending on whether the lake's emissaries or chasms were clear. Regardless of Pausanias' matter-of-factness, the building of dams and canals was a huge undertaking, requiring the services of skilled designers, stonecutters, and masons, as well as unskilled workers. The manpower might have been an entire community set to carry out the orders of a chief engineer and his group of skilled specialists. Such men would have been mercenaries, hired by particular kings for particular projects much in the way that stonemasons were commissioned in the Medieval period to build the great cathedrals of Europe. Mesopotamia in the third millennium used hired experts to design the great canal systems that were then dredged and walled by masses of expendable slaves. Not so long ago it was assumed that those Near Eastern artisans traveled through Mycenae, working wherever they were needed; for how else, it was asked, could the Mycenaeans have learned such complex engineering techniques? More and more, however, scholars allow the possibility that the Mycenaean engineers were essentially self-taught, although they might have been influenced by Near Easterners and by the idea of canalization. And possibly, too, the Mycenaeans learned how to organize group labor forces from the Near Easterners. About this last point the archaeologist Colin Renfrew has raised objections. Some sort of community effort was the major factor in the building of the monumental ancient Neolithic temples, or henges, scattered around northern Europe, and these peoples learned neither their building techniques nor their organizational scheme from the East. The weight of evidence by analogy would suggest that the Mycenaeans were capable of both initiating and carrying out their civic works independently, and that they, as other cultures did, employed specialists as architects.

Completely demythified, Heracles becomes the hired expert in the employ of the king of Mycenae; folk memory would have heroized his labors and eventually linked them to tales of a semidivine son of Zeus. Looked at in this unromantic light, other details in the tales of the labors yield their "true" meaning. The fearful Eurystheus, cowering in his jar and peeping over its rim at the returning hero and his capture, is a comic reminder that it was common practice to use large pithoi both for the storage of oil and grain, and as burial vessels. In times of danger, the pithoi were buried upright in the floors of houses so that foodstuffs could be accessible during long campaigns. At Troy VII, the city destroyed as a result of the Trojan War, the underground pithoi gave the city the added advantage of keeping their food stores hidden away from the enemy when the walls were stormed. To interpret consistently, of course, Eurystheus in his jar implies that Heracles is a source of danger rather than savior from it. But then, thinking back to our comments about the political ties between Tiryns and Mycenae, we can assume that relations between the two rulers were not always the best. The suzerain always appears in the labors as an imperious coward who imposes impossible tasks on his brave and dauntless baron. Inequity between king and retainer is, moreover, a recurring feature in myth and folktale, for a king's concern is to hold sway and a hero's is to assert his prowess. A hostile attitude between the two is more likely to leave its imprint on myth than a friendly one, for the unfavorable characteristics of an overlord provide an excuse when suzerainties break down.

To show that the style of the final labors differs radically from that of the first six, a single example will have to suffice. Unlike the earlier ones, these last tasks have a purely mythical and even mystical significance.

When Heracles has completed ten labors, he expects that his servitude has come to an end. Eurystheus, however, discounts the second and fifth labors because Heracles has been helped by Iolas and by the River Alpheios, respectively. The king therefore sets two more tasks. The eleventh labor is to fetch Hera's golden apples from a tree planted in her own divine garden, the Hesperides. The garden lies on the slopes of Mount Atlas, guarded by the watchful dragon Ladon. After traveling many months in a westward direction, Heracles encounters the sea god Nereus, who alone can advise him how to accomplish his task. The god resists Heracles' demands by undergoing many changes. Eventually, however, he capitulates and tells the hero not to pluck the apples himself, but to employ Atlas as his agent by relieving the giant of his burden of holding the earth on his shoulders. By means of a cunning ruse, Heracles tricks Atlas into securing the apples and then journeys with them back to Eurystheus. The astonished king, who expected that by setting this task he would rid himself of Heracles forever, has Hera's nymphs return them to her garden, since it is unlawful to keep the goddess's property.

Enchanted fruit in a magical garden inhabited by a snake is a feature of so many myths about immortality that merely to call attention to it is tantamount to comment. The snake's habit of shedding his skin has made him a symbol of rebirth to many cultures. The garden, too, which only the gods enter freely, is a primary symbol of Eden, where none toil and intemperateness is unknown. Finally, fruits have stood for the token or agent through which paradise and everlasting life can be tasted, consumed, and so gained. Trees themselves often represent the life cycle, and are so understood in the familiar phrase "family tree." Lastly, the location of the garden in the far west, beyond the rim of the world men know and over which the sun travels daily, completes the symbolic equation. Heracles, like Theseus and the Sumerian Gilgamesh, has been sent out to find the gift of life. Since ultimately the apples are returned, one can say that like the other demimortal heroes, he is denied it. The interview with the protean sea god is one way of demonstrating the difficulty of the quest: other heroes, too, are helped by charmed and omniscient strangers. The trickery of the giant Atlas is simply a variant on an ancient folktale motif in which an oversized, brutish demigod is outwitted by a purposeful and clever mortal. Jack the Giant Killer and Odysseus the killer of the Cyclops are kinsmen to this Heracles.

Considering the faulty chronology of the traditional Mycenaean king list, reviewed briefly at the start of Chapter V, Heracles' service to Eurystheus is rendered during the period *before* 1300, while Mycenae was growing from a small city to the most powerful state in the empire. Works like the fortifications of Mycenae, Athens, and Tiryns, with their plans of cisterns and reservoirs, all were attributed to Heracles' skill. Yet they were not built until c. 1250, the period when the Mycenaean empire was under attack. The dates of the other engineering works are distributed over the years between c. 1400, when the earliest wall of Tiryns was built, and 1250. Mycenae's palace and Citadel were probably constructed about 1340 or 1330, perhaps by the same king who constructed the Treasury of Atreus as his burial place. These works are roughly contemporary with the final extension of Tiryns and the replanning of its palace. It is even possible that the same artisans were employed to build at both cities, for architecturally they are very similar.

It is apparent then that Heracles' stories make nonsense of any attempt at dating or sequence. His enormous popularity among the later Greeks leads to the supposition that he was beloved from the days of his Mycenaean birth and episodes accrued to him throughout Greek history. On only one point do archaeology, chronology, and Heraclean legend shed light on one another, and that is in the probability that the labors express the mid-fourteenth century, the period when Mycenae began to exert its power over nearby cities and hill baronies. With this in mind, Heracles' labors seem to be a mythological expression of Mycenae's efforts both to bring new lands under its dominion and to police its existing protectorates. That much can be inferred also from the language Herodotus uses in his account of the end of Eurystheus' reign. According to him, the Heracleidae (sons of Heracles) were "refused shelter by all the Greeks to whom they applied in the hope of escaping slavery under the people of Mycenae." Athens alone received them and then, with their help, brought down the tyrannical ruler Eurystheus in a "victorious campaign against the masters of the Peloponnese."

4

When Eurystheus dies the Mycenaeans are advised by an oracle to choose a prince of Pelops' house to rule over them. The house has been accursed ever since Pelops' treachery in the winning of Hippodameia, and now another violent chapter is to be written in the family annals. The brothers Atreus and Thyestes are sent for from Midea, and a debate follows over which one is to take the throne. Atreus claims Mycenae by right of primogeniture and also as possessor of the horned lamb with the golden fleece.

This pledge of sovereignty originated in a vow made by Atreus to sacrifice the finest of the splendid flocks left to him and his brother by their father, Pelops. The god Hermes, eager to avenge the death of his votary Myrtilus, the charioteer murdered by Pelops, overheard the vow and coaxed his friend the Goat Pan to fashion a horned lamb with golden fleece and place it among the brothers' flocks. Knowing Atreus' greed, Hermes calculated that Atreus would claim the golden creature and thus precipitate a fratricidal war. Atreus kept his vow; he sacrificed the lamb's flesh, stuffed the fleece, and locked it in a chest; then he boasted about his possession to all. The jealous brother, with whom Atreus' newly married wife, Aerope, had fallen in love, agreed to be her lover if she would secure the fleece.

In the council hall, during the debate among the elders over the successor to the vacant throne, Thyestes cleverly coerces Atreus into admitting that the holder of the fleece should assume rule. When festivities are under way to proclaim the new king, Thyestes displays the lamb Aerope has brought him and is thereupon pronounced the rightful king. Zeus, who favors Atreus, prompts him to induce Thyestes to forfeit the throne if the sun is ever observed to go backward on the dial. Whereupon the great god reverses the laws of nature: Helius turns his horses' heads about toward the dawn and the stars retrace their courses. That night the sun sets in the east; Atreus ascends the throne doubly enraged with his brother over the discovered adultery and banishes him forever. After a time Atreus, feigning forgiveness, recalls Thyestes with an offer of half the kingdom. A banquet is ordered to celebrate his return and Thyestes eats heartily. When he has done, Atreus sends in to him the bloody heads, hands, and feet of Thyestes' three sons to show him what he has eaten. Thyestes recoils, vomiting, and lays an enduring curse on the seed of Atreus.

A series of hideous events follows. In one episode Thyestes seduces his own daughter Pelopia, who kills herself when it is revealed to her; in another, the son of their incestuous union kills Atreus at his father's command. Thyestes then becomes king of Mycenae and another golden-fleeced lamb appears among his flocks. Thereafter, every Pelopid king is confirmed in his kingship by the manifestation of a similar lamb.

Many and ingenious are the interpretations that have been made of this story in all its gruesome detail. The Romans Lucian and Polybius thought that at the time that Atreus and Thyestes quarreled over the succession, the Argives were already habitual stargazers, so they agreed that the best astronomer should be king. Robert Graves thinks the story refers to the custom that the king "reigned until the summer solstice, when the sun reached its most northerly point and stood still; then the tanist * killed him and took his place, while the sun daily retreated southward towards the winter solstice." The element of omophagia (the eating of raw flesh) has been compared to Kronos' vomiting up of his children, and both myths are seen as metaphors for primitive confusion over the sexual role in the birth process. The golden fleece has inspired its own anthology of decipherments, some of them discussed more fully in Chapter IX. Rivalry between Argive kings features in the myth of Acrisius and Proetus, is implicit (although different) in the labors of

---

* The elected heir of a living chief in a system that limited choice to the chief's kin.

Heracles, underlies the anger of Achilles in the *Iliad*, and was probably a constant factor in real life. Its causes must have varied, as they do in these literary examples, from simple greed to complex sociological and political issues. Atreus and Thyestes are very like the Biblical Cain and Abel, who were farmer and husbandman, respectively; or, as some Hebrew scholars think, representatives of contending agricultural and metalworking tribes. The Pelopids seem to have acquired some of their power through sheepherding, at least in this episode of their history. During the time setting envisioned for this myth, the late fourteenth and early thirteenth centuries, Mycenae was probably learning to exploit the copper ore in the mountains of Argolis. A. J. B. Wace, the late archaeologist, has suggested that working mines in those hills behind Mycenae might have been one source of the city's wealth that increased so markedly in the period. If this were so, an economic as well as ideological rivalry between miners and sheepherders is easy to imagine. Innate jealousy between groups whose sources and standards of prosperity differ is in any case well-known. The golden fleece might then represent an ideal compromise between the two groups—a symbolic declaration that copper magnates and husbandmen alike had equal voice in the election of a single ruler. The minor detail in the myth that suggests so democratic an arrangement is the council, called to decide on a king before Atreus' ascension to the throne. But then, this could be an interpolation in the myth from the Classical Age.

Historically, Greece was a country that found little or no obstacle to embracing a variety of religious beliefs. Yet there may have been ideological battles to be won before synthesis or coexistence was achieved between, for instance, the religion of Zeus and the pre-Greek mother religions. One mythologist has theorized that there was bitter, sporadic factionalism in Greece during the second millennium between worshipers of the goat and bull gods. Symbolism in the story of Atreus and Thyestes lends itself to the possibility that their rivalry represents the conflict between these two religions or, more accurately, cults. Worshipers of the goat god were cultivators of the vine. Their rites were orgiastic expressions of the fertility principle, earth-oriented and secret, like the chthonic aspects of the Dionysian religion. The countryside best suited to viticulture is hilly, an environment that also suits the goat, and so it would follow that the goat people were inhabitants of the hills. Differences between them and the peoples of the plains might have had their basis in the different economic orientation that geography implies. For the plains people were agriculturists, keeping domestic animals, especially cattle. Among them, the bull was the manifestation of the deity who from high antiquity was associated with the sun. The sun bull was a sky god, linked only through sacred marriages to terrestrial fertility gods, and generally opposed to chthonic cults. A series of folk traditions created a link between the bull and the bee, often thought to have been born as a result of spontaneous generation from a bull's carcass. Since the bee makes honey, or nectar, and from honey mead is concocted, the bull god came to be further associated with drinkers of mead. Hill folk or plainsmen, drinkers of wine or mead, worshipers of the goat or the bull, all thus became symbolic references to opposed ways of life. Bull worship, moreover, is the old established religion of Mesopotamian cattle breeders; therefore, the distinction between hillmen and plainsmen of the later worshipers is only a development of a more ancient geographical and cultural division between Near Easterners and Greeks. Near Eastern settlers in Greece would readily have adopted the bull god who so closely resembled their own, and would have fought against the followers of the goat, native to the mountainous mainland.

Several problems exist in this oversimple outline. One is that no one knows who introduced the vine into Greece. The consensus is that when the Greeks came it was already there, yet not cultivated as a crop until the Greeks were well established in the second millennium. If that is the case, and since the Greeks brought a bull god named Zeus with them, why did not wine become associated with Zeus? Homer, nevertheless, says the Olympian gods drink (eat?) ambrosia, a nectar food. Another unexplained factor is that the goat religion sounds very like the worship of Dionysos, about which there is no consensus whatsoever: not about when it was originated, where, or by whom. Perhaps, too, a theoretical conflict between members of a bull cult and a goat cult would be more convincing if there were prominent sculpture or monuments depicting these beasts in contexts of veneration. Although there are many representations of bulls and goats in Mycenaean (and later) art, none is so imposing as, say, the two great stone lions over the entranceway to the Citadel of Mycenae. Tradition says that lions are the emblem of Pelops; he originated in Asia Minor, where lions as symbols of rulers have a long history. The Pelopid house kept their founder's emblem as a sign of their enduring sovereignty. It is, of course, possible that the cult standing of the king mattered somewhat less than his genealogy. But that is, admittedly, a guess that may have meant little or nothing in the Bronze Age. (See Illus. 34.)

If then there were skirmishes between goat men and bull men, they might be expected to have taken place well before the building of the Lion Gate in 1250 B.C. The little material evidence that might be called upon to support the theory that the mythical brothers reflect an historical rivalry is not earlier than, but contemporaneous with, the date of the Lion Gate. In the middle of the thirteenth century, the town of Mycenae was expanding. It was then a fortified citadel; the megaron section of the palace had been built; the ramp and approach up the hill toward the palace had been laid out and walled; new tholos tombs were constructed some distance away; and several small but rich houses were clustered on the hillside beyond the walls. Apparently, when these houses were built

34. The Lion Gate at Mycenae.

Mycenae was enjoying a period of peace, or else they would not have been placed outside the city's walls. The period was also one of relative prosperity, for the houses seem to have belonged to palace officials and merchants engaged in the manufacture of perfumed oil and other luxury goods, and many were found to contain rich furnishings of ivory and precious stones. At about 1250 B.C. these houses were thoroughly destroyed by a fire that must have come unexpectedly since valuables were left *in situ*. A. J. B. Wace has attributed the destructions to the upheaval caused by the quarrel of Atreus and Thyestes.

There are three sets of "facts" which seem to be linked: the destruction of the private houses outside Mycenae's walls, the supposed warfare between worshipers of the bull and the goat, and the mythical quarrel between Atreus and Thyestes. Since Wace himself has suggested that the destruction of the lower town might be associated with the Atreus and Thyestes myth, and since so many archaeological data have been found to correspond to mythological tradition, his idea is perhaps more than good guesswork. An especially provocative find in the House of the Sphinxes is a set of seal impressions representing a man standing between two wild goats. Might this house owner have chosen a goat for his signet because he was a follower of the goat cult? Perhaps a more persuasive point in this connection is that archaeological and mythical chronology coincide surprisingly well. If it is assumed that Atreus is just coming to manhood in 1250 B.C., when the quarrel with Thyestes over succession takes place, it is just plausible that thirty years or so elapse before his son Agamemnon takes the throne. (See Chronology, Appendix I.)

There are, nevertheless, other explanations for the destruction of Mycenae's lower town. Some archaeologists have assumed that the burned-out houses are the first and earliest depredations of the invaders from the north who fifty years later were to devastate Mycenae entirely. And still others have pointed out the difficulty in making statements of any sort about military engagements. The Mycenaeans must have had many military encounters of a local character for which we have no evidence. They are simply deduced from the remains of weaponry, vase paintings, frescoes and other works of art, and like evidence that the Mycenaeans were a warrior aristocracy. Since overland travel was always difficult in the mountainous Peloponnesos, bands of warriors might have used sea roads and skirted coastlines to get from place to place, and such roads leave no traces. Hostile engagements might have been coastal affairs of a hit-and-run nature; of these too we would not expect to find traces. By the same token, battles—if battles there were—between bull worshipers and goat worshipers might well have taken place and left us nothing but myths as clues to their causes or duration.

In dramatic retellings, sensational elements of the myth have been exaggerated at the expense of ideological ones. Certainly, adultery and cannibalistic feasts are more immediately horrible than ideological rivalry. Still, golden lambs, the intervention of the gods, the council of elders, all those elements introduced into the story in a minor key, so to speak, indicate that the myth's core has to do with the political repercussions of the royal brothers' far-reaching differences. Their geographical disparateness, the sources of their wealth, and the implications of their opposed religious loyalties must have been highly significant when succession was at issue. Read in this way, the awful curse on the house of Atreus is the result of a bloody act of personal vengeance, not directly related to the initial causes of the brothers' quarrel.

The archaeological remain traditionally associated with Atreus is, of course, the so-called Treasury of Atreus. Both Wace and other archaeologists agree that the Treasury and the Lion Gate were built contemporaneously. Wace, however, suggests that the building took place around 1330 B.C., too early to fit the family chronology. George Mylonas suggests that both monuments were built around 1250, the date most attractive to the theory outlined above. The Treasury of Atreus is not a treasury at all, but the most outstanding example of a tholos tomb, and perhaps the most ornate. It was conceived and executed in monumental proportions, in elaborate carved detail, and in high color. The curved inner walls of the chamber forming a huge vault were probably faced with bronze rosettes and other decoration in bronze to enliven the dark interior, for small holes dot the surface at regular intervals and some have remnants of bronze nails in them. Parallel rows of bronze nails on the walls at each side of the threshold held a huge wooden frame in position. Fragments of the facade are scattered in museums all over the world. In its original state, it was covered with slabs of stone. The lower part was made in green stone ornamented with chevrons, spirals, and petals. The upper half was finished in two tones of red marble from Lakonia, and carried a design of spirals and split rosettes that ran upward toward the relieving triangle. (See Illus. 35 and 36.) It is impossible to be sure whether the Elgin slabs in the British Museum, showing parts of charging bulls, belong to the facade, or, as has been suggested, they came from some interior decoration of a side chamber. The latest investigations prove that these slabs had been worked in the neighborhood of the Treasury and definitely were part of the finished building. Does the decoration have any relationship to Atreus' supposed affiliation with the bull cult? The grave itself was looted long before Pausanias observed it, therefore there are no clues from grave goods. But apart from any of its possible associations with the Atreus myth, its lofty proportions and impressive construction testify to the high degree of excellence that architects at Mycenae had achieved in the thirteenth century.

It is conceivable that the prince who built the Tomb of Atreus enlarged and refortified the palace, for the Treasury is only one building of the complex at Mycenae that had been erected by 1250. Fragments of walls, filled-in rooms, bits of discarded frescoes, along with shards of different periods and reused stone blocks, indicate that there had been an earlier palace, built sometime between 1580 and 1400. A second palace, belonging to the foundations now visible, was constructed over the first. It was apparently designed to take advantage of the natural hilltop setting, and must have presented a stepped or terraced appearance. The main unit of the early palace was the megaron, or great hall, facing south to avoid stiff north winds that sweep the site even now. Judging from destructions, additions, and alterations, it would seem that the megaron of this earlier palace was repaired and incorporated into the second palace. Domestic quarters lie in the eastern area, but their extent is still undetermined. Homer's reference to Mycenae as "the city of wide streets" is consistent with vestiges of a main road, leading to the palace from the Lion Gate, along the gentler northern slope of the hill. In late Mycenaean times, a great staircase completed the entrance area up the ramp and zigzag embankment. Outside the gate there was a cluster of small buildings that may have been inns for travelers, or perhaps booths for traders. (See Illus. 37.)

The plan of this second palace is dominated by two corridors, north and south, placed at different levels to separate state from private apartments. The main room of the megaron was paved with a border of gypsum slabs; the remainder of the floor within the border was covered with painted stucco. Four superposed coats of stucco have been distinguished, indicating that the floor was renovated from time to time. One wonders what would have caused the need for such frequent repair. The surviving walls were deco-

35. The Treasury of Atreus: architectural drawing of the facade.

36. Detail of the design in the relieving triangle and in the half-columns.

rated in fresco. Although badly damaged by fire, several fragments show recognizable horsemen and soldiers as well as women in front of a palace, standing on a rocky ground. Another section of fresco is reminiscent of the Silver Siege Rhyton: it seems to have represented a battle, waged before a fortified citadel, while its women watched from the walls. In the room of the fresco, with its throne and its central hearth ringed by a painted flame pattern, the business of state was carried on. Visiting foreign leaders or officials were seated on benches affixed to either wall, with benches lining the entrance hall. Homer describes just such a megaron in the palace of Alcinous.

The fact that Mycenae's second palace is larger and more elaborate than the first suggests that there was an increase in the quantity and the quality of life between the two construction dates. Since a Mycenaean palace was not only the residence of the king but also the governing center of the province, it sustained a considerable social and economic life. It quartered craftsmen, minor officials, tourists, and servants, who, if they were not permanent residents, were constantly in and around the palace area carrying on its work and making its domestic and foreign contacts. The permanent residents included a household staff of slaves and servants, carpenters, potters, tailors, woodcutters, and metalsmiths, who either had quarters within the palace or visited it daily. In addition, there were the women who cooked, prepared the oil, meats, and grain, and did the cleaning. Weaving was a skilled task of the royal women, who taught it to the younger women and servants under their supervision.

In the last ten years a group of four substantial houses have been excavated outside the walls of the Citadel. These are the dwellings that may have been destroyed as a result of the quarrel of Atreus and Thyestes. At first it was thought that these houses were dependencies of the palace, sheltering officials or noblemen who were responsible for exporting oil and luxury goods abroad, because most of the Linear B tablets at Mycenae were recovered from them. Closer inspection of the houses—named West, Oil Merchant, Sphinxes, and Shields—and decipherment of their tablets prove that they were independent sites of industry and commerce. The tablets record lists of rations, personnel, and spices used in the oil processing that was carried on in the House of the Oil Merchant. His eastern basement consisted of eight rooms, where large pithoi of oil were stored, and had a heating system so that oil did not congeal in cold weather. In the corridor stood thirty large stirrup jars filled with oil, sealed and stamped with a signet, waiting to be shipped away. Burn marks along the corridor indicate that whoever set fire to the house knocked off the spouts of these jars so that the oil would blaze as it ran out.

The houses of the Sphinxes and of the Shields were named after the design on the ivory furniture inlays found among the debris. They, too, contained many storage vessels and decorated

37. Aerial view of Mycenae from the west.

jars of high quality. Remaining parts of stairways to upper floors of
these houses suggest that the merchants lived above their working
quarters in very pleasant surroundings. Frescoes decorated the
walls, furniture was adorned with faience, and ivory was in daily
use. All the equipment necessary to the routine of everyday living
was well made: kitchens, hearths, altars. The merchants of these
two houses may have acquired their wealth through the labor of
workers in blue glass paste, used in jewelry, and in the manufacture
of cloth, for the Linear B tablets affirm the existence of both sorts of
industry. They also list numerous women of Hellenic and barbarian origin who formed a domestic staff. Perhaps the most curious
feature about these factory-residences is their lack of any indication
of what sort of currency was used. There is evidence of what was
bought and sold but not of the negotiable tender. It is generally
believed that oxhides had a fixed exchange value during the Middle
Helladic period. Two finds dating to the Late Helladic period
suggest that copper ingots may have begun to replace oxhides as
currency. One is a hoard of copper bars in the little palace at Hagia
Triada on Crete. The other is the freight of copper ingots shaped
like hides found in a wrecked ship sunk in the southern Aegean.
Were the ingots a supply of cash this merchant ship had earned in
the sale of its original cargo?

Discoveries of this sort have changed our picture of the late
Mycenaean world in two important particulars. When Linear B
tablets were first discovered, it was taken for granted that their
complicated lists of peoples and possessions referred to operations
conducted by and from the throne. And in many cases that was
true. The ruler managed his economic affairs with the help of
scribes whose business it was to keep his records. Because the form
of the script was fairly rigid, and because no letters, literature, or
occasional writings turned up in the course of excavations, it was
assumed that literacy was the specialty of a few trained men, and
these in the employ of the throne. As it came to be proved that the
houses outside Mycenae's Citadel had been owned by independent
businessmen, so the supposition about literacy had to be revised.
Most of the Linear B tablets at Mycenae, in fact, belonged to these
"merchants' " houses, and it is doubtful that all of them employed
scribes. More than likely, the Linear B script was used by a fair
number of the upper-middle class in the ordinary conduct of its
business life. Tax gatherers and accountants, manufacturers and
traders, wealthy individuals as well as administrators probably
engaged in some correspondence about their affairs as well as kept

books about them. Even inscriptions on storage jars would have been useless unless the people using those jars could read their legends. In short, reading and writing might have been more common than was at first believed. Perhaps the breadth of such literacy was minimal, limited to numbers, phrases, terms, and like words that were useful. But then, in the absence of more tablets, the capacity of Linear B to express complex language structures cannot be known.

A second revision of the image of society conveyed by these houses is a corollary of the first. Palace centers were not only the strongholds from which warriors set out in hopes of conquest, nor only the nerve centers of overseas trading enterprises, but self-sustaining towns with well-developed local industries supplying domestic as well as foreign consumers. A glance at the variety of occupations engaged in at "the city of wide streets" illustrates the range and composition of this middle-class society. There were architects and masons; smiths and workers in copper and bronze; potters, oil makers, painters, gem-cutters, woodworkers; all the artisans engaged in the manufacture of cloth, from weavers and spinners to fullers and tailors; wine makers, butchers, tanners, and shoemakers; horse trainers, harness and chariot makers; cooks, bakers, farmers, swineherds, and shepherds. If the city was on the sea or controlled access to it, the list would have to be extended to include wheelwrights, oarsmen, sailmakers, and others skilled in the shipbuilding arts. Each man would have been trained specifically in one profession and so, one imagines, would also be responsible for apprentices and servants who did the more menial jobs associated with his particular craft. The group of independent houses and their industry, placed outside the walls yet engaged on a smaller scale in the same sort of activity managed by the palace, gives rise to speculation about their relations to the ruler. It has been suggested that the owners owed services of some sort and taxes to the sovereign, but were self-reliant in their own upkeep and their ventures in trade. Perhaps there were other, similar groups of houses located around the central fortification. The many place names on the tablets suggest that each such group had its own name, just as each hamlet and farm community has today.

VIII

Agamemnon's World

Agamemnon, the son of Atreus and perhaps the best known of all Mycenae's kings, assumed the throne after Thyestes' death. His story is linked to the ten-year-long war he commanded against the Trojans and to his tragic homecoming. Homer's *Iliad* and Aeschylus' *Oresteia* are traditionally accepted by all as the sources for these events. In fact, everything about Agamemnon's life and tenure as king of Mycenae before his departure for Troy is to be inferred from these works, although additions to his life story in the way of prefaces and sequels have been written by others, notably Euripides. Since justice cannot be done to the poems and plays, a summary account of the highlights of the tradition is offered here by way of substitute.

Menelaos and Agamemnon are the third set of mythological brothers who rule in the Peloponnesos: Menelaos in Sparta, Agamemnon at Mycenae. When the Trojan prince Paris abducts Menelaos' wife Helen, all the Argive princes who once sued for her hand and then vowed to support her final choice of husband assemble in war council. It is agreed that their combined forces will meet at Aulis and from there sail to Troy. The list of princes and their armies is long, distinguished, and their amassed strength must have been formidable. The largest fleet of one hundred ships is Mycenae's; Knossos ranks second with her contribution of ninety ships. At Aulis the armies lie becalmed for lack of a strong wind and petition the gods through the seer Kalchas for guidance. He announces that Agamemnon must sacrifice his daughter Iphigenia to the goddess Artemis in order to appease her for his killing of a sacred deer. Under pretense of marrying her to the great hero Achilles, Agamemnon sends for the girl. Just as she is about to be sacrificed, the goddess relents; Iphigenia is taken up in a mist and spirited off to the land of the Tauroi (the Crimea), and a hind is placed on the altar in her stead.

After all manner of other delays the fleet draws up on the beach before Troy and the Greeks settle into a long campaign. Paris, as is appropriate, is the nominal head of the Trojan war party; his elder brother Hector becomes the actual Trojan leader and scourge of the Greeks. Their most brilliant hero is Achilles, whose bitter quarrel with Agamemnon over booty from a raiding party almost costs the Greeks the war. Homer does not paint the "king of kings" in flattering colors: his most constant epithets carry a sense of greed and pride, attributes he might well have acquired as sovereign of the rich and powerful city. Ten years of warfare elapse before Troy falls to the Greeks. During the long siege, affairs at Mycenae are in the hands of Agamemnon's wife, Clytemestra, and her lover, Aegisthus, the son of the incestuous union of Thyestes and his daughter Pelopia. Aegisthus now carries on the feud begun by Atreus and Thyestes by plotting the death of the homeward bound Agamemnon. Clytemestra is a willing partner in the planned crime for she is enraged and embittered by the sacrifice of Iphigenia, that she assumes has been carried out. Guards are stationed in the watchtowers along the mountain passes with instructions to light fires as a signal of the returning ships' approach. The war leader's homecoming is an elaborate occasion filled with pretended fondness. Although Aeschylus does not mention them, Agamemnon must have brought gifts, slaves, and his share of the booty from Troy. All sources, however, mention his concubine Cassandra, a princess of the royal Trojan house famed for her gift of prophecy. When the king is being bathed and anointed for his homecoming celebration, the adulterous pair set upon him and kill him. Cassandra meets the same fate. It is to avenge Agamemnon's death that his son, Orestes, later kills his mother and Aegisthus. With his act the curse laid on the house of Pelops is finally played out.

2

In 1941, during the course of road building on the outskirts of the ancient site of Aulis, a long, narrow Temple of Artemis was discovered at the place where Agamemnon was supposed to have sacrificed Iphigenia. The temple, whose identification is certain from the inscription on a statue base, dates from the fifth century and therefore does not indicate anything about the historicity of the famous Greek expedition. It is, instead, one of many examples of the interest and veneration with which the Classical Age looked back to the Heroic one. In fact, the gathering at Aulis has always caused wonder, for why should a commander-in-chief from Mycenae rally his forces at a Boeotian harbor instead of one in the Argolid? There is no answer. A myth connects facts from different ages in an arbitrary manner and it is folly to expect consistency. Tradition is firm about Aulis, and on its behalf it must be said that Aulis is the only harbor on the western coast of Boeotia well protected from weather and occasional·marauders from the open sea. A glance at the map on page 89 will show that there is, moreover, sufficient area for the massing of a fleet of such considerable size. As for Iphigenia's dramatic visit to the temporary camp, human sacrifice was never a feature of Greek religion and wherever it does appear in myth it is usually attributed to some vestige of an older, eastern religious practice. Iphigenia is often associated with the goddess Artemis as either victim or priestess. Her name, "mightily born," is a title of the goddess, and she is often thought to be an avatar of the deity rather than a princess of Mycenae's royal house. In this myth she might be; for tradition says that after her rescue, she became a priestess of the Taurian Artemis, who was worshiped in savage fashion: all strangers were sacrificed to her. Perhaps because of the linguistic identity of the two females, the ancient brutal ritual became confused with this incident in the battle poem.

The saga of the Trojan War is so historical-sounding in its details of ships, their deportment, men, weapons, fighting styles, customs and procedures, codes of behavior to enemies and allies, geographical specifications, and the like that it is difficult to conceive of it only as a saga built on a famous older siege poem. A century's worth of excavation at Troy has not yet made it permissible to call the *Iliad* the record of an historical event. The *Iliad*, like the *Odyssey*, has been a mine of information about life and warfaring in the Mycenaean Age, much of it verified by Linear B tablets: the heroes' dress, the way chariots were used, the method of hurling spears, the use of trenches or ditches as strategic fortifications, the funeral games on a hero's death, the kind and occasion of sacrifices to the gods. Hector, Priam, and Tros are named on the tablets at Pylos, a fact suggesting that people in the *Iliad* were known, at least as fictional characters after whom ordinary men may have been named. (See Illus. 38.)

The war itself, however, like its cause, remains stubbornly ambiguous. An historical association of some sort between Mycenae and Troy is completely affirmed, for the Greeks had been trading with Priam's city ever since their ancestors left Troy to settle on the mainland. It was probably a combination of ancient remembrance and ongoing commerce that gave rise to the tradition that Heracles built the walls of Troy, as well as to the conflicting legend that Poseidon and Apollo were hired by the Trojan king Laomedon to build them. But the nature of the Greek venture on the Asian mainland in c. 1200 is complicated by the record of two centuries of trade, by references of an equivocal sort to Greek relations with the Hittite empire, and by that empire's relation to other Asian kings. The best and most comprehensive study of the historical background to the Trojan War has been the work of Professor Denys Page, who sees Homer's poem as a supplement to events written about in Hittite and other Asian records. These, consisting of letters and other diplomatic "papers," incorporate references to political problems on the Asian mainland from which a sequential history has been painstakingly deduced. The following is a summation of his interpretations which, for simplicity's sake, omits the excruciatingly difficult philological problems he has had to resolve. Conservative linguists, for instance, still debate whether the Hittite mention of the king of the *Ahhijawa* in the Tawagalawas Letter should be translated as "king of the Achaeans" or whether *Attarissiyas* is a transcription of Atreus or Agamemnon (Greek Ατρειδης). Argument either way becomes especially impenetrable because Hittites did not always refer to foreign leaders by the names familiar to us. Tutankhamen in their records is given his pharaonic title, Neb-Kheper-Ra, and that is misrendered as *Niphururia.*

During the first half of the thirteenth century B.C., Hittites controlled the greater part of Asia Minor, except the northwestern sector (see Map 2). Sometime thereafter, however, Hittite power began to slip. King Tuthalijas IV (c. 1250–1220) faced a series of

38. An implicitly historical representation of the Greeks' Trojan Horse, on wheels, carrying warriors.

foes: he was challenged by Arzawa, the leading principality in the south which revolted and had to be subdued. Then a former confederate, Attarissiyas, provoked battle with the Hittites on the Asiatic mainland. In the northwestern sector of the continent, the league of cities led by the kingdom of Assuwas (the word is thought to be Asia) was issuing threats. In the following king's reign, c. 1220–1190, the league of cities made inroads on the empire; the Hittites lost Arzawa and Hittite dominion receded forever from the continent. In the power vacuum created, the growing ambitions of the Assuwas league of cities came into direct conflict with the Achaeans who exerted influence over the coastal region and who had been allied with the Hittite nation. The natural consequence was a clash between these two powers; but of this there is no documented evidence, for the darkness of the subsequent Dorian era hid the scene for several hundred years. In the new dawn, only the Greek epic poems preserve the story of a war between Achaeans and a league of cities on the northwestern mainland. Somehow within this framework the fall of Troy took place. Professor Page is not certain that Troy is actually named in the membership list of the league of cities: it depends upon an equation of *Truisa* and *Troia,* and on whether Troy's fall took place in the reign of King Tuthalijas or in that of his successor. His guess is that the Achaeans attacked Troy soon after the defeat of the league under Assuwas by Tuthalijas in c. 1230, given a decade either way. It was the moment when the Hittites left the northwestern region and when the kingdom of Assuwas had barely recovered from a defeat.

What would have provoked the Achaeans to fight? As was pointed out, the Achaeans had been trading successfully for centuries with the many cities on the coast from Troy to the Egyptian Delta (except the central western coast). Ordinarily the channels of commerce were peaceful; occasionally they must have been combined with a quest for new homes and new wealth to be won by the sword. Achaeans were at the apex of their prosperity when the Hittite decline removed the last obstacle to an exploitation of the highly coveted western shore. The attack on that coast is thus "the last chapter in the tale of two hundred years of economic penetration in the East," as Professor Page says, and "the *Iliad* illustrates a chapter of the story recorded in the Annals of King Tuthalijas."

Read in this way, the *Iliad* becomes an historical source at odds with the annals of the Hittite king in one major particular: in Homer, it is Troy, not Assuwas, that leads the league of nations. Then, too, the Greeks in the *Iliad* are an expeditionary force from the mainland, whereas the Achaeans—the men of Ahhijawa—known to the Hittites are from Rhodes. Professor Page does not see these differences as significant since the Hittite documents are fragmentary and tell only a portion of the whole story. It is natural enough that the *Iliad* concentrates only on the siege of Troy, for that city had long been one of the strongest and wealthiest fortresses on the coastline from the Dardanelles to Syria. The important point is that the event commemorated in the poem fits into the historical background and adds to it by showing 1) that the struggle for power was not limited to the center and south but extended to the north also; and 2) that the Achaeans came not only from the colony state Rhodes but also from the mainland.

The one other important piece of evidence for the historicity of the *Iliad* is the long Catalog of Ships in Book II. The catalog is an order of battle and lists the commanders, their places of origin, and the number of ships they provided. It has been demonstrated, but not universally accepted, that both the Greek and the Trojan catalogs are authentic inheritances of the late Mycenaean period and are connected with an overseas expedition. Page believes they were preserved independently of the poetical tradition that culminated with the *Iliad* because some of the listed contributions of ships to the fleet are clearly numerical exaggerations intended to flatter either the donor or his country. The figure, for example, for the Thessalian districts, not all of which are maritime, is 1,186 ships, an absurdly high number. Considerations of vocabulary and meter further support the idea that the Greek catalog was a separate composition incorporated into the *Iliad* at a late stage of its development. The numbers of ships, therefore, are mostly unreliable. Conversely, the names of people and places in both catalogs are, for the most part, true. They seem to have altered only slightly during the long period of the catalogs' oral transmission, both before they made their way into the *Iliad* and afterward, when the entire poem was known only orally. The problem then can be stated as follows: the poem as an entity can be shown to have an historical context; parts of the catalogs, although composed separately, also seem to be historical. Do both the poem and the catalogs refer to the same event, a siege of Troy? The highly respected scholar Walter Leaf thought that the Trojan catalog represented a state of affairs that could not have existed after the Trojan War, when the political and geographical complexion of Asia Minor changed entirely. Nor could it have reflected any period long before the war, when the Hittites, who are not mentioned, were the dominant power. It followed therefore that the catalog was a "metrical narrative" of the war in nearly original form. Leaf was impressed by the quantity of accurate information that the *Iliad* gives about the Troad, knowledge that must have been acquired well before the Ionian migrations of the post-Mycenaean era that made this neighborhood of Asia Minor "Greek." The Trojan catalog must be of Mycenaean origin, he thought, and his reasoning seems conclusive. First, the Trojan catalog is meager compared to the Greek one; had it been composed after the war by an Ionian poet, he would have known more about his Asian neighbors and their history. Secondly, if it is conceded that the catalog is a Mycenaean composition, why would Mycenaeans make a list of people and places in Asia Minor unless they purposed an expedition into the area? Poets could not have known what they did unless Mycenaeans had visited Asia Minor either before, during, or immediately after the war.

3

Controversy over the historicity of the catalogs and the *Iliad* may never be settled; only a summary glimpse of their complexity has been attempted here. But if the Greek catalog is history, it

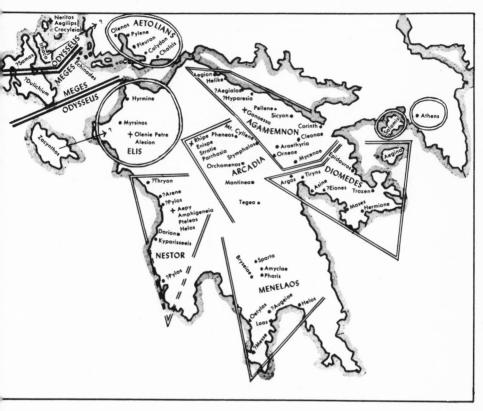

39. The Argive principalities according to the Homeric Catalogue II.

validates the political and geographical conditions of Mycenae given in legend. In the early days of the kingdom, when it was governed by the Perseids Acrisius and Proetus, its territory extended to Dendra-Midea in the west, to the Argolid coastline on the east, and to Tiryns, ten miles away in the south. In the reign of Eurystheus, we discovered, Tiryns with its surrounding plains was a subsidiary kingdom of Mycenae, and the implications of the Heraclean labors were that new and larger lands were being brought under Mycenae's sovereignty. The catalog vindicates these legendary boundaries by showing that in the later thirteenth century Mycenae was still occupied by the overlord of the Achaeans. It adds that his personal dominions now extended outward to important areas of the north and northwest, like Corinth and Helice. And he also remained supervisor of the Argive plain and its fortresses, although the major one, Tiryns, was ruled by Diomedes. (See Illus. 39, a map of the Argive principalities according to the Catalog.)

The remainder of the *Iliad* makes it clear that the overlord commanded the allegiance of *all* the Greek kings, from Odysseus, who ruled in the far-western Ionian islands, to aged Nestor at the southern extremity of the mainland. That was, at least, in times of war. Does that imply that Mycenae was the government seat of a Mycenaean empire? It is an issue over which academic battles have been joined but not decisively won. Scholars who argue against the concept of a Mycenaean empire point out 1) that the natural land barriers prevented full unity; 2) that all the citadels had fortified walls; 3) that in poetic records Greek fought against Greek; and 4) that at the end of the era nearly all of the palaces were burned although there were no foreigners (a debatable term) in the land. Supporters of the idea of empire or hegemony of some sort place great significance on Agamemnon's power to gather all the major cities under his sole authority to fight with Troy. And they also consider the extensive roads, connecting province to province, as a strong argument for some kind of unity. Arguments that fall in the middle ground emphasize that political control was likely to have been personal, and any general organization of the principalities was likely to have been governed by both kinship and the conveniences of trade. About the position against the idea of a Mycenaen empire, and about the cautious stand of the uncommitted, a good deal can be inferred from the information given thus far on the development of the Mycenaean mainland. More, however, needs to be said about the reasoning of scholars who call attention to Mycenaean roadways as an indication of political unity.

Mycenae's road system was extremely sophisticated for its time. It created a network among the important towns of the Argolid and Messenia, of Boeotia and Attica, too. Stone bridges forded streams and steep grades; reinforced culverts took care of water runoff. The roads outward from Mycenae, toward Tiryns in the southwest and Corinth in the north, have had careful study. They average between two and three and one-half meters in width so that two chariots could pass each other with relative ease. Between nearby cities and close to the city itself, the surfaces are stone-paved; in fact, one can still trace wheel ruts through the Lion Gate. Farther away from the city centers, the surfaces are either graveled or made of packed dirt with boulders or guard stones as retaining edges. The extent and upkeep of the system argue that good communications between provinces and towns—better than the mountainous geography would lead one to expect—were of great importance.

The roads, however, were more than a feat of advanced technology and more than evidence of continuing contact between citadels. They were public works, requiring for their execution corvée laborers already charged with carrying out the huge amounts of tomb building, wall building, citadel building, and hydraulics works that have already been cited. Without a large increase in wealth, population, and power, such services to the state could not have been rendered. According to many historians, the late Bronze Age was supposed to have been a time of declining wealth and fear of invasion. The great spurt in building activity was a defense against that fear. But the decline in wealth can only have been relative to some estimate of earlier Mycenaean prosperity. From the fourteenth to the second half of the thirteenth century, archaeology records a continuous increase in wealth. Furthermore, as more than one observer has commented, the ability to command manpower service on such a large scale, and to direct it with success, implies a closely supervised state organization. Whatever the threats of attack, domestic and foreign, they did not weaken the organization of the major centers—not, that is, until after the Trojan War. And finally, the character of all this building and construction is oriented around kings, implying that theirs was the greatest share of the century's capital gains. The simultaneous rise of a mercantile class had not yet reached proportions of threat to royal power.

4

High in a watchtower atop a mountain near Mycenae, a guard sees the caravans of the returning king's party approaching the city. He lights a bonfire, thereby relaying his message to guards at Mycenae's Citadel, who immediately inform the queen. She gives orders: rooms are to be readied, food prepared, wine jars carried from storerooms to the pantries off the central megaron. Braziers are lit, and water is fetched from the cistern deep below the palace walls. She has her plans. A carpet is spread over the entranceway and Agamemnon and Cassandra alight from their chariots. Householders line the way to welcome their sovereign; the queen greets him fondly. While wagons are emptied of wonderful gifts and prizes of war, while his retinue find their places among the palace people, while the scent of roasting oxen promises a banquet, the king is invited to bathe. Bath pourers assist him in his silver bathtub until Clytemestra sends them away. Then she stabs him.

Did any of this happen? From what has been reconstructed of daily life at Mycenae, all of it is conceivable, much of it routine, and only the silver bathtub an outright fabrication. Yet even the way that detail found its way into the story is understandable. Watchtowers and guard stations were posted at strategic points in the vicinity of most large palaces. To some extent, the Citadel of Mycenae was its own lookout point, for the hilltop commanded a panoramic view of the surrounding countryside. Moreover, the city was fortified against surprise attack and therefore guards and lookouts might have operated in small units of two or three men at survey posts spread outward in a concentric network that could survey considerable distances. Aeschylus says the watchman near Mycenae lit a bonfire; but that would have been too imprecise a method of sending messages if the approaching visitor had been unexpected. Then probably a runner or, if the terrain allowed it, a chariot would have been dispatched with more specific tidings.

Preparation at the palace would have begun immediately. Perhaps an ox was spitted and set to roast over the central hearth. Oil lamps and braziers would have been set out in the megaron, and the heavy Greek wine mixed with water. The more laborious task would have been to fetch water. Some idea of water systems has already been gleaned from earlier discussions. The system at Mycenae was awesome. The original palace depended on rain and perhaps a few wells (this is contested) for its water supply in times of siege, for there was no spring on its rocky hill. This serious shortcoming was remedied in the closing years of the thirteenth century by the construction of a remarkable underground cistern and aqueduct immediately outside the northeast walls and completely hidden from view. The water drawer would descend a stepped passage leading underground through the north wall (sixteen original steps remain). He would arrive at a doorway that opened onto a rectangular roofed platform. A second door led into a second section that descended twenty or so steps farther down a passageway that ended in a landing some 2.8 meters below the level of the first. A third and final section began at right angles to this landing, proceeding another fifty-four steps down, about 12 meters deep, to a well-like reservoir measuring 1.6 by 0.7 meters and 5 meters deep. The steps and walls of this third section were covered with a thick coat of watertight plaster; the steps of all three sections were made of limestone; the roofs were constructed either of corbel vaults or of huge slabs laid horizontally across the walls. Water was supplied to the reservoir through an underground conduit of terra-cotta pipes that ended in an opening in the reservoir's saddle roof. The origin of the water source is not known since excavation has not continued for the length of the pipes. If, as has been surmised, the source was a spring on a neighboring hill, the Mycenaeans must have understood the principle of water finding its own level, a seemingly simple idea that was elaborated only in the modern age. For the springwater would have had to travel down into the small valley formed by its own hill and then up again into the palace's cistern. Miles and miles of Roman aqueduct sloping gradually to control the grade level of its conduits might not have been constructed had the Romans understood this principle. (See Illus. 40.)

What of the gifts that Agamemnon brought home with him? It must not be supposed that these were odd trinkets or tourists' mementos to distribute among his family. They were substantial objects that added to his store of treasure and kept him in supply of gifts for the many occasions when one was called for. In the Mycenaean world there was scarcely a limit to the situations in which gift-giving was expected. Rewards, prizes, payments, fees, bribes, dowries, "gifts of wooing," all fell under the rubric "gift," and gift exchange governed the conduct of domestic and foreign diplomacy. One set of tablets at Pylos, headed "What Pu-ke-qi-ri saw when the King appointed Sigewas *damokoros* [mayor?]," lists the following objects that were probably gifts given and received on the occasion of his appointment: decorated pots, boiling pans, tripod caldrons, fire tongs; furniture: tables, chairs, footstools inlaid with ivory; colored glass, gold, and precious stones. Another tablet, this one from Knossos, carries the words "for guests" before the names of certain clothes, proving that the rules of hospitality included gift-giving. Odysseus is made welcome with embroidered robes at the Phaeacian palace of Alkinoos in just such a ceremonial fashion.

The practice of gift-giving may have been adapted from the Near East, where similar collections of gifts are recorded. A fragment of a Mari tablet shows that the king's appointment of a mayor, a parallel to the *damokoros* at Pylos, was accompanied by a gift of silver and sheep. The wedding gifts of Queen Akhatmilku at

Ugarit included jewelry, gold vessels, clothes and fabrics, chairs, footstools covered with gold, ivory, and lapis lazuli, bronze implements like cooking pots and fire tongs. Agamemnon himself proposes to give Achilles seven towns in Messenia when he is trying to bribe the hero into returning to the battlefront at Troy. The Mycenaean love of display is only one factor in the richness of such gifts, that occasionally found their way into graves and tombs. The other is that seemingly mundane items like cooking pots and caldrons were convenient forms for carrying and distributing metals, in this age perhaps more precious than gemstones. The utilitarian ware was often melted and recast into weaponry and armor. But in any form, metal constituted the visible wealth of its owner. Even copper ingots, which might have been used in this period as currency, were more likely to have been converted into usable objects than stored in ingot form.

Agamemnon probably was murdered. The combination of barbarity and splendor so often attributed to Mycenaean art, building, and myth suggests that these people did not shrink at violence. Traditional accounts of his murder differ in interesting ways. Homer sketches Aegisthus as a devious and weak-willed character who does the actual killing with a sword and twenty men

40. The underground cistern at Mycenae.

41. Aegisthus stabs Agamemnon.
Electra rushes up on the right.

to back him up while all are at dinner in the megaron. Clytemestra supports her lover as he kills her husband; and then she stabs Cassandra without assistance. Perhaps Homer's murder scene did not survive as well as Aeschylus' because it is so pictorially difficult for artists to represent: the tangle of corpses, wine bowls, tables heaped with food, etc. Other poets introduced the ax as a weapon, brought Agamemnon's children on to the scene of the crime, and changed the latter to the famous bath. Aeschylus simplifies the scene further by having Clytemestra perform the deed. (See Illus. 41.)

A room in the northwest corner of Mycenae's palace, near the domestic quarters, with a stepped red-stucco floor and a drain, caused some excitement when it was discovered since the drain suggested it was a bath. Guides leading tours through Mycenae repeat the identification, pointing to the red of the stucco as the bloodstains caused when the king was killed. In spite of their enthusiasm, better-preserved examples of similar rooms at Tiryns and Pylos show that the position of the drain at Mycenae makes it unlikely that the room was a bath. The floor of the bath at Tiryns, for instance, is a single limestone block. Along the edges and at specified distances there are small holes meant to receive dowels by means of which wooden paneling was secured to the floor. The room's drainage outlet, cut in the floor block, leads out to a paved court and a larger drain. The vestiges of the drain at Mycenae, in contrast, do not lead to any part of the palace's main drainage system.

The bathtub may have become part of the myth through a misunderstanding of a silver larnax that the king possessed—the

Greek words for bathtub and sarcophagus are identical, and their general shape and size are nearly so (see Illus. 42). Larnakes were used for burials on the Greek mainland in the period of the Trojan War, although Homer knows them only as bone receptacles after cremation, or as tubs. Early tomb robbers, finding such larnakes with distorted corpses inside them, may have explained them with tales of murder and torture. Indeed, looking at them, one finds it difficult to imagine them accommodating a full-sized corpse unless it was doubled up and twisted in a frightful manner. The curator of the Museum at Thebes, where a substantial collection of larnakes from Tanagra is housed, assured me that an adult body fitted quite comfortably when laid on its back with the knees drawn up. The point is perhaps better appreciated when it is recalled that the skeletons found at Pylos (see Chapter XI) had massive bones and were taller than the average westerner today.

Larnakes originated in Crete, where many have been found. Although Mycenaeans might have known about them since their fifteenth-century "invasion" of the island, they do not seem to have adopted them until the late thirteenth or early twelfth century, when Crete was Mycenaean. Their use is one of several minor variations in burial practices in the period of the late empire at different places on the mainland. By confirming what is known from art, poetry, tomb contents, and the like, the paintings on the larnakes show that there was an essential continuity of funerary custom from the fifteenth to the twelfth centuries. Placing the body in a clay coffin instead of directly on the floor of the tomb was the only major innovation.

Homer's account of Patroklos' funeral is the most complete picture extant of the last rites rendered to an important person. To his poetry can be added the evidence of tomb art, myth, offerings to the dead, and paintings on sarcophaguses to deduce that the cere-

42. Mourning women in procession on a painted larnake from Tanagra.

monies for Agamemnon must have been splendid. Although there were variations in the ritual, especially late in the twelfth century when styles and practices from many sources were being fused, some features seem to be constant. The king's body would have been washed and anointed with precious oils, then dressed in a fine robe and arrayed with his favorite rings and jewels. Perhaps while this was being done, the palace goldsmith would have put the finishing touches on a mask in the king's image he had long since prepared. A litter bearing the masked king and some of his personal effects—a particular dagger or sword—would have been accompanied by a procession of wailing women in stylized postures of grief. Recently discovered painted larnakes from Tanagra and Perati depict such processions vividly: the women's bodies sway, moving to the sound of their lament (?); their arms are upraised over their heads; and in some instances their hair is torn out and their cheeks are grooved with blood. Since this same raised-arm gesture was first found on tiny female figurines in the graves of children, the figures were thought to be divine nurses, ready to serve the helpless children on their journey to the other world. As more such figurines were found in a variety of graves, the identification was suspect. But it was not until they were compared with the paintings on larnakes that their true nature as representations of mourners was understood. (See Illus. 42 and 43.)

One curious detail in the paintings on the Perati larnakes is a little tail-like appendage at the side of the women's long dresses. It has been suggested that the "tails" are locks of hair tied to the robe at the girdle, ready to be laid on the grave in the final moments of the funeral ceremony. In Aeschylus' dramatization of the Agamemnon saga, Orestes places a lock of his hair on his father's tomb in just such a gesture of veneration. Still, no explanation of the "tails" is universally accepted.

A chariot cortege may have replaced the litter in some processions. Several compositions on vases with funerary scenes show the dead man carried in a chariot. He is in an upright position so that he is in full view, but he is armless and wrapped in a shroud to emphasize his contrast with the living. The chariot was armed with sword, javelins, and quiver and its teams of horses often were slaughtered in the dromos of the tomb.

Painting on the famous Cretan sarcophagus from the Hagia Triada indicates that tables, with colored cloths, heaped with food and bound animals, were carried in procession to the graveside. (See Illus. 44.) There, after the body was laid in the tomb, the

43. Gold face mask found at Mycenae.

animals were slaughtered on a block sacred to that purpose by a priest wearing a long heavy robe. The scene of sacrifice on an agate gem from Chamber Tomb 47 at Mycenae is symbolized by a double ax used to stun the animal. On another gem from Vapheio, the priest standing at the block or table is making an incision in the abdomen of a wild boar. The beast's blood was caught in a special vessel so that, at some point in the ceremonial proceedings, it could be poured into the earth in a libation, either to the earth gods about to receive the new dead or to the dead man himself. Horses, dogs, oxen, and sheep were the usual sacrificial beasts, but there might also have been human victims on very rare occasions. Homer says that at the funeral pyre of Patroklos, Achilles sacrificed twelve Trojan prisoners as well as many animals. On the other hand, there is no certain evidence that this practice is Mycenaean. Skeletons found in the fill above the door of Chamber Tomb 15 at Mycenae originally led to the belief that they were examples of immolations. Later other explanations were considered more plausible. The sacrificed animals were eaten at a final meal which was taken after the corpse and its gifts had been interred and the landfill put in place. Drinking cups in huge quantities found at some grave sites suggest that a feast—or at least a toast—by many members of family and friends was not unusual. In the Archaic Age it was also customary at this stage of the ceremony for singers to perform a funeral dirge extolling the dead. The call for singers at Hector's bier in the *Iliad* is the only indication we have that this too might have been a Mycenaean practice.

Moving a stele or cenotaph into place was the final act performed at the site before the mourners dispersed. Ceremonies for a nobleman or king were not officially complete, however, until the last of the funeral games had been played out. Athletic contests and chariot races of the sort continued annually at Olympia were a tribute to the dead in which young noblemen displayed their gymnastic skills. Wrestling, spear hurling, foot and chariot races might have continued for up to ten days, extending the lavish funeral display that the Classical Age was to find so extravagant. The games are too well illustrated in Mycenaean art to doubt that the myth of Pelops and Homer's *Iliad*, too, were reflecting real customs.

5

The more information that accumulates about funerary and burial ceremonies, the greater the scholars' frustrations. Monumental tombs, elaborate grave gifts, costly ceremonial equipment, ritual art, Homeric descriptions are all hollow signs without meaning. No one is certain and few opinions are clear about the

44. The Hagia Triada sarcophagus. Mourners bear gifts for the dead and animals for sacrifice at the gravesite.

nature of Mycenaean religious beliefs, yet many of its practices are now known. Jars of foodstuffs placed near the corpse along with furnishings that were important to the person in life suggest that the family was preparing the dead for another life. Children were furnished with beloved toys, warriors with their best weapons, women with cosmetic boxes and household articles, many dead of both sexes with cooking utensils and fire pans. These objects seem to reflect an attempt to make the new life less strange. Yet others interpret the splendid funeral honors and the nature of funeral gifts as farewell gestures before a journey, rather than as tools with which to begin a new life. The rites for the dead, they say, are essential means for him to arrive at his destination. Without them he might wander helplessly between two worlds like Homer's El-penor, begging for a proper burial so he may rest. In the world of "shades," Elpenor is "strengthless and will-less, more than a memory but less than a being." Evidence from Homer, however, is double-edged. If the *Odyssey* is read as a Mycenaean document, it can also be argued that the Heroic Age believed in a life after death. The hero descends to an underworld of shades, and after pouring a blood offering reminiscent of those poured during funeral sacrifices, he is able to talk with the ghosts of his mother and Achilles. Strictly speaking, Odysseus' meeting with the ghosts only implies that a concept of soul, or psyche, was current in Homer's time, and that he reflected it in his poetry. Still, on one of the painted larnakes from Tanagra, referred to above, a single female figure floats or flies in the air. Her robe does not move in the wind, but her arms curve upward and fan outward into little wings that are drawn back as she flutters aloft. After the Dark Ages, winged gods and other beings became an artistic convention. In the twelfth century, however, elements in mythology and cult were more fluid, forming and shifting under the impact of innovations brought about by the breakup of the Aegean communities during and after the Trojan War. After examining the little figure Professor Emily Vermeule asked, Could this painting be the first representation of a dead woman's soul leaving her body? Did, then, the Mycenaeans believe in a duality of mortal body and immortal soul?

Or, to take a related concern, some graves indicate that gifts continued to be brought to the dead long years after his burial. At Tomb 520 at Mycenae, and at Prosymna, deposits of Geometric-style pottery shards were found above the grave fill. More such fragments of vessels, figures of horsemen, and unstrung pearls were found in the dromos of the tomb of Clytemestra. Could the dead have been the object of a cult in Mycenaean times, as some scholars have supposed? The very idea of a sacred precinct marked out by the grave circles at Mycenae seems to support the idea, and the proved existence of hero cults in post-Mycenaean eras does also. The supposition is that hero cults rose out of an earlier, possibly Mycenaean, veneration of the dead. Arguments in opposition point out that to prove a cult of the dead, it would have to be established that gifts and rituals were renewed regularly or seasonally and that graves were carefully tended and kept intact. Of these there is no evidence. Still more important, countless graves indicate that once the bodies of the dead had decomposed, the bones were heaped aside unceremoniously to make room for fresh corpses.

Not all the indirect testimony of poetry and art, or the tantalizing lists of gods on the Pylos Linear B tablets, or the numerous objects of cult unearthed by archaeologists have enabled a reconstruction of an organized system of religious belief. As Martin Nilsson says, "Minoan-Mycenaean religion is a picture book without text." All is conjecture and hypothesis, much of it based upon analogy with later Greek and other religions. The references made in these chapters to Mycenaean gods and their cults are still unassimilated into a whole theology with an attendant doctrine and code of ethics. Shrines and sanctuaries are few and poorly documented, their many small votive objects susceptible to widely divergent interpretations. It is only in the last few years, in fact, that undebatable evidence of a Mycenaean cult practice has come to light. It has caused a reexamination of many long-held theories.

In 1968 and 1969, the archaeologist William Lord Taylour found two separate buildings intended for cult purposes on the site of the Citadel House at Mycenae. Apparently they had been built c. 1250 and destroyed thirty years or so later. The two buildings had three architecturally distinct areas in which three equally distinct cult scenes were enacted. There was a temple complex, consisting of a room with an asymmetrical arrangement of platforms, and a storeroom in which had been sealed a group of idols whose like had never before been found on the mainland. There was a fresco room, built after the temple and then deliberately filled in when it fell into disuse; and there was a shrine which Lord Taylour associates with "intimate and private worship." The other find in the storeroom was a collection of about seventeen broken clay snakes in a naturalistic style, again with no parallel in the Aegean. Snakes are prominent in Minoan religion as guardians and protectors of the home and are closely associated with the Great Mother, or Nature

Goddess. Only at Mycenae have they been found modeled as separate entities, unattached to another figure, and in a religious context. The snakes do not seem to belong to the idols, which are made in such a way as to suggest that they either grasped objects in their hands or had objects affixed to their bodies.

The idols show a high degree of individuality: of twelve large, forbidding ones, five are female, four are male, two are hermaphroditic, and one is unidentified. There are seven others, smaller and in fragmentary state, also more of them female than male. Where arms or stumps of arms exist, they are raised and extended outward in a blessing (?) gesture; one holds a hammer-ax, another has a snake at her side. Only one tall figure in the collection was found *in situ* on a platform in the temple, before her a table of offerings. Her eyes bulge formidably; her nose and chin are more prominent than these features are in contemporary painted representations; and her neck and chest are pierced with an arrangement of holes that probably were to secure clothing and jewels in place. Taylour conjectures that the idols, stored next door to the temple, might have been taken out and positioned on the platforms according to some schedule or calendar of worship. Since the platforms have graduated heights, the figures placed on them may have had different statuses. Not all the figures necessarily belonged to the temple cult; some antedate the construction of the temple and therefore may have been carried from other shrines to the storeroom for safety.

The character of the temple, with its platforms and forbidding idols, seems to Taylour to be clearly Mycenaean. The room of the fresco, on the other hand, seems Minoan in spirit, dominated as it is by the central figure of a goddess dressed in the ceremonial open-bodiced Minoan style. Her skin is white, whereas two small male figures higher up in the composition are given red skins, the conventional color for men in Minoan art. Another, smaller goddess or priestess stands to the left of the central figure and salutes her with a raised object that looks like a very un-Minoan spear. Her companion, a hooved animal incompletely represented, suggests that she may be the Minoan Artemis, Mistress of the Animals. The small L-shaped shrine with its low platform on which a kindly faced, blessing goddess was found is neither distinctly Minoan nor Mycenaean in design, although all the many pots found on the floor are unremarkably domestic. There are other figures in the fresco, each with its own character and each therefore representing a different god or goddess, possibly of differing rank.

The effort to characterize the rooms as Minoan or Mycenaean must be somewhat gratuitous, for the three areas are unlike any of the places identified as temples or shrines either in Mycenaean territories or on Crete. In fact, the shrine at Mycenae is the only one on the mainland, with the possible exception of the one at Eleusis, whose identification as a shrine has not been challenged. What is perhaps still more significant is that Mycenae's cult areas are unlike any of the shrines and sanctuaries depicted on gemstones and rings, hitherto a major source of information about cult and religion. The recurrent elements in gem art are tripartite shrines, horns of consecration, and double axes; sacred trees, goddesses in bell-shaped skirts, and daemons in either ferocious or sacrificial postures (see Illus. 33). Almost none of these emblems are represented at Mycenae or at the few other places designated tentatively as shrines. The only exception—what may be the remains of a set of horns of consecration, possibly from a destroyed shrine—has been found at Pylos. It may be that gem designs had become stylized and fixed evocations of cult long after they ceased to represent a living cult practice. The artist perpetuated a schema whose elements were significant to his patron not because they were literal, but because they were aesthetic and symbolic. The only correspondence between representations of cult in gem art and the rooms at Mycenae is that both show the cult place as a separate building. An interesting corollary is that precincts once sacred remain sacred, tending to illustrate that there is a continuity of places of worship if not of forms of belief. Under several temples dating to the Archaic and later ages, Mycenaean shards have been found; at Mycenae a temple to Athena stood over the site of the palace where Taylour's sacred buildings were excavated.

Taylour's attempt to distinguish between Mycenaean and Minoan styles illustrates a recent school of archaeological thought. Decades ago, Martin Nilsson theorized that Mycenaean religion was "indistinguishable" from Minoan. The latter was supposed to have supplied the uncultured mainland people with the types and forms of cult objects which were afterward represented in small monuments, votive figures, and gemstone art on the mainland and in Crete alike. As distinctions between the two peoples became more and more apparent, and as the strength and independence of the Mycenaean civilization were better documented, it was conceded that the claims for Minoan influence in religion, like that in art, had been excessive. The Greek-speaking Zeus worshipers had adopted many Minoan customs and artefacts, had even come to employ Minoan artists who were responsible for the similarities between Crete and mainland cult equipment, but they retained many more ancestral beliefs than they abandoned. Now statements made about Mycenaean religion are tested for their basis on shrines, representations, art, cult objects, and the like found on Mycenaean soil. These, however, to repeat the complaint made above, are not as plentiful or as intelligible as one might wish. For this reason Taylour's finds vie in importance with the religious tablets found at Pylos, and any speculations about the nature of Mycenaean cults must take both into account.

After a headnote without interpretation, Side B of Pylos tablet Tn 316 lists a series of gods and their gifts.

Poseidon	1 gold cup	2 women
Pere	1 gold bowl	1 woman
Iphimedeia	1 gold bowl	
Diuja	1 gold bowl	1 woman
Hermes	1 gold cup	1 man
Zeus	1 gold bowl	1 man
Hera	1 gold bowl	1 woman

This one large, hastily written tablet takes Homer and myth out of the realm of imaginative poetry and into Mycenaean life and society. Here are the biased, quarreling gods of the *Iliad,* Agamemnon's protectors and enemies as well as Pylian Nestor's. Other Linear B tablets refer to more of the Olympians. One from Knossos refers to *Potnia Atana,* which may translate as "the lady of Athens," or Athena; another refers to *erinu,* perhaps a variant spelling of Erinyes, the Furies in Aeschylus' dramatization of the Agamemnon story. Others of the gods mentioned, like Iphimedeia and Diuja, were entirely forgotten in later times. Mycenaean heaven must have been crowded with deities: twenty-four on the Pylos tablets, eleven on those at Knossos, more than twenty represented by idols and frescoes at the Mycenaean sanctuary. Even if some are duplications, the numbers are large, the diversity surprising. Some gods, like Demeter, familiar from epic do not appear at all. Others, like Poseidon, seem to be overwhelmingly popular. Withal, the variety and number are typical of the Greek religious spirit of welcome toward new gods and continuing veneration of old ones. In addition to the chief gods of the pantheon, each locale or tribe had its own favorites, so that not every god worshiped at Pylos was also worshiped at Mycenae. Nor is it clear whether a Pylian visitor to, say, Athens would have recognized all the gods of that city. The divinities prefaced by the title *Potnia* ("lady" or "mistress"), for instance, may be local avatars of one major female deity, in just the way that the Virgin of Guadalupe and the Madonna of the Flowers are regional manifestations of the Virgin Mary. Or, since *potnia* is simply a form of respectful address, these may be different goddesses whose identities were too locally based to have been remembered by descendants of the Bronze Age Greeks.

Pylos text Tn 316, partially quoted above, lists a total offering of thirteen gold vessels. To John Chadwick, the foremost inter-preter of Linear B, that was "too rich a treasury for any ordinary ceremony." He thought the Pylians were making a supreme plea for all heaven's protection from imminent disaster. Consequently, the mysterious references to men and women, which might ordi-narily be interpreted as a gift of slaves to the deities, he read as outright sacrifices to them. The rarity of human sacrifice in Greece has already been mentioned. Dedicating people to serve the gods was, however, a common practice. Such priests or servants do not seem to have been connected to a sanctuary or shrine; yet, ac-cording to the tablets, they held extensive tax-free lands. One priestess at Pakijana is portrayed on a Pylos tablet in argument with the community over the terms of her landholding. She wants it declared property of the god; the community says she must pay taxes—something she can well afford since she owns a personal slave girl and two male slaves. Sometimes these religious officials inherit their positions and own lands as citizens. Men of noble blood, called either *tereta* or *telestai* on the tablets, have religious as well as military obligations. Yet probably their landholdings are the rewards of their rank.

Neither the tablets from Pylos nor those from Knossos contain religious laws, prayers, or dogma of any sort. References to holy days are the only trace of a religious system. The diversity of religious functionaries on the tablets, nevertheless, implies a large religious *organization* separate from the civil one. At Pylos there were key bearers, sacrificers, barley sprinklers, and fire tenders in addition to the priests and slaves already mentioned. Some of the offices were honorific, conferred by the king as a reward for ex-traordinary service. For the king remained a central figure in this religious society, with the ultimate responsibility for carrying out the community's obligations to its gods. He was not a demigod, as early stories about Minoan divine kings would have us believe, but an archbishop, as it were, who delegated and oversaw tasks.

6

According to Aeschylus, after Agamemnon's death and burial his daughter Electra comes to his tomb in anguish and invokes his aid. Confident that the dead can hear, she cries out:

> I myself pour these lustral waters to the dead, and speak, and call upon my father: Pity me; and pity your own Orestes . . . By some good fortune let Orestes come back home. Such is my prayer, my father. Hear me; hear.

When Orestes does return, both children together return to the tomb and call upon their father. Electra begs him to contrive Aegisthus' death; Orestes reminds Agamemnon of his cruel murder in order to persuade him to materialize and watch the vengeance being planned.

> ORESTES: Will you not waken, father, to these challenges?
> ELECTRA: Will you not rear upright that best beloved head?

The invocation ends with the children's conviction that they are in Agamemnon's presence. Orestes carries out the murders of Aegisthus and his mother in the name of honor to the dead king and his house. He is then, however, hounded by the Furies, those ancient chthonic viragoes whose blood-logic now demands his death for matricide. Through the arbitration of Apollo, Orestes is tried before Athena and a jury of twelve Athenians. The obligation to avenge the king's death is weighed equally with the crime of matricide, and, after being purged of bloodguilt, Orestes is exonerated. Aeschylus creates a triumph of law while giving to the Furies, "daughters of ancient Night," their due worship in a new guise as protectors of the family. They are guided back to their chambers in the deep of the earth by Athena.

The poet's version of the events following Agamemnon's murder plunge us even deeper into murky suppositions about the cult of the dead, the belief in the soul's immortality, and popular religious attitudes. The faith of Electra and Orestes in the power of the dead is unquestioning. So is Electra's confidence that her libation, poured directly into the tomb, will invigorate her father's shade. The poetic act is reminiscent of funeral libations poured at the graves of the Mycenaean dead. It also recalls Odysseus in Hades, pouring out blood to induce his mother's ghost to speak.

The scene with the children at the tomb is the polished dream of a great playwright, not to be read as strictly historical. It represents, nevertheless, ancient popular tradition that was still evocative to Aeschylus' audience. Since Mycenaean religion is without codification or doctrine, it is impossible to distinguish between formal beliefs and simple magic. The Mycenaeans might have prepared the way for the later opinion that they practiced a cult of the dead by their awe-inspiring tombs and an oral tradition that glorified their heroes. But not all the dead were buried elaborately; and not all the population were heroes. It was possible then, as now, to hold contradictory ideas simultaneously, one dogmatic and theological, one unarticulated and informal. The dead do not return to earth; but no one knows what sources of energy their world may contain. Hero cults founded by cities in the expectation of benefits, or to avert the wrath of the dead, were an important religious phenomenon in the post-Mycenaean eras. Their genesis, scholars believe, was an outgrowth of earlier popular sentiments about an afterlife, essentially prereligious and akin to nearly universal superstitions about ghosts. So Agamemnon, a powerful king in life, might yet have powers in death. Orestes' bones, for instance, acquired a significance for the political stability of Sparta that relics of Christian saints have for the sanctity or efficacy of shrines. It was said that the Spartans, after being consistently beaten in their wars with the Tegeans, sent to the oracle at Delphi to discover how to ensure victory. They were told to recover Orestes' bones from Tegean territory. After they did so, the Tegeans were defeated.

The chthonic *(chthon,* "earth") aspects of Aeschylus' drama are more formally related to the dark side of Greek religion, rooted in the pre-Mycenaean ages. Chthonic spirits dwelt in the earth and performed two functions: they received the bodies of the dead, and through their assurance of fertility they provided the means of life. The agricultural nature of these underground spirits was most often emphasized by the later, Olympianized Greeks. But their pre-Greek affinity to terrible mother goddesses with dual roles in the worlds of the living and the dead remained strong. The characters of Hera, Demeter, and Artemis all illustrate these twin aspects in many myths. The late episodes of the Agamemnon myth cycle, on the other hand, tend to exaggerate the pre-Olympian, chthonic character of Greek religion. Could these episodes incorporate a genuine reminiscence of chthonic cults at Mycenae? Might William Lord Taylour's temple-shrine complex with its preponderance of female idols and its seventeen snakes—familiar chthonic manifestations—have been the setting for such cult worship by an historical Clytemestra? Taylour's discussion of the buildings, referred to above, makes a provocative point. One wall of rough-hewn rock is intentionally exposed in the temple, whereas the other walls are finished with cut stone. There seems to be no architectural reason for such a design, and Taylour surmises it had a religious significance. There are no shrines, to chthonic or other gods, with which to compare the feature, therefore nothing can be proven. Rock, nevertheless, is regularly associated with sacred snakes, as well as with the caverns and grottoes housing chthonic spirits.

There remains a final point to be made about Aeschylus' treatment of the chthonic Furies. In the Classical Age, when he wrote, a state of compromise had to be legislated between old, persistent superstitions that the blood of a murdered man called out for vengeance and a new, morally enlightened view that wanted a suspected murderer tried in a court by the state. In the old view, it was the responsibility of the dead man's family to purify the land of the pollution caused by the killer; therefore shedding more blood was an essential, if primitive, obligation. The appeasement of the Furies in the play therefore illustrates a political reality. Even after homicide became the sole concern of state courts, the idea of infection or miasma as a consequence of killing remained strong and ceremonies of purgation were mandatory. Orestes at his trial makes a plea for humanitarianism and against blood feuds by crying out: "The miasma of matricide *can* be purged away . . . it was driven out at the shrine of Phoibos with slaughter of pigs in cleansing rites." He also is purified, for the curse on the house of Atreus ends with him.

7

Agamemnon's saga begins and ends with violence at home; his career is spent in violence abroad. These circumstances serve as markers that help to fit his saga into the chronology of Mycenae and the Mycenaean world. Everything, however, depends upon a consensus for the date of the fall of Troy, as a glance at the following chart will show.

c. 1350–1340   The first cyclopean Citadel of Mycenae is built. (Perseus reigns?)

c. 1330   Large-scale palace construction at Mycenae, Tiryns, and other sites. Expansion and prosperity.

c. 1250   Second Citadel of Mycenae built, along with the Lion Gate and the Treasury of Atreus. The town outside the gates of Mycenae is burned. (Atreus reigns?)

c. 1230–1200   Northeast extension of the Citadel and the construction of underground fountains at Mycenae, Tiryns, and Athens.

c. 1230   The Hittites abandon the northeastern regions.

c. 1200   The fall of Troy. (Agamemnon rules?)

c. 1200–1190   Widespread destruction of Mycenaean sites, including Mycenae. Migrations of Mycenaeans. (Orestes rules?)

c. 1187–1180   The two large-scale battles of the Sea Peoples: Sea battle off the western Delta of victorious Egyptians (under Rameses III)—Menelaos' visit to Egypt. Triple battle among Hittites, Cypriots, and Egyptians off Cyprus.

c. 1150–1120   Final destruction of Mycenae and Tiryns. The Dorian invasion, "the descent of the Heracleidae."

Thucydides says that the end of Mycenae came eighty years after the fall of Troy, or in 1190. Ancient chronologers date Troy's fall to 1180. Either way, there is too long a time between the documented collapse of Hittite powers in the north and the legendary war itself. Agamemnon then has to have reigned almost one hundred years after his father, Atreus; and the final destruction of Mycenae then should be dated to 1100, a later date than archaeology accepts. If, on the other hand, the date of the final destruction of Mycenae is reckoned as closer to 1200, an opinion favored by some archaeologists, the battle of Troy must have come very shortly after 1230, and both Agamemnon's return and his city's fall would have become contemporaneous. The chart given above is a widely accepted compromise between ancient history and modern archaeology—although it is based entirely on scientific rather than mythological information.

From 1250 on to about 1200, the localized destructions and the threat of further warfare signaled by the building of fortifications and underground fountains seemed to be the responses to Greek aggression against Greek. Legend shows that the mainland states were constantly attacking one another all through the thirteenth century. Two wars against Thebes, the Theban war against the Orchomenians, the Athenian attack on Eleusis, the attempts to burn Mycenae are only the most familiar episodes in an age of antagonism and dynastic rivalries. A seeming contradiction lies in the fact that in this same period, Mycenae and other centers of Mycenaean power rose to energetic heights to carry out formidable kinds and amounts of construction. Very probably population had increased to numbers that would sustain the heavy demands made on it by huge corvées of labor in nearly continuous activity. In any case, far from weakening Mycenaean resources and power, the troubles that erupted seem to have called forth great expenditures of both. Perhaps the momentousness of this period and the next can be inferred from the fact that it provides the stimulus for a large proportion of Greek myths and most of Homeric poetry. Only part of that stimulus, nevertheless, should be attributed to domestic upheavals. Troy's final days, the disintegration of Hittite power, the depredations of the so-called Sea Peoples, and the Dorian invasions all occur within a short time of one another. Apart from the spiraling effects that one outbreak of violence may have on another, the interrelatedness of these events is not well understood. Nor, of course, do myths attempt to understand them, either causally or otherwise. They concentrate instead on the personal trials of their heroes, presenting events as though they were atypical and each hero as unique. It is not the business of myth or epic to analyze or synthesize; they are oblivious of their common patterns and themes, just as they are indifferent to historical time and context. We, however, cannot fail to notice that the saga of Agamemnon, like that of Odysseus, concludes in danger, struggle, and dissolution. Nor can we fail to observe that the myths themselves end with the end of these families. Aegisthus' usurpation of the throne and Orestes' strategy to regain it are implicit in political instability. It may be imagined that their struggle over succession was no more outstanding than other such moments memorialized in legend, especially since succession was a monotonously predictable motive for murder, often correctly interpreted as a mythical expression of tribal warfare. What is noteworthy, nevertheless, is that the other returning heroes of Troy also confront households that have deteriorated into shambles of misrule. What must Nestor have found at Pylos, Diomedes at Tiryns, Odysseus at Ithaca? Some of the heroes meet with storms at sea—a favorite metaphor in myth for undefined but grave troubles—as they try to make for home. Survivors are only temporarily exempt from disasters ashore that force them into warfare, emigrations, and relocations. Mopsus, the son of Apollo and Teiresias' daughter, finds himself in dispute with a fellow hero, Amphilochus, over sovereignty of a city they have founded jointly in Cilicia. To decide their rival claims they kill each other in single combat! Is this an expression of localized warfare between tribes in southwestern Anatolia, where whole cities were in revolt against centuries-old allegiances? Neoptolemus, Achilles' son, reaches home at Iolcus; but myth says he does not stay to enjoy it. For reasons that are annoyingly and suspiciously omitted, he builds a new city on the west coast near Lake Pambotis. The ships of the great Diomedes are wrecked on the Lycian coast and he himself barely escapes becoming a human sacrifice to Ares before he finally reaches his home. There he finds his wife has installed her lover as ruler.

A feeling of unsettlement and dislocation pervades all these tales. Some of them, and they have not all been summarized here, refer to the very tribes and countries we know to have been involved in the career of the Sea Peoples. Myth says that Rhodians under Tleptolemus were assisted in their fight against the Lucanians (of Lukka?) by Philoktetes; and Rhodes was certainly a host to tribes from Asia Minor, like the Lukka, who were causing trouble for the Hittites. Egypt, which bore the brunt of several attacks of the Sea Peoples and documented them, is mentioned several times in the tales. The identity of these so-called Sea Peoples is one of the mysteries of the Late Bronze Age. Egyptian records refer to some of them specifically and illustrate others in their relief sculptures. In the fourteenth-century Amarna Letters among the Egyptians, Hittites, and Cypriots, four groups of Sea Peoples are identified: Denyen (Danaans living in Cilicia); Lukka (Lucanians [?] in Lycia opposite Rhodes); Shardana (Sardinians?); and the Shekelesh (Sicilians?). The change in political and commercial patterns of life created by the fall of Knossos seems to have plummeted these tribes into piratical or mercenary activities. Apparently they were known to Mycenaean sailors and, as we have seen, they make appearances in Mycenaean myths.

In the critical battle of Kadesh, c. 1286, Sea Peoples fought on both Egyptian and Hittite sides. With the powerful Hittite Muwatallis were allied the Lycians, Dardana, and other Aegeans from the Levant. Although the Egyptians under Rameses II were victorious, their losses to the massed strength of the Hittites were such that they withdrew completely from Syria and the Levantine coast. It was their retreat that left the Levantine ports free for the further expansion and consolidation of Mycenaean interests in the area. About their activities we hear through the Hittite grandson of Muwatallis, who campaigned against the cities of western Asia Minor in about 1250. He was irritated by the Mycenaeans' refusal to become his vassals, for their independence interfered with the allegiances of the Anatolian cities. Some of these eastern Mycenaeans were legitimate colonists at sites like Miletos, Ephesos, and Rhodes; others were pirates, drifters, traders, mercenaries, and temporary settlers at more than thirty coastal and island sites. The chief center of Mycenaean power was probably on Rhodes, and other centers may have been organized in a loose federation under the Rhodian king. The Hittites referred to them as *Ahhijawa*, a pronunciation of either Achaiwa (Achaians) or Argeiwa (Argives): in Homer the terms are interchangeable for the Greeks at Troy.

By 1233 some of the Achaiwa had swelled the ranks of other Sea Peoples against the pharaoh Merneptah. Nearer to home the pharaoh also had to deal with a Libyan uprising of charioteers, some of whom, according to Greek tradition, were migrant Trojans. At this time the ships of the eastern Mycenaeans were carrying cargoes that were formerly the exclusive monopoly of Hittites and Mitannians. In addition to the traditional bronze and luxury items, they ferried iron, the new metal in the Aegean, and the new Anatolian cut-and-thrust swords, as well as the new fashion for cremation burial, to points on the east coast of the mainland like Perati and Mycenae. This was the moment when such sites were recovering from the first wave of destructions, a time of brief reprieve when some cities built additional fortifications. The adventures of the Sea Peoples reached their height in a sea fight off the western Delta, won by the Egyptians c. 1187, and in a second battle among Hittites, Cypriots, and Egyptians off Cyprus in 1180. The first, fought in the eighth year of Rameses II's reign, is memorialized by reliefs in Rameses' temple at Medinet Habu. Danaans, Philistines, Alasians (Cypriots), Shekelesh, and others were again on the side of the Egyptians. Some of these peoples are identified in the reliefs by their costumes.

The second battle was still larger, involving three waves of Sea Peoples' ships against the Hittites under Suppiluliumas II, who also enlisted some Sea Peoples as allies. Although the Egyptians won the first and the Hittites the second of these campaigns against Sea

Peoples, their governing systems were too weakened for them to maintain the advantages of victory. Both nations were eclipsed by great movements of land and sea tribes from the north and east that eventually resulted in the emergence of the Philistines and the Assyrians as strong powers. By the middle of the twelfth century their empires came to an end, just when the Mycenaean mainland cities also gave way to the new Dorians. One generation after the Delta and Cyprus sea battles, Mycenae was destroyed for the last time.

IX

Jason, Argonaut and Merchant Prince

Legends of the early Greeks do not always focus on the actions of a god or the trials of a hero. Sometimes they are about a mysterious people like the Pelasgians, those descendants of Pelasgus who is said to have inherited one-third of the Peloponnesos from his semidivine father. Whenever folk memory was put to explain an unfamiliar custom, an alien-sounding phrase, or a partially remembered place, it attributed it to the Pelasgians; and so they slowly assumed a confused legendary life. Such a tradition borrows credibility from a gap in real history and reliable geography. And, in fact, the Pelasgians have become ever more imaginary as material evidence of life in the Peloponnese has taken on the contours of a concrete reality.

The Minyans of Thessaly were another legendary people often made responsible for fabulous and inexplicable events. Unlike the Pelasgians, however, the Minyans have become historical. Before the explosion of archaeological discovery in this century, they had no more substance than the names of their major heroes: Minyas, the eponymous ruler; Achilles, who led the Minyan contingent to Troy; and Jason, a favorite son who led the famed expedition of the Argonauts. Slowly, however, they have emerged from the realm of fancy and we now know a good deal about these rich and adventurous people. Their story is fragmented and still incomplete. In many respects, Minyan history parallels that of other Mycenaean tribes, and so it is legitimate to include Minyans under the rubric Mycenaean. In other respects, it remains wholly disparate, sharing the fortunes of backward and remote Thessaly rather than those of the energetic and rapidly developing Peloponnese. In the general sense that the term is used, Minyans are Mycenaeans; and when Jason takes the legendary stage, their traditions are nearly undistinguishable. Long before his famous exploits, however, the Minyans were establishing their name as a separate tribe of new Greeks living in the far, wild north.

Tradition has it that the Minyans originated in Thessaly but made their chief center at Orchomenos, in Boeotia. With relative speed they seem to have strengthened their home at that site and then to have imposed their influence over a wide geographical arc. The telltale evidence of red-on-white pottery ware from the Argolid to the Troad seems to offer a tentative archaeological basis for the spread of the clan of Minyas. The quantity of these pots, called Minyan ware, at Troy, Iolcus, and Orchomenos (see Map 2) has led one historian to surmise an especially close connection between the two major cities, the latter of which used Iolcus as its port. But the precise relation between the pottery and the spread of the tribe is far from clear and must be left open for further research. The weight of archaeological evidence for the existence of the Minyans as real rather than purely legendary falls instead on the architectural remains at Orchomenos and Iolcus.

What first attracted Schliemann to the area of Orchomenos was the report, by a local farmer, of a thunderous noise like the boom of an underground explosion, coming from the hill covering the site. A few years later, when Schliemann began digging, he found that the roof of a huge chamber tomb, which had held up the ground weight of three millennia, had finally caved in. Unfortunately, Orchomenos was the victim of careless workmen and the vicissitudes of politics. Pottery and tools were heaped up in disorderly levels as a result of the poor supervision of diggers, and the intervention of two world wars among scientific digs gave the local inhabitants ample time to plunder the tomb. As a result the finds were relatively poor, and precise dating is impossible. There is little doubt, however, about the relative age of the site, for its oldest stratum is Neolithic; the site preserved a level of settlement that was burned and overthrown by force by the next inhabitants, who built with the familiar megaron shape. Both the burned layer and the rectangular houses offered the same silent evidence of Greek-speaking invaders that we have already met in Chapter II. The story told by stratification at the site seems to be unexceptional until the period of the tholos tombs scattered in the neighborhood. One of them, excavated by Schliemann, has been identified as the marvelous Treasury of Minyas that Pausanias described to his readers in particular detail. In undisguised annoyance with the Greeks for being "wonderstruck" by exotic buildings like the pyramids while ignoring their own marvels of construction, Pausanias explained that Minyas was so much wealthier than his predecessors that he needed and therefore built a great treasure-house to store his riches. The splendid structure

> is built in stone, the shape is circular but the top does not stick up too sharply; they say the topmost stone is a keystone holding the entire building in place.

In fact, modern studies of Mycenaean architecture agree that the vaulted dome on most tholos tombs is indeed built up by successively narrower layers of stone that are then held in place by an uppermost "keystone." Pausanias' eye did not mislead him about that, although of course the building is not a treasury. Fragments of its elaborately decorated facade, much of which may have been intact when Pausanias saw the building, hint at how the tomb may have acquired its label as a treasury. But even without its ornamentation, the tomb itself is a sufficient indication that the buried chieftain was important enough to command great attention, and wealthy enough to support the artists and artisans who erected the fabled structure.

About Minyas himself it is said that he migrated from Thessaly to Orchomenos, where he founded a kingdom. The persistence of the notion that Minyas amassed great wealth is based partly on the splendor of his tomb. From the number of associations of his name with expensive enterprises, however, one must be open-minded about the likelihood that the tradition had some other basis in fact.

Boeotia is a farm-rich province—one of the few on the mainland in a position to trade its surplus for other amenities. Surplus is the key to the difference between subsistence and luxury economies. As soon as more agricultural produce than necessary is available, some workers can be freed from the need to farm or herd animals and can become artisans, potters, builders, and the like. Alternatively, a surplus can pay for these services performed by outsiders. Smiths, for example—perhaps the most valuable craftsmen of the age, and traditionally itinerant workers—might share their specialized knowledge of metals with many communities in turn and carry away news as well as payment in goods. Social and economic diversity, then, is born of surplus. A simple trade of useful commodities can take place when communities are still basically self-sufficient. But well-developed trading enterprises depend upon surplus and the diversity that surplus supports in order to function in an ongoing way.

The Minyans, in fact, are known as traders who became wealthy enough to found several cities in Boeotia, Thessaly, and far western Pylos. It is possible that these sibling states sent tributes back to the dynasty seat. Orchomenos, moreover, was prosperous enough to undertake one of the most remarkable feats of engineering in the ancient world—the drainage of Lake Copais. Copais was at once the largest and shallowest lake in Greece. Or, more accurately, it was more of a marsh than a lake: high in the winter, when it was fed by rainfall and melting snows from Mt. Parnassos and Mt. Helicon; a marshy plain in spring where cattle and swine browsed and crops were sown and reaped; and by the end of the summer so dry that a network of cracks and fissures crisscrossed its surface. This is the ordinary cycle of the lake's changes in modern times and there is no reason to believe it differed in antiquity. Strabo and Pausanias both tell of drowned cities built on the margin of the lake, just as nineteenth-century travelers told of villagers forced to flee before the quick rise of the waters in late October and November, a rise which left vineyards and cornfields underwater when natural drainage outlets were clogged or slow. In spite of the hazards, villagers returned when the waters receded, for the rich alluvial deposits enormously increased the yield of these lands. On the higher, arable portions of the lake, two crops a year was normal. It was on these fat lands that the Minyans grew rich and Orchomenos became a symbol of affluence.

The Minyans did not expose their wealth to natural risks. When French and then English investigators in the nineteenth century drained Lake Copais, they uncovered a vast complex of prehistoric engineering that extended across its basin into surrounding hills. The Minyans had guaranteed the lake against flooding the ninety square miles of its basin by crossing it with canals at its north and south ends and through its middle. These led to the largest of twenty-three natural outlets, or *katabothrae,* as the Greeks call them—subterranean chasms or fissures in the mountainous margins on the north and east shores of the lake which carried the waters to the Euboean Channel at Larymna (see Map 3). Then, in addition, the ancient engineers undertook to secure a more certain and regular discharge of the waters by tunneling through from one of the *katabothrae* at Binia to the Bay of Larymna. Over the low Pass of Kephalari, in a line of 2,230 meters, they sank sixteen shafts from eighteen to sixty-three meters deep, and for a distance of five hundred meters had actually tunneled from shaft to shaft.

To guard this great drainage system on which their prosperity vitally depended, a chain of forts was built on the high ground, made higher by the earthworks bounding the canals. The central one of these fortified posts was situated on Gla, a great rock island springing directly out of the lake about a half-mile from the eastern shore. Its face is almost perpendicular, rising to a height of about seventy meters above the plain, and one of the canals passed under its eastern wall. Following the very edge of the island rock so as to utilize every foot of space, the fortress wall, some twenty feet thick, ran two miles in circuit. Within the ramparts was not only a small citadel but a community whose exact nature is still undetermined. Gla is too bare, rocky, and dry—there are no springs on the island—for it to have been a city. Yet the fortress contained a sort of palace with a long megaron, two hearths, and long buildings with many rectangular rooms or divisions. The dissimilarity of its floor plan to other Mycenaean citadels, its paucity of household furnishings and artefacts, its absence of burial places, along with the nature of the entire complex all taken together have led to the belief that Gla was a military barracks, perhaps the administrative center for all the fortresses. Its rectangular divisions would then have been stables, and the huge space within the walls a yard for horses and chariots. That there were chariots is proved by the existence of wheel ruts in the network of roads built along the canal embankments that connected one fortress to another and to the great palace at Orchomenos. Manpower in the barracks could have been drawn from the population along the lake shores which, archaeologists tell us, were more thickly populated than at any other period in the area's history.

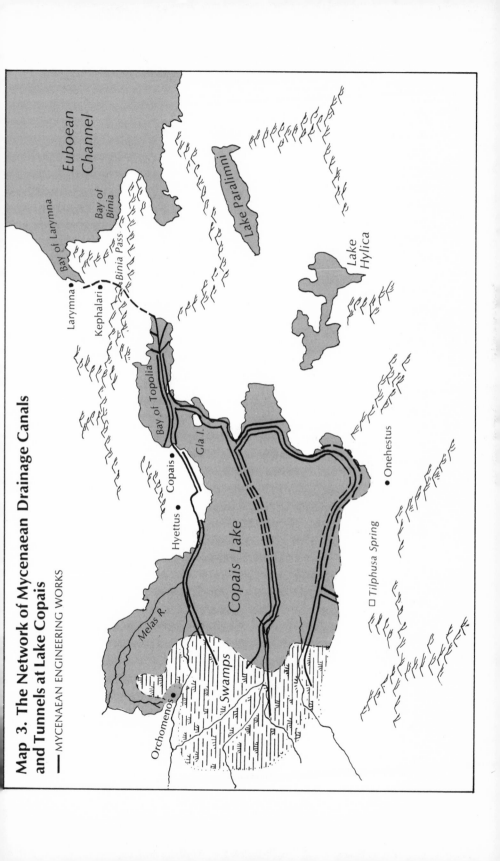

Map 3. The Network of Mycenaean Drainage Canals and Tunnels at Lake Copais

— MYCENAEAN ENGINEERING WORKS

Euboean Channel

Bay of Larymna

Bay of Binia

Larymna •

Kephalari •

Binia Pass

Lake Paralimni

Lake Hylica

Bay of Topolia

Copais •

Gla I.

Hyettus •

Onehestus •

□ *Tilphusa Spring*

Copais Lake

Melas R.

Swamps

Orchomenos •

2

Minyas' fame was eclipsed only by that of his descendant Jason, leader of the Argonauts. His saga is a blending of possible fact with probable fiction, filled with incidents of naturalistic phenomena and supernatural intervention. To ask which of the component parts ought to predominate is like asking whether the tale begins with the words "Once upon a time." Does fancy take the imagination under its sway, or do the wonders of fairyland only color the narrative of a real voyage to a real place?

In its most elemental form, the *Argonautica* is the record of a journey to the Black Sea made by Minyans of Thessaly in the middle of the thirteenth century B.C. This enterprise, marvelous in itself, was elaborated in its many retellings by stock episodes and characteristics from folktales about quests and journeys. It was probably a king's daughter in one such folktale who came to be identified with Medea. Originally she was a Near Eastern deity, worshiped in the Black Sea region, Thessaly, and Corinth. In the final form of the *Argonautica,* the princess Medea still had traces of her twin birth. As the saga grew, it became associated with the Minyan myth of Phrixos and the Ram, a grisly tale about human sacrifice at Orchomenos. From this story came the idea of the golden fleece, the object of the Argonauts' quest.

Then, sometime during the Iron Age, dim remembrances of Bronze Age trade routes, especially the one for amber from the Baltic, connected themselves to the saga. By this time Minyans had settled in places far from their original homes, and so new names and new heroes found their way into the growing story. The colonization of the Black Sea brought still further enrichment to the saga in the form of details and local traditions from neighborhoods once foreign. It was in the same period, during the eighth and seventh centuries, that the western Mediterranean was reopened to the Greeks, and it generated a whole world of sea stories located in that hitherto unknown region. These, too, found their way into the Jason saga.

In the sixth century, the spread of Orphism introduced a modern religious element—the idea of purification for sin—into the older forms of worship that the tale had incorporated. It was left to the fifth century to put the finishing touches on the geography, and then to the Greek dramatists to give personalities to the chief characters. But finally, it is through Apollonius Rhodius, in the third century B.C., that we have the first full written account of Jason and the Argonauts.

These steps in the growth of the Jason saga can be of only indirect concern in the following pages. Using as a guide the progress of the finished saga, from its preface in the myth of Athamas to its epilogue with Medea at Corinth, we can discover instead those points at which the saga touches history. Briefly summarized, the story line common to most versions of the myth goes as follows. Young Prince Jason comes to Iolcus, in Thessaly, to claim his rightful throne from his devious uncle King Pelias. Frightened because an oracle has predicted his fall to a man of Jason's description, Pelias persuades Jason to fetch some golden fleece from Colchis, fully expecting him to die in that distant and unknown place. A ship is outfitted, many heroes are drafted to serve as companions, and the Argonauts set sail. After several wonderful adventures, they reach Colchis and meet its king, Aietes, and his daughter Medea. Although the king places terrifying obstacles in his way, Jason, with the help of Medea, secures the fleece, and then all make their way back to Iolcus. Their unlooked-for return is clearly unwelcome; nevertheless, the regime of Pelias is overthrown and the couple succeed to the throne. The saga deserves fuller elaboration, and parts of it will be returned to again in more detail at intervals during the progress of this chapter.

The preface to Jason's story begins in the related myth of Athamas, the Aeolian who rules over all Boeotia. On Hera's command, the king takes as a wife Nephele (her name means "cloud" or "cloud fairy"), who bears him two children, Phrixos and Helle. Ino, his second wife, hates and plots against the children. When the land suffers a famine, brought on by Ino's tricking the women into roasting the year's seed corn, her false messengers return advice from Delphi that either Phrixos or Helle is to be sacrificed. As a choice between them is about to be made, they are rescued by their mother, who sends them away on the wings of a magical golden-fleeced ram. They fly toward Colchis without incident until they reach the Hellespont (the Dardanelles), where Helle, the place's namesake, falls off the ram. Phrixos arrives safely in Colchis, is received kindly by King Aietes, and is given his daughter in marriage. Then the ram is sacrificed to Zeus and his golden fleece hung carefully in a grove guarded by a dragon. Phrixos lives out his days in Colchis uneventfully.

This part of the myth is complete in itself, its kernel being the sacrifice of a householder of Athamas. Herodotus says that such a rite was practiced in Thessaly even in historical times in order to avert the calamities of drought, crop failure, and hunger. Pausanias verifies the practice of sacrificing householders of Athamas, but further records that the sacrifices took place at Mount Halus as part of the cult of Zeus Laphystius. Geography becomes confusing here, because Mount Laphystion is in Boeotia, near Orchomenos, whereas Mount Halus is surrounded by the field of Athamas in Thessaly. The source of Pausanias' statement that these sacrifices took place on Mount Halus is unknown. But since there is no other mountain with this name, it is probable that the Boeotian mountain was the original site of the cult to which Athamas belonged, and that the cult, like many another, was transferred to different locales. Many homes of the cult were traced to the neighborhood of Lake Copais. Plutarch, for instance, mentions a human sacrifice at Orchomenos in a family that claimed descent from the Minyans.

Since human sacrifice was distasteful to Classical sensibilities, and in any case had long since been abandoned, traditions that referred to the practice either were suppressed outright or were minimized by the substitution of gentler details. The confusion on the ritual level of Athamas' story as we have it is due to such impulses. Phrixos' escape on the back of a ram represents later, more sophisticated religious ideas than human sacrifice. His flight does not grow out of the original narrative as a result of his mother's fear for his life, but is the intentional part of a rite of purification in which a town expels the evil in it by making a sin offering. Phrixos is a scapegoat, not a sacrifice, who carries off with him some offensive evil. His escape, therefore, is conditional upon his not returning to his home. Ritualists, looking at the tale from their viewpoint, link Jason's quest to the older myth at this juncture. Jason's function is to return the fleece and thus symbolically to bring forgiveness to the clan for Phrixos' expulsion. The idea of forgiveness is still more modern and is inconsistent with purification rituals. Purity can be attained by the performance of a simple magical act. Forgiveness is purely conceptual; there are no external tokens, rituals, or signs to indicate that it has been won. The essence of the scapegoat-sacrifice is that it expiates sin and puts man back into a right relation with the powers of the universe. To bring back the fleece—that is, part of the ram that was sacrificed in Phrixos' stead—is to violate the assumptions of the ritual by bringing back the evil.

The role of the fleece in the basic myth reflects still another ritual also associated with Athamas' household. Each year at the hottest time of the summer, men dressed themselves in sheep fleeces and moved in procession to the top of Mount Pelion to propitiate Zeus Acraeus, the rain giver. According to some accounts of this and similar customs having to do with weather magic, the priest wore a fleece robe with purple or black edging in imitation of dark-edged rain clouds. This ritual explains the curious name for Athamas' first wife, Nephele: "cloud fairy" is consistent with the longed-for rain cloud. The connection between Athamas and this particular weather ritual is implied by his supposed founding of the town of Acraephia, on the east side of Lake Copais. Perhaps the fact that Athamas' sons are eponymous heroes of several other towns in Boeotia is a clue to other localizations of these Minyan rituals.

The myth of Athamas' son, a Minyan and king of Orchomenos, is connected with that of Jason and the Argonauts simply because the fleece gave the adventurers something fabulous to search for. A storyteller's impulse for neatness is probably responsible for the family tree that links Athamas' branch of the tribe to Jason's. The results are neat indeed (see below) for they place the provinces of Boeotia and Thessaly under bonds of kinship to each other. Their connection here illustrates the point made earlier about the indistinguishability of Minyan and Mycenaean peoples, in spite of the separateness of Thessalian culture. No special political significance is made in the Athamas myth of his relationship to his brother—although one can be inferred from other such Bronze Age genealogies. That of the house of Atreus comes immediately to mind. Instead, the interrelatedness of the characters is meant to rationalize Jason's claim on Pelias' throne, and to explain through the fact of kinship why Pelias should be haunted by Phrixos' ghost. To both intentions, a cheerful suspension of disbelief is probably the best response.

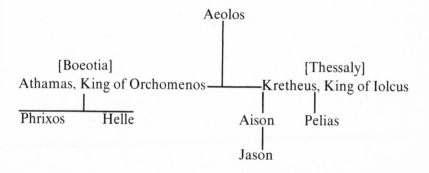

When Kretheus dies, his son, Aison, and stepson, Pelias, struggle for the throne. Somehow, Pelias is victorious over the lawful heir—primogeniture is decisive—and Aison's family is dispersed. Jason is spirited away by his mother to the cave of the wise centaur Cheiron, where other young princes are being trained for manhood. During Jason's long heroic apprenticeship, Pelias is warned by an oracle to beware his death at the hands of a one-sandaled man. Approaching Iolcus years later, Jason loses one of his sandals in the current of a rough stream. He continues on to the palace with one foot bare, so that Pelias, meeting the young prince, is immediately mindful of the oracle. Pelias then tells Jason a sad tale of being haunted by Phrixos' ghost, who is demanding the return of the golden fleece. Jason is induced to set off in its search and at once begins preparation for his expedition. With the help of Athena, Hera, and fifty heroes, his departure is made ready.

Now a threat to an unlawfully held throne, delivered by an oracle and made good by a young prince in disguise, is a familiar theme in Greek myths. It recurs in the Oedipus story and in that of the house of Atreus, in both with horrible effect. At one time it was fashionable to see in the theme a reflection of the rites that governed kingship in certain primitive cultures. Anthropologists thought that a king kept his office so long as he could defend it against stronger claimants. In some tribes, they thought, the king was also the symbolic guarantor of the crops and the harvest. Often, at the end of his reign, the king or a surrogate was ritually sacrificed to renew the magical strength of his government over men and nature. Late myths in which kings are displaced by younger men were therefore read with an eye to these ancient ideas about fertility and kingship. Vestiges of such fertility cults are well documented in Near Eastern religious myth cycles that had a profound influence on Greek myth and ritual. Whether or not the theme here is essentially Near Eastern is disputed. Today mythologists tend to prefer interpretations from an economic or political standpoint. In their view, kingship probably *was* an uncertain privilege, surrounded by magical signs of approval; but it was certainly vested in a dynasty whose wealth spoke for its power. Struggles over the right to a throne must always have involved men who first possessed riches, and then that combination of genealogy and magic that would satisfy the tribe's rudimentary socio-religious code.

Stripped of its ritualistic overtones, the myth's action simply says that Jason comes to set things right: to establish order by laying to rest Phrixos' ghost and restoring the throne to the sons of the firstborn. Commentators in post-Classical eras have sometimes complained of the immorality of having gods predict the outcome of men's petty quarrels. The evil usurper Pelias should not have been warned of his coming fall to a virtuous, one-sandaled young man. (There may be a shred of custom in this detail, for the Magnesians took their fighting stance with the left foot bared and placed squarely forward from the body for a firm grip on the slippery earth.) But on the whole, an unlawful king who tries to hold on to his throne by devious means, and who is ousted by a young claimant that has successfully completed some impossible task, is the stuff of folktale.

3

The adventures of the Argonauts seem to be the genuine reminiscence of a Minyan trading voyage at some point early in their history—early because the Minyans are known from the first as traders and evidence of their accumulated wealth is certain by the seventeenth century. Jason's ship, the *Argo,* is fabled as the first seagoing Greek vessel. The claim can be taken to mean that it was the first ship large enough to sustain a long journey by many men; or it may imply a reference to the earliest joint venture by a group of important men—perhaps a kind of collective of Minyan kinsmen. Or it may be nothing more than a poetic evocation of the voyage's epic stature. At the very least, any one of these reasons implies the tale's antiquity, for no ordinary journey need be memorialized by the paraphernalia of heroes and heroic machinery. If, then, the myth celebrates a real voyage under the guise of its folktale trappings, what kind of an expedition in what sort of "first ship" might this have been?

Although the storyteller does not know so, oceangoing vessels had been setting out to sea from ports like Iolcus in Thessaly for thousands of years in search of obsidian. The black volcanic glass was used for tools and weapons by Neolithic peoples all over the south and west Aegean since the sixth or seventh millennium. Although it is found wherever there has been recent (geologically speaking) volcanic activity, the most suitable obsidian must be glassy and tend to fracture conchoidally. The Cycladic island of Melos, Giali in southern Anatolia, and the Carpathian Mountains are all locations from which this high-grade obsidian is thought to have come. But until spectrographic analysis, no one knew which sources had been tapped by which groups of Neolithic peoples. Now, by identifying the values of trace elements that vary among sources, it has been determined that Melos supplied obsidian to most of the Aegean from the Neolithic to the Middle Bronze ages. The difficulties for these early peoples of building log rafts with stone tools, of acquiring a knowledge of the sea and its treacheries, and of learning sufficient astronomy to navigate by cannot be minimized. Such feats imply a level of technology one might think incompatible with Stone Age cultures.

One school of archaeologists thinks that early peoples had no sense of proprietary rights to mines or raw-material dumps. One simply landed at an ore site, took what he wanted, and left the way he had come. Others suppose that the birth of a commercial instinct is implied by obsidian expeditions, and that some goods had to have been traded in exchange. In either case the questing sailors would have had to be laborers also, first working the mines at the site, then carrying back the material, and finally learning how to flake it properly at home. The entire enterprise was both risky and arduous, and at the very least proves that successful sea journeys in the most primitive of vessels had played an important role in the life of the Aegean well before the merchant Greeks came.

It must have been the Neolithic sailors in Thessaly who taught the horse-taming, land-oriented new Greeks the fundamental techniques of seamanship. For within a relatively short space of time these newcomers were venturing up and down their coastline, widening trading contacts and making new friends and enemies. In spite of the limits of their schooling, however, it was the newcomers who influenced the crucial developments in maritime history. In the second millennium the Greeks built the first truly seaworthy ships. Sailing craft and galleys both appeared in this period, and the rig the Greeks designed was to become standard in the ancient world for centuries. Aegean workmen invented the brail, a device for shortening sails, and devised the hull that was to be the proto-type for later galleys. By about 1600, most ships were probably the product of Cretan and Levantine shipyards. Their ready supply of lumber and their unbroken tradition of sea-oriented activity make it likely that they assumed the responsibilities for building and selling ships on a large scale.

Where Jason's ship is built is never mentioned. But "the far known *Argo*" can have been large enough and technologically sophisticated enough to accommodate Jason and the fifty heroes who become his companions. Fifty seems to be an arbitrary large figure, for there is little agreement about the number of Argonauts in different versions of the saga. Each storyteller must have added his city's favorite sons to the patriotic roster whenever the tale was told. Looking at the heroes in this way may explain their relative inactivity in the tale. There is little for them to do, and that little not at all individualized. It is therefore fair to assume that in the original lost ballad cycle about a Minyan journey, the heroes are not companions of Jason, but incarnations of real men to whom supernatural as well as patriotic powers accrued. The legend in its final form thus includes lists of local heroes, respected by their clans and remembered in cult. Heracles is the most famous member of this section of the Argonauts' roster. Sometimes a hero's father or grandfather is added to the original group supposed to have sailed with Jason as a way of establishing the hero's genealogical reputation. Many fathers of the Trojan War heroes became Argonauts in just such a fashion: Peleus, father of Achilles; Telamon, father of Ajax; and so on. If we reckon the date of the *Argo*'s voyage by the presence of this latter group of heroes, it has to take place no later than c. 1250 B.C., roughly two generations before the War. Eratosthenes dates the voyage of the *Argo* to 1225 B.C., although Eusebius puts it at some earlier time, between 1263 and 1257. The difficulty about accepting any of these dates is that they are based only on genealogies and therefore argument about them tends to be circular. Material evidence is crucial but fragmented. If, for example, Minyas' tholos tomb at Orchomenos is dated to 1300, and two generations of about twenty-five years each are calculated as having elapsed between him and Jason, both literary and archaeological chronologies place the *Argo*'s journey at about 1250 B.C.

Here a digression and brief proviso about dating the saga are in order. First, trading voyages must have been undertaken regularly during the period when the Minyans were acquiring their great riches, say, up to and including the thirteenth century. Then, some of the heroes named fix a memory of the journey at about 1250. Thirdly, the geography of the journey was elaborated by storytellers *after* explorations of the Black Sea in the eighth century. These travels may have been reminders of early Minyan expeditions and so places and place names from the two separate periods may have become fused in late versions of the saga. The *Odyssey* landscapes (see Chapter X) may have undergone similar confusions. Lastly, some religious elements in the tale, like Orphism, can only be additions made by pre-Classical narrators to the body of an already existing narrative. For all these reasons, dating the saga is largely a matter of recognizing that it is formed of several elements from several periods of time, even though these pages are biased in favor of the saga's Bronze Age origins. This said, we return quickly to the *Argo*'s gangway.

Tradition says that the Argonauts set sail from the harbor of Iolcus, near modern Volo, in Thessaly. Here archaeological finds correspond just as closely to myth as they do at Orchomenos. Although Mycenaean pots and jars are scattered all over the area, none are so numerous or so important as they are at and near Iolcus. The remains of very old habitations have been unearthed there recently and trial excavations have revealed an extensive and well-built palace. The lowest floors of this palace are laid upon Neolithic levels, and therefore the early date of the citadel is undisputed. Upper strata seem to indicate that the palace was continuously inhabited into late Mycenaean times, although that cannot be said with certainty until excavation reports have been published. More evidence of the importance of Iolcus comes from the surrounding neighborhood, where rich tholos tombs with many gold-studded artefacts have been found. It is exciting to read into the palace and tombs a connection with the *Argo*'s heroes. Could they not have been real men who returned to Iolcus to live out their lives and be buried in splendor? The question is perhaps less ingenuous than it might seem to be, given the probability that the fabled expedition was born of actual experience. Since that is so, the more apt question is: Where were the true Argonauts going and why?

4

If we take "true Argonauts" to mean Minyans, it would have to be assumed that they had set out in quest of something more substantial than golden fleece. One philologist has suggested that the adjective "golden" is a storyteller's afterthought, added to make sense of a basic confusion about the Greek word for "fleece." In both Classical and pre-Classical Greek the term for "wool," when contracted, sounds very much like that for "hollow" or "cavity."

Words that sound nearly alike but have very different meanings occur in all languages, and an original error which yet fits in context can be perpetuated with confusing results. So the phrase "a quest for the fleece" might have been "a quest for cavities" or "caverns," that is, holes in the earth—or, more obviously, the openings to mines. Mining in the Black Sea area had already progressed to a fairly sophisticated level of proficiency during the second millennium, when Mycenaean merchant sailors began to journey there, perhaps at first in search of metals. It seems certain, moreover, that voyages to Colchis especially for gold were being made long before the time of Homer. Nothing says that they were successful, for the area is not known to be an *important* source of the precious ore. But the quest for gold is a universal adventure that poets and ballad singers might well have linked fortuitously both to Jason's mission to pacify Phrixos' ghost and to the cult significance of the golden ram.

Assuming that some such link was made by singers, another interpretation presents itself. In the interest of good narrative, Jason's quest would remain important to his story in all its versions. His original goal, however, would have been a golden ram, not its fleece; for the ram was the symbol of kingship, and gaining the throne of Thessaly was the underlying motive for the struggle between King Pelias and Jason. A golden ram's-head scepter is often pictured in archaic art in the hands of a king. The additional fact that it was probably the king, the bearer of the golden ram, who officiated at rain-making ceremonies like that described above only strengthens the connection between golden ram and golden fleece.

Identifying the fleece was a popular game played by many ancient writers. Suidas, one of the more romantic ones, believed the fleece to be a book about gold that was derived through alchemy, written on parchment—or skins, misunderstood as fleece. Hence, the quest for the fleece was the quest for a book about alchemy. The Colchians, he reasoned, were kin to the Egyptians, on Herodotus' say-so; the Egyptians were experts in alchemy; therefore the Colchians were also interested in alchemy. Somewhat less tortuous was the idea of the Roman Strabo. He thought that the Argonauts went to the Black Sea in search of alluvial gold. Apparently natives on the Colchian Phasis (see Map 4) were reported to have collected the ore by laying fleece on the riverbed. The nuggets that silted down onto the wool as waters washed over it would then be retrieved and traded as private hoards. The relatively small amounts that might have been accumulated in this fashion scarcely could have been sufficient to motivate the mounting of the Argonautic expedition. It would have been a sufficient amount, however, to gild the fleece and give it a fabulous reputation. And that in turn might have prompted an exploration for the source of the gold.

There is no better evidence than this for golden fleece. What other objectives the Argonauts might have had is suggested by the routes they took, as these are reconstructed from descriptions of places in the saga. A consensus of ancient writers says their destination was Colchis, far on the east coast of the Black Sea. Only Apollonius gives a full account of their journeying, enumerating in fanciful detail the steps on their outward and return voyages. Although it is extraordinarily difficult to reconstruct geographical data across the bridge of darkness that separates the Bronze Age from more recent historical periods, the *Argo*'s route seems to parallel in many respects those taken by European as well as Mycenaean traders in amber in the second millennium. Since Apollonius wrote in the third century B.C., scholars long believed that his verbal maps referred to the eighth-century period of Greek exploration and colonization in the area of the Black Sea. As Mycenaean remains continued to turn up at widely scattered sites all over the Mediterranean basin, it came to be recognized that in many cases the colonizing Greeks were following in the footsteps of their second-millennium ancestors. It may be true therefore that Jason blazed the trail to the Black Sea for his eighth-century descendants to follow. To this conjecture a proviso must be added: amber does not originate in the neighborhood of the Black Sea. Its major source throughout earliest antiquity was the far-northern Baltic states. To get there, however, involved an arduous trek by sea and river channels that crossed the central European continent and skimmed the coastal waters of the Atlantic (see Map 4).

Subscribers to the view that the Argonauts went to the Black Sea in search of amber argue that the north shores, especially at the river mouths of the Danube and the Don, would have been posting stations for traders and natural depots for goods traveling south. Therefore even if no other, European, destination is hypothesized for the *Argo,* it could have collected amber, that had originated in the Baltic, from depots in the Black Sea area. As for the *Argo*'s hypothetical crisscross of the European continent, several traditions say that the *Argo* did not return to Iolcus the way it came. Jason and Medea visited her aunt Circe, whose island country was supposedly located in the northern portion of the Mediterranean,

Map 4. Continental Trade Routes
in the First and Second Millennia

•••• AMBER ROUTES
◄━━ HYPOTHESIZED ROUTES OF
         ARGONAUTS

Volga

Dvina

Bromberg

Rhine

Elbe

Oder

Vistula

Kalisch

Dnieper

Dniester

Bug

Don

Rhone

Po

Drave

Save

Danube •(Ister)

Dodona

Iolcus

Hellespont

Sinope

Colchis
(Phasis)

Gades

"Pillars of
Heracles"

Syrtis Minor

Crete

Lake
Tritonis

Syrtis
Major

N
W   E
S

near Corsica. This visit alone would have involved the couple in an overland march along the same east–west rivers on which amber traveled. Since we know that the journey of the Argonauts took place in Mycenaean times, it can be assumed that the itinerary of the *Argo* was devised according to routes known to geographers in the first millennium.

But that is only an assumption, for proofs that the Mycenaeans knew central Europe, or at least its major rivers, are debatable. As several instances in this text show, objects move from place to place by many means, so that their appearances and reappearances do not necessarily imply direct contact between the peoples of those places. What geography was known to the prehistoric world can, nevertheless, be learned from hypothesizing a route between an object's place of origin and its place of eventual discovery, taking into account, of course, natural land and water barriers. The method has taught us that ever since the Neolithic era, central Europe had been in commercial relations with the Near East. The trading routes used traversed the central Balkans by the Morava and Vardar rivers to the Aegean Sea, and went from thence along the western and southern coasts of Asia Minor, leading to Cilicia, Cyprus, Syria, and Palestine. At various places along this route, finds or dumps of amber and faience beads have been identified. The sites of faience and amber are analogous, as are their uses in ornaments, necklaces, pins, bracelets, and the like made in the Near East and then traded throughout Europe. The Polish cemetery of Mierzanowice in the Opatow district, for example, was the site of one such hoard of ornamental copper plates, bone buttons and pins, arrowhead flints, faience and shell beads, necklaces of boar's tusk, and corded-ware pots—all objects collected from the various cultures crisscrossed by this route.

During the second half of the third millennium the appearance of new peoples is reflected in the changed composition of these occasional hoards on the major routes. The great expansion of the Eurasiatic steppe peoples meant that local culture groups formed in the eastern Balkans, western Anatolia, central Europe, and, of course, in the Aegean, where we have already met them as the new "Greek" invaders (see Chapter IV). Apparently some of these peoples, called by anthropologists the Kurgan pit-grave people, came to the Black Sea area about one millennium earlier than they did to other regions. The region was still forested and no older, developed culture had left its imprint there. This meant that whereas elsewhere older Neolithic cultures either had disintegrated when metallurgy and the horse were introduced, or had been absorbed into the new culture groups, lending them features and colorations that blurred the distinctions between older and newer social structures, in the Black Sea area clear traces of the Kurgan peoples were retained for a considerable length of time. In addition, the area was settled and materially ready to trade earlier than was Anatolia or the Aegean, where transitional structures of social life were in flux. For these reasons long-established trade, like that in amber, was only briefly interrupted during the climax of the migrations in 2300 to 2200 B.C., and was then reestablished relatively quickly, sometimes along the same previously traveled routes.

Amber beads appear again definitely at about 1800 B.C., in grave offerings of ring pendants worn around the neck, perhaps as solar amulets. Schliemann found large quantities of such amber necklaces in Mycenae's oldest grave circle, dated to c. 1650. By the end of the seventeenth century, shaft graves and tholos tombs elsewhere also contained amber spacer beads more often than not, suggesting that trade was well established and was now growing more extensive. The remarkable fact is that *all* the Mycenaean beads found at points as disparate as Pylos, Elis, Anvi (in Crete), and Mycenae are of Baltic origin. Chemical analysis has shown them to contain a high percentage of succinic acid, not present in the amber found in Iberia southern Italy, and Rumania. Mycenaean sources of supply as well as trading routes can be determined more accurately than can those of earlier periods by mapping the location of amber finds with the same acid content.

Amber came south along three major trails, each of which has been suggested as the route of Jason's homeward voyage (see Map 4). From sources in Lithuania, Poland, and East Prussia, the stone was transported to the lower Vistula, made its way via the Notec or Warta River to the Oder, and then passed through Bohemia and Slovakia to reach the Danube. From there it crossed the Alps, then hugged the east coastline of the Adriatic and entered Mycenaean Greece. Another route, beginning also at the lower Vistula, took the Dniester River from the Oder, and ended on the north coast of the Black Sea. East of the Vistula, amber beads do not occur in the quantities that they do in central Europe and in Greece. Nevertheless a third route seems to be traceable along the Baltic coast to the Rhine, south to the Rhone (or the headwaters of the Po), from thence (probably by ship) through the northern Mediterranean, through the straits of Sicily, and across the Ionian Sea to Greece.

Among those favoring the last route there is a group who hypothesize an alternative course from the mouth of the Rhine, along the coast of France and Spain, to the Mediterranean via Gibraltar. Of the three routes this last would have been the least plausible for the Argonautic expedition. But as the amount of specific geography in the tale is equaled by the numbers of mythical places, there are large areas to be dismissed as fairylands.

The rationalistic spirit of the twentieth century finds it hard to imagine why anyone would undertake so hazardous a journey for a purely aesthetic—and not very rare—stone. There is no evidence that it had the commercial value of, say, diamonds now or even gold or copper in the same period. It had instead properties with higher claims on the imaginations of semibarbarous men, and those were magical. From the time of the Stone Age, tiny figurines of amber were worn as talismans against the evil eye and to ward off the physical ills of rheumatism, diseases of the lungs, toothache, and respiratory infection. Centuries later, during the new science of the Classical era, Hippocrates and Galen complained that their patients put more faith in the curative powers of amber amulets than in their medicines. There is no reason to believe that the centuries intervening between Neolithic and Classical times wrought any change in men's belief in the medical characteristics of the stone. Instead, the passage of time gave the gem additional values connected with the worship of the sun. The Greek word for amber, *elektron*, means "substance of the sun"; as late as Thales' time it was thought that amber had captured the "soulfulness" of the sun's matter. We still retain a trace of the sun worshipers' concept of its life-giving force in our word *electricity*, the power from the sun to give light and heat. In the time of the Minyans and Mycenaeans, amber may have come to men's attention as a result of their search for tin, for several of the same routes used for the transport of amber were crossed by the traders in tin. This is not to suggest that the material for the manufacture of their physical weapons ever eclipsed an interest in their spiritual ones; the importance of the two substances remained separate and equal, although the trade in amber fell off markedly after the middle of the fifteenth century, whereas that in tin remained constant until the coming of the Iron Age in the twelfth.

At the height of the amber trade, between 1650 and 1450 B.C., contacts between Europeans and Mycenaeans must have become more intimate. Yet no Mycenaean objects or artefacts dating to the early period of trade have been found in Europe—not even pottery.

It is possible to surmise that the Greeks traded perishable commodities and foodstuffs, carrying their empty jars back with them for reuse. But this is an accommodation to the unknown and cannot be said outright. One archaeologist speculates that in the high-trading period they may have exchanged artisans for the finished amber beads since the characteristic Mycenaean spiral design appears on several European monuments and pots. These, of course, might have been merely European imitations of Mycenaean originals, as is a startlingly accurate metal cup handle of Mycenaean shaft-grave design found in a Saxon cemetery. Isolated finds like these do turn up in still more unlikely places, suggesting perhaps that they were retraded over and over again, beginning their cycle at some place nearer their homes. The major question about Mycenaean artefacts in Europe and in the Euxine also is simply, Why are there not more? The several nests of pots at Ak-alan, on the south coast of the Black Sea near Amnisos, for instance, are rather slight evidence on which to post a trade route. The answer is twofold.

River lanes and sea channels do not leave traces. Posting places along rivers and coastlines are the only ambiguous evidence that can be added to the scientific assessment of currents and wind lanes that carried traffic in predictable patterns, thwarting *unnatural* destinations. If we count the voyage of the Argonauts as an authentic remembrance of Mycenaean trade journeys along the water route to Colchis, we also need to reconstruct the route to Colchis taken by the goods other than amber that these traders came for. Did gold or horses or precious perfumes travel from their sources in the east and north to the Black Sea coast ready to be transferred to the Greeks? Confirmation comes from a curious set of inferences. About the most important of these, the least is known. Late in 1947 a sizable Russian excavation of Trialeti, a town in the Caucasus, uncovered burials of late Bronze Age chieftains whose tombs were rich in gold and silver. This bare fact proves that precious metals did exist in Colchis in the period postulated for Jason's quest. A larger piece to the puzzle comes from eighth-century political geography, which, it was suggested above, has important analogies to the Bronze Age trade routes. In the neglected annals of the kingdom of Urartu (present-day Armenia) there appear frequent references to the kingdom of Kulhai, or Colchis. What made Urartu rich in antiquity and makes Armenia strategic today is the natural road running north and south through the Aras Valley on the Russo-Turkish border. It travels east of the Armenian mountain mass, down from the central pass of the Caucasus to the northwest corner of Iran, Azerbaijan. During the eighth century, the kings of Urartu and the Assyrians south of them struggled constantly for control of a north–south coastal strip between Assyria and Lake Urmia, which linked the Aras Valley in the north and Azerbaijan in the south. Along this road the caravans from the east flowed. By the middle of the century the Urartians pushed to the northwest and conquered Kulhai, or Colchis, exacting a heavy tribute of gold, silver, bronze, and horses. This meant that the Urartians could connect up a long trade network to the Black Sea at Trebizond, in the heart of Colchis, and thus make contact possible between the Mediterranean world, the Caucasus, and the Iranians in the south. The well-known resistance of trade routes to change is a strong argument from silence that what was true in the eighth century was at least possible in the thirteenth, in spite of the different alignment of political powers. But it is not necessary to prove more than the probability that Colchians could have supplied valuable metals to Mycenaean voyagers, just as they did to eighth-century ones.

5

Identifying Colchis as the true destination of the Argonauts was not problematic simply because on that point of geography there was a consensus among ancient writers. In isolating ports of call along the *Argo*'s outward journey, however, only the legend's place names can be a guide and these offer vexing problems. Place names change and therefore mapping them, if they are "real," is a laborious inductive process. Or their reality may contribute nothing either to the poem's understandability or to the feasibility of a hypothesized trade route, since the same reasons of patronage that urge a storyteller to insert the name of a local hero will prompt him to add the name of a local place. It is thus sometimes said that the *Argo* was built at Argos; or that Thespiae's harbor, Tipha, was at ancient Sipha in the Thespian Argolid. It can, nevertheless, be shown that many of the *Argonautica*'s places are actual.

The *Argo* made her first landfall on the island of Lemnos, situated almost directly east of Iolcus. (It was still a necessary stopover on the way to the Hellespont in Herodotus' day.) We are told that a year before the *Argo*'s arrival the Lemnian women had murdered all their men because they had made concubines of Thracian girls captured during raids. ("This state of affairs came about," Apollonius says, because "the women of Lemnos had neglected the cult of Aphrodite. As a punishment, the goddess afflicted them with a foul odour so that from disgust the men allied themselves with captive maidens. . . .") Now when the *Argo* comes in sight, the women assume it is a Thracian retaliation so they don the armor of their dead husbands and rush to defend themselves against attack. Jason's herald sets their minds at rest and they call a council to plan their strategy. The wise elderly nurse of Queen Hypsipyle points out that their race will become extinct if they do not entertain these men. A truncated version of the massacre therefore is told to the Argonauts, who are all warmly welcomed to the island that they later gallantly agree to repopulate. Hypsipyle offers the vacant throne to Jason, which he politely declines, and all questing is abandoned for entertainment until Heracles angrily calls the Argonauts back to duty.

From the earliest days of seafaring until well into the modern era, piracy was a lucrative and much-practiced activity in the Aegean. It can be assumed as the kernel of actuality in many legends. That much of the story of the Lemnian women is probably true. The remainder seems to be an interpolation designed to explain away the island's former custom of gynocracy. But about this there is little agreement. Scholars who have championed the supremacy of mother goddesses as sociological fact are certain that on Lemnos matriarchy took its extremest form as man-murdering Amazonism. The women of Lemnos, they think, "found greater pleasure in the warlike life of the Amazon than in the fulfillment of their feminine calling." * Therein lies the true meaning of the massacre. Aphrodite is hostile to the women for neglecting her law that marriage and childbearing are women's highest duty.

Other scholars relegate the massacre of the men to the realm of pure invention. Since it was inconceivable to the Greeks that women governed and held office in a viable heterogeneous society, it must be, they argue, that the Lemnian women massacred the men in some fit of anger. The women were then forced unwillingly to assume the roles of warriors and statesmen that they held when the Argonauts arrived. The story of the massacre persisted in the Greek literary and historical traditions. Herodotus, typically, thinks the

---

* J. J. Bachofen, *Myth, Religion, and Mother Right* (Princeton, 1967), page 174.

tale at once implausible and true. Aeschylus, in his play *The Liba-tion Bearers,* has the chorus revile Lemnian women as the foulest of any that legends tell about. So detestable was their act, the chorus says, that a hideous crime is named Lemnian in memory of their wickedness. Some idea of the tenacity of the tradition can be gathered from the fact that purification rituals were still being performed on Lemnos during Classical times. Yearly the island was purified from the guilt of the legendary massacre by sacrifices offered to the dead. The ceremonies lasted nine days, during which all fires were extinguished on the island and new fire was brought by ship from Delos. Whether the literary tradition preceded or followed the annual ritual is impossible to say.

Apparently a gynocracy did exist for some time in vestigial form long after patriarchy was the universal rule. On a number of Aegean islands including Lesbos, Lemnos, Naxos, and Kos, suc-cession to real property was matrilineal at the end of the eighteenth century A.D. We can be grateful that so many British, making the grand tour of Europe that the eighteenth and nineteenth centuries considered so essential, recorded their observations of foreign cus-tom in diaries and letters. From these we learn that on Lemnos the eldest daughter took as a dowry the family house, its furniture, and one-third or more of her mother's property. When they married, younger daughters were equally entitled to whatever house the family then occupied as well as a share of the remaining property.

As for the remainder of the story of the events on Lemnos, it is just possible that the offer of the vacant throne to Jason was more than an elaboration of the deference due to a hero. The Lemnian state seems to have been particularly unstable in Homer's day and in fear of reprisals in the form of raids from the nearby coasts. Perhaps then the reinforcements to Lemnian defenses offered by the Argonauts were an attraction that came at an opportune time. Homer tells us, in the *Iliad,* that Jason's son Euneos was king of Lemnos at the time of the Trojan War. Another persistent tradition says that the Minyans settled Lemnos after being pushed out of southern Thessaly by Achaeans, themselves dislocated by the first wave of Dorians. In Homer's day, the island's ruler claimed his descent from the Minyans, as did others of the island's populace. When the threads of history and fable are sorted out, there seems to be some reason to see the Lemnos incident as a record of a real Minyan settlement on the island.

Since nothing like a Mycenaean "map" has ever come to light, we are left to interpret descriptive clues in order to identify, for instance, the Symplegades, or "clashing rocks," where Jason is stopped on the outward voyage, rocks he "conquers" by magic on the return one. What such clues lack in geographical accuracy they make up for in poetic evocation. For example, Apollonius, through his spokesman, Phineus, tells us that at the end of the Strait of the Bosporus are the Cyanean Rocks.

> To the best of my knowledge, no one has ever made his way between them, for not being fixed to the bottom of the sea they frequently collide, flinging up the water in a seething mass which falls on the rocky flanks of the straights with a resounding roar.

Since the rocks clash together and crush any ship that tries to pass between them, the Argonauts let loose a dove as a test pilot. As soon as the rocks have caught her tail feathers and recoiled again, the crew puts on a burst of speed and rows through safely, losing only the *Argo*'s stern ornament. Thereafter, in accord with a prophecy, the rocks remain rooted.

An episode like the foregoing cries out for rationalization. Wandering rocks shrouded in sea mist would be the stuff of hallucination if we were to condescend to the storyteller. But there is no need to do so since amber merchants and other ancient travelers have reported rocklike ice floes from the Russian rivers adrift in the Black Sea. With these reports were combined descriptions of the dangers of navigating the Bosporus, down which the current, swollen by spring thaw, raced at five knots.

Another description, although not one of place, casts an unintentional light on Apollonius' tale of the Cyanean Rocks. This time he wears a mask of pure fancy which covers up very unexceptional facts. As the *Argo* nears the island of Ares, we are told, huge flocks of birds mistake it for an island and fly over it, dropping bronzed feathers and wounding one of the men. Donning their helmets, half the men row while the other half protect them with shields against which they crash their swords. The fearful clamor drives off the birds and permits the *Argo* to make a landfall. Now, according to ornithologists, each year in early May thousands of larks, kestrels, harriers, ducks, and other birds migrate north from the Sinai Peninsula to their usual sanctuary on the islet of Puga near the Kessab River east of the Bosporus. When massed, their numbers darken the skies, a sight that would be terrifying to superstitious sailors. Since Ares is the island's god, its inhabitants, whether animal or man, can only be hostile, hence the attack on Jason's men with bronzed feathers. An interesting bit of information is offered here. If Jason meets the birds in early May, he must have maneuvered the Bosporus well before the current became too powerful—say, no later than April 1.

Not all the descriptions so obliquely given are yet so successfully identified. Before meeting the Stymphalian birds, the Argonauts have stopped at the city of Mariadyne, at Sinope, sailed past the country of the Amazons, and continuing along the south shore, also passed the country of the ironworking Chalybians. Since some places are actual, like Sinope, it is tempting to assume that all are. But *Mariadyne* is a corruption of a Sumerian word meaning "high fruitful mother of heaven," and not a place at all; Sinope was a Greek outpost in the colonizing days of the seventh century; Chalybians comes from *chalybs*, the Greek word for "iron"; and Amazons are no less fabulous today than they were in any earlier century. This combination of real and fairy-tale place is one of the characteristics of the Jason myth; so much of it has a rational tone of voice that careful distinctions need to be made between rationalized folk memories and actual observations. Apollonius after all is writing a romantic folktale built on a journey motif. Like any travel book, his is filled out with digressions that deal with the cultural phenomena his heroes encounter. As we have already seen, these phenomena have some reference to the seventh or eighth century, when the Greeks began to explore the Euxine with a view to colonizing it. Since it also seems that Mycenaeans made tentative ventures into the area in the course of their amber trade, three possible frames of time reference overlap here and need to be discriminated wherever it is possible to do so. On many occasions, however, no period of time applies since fancy is timeless. Whereas a reference to ironworkers cannot have meaning in any time before iron became current (in the twelfth century at the earliest), a reference to Amazons, in spite of Homer's notion that they fought at Troy, can be valid or not in any context, at any time, if the storyteller so wishes. Valid not because they existed as tall women with one breast (one was removed for the convenience of drawing an expert bow), indefatigable stamina, equally energetic horses, and a utilitarian attitude toward men. Not one anthropologist credits any reality to the myth of matriarchal warrior bands defending their cultural isolation against the advances of Greek heroic society.

The argument for matrilineal and matrilocal customs in

prehistoric Greece is quite a different matter that has been touched on in several different contexts. It is possible that some form of either of these customs was current among the peoples who gave their characteristics to Amazon legends. As for the Amazons' reputation as warriors with the bow, a new set of hypotheses must be reviewed. Jason at one point sets out to conquer not the Amazons, but their descendants the Sauromatians, who were sired by Scythian men. The story goes as follows. Heracles, during his ninth labor, captures three shiploads of Amazons. The women quickly break their chains, kill their guards, and then, not knowing how to man a ship, drift across the Bosporus to Scythian country. After capturing a herd of wild horses, they set out to ravage the land. When the Scythians inadvertently discover that their invaders are women, they offer marriage instead of war and are accepted with conditions: 1) they must move to the eastern bank of the River Tanais; and 2) their female children must preserve the Amazon custom of killing a man in battle before taking a husband. Apart from the story itself, several elements here are significant. Requiring the husband to move to the bride's home may be an echo of matrilocal custom among peoples in the area—it is known among some primitive societies today. Secondly, Amazons are always associated with horses and nomadic warfare, and often, as in this tale, connected in some way to the Scythians. Descendants of these marriages between Scythians and Amazons are called Sauromatians, the very people with whom Jason is required to do battle for King Aietes before he may take the golden fleece.

Jason's brief encounter with Amazonian descendants is not the only source of Amazon legends. There were many tales about these peoples, probably for the very reason that they were founded on erroneous "facts." Homer would have us believe that Amazons were the traditional enemies of the western Anatolians, for when King Priam surveys the massed Greek forces at the walls of Troy, he likens them to the terrible force of Amazons he was once called upon to combat. Priam's enemies come from the east; that is to say, from the European side of the Black Sea. In the sequel to the *Iliad*, the *Aithiopis*, the Amazons reappear as allies of Troy instead of as enemies, and their queen, Penthesileia, is a Thracian, that is, again from a country on the European seacoast. As these places became known, however, and no Amazons were found, Ionian geographers pushed the Amazons' homes farther eastward. Hesiod placed them on the Asiatic side of the Black Sea around the River Thermodon (see Map 5) and gave their principal city as Themiscyra. By the time of Strabo, the entire Euxine had not yielded one Amazon, so they became a factitious people to historians; yet were merely pushed farther east into the Caucasus by everyone else. Strabo wrote:

> There is a strange thing about the legend of the Amazons. Our accounts of other peoples make a distinction between mythical and historical elements, for statements that are ancient and marvellous and fictitious are called myths, but history seeks truth, whether old or new, and contains no marvellous element, or rarely. But the same stories are told now about the Amazons as in ancient times, although they are marvellous and incredible. For instance, who could believe that an army of women or a city or a tribe could ever be organised without men, and not only be organised but attack the territories of other people, and not only overpower the people near them to the extent of advancing to what is now Ionia, but even send an expedition across the sea as far as Attica? Even at the present time these tales are told about the Amazons. Themiscyra and the plains that lie around the Thermodon and the mountains above them are mentioned by all writers as having belonged to the Amazons, but they say they were driven out of those regions. Only a few writers make assertions as to where they are now, but their assertions are unsupported by evidence and are beyond belief, as in the case of Thalestris, queen of the Amazons, with whom they say Alexander cohabited in Hyrcania in order to produce a child. This assertion is not generally accepted. Cleitarchos says that Thalestris set out from the Caspian Gates and the Thermodon to go to Alexander, but it is more than six thousand stades from the Caspian country to the Thermodon.

Even Plutarch wrote as a serious historian when describing the Amazon attack on Athens, recorded in the Parian Chronicle as having taken place in 1256. Herodotus alone straddled the ground between skepticism and credulity by verifying the reality of the Amazons but supposing them to be extinct. He allowed, however, that their descendants were the Sauromatians, whom he placed on the north shore of the Bosporus.

The Sauromatians of Herodotus' time were probably a nomadic Scythian people living east of the Crimea. He thought their women were still Amazons who "hunted on horseback with their husbands, sometimes even unaccompanied; in war taking the field and wearing the same dress as their men." This image of the Amazons is comparable to a report by an envoy to the grandson of Jenghiz Khan, sent out by Louis XIV of France. The envoy claimed that the Mongol women "sit on horseback bestriding their horses

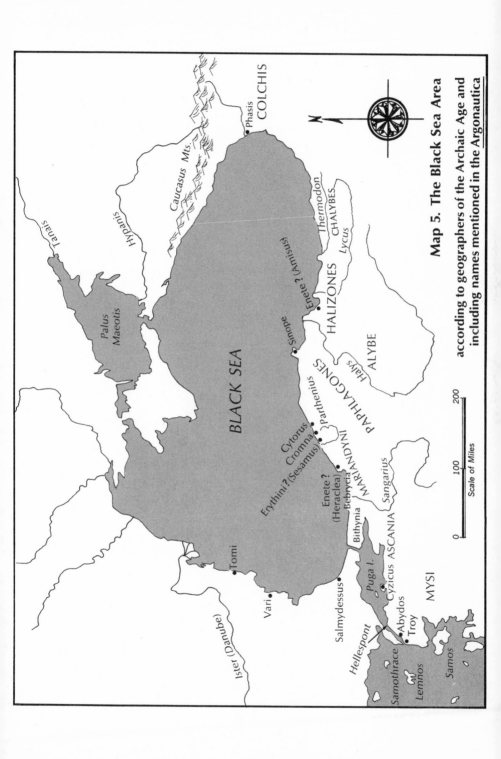

Map 5. The Black Sea Area

according to geographers of the Archaic Age and including names mentioned in the *Argonautica*

like men. Moreover, their women's garments differ not from their men's, saving that they are somewhat longer. When a great company of such gentlewomen ride together and are beheld afar off, they seem to be soldiers with helmets on their heads carrying their lances upright." *

The beardlessness of Mongol men probably added its weight to support the idea of an army of women with customs and habits very like those described by the envoy, Friar William, and by Herodotus. Additional tales of Amazonian military exploits may have been a traditional memory of raids from the east Caucasus that devastated Anatolia from Hittite times onward and probably did so in prehistory. Herodotus gives us the first record of a Scythian raid by the "Cimmerians" in the mid-seventh century. They were phenomenal horsemen and bowmen, and merciless to their enemies, whose scalps they took as trophies; the horror of their destruction of Phrygia survived vividly for centuries. The supposition is that they entered Asia along the east edge of the Black Sea and fanned out westward, even to attack several Ionian coastal cities. During the course of Scythian depredations in Asia Minor, they devastated the Median kingdom, became involved with the Assyrians, contributed to the fall of Nineveh, blasted through Syria, and were stopped only at the borders of Egypt. As a punishment for plundering the Temple of Aphrodite (Astarte) in Palestine, Herodotus says, the goddess afflicted them with sexual impotence. This element of effeminacy also may have contributed to Amazon legends which the Cimmerian raids must have kept fresh in mind. Perhaps stories of Ionian cities being founded by Amazons are based on these experiences.

A fifth-century Greek met only Scythians who had been captured and made slaves of the state. In Athens, for instance, they sometimes served as policemen. The most famous vase paintings of Amazons show them on horseback in the same Scythian costume that came to be standard for archers and police (see Illus. 45). To an eighth-century explorer of the Black Sea, Scythians were as exotic as redskins were to the British in the sixteenth century. To a Mycenaean amber merchant, they could not have been any less alien. It must be recalled that no one, least of all women, rode horseback until late in the Empire period, and then only rarely. One interesting aside about women and horseback riding is offered by a pair of women's felt boots found in a Scythian grave of 300 B.C.

* John Forsdyke, *Greece Before Homer* (London, 1957), pages 106–7.

45. In this vase painting of a warlike encounter, the Amazon on horseback wears Scythian costume.

in the Altai Mountains. The soles are so heavily and richly embroidered with beads, it seems obvious they were meant to be displayed as the wearer was carried in style. The absence of the familiar distinction in social roles between Scythian men and women doubtless impressed itself strongly on Greeks, especially in the Classical period, when women were economically and socially invisible. One ventures to guess, therefore, that stories of Amazons were circular: they were buttressed by tales of Scythians on which the Amazon tales were originally founded.

6

Thus far the Jason myth has taken us over episodes that only minimally distort some real reminiscence, either of place or ethnography. Many of the saga's details are even more rationalized, or are simple observations of fact. For example, the saffron-colored crocus that Medea uses to make a potion that will protect Jason against the breath of fire-breathing bulls is still collected for medicinal purposes today. The drug made from the plant, called colchicine, is a specific against the pain of gout and relieves rheumatic attacks. Widely cultivated in the Old World, four thousand of the dried stigmas of the flowers make only one ounce of saffron, then as now used for flavoring and perfume as well as medicines. A dilution of the aromatic was sprayed in Greek and Roman theaters to sweeten the air and reduce the likelihood of contagions. So, too, another of Medea's potions made from the juice of the stem and leaves of the juniper tree was and is used as incense and as a soporific.

The more purely imaginative and thus more purely mythical portions of the saga have to do with the characters themselves and their adventures in Colchis. After the journey reaches its climax and the quest is ended, the myth contains few economic or geographical reminiscences of the Bronze Age. Now it captures pictographically, as Robert Graves says, a greater number of social and religious traditions. Folktale motifs also increase, as do incidents that have their source only in vase paintings of the Classical period. Apollonius' digressive tale of Eros and Ganymede playing at a game (dice?) with knucklebones probably derives from a painting by the elder Pliny. The vivid description of Jason, limp in the jaws of the dragon guarding the golden fleece, is also probably inspired by Classical art. (See Illus. 46.) This turning toward the fabulous in the material of the final chapters is heightened further by Apollonius' inclusion of the embroideries of other storytellers who added exotica to the bare quest-and-return plot. His most responsible and by the third century most orthodox sources of the Jason saga were, nonetheless, the Greek dramatists, whose interest in any myth qua myth was always subordinate to their interest in heroism and the heroic task. On the whole they were concerned with Jason's character, his complicity with Medea, and the moral dangers implicit in gaining the fleece. Apollonius' attraction to romance and to fairy tale precluded his taking up the heroic tradition where the dramatists left off.

When Jason finally reaches Colchis, King Aietes is not of a mind to relinquish the fleece. Probably in the lost early ballad cycle it was explained that the presence of the fleece was magically essential to the continuance of his kingship. Be that as it may, Aietes sets the impossible terms on which he will allow Jason to achieve his goal. He may take the fleece if he will first plow a large field with a pair of fire-breathing brazen bulls and then sow it with the teeth of Cadmos' dragon, now under Aietes' care. Jason will then have to conquer the armed men who will spring up from the "seed." Understandably enough, Jason despairs of accomplishing the task until Medea, Aietes' second daughter, comes to his aid. Induced by the goddesses Hera and Aphrodite to fall in love with Jason, and promised his faithfulness forever, Medea undertakes to help him. Now Medea, like her aunt Circe, is an enchantress. She gives Jason a lotion made of saffron-colored crocuses as a protection for him and all his weapons against fire for one day. His own strength and skill enable him to master the bulls and plow the fields. The sown men he disposes of as Cadmos did: by tossing a quoit among them to set them fighting one another. Aietes, discomfited by Jason's success and suspecting Medea, repudiates his bargain and threatens to burn the *Argo*. Medea, therefore, secretly

46. Jason, limp in the dragon's jaws. The standing figure is Athena; the golden fleece hangs on a tree branch in the background.

makes his plan known to the Argonauts and leads them in the deep of night to the grove where a dragon guards the fleece. She charms the monster by dropping juniper on his eyelids, and they make off with the coveted fleece. Immediately they are overtaken by Aietes' son, Apsyrtos; but Medea, without a pause, kills her brother and strews his limbs in the way of her father. He, stopping to retrieve them, loses the fugitives. Their mission accomplished, Jason, Medea, and the Argonauts set off on the homeward journey.

No explanation minimizes the bloodiness of the tale at this point. And no explanation should try to counteract the mysterious effect of intrigue between gods and men, and men and each other. Yet the plot here is made up of thinly disguised rituals and customs. Bronze bulls were the symbol of the sun god Helius, to whom foreigners were sacrificed in some parts of the world. The grisly practice is recorded by Pindar in a Pythian ode. He claims that the Rhodian colony of Agrigentum roasted prisoners in the belly of their brazen idol. To this element of the tale has been added the task of plowing a field in one day, a task that would have been imposed on a candidate for kingship. He would have performed this ritual act easily, although he might have had more difficulty in wrestling with a bull and competing in a mock battle with men in beast disguise—the two other ritual acts implied by the episode.

A different shadow of primitivism is cast by the ordeal with a dragon and the command to sow the dragon's teeth. In Cadmos' myth (see Chapter III) emphasis falls on the warlike attributes of the sown men. When they reappear in the Jason story they are still quarrelsome; but it is the fact of their generation from the earth that is important. Jason ritually plows and then reaps in a symbolic exercise of the idea that men are autochthonous, that is, born from the earth. Why is the seed a tooth? Jane Harrison suggested that it is partly because of the resemblance between a gleaming tooth and a seed of corn, the means of vegetable "reincarnation." And partly because the tooth, presumably like some warriors, is practically indestructible. The major symbol of regeneration, however, is the dragon, or snake, himself. In the case of Cadmos we discovered that men were symbolized by snakes, or pictured as killing snakes, or standing near coiled snakes on their grave stelae not because these were representations of actual incidents in their lives, but because the men were snake men. That is to say, they revered the creature as a magical illustration of their human regenerative aspect. So in the case of Jason we find again a huge coiled snake which must be killed in order for him to survive. The chthonic quality of the snake, that is, its association with the underworld because its home is the ground, is hinted at in the vase painting (see Illus. 46) of the fleece-taking episode. The limp hero is being disgorged, literally reborn, from the jaws of the snake, just as the sown men are thrust up from the earthy element, and just as in somewhat more obvious fashion a snake is reborn from his own skin. It is noteworthy that the vase painter is more conscious of his snake theme than he is of fidelity to his narrative, for the figure protecting the hero is Athena, always associated with snakes, rather than Hera, Jason's patroness in the story.

In the murder of Apsyrtos an echo of the regeneration theme plays through the major one of human sacrifice. Aietes' collecting the dismembered body in order to make it whole once again for a proper burial is a restatement of the idea of the generation of whole men from one part, or from a tooth, or from a seed. Probably, killing Apsyrtos was a fictionalized version of a propitiatory sacrifice to a local god to ensure a safe return voyage. Storytellers in ages after human sacrifice had been abandoned tidied up the morality of the myth by changing the plot. In one such tamer version, for example, Apsyrtos remains in pursuit of Medea and Jason until they reach the mouth of the Danube, where the Argonauts then ambush and kill him. Only when Aietes' men are spied at close range do the Argonauts dismember the body as a delaying tactic. The disguised element of human sacrifice is present in all versions. In that just referred to, Medea is made to appear less monstrous; the responsibility for Apsyrtos' death nonetheless still falls on the unhappy couple. They are prevented from rejoining the *Argo* by a magical piece of the oak-tree oracle at Dodona that has been built into the ship. It speaks their guilt aloud and requires them to be purified of the murder. To accomplish this, they set out overland for Aeaea, the first home of Circe, in order to be healed by her.

Perhaps the events in Colchis strike us as more imaginative than the journeyings simply because they are so unremittingly primitive. Their content evokes echoes of idea and custom too barbarous to have been accepted even by the Archaic Age. Heroes reborn out of the netherworld of a snake's belly and men springing up from dragon's teeth are representations, or rather mythic translations, that hark back to a chthonic view of the underworld as the source of all life. They are not metaphors but literal expressions that conceive of the earth as a nurse to animals and men, and they therefore refer to a stage of magical thinking that did not understand the reproductive function of sex. The antirationalism, the darkness of such cults is in direct contrast to the lighter, clear-eyed worship of the sky god Zeus as father, yet it remains there to be half glimpsed, lurking in the background of so much Greek poetry. Often it is dismissed as mere poetry. There is no doubt, however, that pre-Greek religion was strongly chthonic, and that that element remained powerful in spite of its suppression in the later forms that Greek religion took. Equally primitive—in the sense here of pre-Greek—is the original nature of Artemis. Medea, in her unromantic and un-Apollonian portrayals, is a powerful and terrible deity whose attributes resemble those of Artemis. (In Apollonius, Medea is merely a votary of the goddess.) Before she was stripped of her primary characteristics by the patriarchal gods of the northmen, Artemis was an avatar of the Great Mother, worshiped throughout western Asia Minor, Crete, and the mainland. Known variously as Cybele, Ma, Mistress of the Animals, and by a name which the Greeks Hellenized into Britomartis, she was the supreme deity whom the new Greeks found wherever they turned. Her function was to protect all life, especially the young of all species, including mankind. The Mistress's cult must have been shocking to the Greek worshipers of the sky god, for its orgiastic nature was in direct contrast to theirs. Although as an Olympian she is the virginal sister of Apollo and the goddess of the hunt, Artemis alone among the Olympian female deities preserved many of the features of her Great Mother past. Her name, for instance, is Lydian, betraying her origins in Asia Minor. Her mother, Leto, is also a non-Greek with an important cult in Lycia. Since the name Leto derives from the Carian, Lycian, and Lydian word for lady, *lādā*, it is more than probable that both mother and daughter are manifestations of the ancient and powerful Great Mother.

What rituals Medea performed are alluded to but not described. Very probably Apollonius did not know the various forms of Artemis worship, for they had long since been disguised under other names. Pausanias describes one grim festival which must have evolved out of a veneration of the Lady of Wild Things. In a hall of the kuretes, he writes, "they sacrifice without distinction all animals beginning with oxen and goats and ending with birds: they throw them all into the fire." (The kuretes [see Chapter II] were the young male ministrants of the Great Mother.) In this festival the Great Mother has disappeared and her rite has been transferred onto her correlatives. In another connection Pausanias tells us that this kind of sacrifice, so hideously appropriate to the Great Mother, was also made to Artemis Laphria. He describes in great detail a highly popular and elaborate yearly celebration at Patrae. An altar is set up and surrounded by a circle of green logs of wood, approached by an inclined plane of earth. Then a procession of virgin priestesses in a car drawn by deer make their way to the center. Following this

> they bring and cast upon the altar living things of all sorts, both edible birds and all manner of victims, also wild boars and deer and fawns and some even bring the cubs of wolves and bears and others full grown beasts. And they lay on the altar also the fruits of cultivated trees. Then they set fire to the wood. I saw indeed a bear and other beasts struggling to get out of the first force of the flames and escaping by sheer strength. But those who threw them in drag them up again on to the fire. I never heard of anyone being wounded by the wild beasts.

The reminder of human sacrifice is strongly felt; the hint of more sublimated forms of worship to come barely anticipated. The celebration is a transition between ancient and Olympianized practice that characterizes one aspect of the Mycenaean world.

Growing plants were also sacred to the mother of all life, therefore in some ceremonies, like the festival of Artemis Orthia at Sparta, a young tree or bough was an important cult object. In historical times young boys were scourged at Artemis' altar in ceremonies that were understood to be tests of their endurance of pain, an important element of Spartan training. In more ancient ceremonies a blow with the sacred bough was seen as the means by which its *mana*, the power of growth, was transferred from the bough to the celebrant. The fundamental idea is magical, for it presupposes that man can enter into a kind of communion with a supernatural power. The rite might even be called a communion, although the term is restricted to instances when men are filled with the power of a god himself, rather than merely in contact with one of his manifestations. The concept nevertheless is very similar.

All these vestiges of Artemis worship are understood in the tale as indirect colorings to Medea's role, rather than felt as immediate contributions to the plot. The official religion of the story is Orphism, that floating body of prephilosophic ideas about the soul, its transmigrations, its imprisonment in the body, the ascetic life of the latter—these and more that found their development in Plato. There is no evidence to associate these ideas with the mythical figure of Orpheus, and in any event this would not be the place to do so. It is clear, however, that the savage underpinnings of the tale,

like its Near Eastern influences, are softened and rationalized by
the addition of Orpheus' name to the catalog of Argonautic heroes.
His role is always minor. Although he is made the hero of six
incidents in the saga, these tend to be ones in which a general
adviser on material and spiritual affairs is needed. For this reason,
and because his cult was not introduced into Greece until the sixth
century, he is a detachable element in all late versions of the story.
Perhaps the Jason saga was adopted by Orphics as a useful symbol
of the diffusion of his religion.

The dramatists saw Medea as a savage eastern witch, conver-
sant with customs and religious practices both horrible and mysterious. So did the vase painters. And so do the Minyan Greek
characters in many versions of the Jason saga itself. Respect for her
powers is so great that when she and Jason return to Pelias' kingdom with the fleece, she persuades his daughters to kill him in a
particularly grisly way. In order to seduce him into belief in her
magic, Medea appears to Pelias in the guise of an old crone. Then
after invoking the aid of Artemis, she removes the illusion of age in
which she has wrapped herself by an apparently magical gesture.
"Such is the power of Artemis," she cries out. Still, the king remains
doubtful. So she cuts up an old ram (the symbol of kingship) and
boils its parts in a steaming caldron. Moments later, she draws forth
a young lamb she has hidden earlier. Promising Pelias similar
rejuvenation so he can beget many heirs, she persuades him to lie
on a couch and be charmed to sleep. Medea then commands his
astonished daughters to cut him up as she has done the ram, and
they innocently comply.

The murder is couched in rationalizations. The small company
of Argonauts have feared to storm the port of Iolcus unaided, and
so Medea has volunteered to reduce the city single-handedly by
murdering the king and leaving the city leaderless. When her deed
is done, she signals to the Argonauts to approach and occupy
Iolcus. Details of this sort are compatible with heroic saga and
belong rightly to evocations of Minyan or Mycenaean deeds. The
butchering of Pelias, on the contrary, returns to the universal
mythic themes of resurrection and rejuvenation. When it seemed
that only one episode in the saga was built on these themes, it was
fair to assume they were intrinsic to the episode and not to its
characters. The themes' recurrence in actions controlled by Medea
make it more probable that they are expressions of ideas basic to
her mythic origins as a goddess of a Near Eastern type. That

identity, and the themes that characterize her supernatural powers, in turn suggest that other elements in the saga may be more than incidentally allusive to Near Eastern myth. Other members of Medea's clan—Aietes, Circe, Apsyrtos—have Semitic names, and in terms of etymology the hero Jason is only nominally a Minyan. The long-sought golden fleece itself has a role in Near Eastern ritual that makes the Argonauts' search for it analogous to Perceval's quest for the holy grail. Taken all together, these elements comprise a Near Eastern substratum to the Jason saga.

Many testimonies of ancient Greek authors confirm that the fleece, meaning the hide together with the wool of freshly killed sacrificial victims, played an important role in the ritual of purification. The person to be purified stood with his left foot on the fleece or, alternatively, was laid out full length on the hide of a sacrificial ram. The fleece itself was not thought to be divine; it was instead magical medicine with the power to purify in the most ancient sense, by ridding one of evil influences or ghostly infection. The magic consisted in the supposition that the fleece would absorb the impurity. The same visible medicinal remedy was used by Babylonian magic doctors who purified the temple for the feast of Akitu by rubbing its walls with the body of a beheaded "sheep of repentance."

Jason's name, Iasion, signifies "healer" and was so understood by the ancients. What little of that mythic personality remains in his saga is reflected in his having freed, or purified, or "healed" the Athamantid clan of their overhanging curse: the obligation to sacrifice their firstborn in atonement for the murder of Phrixos. Herodotus says the custom was still being practiced in his time. According to the first version of the myth, however, Jason accomplishes the clan's purification simply by returning the golden fleece from Aia. It is clear then that long before he became an epic personification of a knight-errant, he was a magic expeller of evil. A hint of this early identity is carried by the saga as a plot detail: Jason's upbringing and education are the responsibility of the healer-physician Cheiron, the centaur, also the tutor of the healer Asclepios. A stronger clue to Jason's association with healers is in his marriage to the saga's chief magician, Medea: she has "healed" a dismembered ram by making it whole and is reputedly able to do as much for men. Such attributes are standard to Oriental healer gods and are therefore strong indications that Jason is a Greek metamorphosis of one of them.

Other parallels to Near Eastern myth are equally striking.

Phrixos is to be sacrificed to stop drought and famine; so the seven sons of King Saul are sacrificed to save the country from famine. Phrixos' sacrifice is averted by both divine interference and the substitution of a ram (which he sacrifices when he reaches Aia); so Abraham's son Isaac is similarly spared at the sacrificial altar and replaced by a sheep. Aia, the land of Aietes, was identified with Colchis only in the sixth century. His name is originally western Semitic and means "hawk." Aia, then, means "the place of the hawk." Aietes' sister, Circe, also has a Semitic name, meaning "eagle," another predatory bird. Eagle gods and hawk gods are well known in the East: the Egyptians have Horus, the Babylonians Zu, the Canaanites Horon (falcon god), and so on. Ultimately these are associated with the sun, and that is the forgotten reason why the Greek inventors of the Jason myth made the sun god Helius the father of Circe, Aietes, and his family. Because the sun travels underground for half of its diurnal cycle, the sun god was further associated with chthonic or underworld shades. It was to the sun that Babylonians appealed for release from the ills caused by ghosts. And so it is to the sun's country, Aia, that Jason has to travel to pacify the ghost of Phrixos.

The implications of these and many other more esoteric borrowings from Near Eastern mythology are that at some time early in the life of the Jason myth it was exposed to Near Eastern literatures. Storytellers, unbeknownst to themselves, preserved evidence of that important contact in seemingly offhand ways. But then, neither did their Greek audiences always understand the hidden allusions and parallels in tales like Jason's. They often took heroes out of their mythic contexts and brought them into their own world of everyday reality with an ease we might find startling. We, of course, insist that fictional characters have other kinds of verisimilitude before we will adopt them as models to be imitated or heroes to be revered. Perhaps that is a limitation of our historical imaginations. The Greeks were more willing to understand myth as history, so it is not surprising to find mythic heroes as respected cult figures with important ceremonial responsibilities. Often, by the time a mythic persona had acquired cult status, there had come to be curious divisions in the body of tradition surrounding his name and he became a split personality, as it were. His cult rites retained elements of his original nature, whereas these were all but obliterated in the stories in which he figured as a quasi-historical or quasi-realistic person. This is precisely the case with Medea. Euripides, for instance, dramatized her unhappy marriage to Jason, his abandonment of her for the Corinthian princess Glauce, and then Medea's vengeful murder of her own children and the princess. And that is how she has been known ever since. In the remainder of the Medea tradition, now practically unknown, she is not a murderess but a savior who knows the healing power of all plants. Still other "facts" about her lineage and character are attempts to explain her cult at Corinth. A lost poem said that Aietes was a Corinthian by birth who later migrated to Colchis. When a rival to the Corinthian throne took possession of Aietes' share of dynastic power, Aietes' mother sent for his child Medea in order to secure the family's rights to rule. When Euripides has Jason rule in Corinth, it is because in the suppressed Medea tradition the throne of Corinth is her royal birthright. So, too, whereas in Euripides' play Medea kills her own children, in the Medea tradition the Corinthians kill them as retribution for Medea's murder of the princess Glauce. Thereafter, Pausanias recorded, yearly sacrifices were made in expiation at the children's tomb in Corinth. After the destruction of Corinth by the Romans, the sacrifices were discontinued; "children," Pausanias said, "no longer pull their hair and wear black garments in honour of the children of Medea." There is no doubt that the cult of Medea was important in Corinth. What is perhaps unexpected is that the impetus for her cult came from the Minyans themselves. At first afraid of the feats of their adopted princess, when she stayed a famine at Lemnos, they became her votaries and celebrated her fame as a powerful healer goddess.

The reality of the Minyans is no longer open to doubt. The reality of the Argonauts, in spite of all that has been said, is still another matter. In 1908 Chrestos Tsountas, the Greek archaeologist, excavated several Mycenaean beehive tombs at Dimini in the westerly neighborhood of Iolcus. Well before it had been suggested that Troy VIIa might have been the city of a real Priam, or Mycenae the stronghold of a real Agamemnon, Tsountas suggested that the tombs at Dimini might be the graves of the real Argonauts. Dimini, like its neighboring Thessalian towns, has a history of occupation going back to Neolithic times. Its strata also record the later invasion of the new Minyan Greek people in characteristic ways: hearths, megarons, and fortification walls appear. The new culture reaches its height of expression in the thirteenth century in the citadel of Orchomenos in Boeotia; in numerous extravagant tombs nearby; in a palace at Iolcus; and in the graves of the mysterious heroes. At the turn of the century, when Tsountas worked, these bare facts seemed fantastical. Now we are prepared to hear Tsountas' guess as prophetic of reality.

X

The *Odyssey*, Folktale and Travelogue

Odysseus, Penelope, Telemachus. These names are so familiar to us that we have only to hear them to call up the romantic world of Homer's *Odyssey:* the golden castle of the immortal Phaeacians, whose ships are "as fleet as the wings of thought"; the nine years of journeying on an open sea to a distant homeland in Ithaca; the clever escape from the cave of the one-eyed giant, Polyphemus; the patience of Penelope, who weaves a shroud by day and unravels it by night to delay her remarriage; the visit to the underworld; Telemachus' journey in search of news of his father; the bloody revenge of father and son on Penelope's lawless suitors. This is a world at once adventurous and yet courtly, magical and yet fully realized in its carefully told detail. How "real" a world was a question the ordinary reader never asked. For the *Odyssey*, like the folktale it so much resembles, like all poetry, was meant to evoke human responses to illusory events. As Marianne Moore said, the poet's job is to put real toads in imaginary gardens.

As all the foregoing pages prove, how "real" is a question now often asked. Since many elements of the *Iliad* are "true," is it not probable that the *Odyssey* also has buried in its poetry some truth about men and events? The obstacle to any such quest for history in the *Odyssey* is in the nature of the poem itself. The *Iliad* is a battle poem involving lists of men and supplies, ships, harbors, and exact locations, the strategies and techniques of warfare—all contributing to an atmosphere of believability out of which questions about history might well arise. The *Odyssey,* on the contrary, is a romance, filled with enchantresses and vindictive gods on one hand and commonplaces of domestic life on the other. In outline it is also a folktale of the hero who returns, one whose magic episodes have captured the imaginations of people east and west, ancient and modern. It is unlikely, therefore, that any one episode in the *Odyssey* will reflect an historical event. Only the credulous would suppose a basis in fact for, say, Odysseus' descent into Hades. But the episodes often do capture a tradition—economic, social, or religious—either of Homer's time or earlier. And still more often the episodes include in their mixture of literalism and fantasy such detailed descriptions of persons and places, of daily activities and customs, that we willingly conceive of their reality, no matter how alien in time and circumstance they may be from our own experiences. Since the next pages will need to refer to details, it might be well to summarize the *Odyssey* here, doing as little injustice as possible to its unique poetry.

The poem opens in the middle of things: nine years have passed since the end of the Trojan War, and all the heroes except Odysseus have returned to their homes. Poseidon, the god of the sea, has been exacting vengeance for the blinding of his son, the Cyclops Polyphemus, and, so we hear, has tormented Odysseus with storms, disasters, and delays on the open sea. Now Athena, the hero's protector, intercedes with the gods on Olympus for Odysseus' return to Ithaca, and, over the objections of Poseidon, the gods agree that the hero has paid his penalty. With this much introduction, the poem shifts to Ithaca, where Telemachus, Odysseus' son, and Penelope, his faithful wife, are contending with the spoilers of Odysseus' kingdom and Telemachus' inheritance. One hundred suitors for Penelope's hand in marriage have stretched the laws of hospitality to the utmost by wasting the lands and plotting against Telemachus' life to take what is left. Athena urges the young prince to seek news of his father for help in restoring Ithaca's rights. Telemachus sets off on an expeditionary search which introduces him to the great world of the old heroes and earns him his manhood.

At this point, we are taken backward in time six years to meet Odysseus, weeping for his homecoming on the beach at Ogyia, the island of the goddess Calypso. Hearing Zeus' message to release

Map 6. The Mediterranean World

Odysseus, she fits him out with a raft and provisions and he sets forth on the unfriendly seas, eager to be freed from her paradise of inactivity yet in no way optimistic about his chances of reaching Ithaca. After much difficulty, he is washed ashore at Phaeacia and is befriended by Princess Nausikaa and the royal family. To them he tells his adventures for the past seven years and we hear for the first time of: 1) his landing at the country of the Lotus Eaters; 2) his adventure with the Cyclopes; 3) the equivocal gift from King Aeolos of the sacks containing the four winds; 4) the near-destruction of him and his remaining crew by the man-eating Laistrygonians; and 5) the year he spends with the witch Circe. It is she who sends Odysseus to the land of the dead for instructions from Teiresias, the blind seer. In Hades he meets the ghosts of the dead Trojan heroes, has a painful vision of his mother, and reaches the nadir of his endurance against the formidable odds of his long journey home. Still to be overcome are the dangerous passage through the devilish straits of rock and whirlpool, Scylla and Charybdis; and the narrow escape from the Island of the Sun, where the last of his crew are killed for eating the sacred cattle of Helios. It is from Helios that Odysseus reaches the protection of the beautiful Calypso. And thus the reader is brought the full circle of his sojourn in Wonderland.

The Phaeacians, whom at least one geographer has identified as Cypriots, have no more success at inducing the hero to remain with them as husband to the royal princess than Calypso or Circe had at winning his lasting love. He is set on a ship as "fleet as the wings of thought" and finally washed ashore on the long-sought beach of his own Ithaca. But his transition to the real world is neither quick nor painless. Athena disguises him as a ragged beggar and casts a mist over the land to make it unrecognizable, at least in part in order to protect the exhausted hero from attacks by the rival suitors. A series of recognition scenes—with an old swineherd, with his faithful nurse, Eurycleia, with his son, and finally with Penelope—intervene before the bloody massacre by father and son of the suitors and the household slaves who have slept with them, and the final achievement of Odysseus' true "homecoming."

This summary shows that the poem has a three-part design. It begins and ends in the real world of Ithaca; the perilous crossings and recrossings of the dark Mediterranean and the supernatural island creatures Odysseus struggles with all belong to a central section many commentators have called Wonderland. The hero himself seems to be the only connecting link between the two unrelated settings of his story: sea nymphs and one-eyed giants have little enough to do with the pragmatic settling of the king's domestic affairs. Nor does Odysseus try to explain the strangeness of one in terms of the other.

As was noted above, in its large outlines the *Odyssey* is a folktale whose elements are common throughout northern Europe. A soldier, discharged after years of service, finds himself unrecognized and unwelcome at his home. A devil or other supernatural agent appears and offers to solve his dilemma if the soldier either will live in a bearskin for seven years (or six, or eight, depending on the particular version) or give himself to the supernatural world. The soldier agrees to live in the bearskin and endures many adventures, some of them humiliating, none of them explainable rationally. At the end of the stipulated time, the devil reappears, cleans his victim and makes him handsome, releases him from his bargain, and then makes him accepted once more among his own people. In spite of the distortion in the sequence of narrative elements, usual in folktales, the parallel is clear. Odysseus is another soldier in service (at Troy) for many years whose return home is complicated by the intervention of both friendly and unfriendly supernatural beings. Poseidon's hostility keeps Odysseus in uncivilized settings among creatures with animal characteristics for many years, until Athena's protection wins Odysseus his freedom. He arrives at an Ithaca utterly strange to him, unrecognized at first by all but his dog Argus, who dies of joy on the spot. At an appropriate moment, Odysseus is transformed from a hoary, weathered beggar into a handsome godlike man; and finally he is accepted by his wife.

Readers will immediately recall tales with similar features. In New York, Rip Van Winkle returns to an unfamiliar world after a long and magical sleep in a mountain or forest stronghold. The folktale motif in his story, like Homer's, is disguised by trappings of authenticity. In Russia, the man who disappears is a doltish peasant whose unlooked-for return after six years is greeted with jeers by a family ashamed of his shaggy appearance. He comes to be venerated by superstitious neighbors because of his reputed familiarity with wood sprites.

These tales and countless others like them recapture in a rude popular form the ancient Indo-European cult of the brown bear, one whose deep hold on the imaginations of centuries of men has little to do with any interest in particular stories based on the cult, but has everything to do with both a resemblance to bears' charac-

teristic hibernation for six weeks of winter and with primitive
speculations about the world of the dead. Myth is more direct than
folktale in its expressed interest in the supernatural. Persephone
and Orpheus are only two of several Olympian gods who return
seasonally from the underworld and therefore reflect ancient prereligious ideas while continuing to exert their powers over later,
more sophisticated religious thought. The primitive cult of the bear,
called Salmoxis, has as its central theme a death and resurrection. It
may have been brought into Greece by migratory Thracian tribes
for Herodotus, that invaluable collector of hearsay, reports a
bear-type story still current in his day among Greeks of the Black
Sea area. The particular importance of the "bear elements" in the
Odyssey is that they point up a relation with sacred legend in the
northern mainland of Europe, especially Germanic and Scandi-
navian Europe. The resemblance between mid-Eastern and Greek
literatures is generally recognized and often overemphasized. The
relationship of European to Greek art, on the other hand, is still
largely unknown. The entire sequence of Odysseus in Hades, for
instance, may combine an echo of the bear cult with Near Eastern
divinity myths as they are known to the Heroic Age. Ultimately, the
northern cult of Salmoxis is not strong enough to hold its own
against either the worship of the pre-Greek mother goddess or the
still later worship of the Greek pantheon under patriarchal Zeus.
Both new religions testify to the antiquity of the bear cult and to the
tales surrounding it.

Once begun, the game of finding resemblances between the
Odyssey and other ancient tales is hard to stop. Sinbad the sailor is
another traveler who spins long stories of his wanderings in strange
and magical places. In his repertory there is a cave episode almost
as barbarous as that of Odysseus and the Cyclopes. In Sinbad's
story it is a wolf who leads the hero out of a place where he was left
for dead. Odysseus escapes from the cave where he should have
died by clinging to the belly of a ram. There are other similarities,
too. Sinbad and Odysseus are wealthy men of affairs with settled
households who, nevertheless, often disguise themselves as beggars
or suppliants. Several of their adventures end with their being
laden with treasures. And both cross and recross perilous seas.

Resemblances and parallels to other popular tales are not
always so subtle. Homer knows that his audience is familiar with
the epic journey of the Argonauts, for example, so he reminds them
of the similarity between Jason's and Odysseus' departures, adventures, and returns. In doing so, he is calling upon tradition in its

most popular form—the heroic adventure story that was Greek history to the Archaic and Classical ages—and he is making his own hero glorious by comparing him to one better known. Even the *Odyssey*'s folktale episodes reflect traditions—albeit of a different order—to the modern folklorist. He reads the tales alert for hints of social, ethnographic, and religious customs of which Homer was probably unaware. Woven into the web of the Circe episode, to take one case, are clues to the northern European and Asian origins of the tale. Homer did not know the literary antecedents of his story, nor did he know that his Bronze Age ancestors were a mixture of Asian and European races. Yet now, if we had only Homer as a guide, we could reconstruct some of Bronze Age cultural history by patient analysis of the story's details.

Its essential features are as follows. Odysseus and his men make a landing on the island of Aeaea. Odysseus strikes through the forest, climbs a rocky height, and spies smoke rising from a stone house which turns out to be Circe's palace. He sends out a scouting party, who are welcomed by the enchantress, fed on a drugged pottage, and then changed to swine at the touch of her wand. En route to rescue his men, Odysseus meets the god Hermes, who advises the hero to threaten Circe's life but not to resist becoming her lover. Hermes gives Odysseus the magic white-flowered moly as an antidote to Circe's poison. Odysseus is neither moved by the lovely singing heard as he approaches her forest clearing nor frightened by the wolves and lions (once men) guarding her castle. The hero challenges the seductive goddess by snatching his sword and rushing on her as though he means to kill her. Shrieking, she falls to her knees, swears an oath against further evil intentions, and offers herself as a lover. Then at his wish she transforms his crew back into men, younger and more handsome than before. Hero and goddess remain together for one year, feasting and resting, before Circe prepares him for his descent to Hades.

Imagine for the moment hearing the tale in the Black Forest. Circe's palace is hidden in a deep wood—where can be found living every witch and loathsome hag known to the Brothers Grimm, including the one who almost cooked and ate Hansel and Gretel. In European versions, the house or palace can be sighted only by climbing an unusually tall tree, or be discovered if some fabulous animal or woodland being leads the way. In Homer, Odysseus finds it by mounting a steep lookout. A friendly god sends a great stag across the paths of the hungry crew, and indirectly that event leads them to Circe's palace. In European versions, a troll or small stranger appears with magic aids or instructions. In Homer, a disguised Mercury brings Odysseus the moly flower as protection against Circe's charms. (Homer seems to forget all about it, for Odysseus neither uses it nor makes any further reference to it.) Wolves and lions surround the palace, to which the crew is drawn by wonderful singing, a common motif; but swine fill the nearby sties. If Circe intends to devour her guests after their metamorphoses, Homer also forgets to say. These and other curious lapses may have been more important in an older version of the tale that stressed the forest setting, the stag, meeting the strange helper, the animals, and the magic flower. Perhaps Homer's "mountain-bred wolves and lions" belong also to that same northern European story. They certainly make for odd zoological companions with swine.

Now, all these "northern" details contradict the goddess's genealogy. For Circe is a sister of Aietes, king of Colchis, known to us through the Jason legend as guardian of the golden fleece. She is thus also an aunt of Aietes' daughter, the baneful Medea. Another twist in Circe's ancestry makes her a daughter of the sun, so she has twin mythic personalities. As child of the life-giving sun, she brings men all sensuous pleasures; as sister of the terrible Aietes, she makes animals of them. Since the Jason legend had been popular from antiquity, Homer could borrow details like these about its personages with a cheerful acknowledgment to his audience that his source was "well enough known." The comment is his own verification that eastern legends were older than his composition, and that they were available to him in some form. He may not have guessed, however, how closely his Circe resembles the lovely and terrible Sumerian goddess of love and war, Ishtar, known by other names (Ashtoreth, Astarte) all throughout the ancient Middle East. Nor, probably, did he realize that Circe, like Ishtar, is an ultimate descendant of the Great Mother goddess, Cybele.

Setting and story elements, then, derive from northern models; the characters and their behavior come from the East, perhaps by the same uncertain path that the great eastern religions made their way from Asia to Greece. Probably their route lay through Crete, where the Great Mother is often depicted with attendant lions. (The animal is a striking feature of her eastern origins because there are no lions in Crete.) Primitive and unchanging, the old religion remained everywhere in the Mediterranean, although Aryan-Greek polytheism occasionally drove it underground. A central feature of the ancient religion, the sacred marriage, can be discerned in the worship of cult figures and minor deities as well as in stories and folk sagas. The mother goddess takes as her lover a young hero king (or her cosmogonic son, or husband) who is nonetheless her victim. Ishtar has Tammuz (Adonis), who dies yearly. She quests for him through the underworld and brings him back after a struggle with the underworld goddess, her "twin." In the Greek version, Aphrodite is in love with Adonis and struggles with Persephone for him; Zeus arbitrates and allots six months of "marriage" to each goddess. The same myth complex gives Aphrodite a son, Eros, and that couple is a misunderstood vestige of Cybele and her son, Attis. In short, no deity was more ancient and none more powerful than the Greek mother, for even after the succession of the patriarchal Olympians in Greece, her worship and her attendant mythos were distributed among the personalities of Aphrodite, Hera, Athena, and Persephone/Hecate. Often, like Circe, she is connected with the underworld—the goddess instructs Odysseus in the way to Hades. Always she is intimately linked with sexuality. Sometimes she is explicitly opposed to a civilizing principle, embodied in a sky god whom she marries when her matriarchy is threatened by his supremacy. In one eastern myth Ishtar, the twin-natured goddess of love and war, tries to usurp all the civilized and societal decrees established by her rival, the sky god Utu. Their otherworld struggle mimics the changeover in the real world from female to male gods and from matriarchy to patriarchy. The female figure is the more primitive, even animalistic; the male god the more cerebral and socialized. Whenever Ishtar wins a round in their battle, men revert to animals; whenever Utu is victorious, his city becomes more diversified in its arts and laws.

Examples of the goddess-hero "marriage" are so numerous that we must content ourselves here with one archetypal version. The partners are the Sumerian hero Gilgamesh, an Odysseus prototype, and the goddess Ishtar, who, together with a mysterious woman by the sea, Siduri, embodies aspects of the later Circe. Ishtar is attracted to the hero, so she tempts him from his heroic tasks and woos him with sensual pleasures. He challenges her love, much as Odysseus does Circe's, by confronting her with a history of her victims, all cruelly metamorphosed into animals or punished in other fashions for the very sacrifice of their manly strength that her love demands. Furious at being spurned, Ishtar begs heaven for aid in destroying Gilgamesh. He again is victorious and thus neutralizes her sexual power. Later his wanderings bring him to a magical place beside the sea reminiscent of Circe's enigmatic island where "east and west are confused." Here Siduri's vineyards and vats of wine are part of her message to eat, drink, and take pleasure as the "lot of man"—the same advice that Circe and her son, Comus, give. Gilgamesh is instructed by Siduri in how to cross the waters of death, much as Circe instructs Odysseus in the way to Hades. A recurrent motif in this myth type is that the "divine" female power victimizes the hero (Circe's name means "hawk") until he somehow escapes. Usually she reveals to him both man's instinctual drives and the way to the spiritual otherworld. The correspondence with many seasonal myths is abundantly clear. The underlying fear of her multiple personality, alternately fascinating and horrible, is equally clear but rarely stated. Ovid, as one exception, writes of the darker side of Circe's attraction. In one of his tales Macareus, a shipmate of Odysseus, tells how it *feels* to be changed into swine. In another tale emphasizing the inevitability of the sexual experience, Saturn's son, Picus, is changed into a bird and all his men into awful beasts for spurning Circe. Apparently, no man is a hero without sexual experience; and with it no man remains entirely heroic. Moreover, the goddess can be jealous as well as vengeful, for, again in Ovid, Circe changes Scylla into a mass of snarling dogs for being preferred by one of her rejecting (and frightened!) lovers. In no country was the Circe episode more popular than in England, where Medieval and early Renaissance translators read it as a moral lesson on lust and bestiality. Their Circe, a post-Edenic Eve, can only be withstood by the reason and fortitude of a truly heroic, i.e., Christian, man. When the allegorizing translator came upon Homer's troublesome detail—after Circe rejuvenates them, the men become more beautiful than before—he brushed it aside as an irrelevance born of the Greek love for supernatural trimmings.

Although no other woman in the *Odyssey* is quite as fierce as Circe, all of them are overwhelmingly powerful. Most are enchantresses, and Odysseus' encounters with them are charged with a vague sexual fear. Calypso's island (her name means "concealer") is a place where heroes retreat into paralyzing indolence. The Sirens' lure is to intellectual prescience, possessed only by gods and half-men like Teiresias. Life with the lovely Nausikaa would be an endless enchantment on a golden island paradise whose very unreality seems to threaten a kind of death. Even Penelope is a magician at weaving a never-completed shroud which promises doom to her suitors. The poet gives her a slightly sinister aura by comparing her indirectly to the murderess Clytemestra. There is no doubt about the superiority of Penelope's intelligence to that of the suitors she deliberately deceives. Nor does she acknowledge Odysseus until she has deceived him also. When they are reconciled, it is through their shared secret about their marriage bed. Penelope, of course, is only mortal, whereas Helen is a daughter of Zeus and an outright sorceress. The major feminine figure in the Trojan cycle, she shows only a shadow in the *Odyssey* of her divine power. She puts a magic potion of forgetfulness into the wine being drunk at the banquet in honor of Telemachus, Odysseus' son. Nevertheless, with only a few lines at her disposal in this poem, she commands the breathless attention of all as she sweeps into the megaron and proceeds at once to name the weeping young Telemachus, still unidentified by her slower-witted husband, Menelaos. Perhaps the scales are tipped in favor of feminine superiority from the outset in the poem since Athena is the protector and the brains of the family. Yet even she, whose power is direct, becomes vaguely sensual in Book XIII. Fear of women as the source of all evil is a theme that characterizes the *Odyssey,* as well as Genesis and Hesiod's tale of Pandora's box.

One exception to all these ominous and charmed women would seem to be the Phaeacian queen, Arete. Yet the poem's action makes her of all the women most resemble the Great Mother herself. Arete is a queen in a land of peace and plenty. She guides the household, settles disputes among the people, resolves the quarrels of the men, and is honored as no other woman by her husband. Nausikaa and Athena both tell Odysseus to apply to Arete for aid, for if her favor is secured the hero may be assured of his return home. When Odysseus enters the Phaeacian palace, he passes the king and appeals to Arete, sitting at her spinning next to her husband and her sons in the midst of the counselors of the Phaeacians—her usual place of honor in the hall. At the conclusion of Odysseus' strange story about the women he has seen in Hades, she breaks the silence first, claims Odysseus as her special guest, and suggests additional gifts for him—to all of which the oldest counselor agrees. Odysseus makes a formal adieu *to her* before she sends women to his ship with stores and presents, playing out the role of the hospitable host usually assigned to men. At least one critic of the *Odyssey,* mulling over the role of women in the poem, has labeled Homer as "domesticated"—by which he means a tamed half-brother of the fierce warrior-lover who wrote the *Iliad.* Still another commentator, finding Odysseus subdued enough to suit the charmed lives of the overcivilized Phaeacians, and assuming Phaeacia to be Cyprus, has concluded that Homer was a Cypriot. And yet a third has judged that any poet so filled with the wonder of woman could only have been a woman.

A less dramatic conjecture about the importance of women in the poem has to do with their postmythic associations with settled life. Odysseus has spent many years of his manhood earning a reputation as a clever but brutal warrior. Speaking to King Alkinoos of the departure from Troy, Odysseus unabashedly describes making a detour to loot a small eastern coastal town, as though to say no hero would have resisted such opportunity. In most of the poem, nevertheless, skillful piracy and raiding are of negative value. Fortitude, endurance, patience, and most of all diplomacy need to be combined with intelligence and strength in order for Odysseus to surmount nine years of obstacles to his homecoming. These virtues a warrior may do without; a wise ruler in peacetime may not. The contradiction between the two sides of Odysseus' character is a result of the poet's uneven blending of images of a brave Mycenaean past and his own peaceful, unadventurous present. Women other than goddesses had minimal roles in the myths and poems of the oral tradition to which Homer was heir. They neither ruled as princes nor warred as heroes. Even the important evidence of Linear B tablets reserves the mention of women to occupations associated with heaven or housekeeping. In fact, were it not for Homer and the ambiguous evidence of graves, they would be almost invisible. Small wonder, then, that those few mortal women who are remembered are powerful or frightening or both.

2

Not all the poem's folkloristic material can be looked at as the top of a submerged iceberg, or made to sustain the interlocking threads of myth, cultural diffusion, and traditional attitudes that lead outward from the Circe episode. In many cases, it is difficult to be certain about which is the oldest thread of an unraveled story, or which the most "factual." At other times, Homer's tale is a variant of a widespread and ancient story without particular antecedents but with many parallels. The Cyclops adventure, for instance, is known from Asia to Poland in 102 versions as the tale of blinding the giant. In the fullest renderings, two narrative situations are brought together. First, a young man contends with a dull-witted giant (or dwarf, or devil) who is tricked in one way or another into relaxing his guard and is then blinded. The giant or other monster is always allied to anarchic and stupid force, and is pitted against a superior, civilized figure. In the *Odyssey* the giant is Poseidon's son Polyphemus, in whose cave the unsuspecting Odysseus and his men have taken a brief respite from their travel. Polyphemus' return to his cave and his gleeful dinners of two crewmen at a sitting force Odysseus to his first stratagem: he feeds the brute a strong, un-mixed wine. Then, while Polyphemus sleeps off his drunkenness, Odysseus and crew twist a hot spit into the ogre's one eye. Desper-ate with pain and rage, he removes a huge boulder serving as the cave door and shouts for help that "Nobody" has blinded him. His people assume he has been touched with Zeus' madness and ignore him. The second element of the basic story involves the hero's disguising himself in an animal skin (ram, ox, goat, dog, or what-ever) in order to escape from the giant's cave. Odysseus and crew cling to the undersides of Polyphemus' sheep, which file out of the cave past the blind giant's searching hands. Once away from Polyphemus, Odysseus taunts him with a final boast of his true identity—a touch added by Homer. (See Illus. 47 and 48.)

The Cyclops episode precedes the first of Odysseus' trials on the open sea, raised in storms against him by Poseidon in revenge for the blinding of his son. Commentators who read the *Odyssey* as a universal story of Everyman see the Polyphemus episode as a "Freudian" parody of the birth process. Odysseus passes out of a dark cave or womb by clinging to the belly of a sheep as an unformed entity—Nobody or No-man—to make a new beginning. Then he names himself. Thereafter, nymphs and dragons and other fabulous beings give the hero various lessons. The sweet-singing Sirens offer him divine knowledge; his stay with Circe is an education in sensuality; he meets the problems of choice with Scylla and Charybdis; and conquers the lure of Calypso's atmos-phere of *dolce far niente.* The hero's victory over the irrational sea by means of his superior wit is a graduation, as it were, from a realm of blind forces into one of control and reason. Eventually he ac-quires his characteristics as a wily trickster, a ruthless murderer, a compassionate leader of men, and a gentle husband.

The divine kinship of Poseidon and Polyphemus is Homer's invention, for the one-eyed Cyclopes have their own place in Greek

47. Odysseus blinding the Cyclops.

48. Odysseus clinging to the underbelly of a very horselike sheep to escape the Cyclops' cave.

mythology. They are three of the original children of Gaea, "earth," and her son Uranus, "heaven" (another sacred marriage?). Immediately after the Cyclopes' birth, Uranus, in an unfatherly gesture, throws his monster sons into Tartarus, the dark place of the wicked. The Cyclopes do not fare much better at the hands of their brothers, the Titans. When the Titans successfully revolt against their old father, Gaea persuades them to free all their many brothers. They do so, and as soon as the new regime of Titans is firmly established under the control of the youngest Titan, Kronos, the Cyclopes are thrown back into the nether regions. Apparently, the unfortunate Cyclopes are not a bit vengeful. When their nephews later war with the Titans, the Cyclopes give them powerful gifts, ensuring their ultimate victory over their fathers. The new gods divide up the world between them. For Zeus, the Cyclopes fashion the thunderbolt; for Poseidon, a three-pronged trident; to Hades they give a helmet that makes the wearer invisible. At some point in time, the three Cyclopes multiply, for Homer says they are a well-known and numerous race whose land is ruled by a godlike master named Polyphemus. It is Homer also who gives Polyphemus his gruesome taste for human flesh. The further barbarism attributed to the Cyclopes of roasting their victims is a later addition to the tale by Euripides (in his play *Cyclops*). Others of the Cyclopes' abominable characteristics belong to the variable and ubiquitous folktale of the giant and not to their place in the mythical origins of the Greek gods.

The *Odyssey* is so rich in information for us that we sometimes forget it was also new and marvelous to its eighth-century audience. Their responses were important to Homer, for many passages show that he was conscious of their milieu, their interests, and their prejudices. The opening of the Cyclops chapter is a perfect instance of the poet's flattering his listeners. Nothing is said about these mythical peoples or the grisly events which will occur inside the cave. Instead, Odysseus describes his landing on a strange coast as though he were surveying the potential of the place to sustain a settled and domestic life. He could not have made more specific observations were he a scout, due to submit a report to some superior at home.

> Not very far from the harbour on their coast, and not so near either, there lies a luxuriant island, covered with woods, which is the home of innumerable goats. The goats are wild, for man has made no pathways that might frighten them off, nor do hunters visit the island with their hounds to rough it in the forests and to range the mountain tops. Used neither for grazing nor for ploughing, it lies forever unsown and untilled and this land where no man goes makes a happy pasture for the bleating goats. I must explain that the Cyclopes have nothing like our ships with their crimson prows; nor have they any shipwrights to build merchantmen that could serve their needs by plying to foreign ports

in the course of that overseas traffic which ships have established
between the nations. Such craftsmen would have turned the island into a fine colony for the Cyclopes. For it is by no means a
poor country, but capable of yielding any crop in due season.
Along the shore of the great sea there are soft water-meadows
where the vine would never wither; and there is plenty of land
level enough for the plough, where they could count on cutting a
deep crop at every harvest-time, for the soil below the surface is
exceedingly rich. Also it has a safe harbour, in which there is no
occasion to tie up at all. You need neither cast anchor nor make
fast with hawsers: all your crew have to do is to beach their boat
and wait till the spirit moves them and the right wind blows.
Finally, at the head of the harbour there is a stream of fresh water,
running out of a cave in a grove of poplar trees. . . . This is where
we came to land.   [Book IX: 103*ff.*]

There is so much here, so very tightly condensed, that it is easy
to miss the main point of the passage. Odysseus talks chiefly about
agriculture, but he assumes that his audience is very interested in
shipbuilding, merchantmen, and overseas traffic. There is also a
note of reassurance in his comments: the harbor is safe and ideally
protected from adverse winds; there is plenty of fresh water. It is
not likely that our hero's aristocratic audience would respond with
more than mild curiosity to such detail. Phaeacian King Alkinoos
and Queen Arete are sympathetic listeners to the sad history of
Odysseus' own misadventures. If, as is often supposed, Phaeacia
was actually Cyprus, it was rich in copper; abundant in lumber and
the craftsmen to turn that into ships; agriculturally prosperous; and
successfully engaged in the trade of grain with Asia, at first through
the Phoenicians and then on its own. The Phaeacians, therefore, are
more than self-sufficient in their "gold and silver" city. They are,
moreover, masters of the sea. Homer says their ships are both
"rudderless" (?) and independent of the whims of currents, of
storms, and even of sailors. We may imagine, then, that all these
topographical details and pragmatic bits of information, about
which Odysseus says he "must explain more," would have been
received with courteous disinterest by his "godlike" hosts. Certainly, the remainder of the noble audience is unequivocally
scornful of merchants. When the exhausted Odysseus declines to
join in their heroic games, a young courtier sneeringly likens him to
a "merchant-sailor"—a painful insult.

If Odysseus had in mind warlike Achaeans, like himself, his
description would have struck a wrong note. Greeks then as now

were seamen, knowledgeable about shipbuilding and related crafts—although whether they would have referred to their ships as "merchantmen" is doubtful. Their chief interest in Mycenaean days, however, was probably less in the natural and agricultural potential of a new land than in its position on a known trade route, its relation to the lands of other tribes, and its possible yield of metal ore, lumber, and luxuries, facts Odysseus does not mention at all. Homer's passage, therefore, seems not to be addressed to either the mysterious, overcivilized Phaeacians or to the hero's own people. It is the poet's contemporaries to whom Odysseus' report would have been fascinating. In the eighth century, Greeks were eking a living out of the rocky mainlands, heavily overpopulated and pressured by social and economic inequities. These men would have clung to the poet's every syllable, perfectly aware that here was a passage in the epic in which the distant heroic world they were learning about had been pushed aside to make room for their own. For a moment Odysseus ceases to be a resourceful mythical king, forced to journey for a lost homeland, and becomes a purposeful explorer and geographer in the forefront of the age of colonization.

About King Alkinoos, Homer's audience might have noted carefully that he was a financally burdensome second son, sent out from his overpopulated land to colonize a distant island. For the Greeks of the Archaic Age were at the start of their greatest period of expansion into the hitherto unknown western Mediterranean. Everywhere in the Aegean there is evidence of a resurgence of energy after the blankness and lethargy of the post-Heroic Dark Ages. Craftsmen and artisans were slowly appearing on the scene, a new middle class began to emerge, and city-states, soon to have standing armies, began to form. By 750 B.C. a great movement out of the pockets of Greece, west to Italy and the Spanish Mediterranean and northeast to the Black Sea area, was under way. At first journeys were haphazard and independent ventures. Slowly, group emigrations were arranged by parent cities to set up new settlements called *apoikia,* a term connoting more independence than our modern equivalent, "colonies." There is not a trace of evidence from a Hellenic Marco Polo to confirm that exploratory trips were undertaken by hardy men in, say, the first half of the century. Yet these must have preceded the expeditions of whole families and their hard provisions. Moreover, the lumber and metals necessary to build and outfit ships for explorers and expeditions alike presumes a supply much greater than isolated localities could have sustained. Therefore, a prosperous trade must have been part of a general and slow increase in wealth over some time. By 800 B.C. there was an acute need for metals, and that was probably a spur to the widening of commercial seafaring, and eventually to colonization itself.

The earliest colony was Cumae—modern Ischia, near Naples—commonly dated to 750. Very like the Cyclopes' country, Cumae was an offshore island from which a landing party might reconnoiter farther without too much risk. All the lands to which the Greeks migrated were already inhabited by a variety of peoples at various levels of cultural development. Some, like the Etruscans, strongly resisted the Greek newcomers; others, like the Sicels (Sicilians), were either reduced to a labor force or pushed inland. Odysseus' comments on the Cyclopes' lack of law-making assemblies, the crude state of their technology, their laziness ("they neither plough nor till the land; crops of wheat, barley, and grape spring up unsown"), and their generally uncivilized condition could well be suggestions to prospective colonizers that these people would offer no great obstacles to an invader with superior ships, crafts, and organizational intelligence.

Stories that made their way back to mother cities about battles against the original inhabitants lent themselves to fantasy as easily as did tales about American pioneers against the Red Indians. Often, too, such stories became attached to the sagas of well-known heroes. It is very probable that the description of the Cyclopes' island was added on to Odysseus' exploits in just that fashion—whether as a memory of some explorer's observations or as pure invention. Linguistic analysis of the style clearly shows the passage to be later than the giant story deriving from high antiquity.

Taking a final look at Odysseus' reconnaissance, we notice the repeated emphasis on the quality of the island's soil, its produce, its natural lushness, and the desirability of its harbor. Homer is here consistent with recent evidence that the motive for colonization in the eighth century, unlike that in the Mycenaean fifteenth, was not chiefly commercial. First information about a new site probably came from traders; but settlers are interested in land. Traders, by definition, return to home bases; Greek migrants were basically agrarian. They settled near the sea; but they can be typified by the Syracusan aristocracy who were called *gamoroi,* i.e., "those who divide the land." Lastly, archaeology shows that a series of social crises which prompted and sustained two long waves of migration from about 800 to until about 600 stemmed from overpopulation.

In Greece after the Dark Ages, the feudal society of kings had been all but eliminated and a tight aristocracy owned much of the best land. An image of the wealth monopolized by this tiny minority can be gathered from vase paintings of the period depicting the full panoply of armor, helmets, body weapons, and greaves worn by this warrior elite. Metal was scarce and expensive. So, too, was horse breeding, essential to the military monopoly held by these nobles—although the actual importance of cavalry has been disputed. By the seventh century some of this capital was being distributed among a small middle class whose origins and growth are obscure but hypothetically linked to the needs of the aristocracy. Farmers, merchants, and shippers begin to appear in the period's lyric poetry, hitherto limiting its references to persons of the nobility. The status of carpenters also can be taken as an indication of a changing social and economic condition, for they were now being employed by "capitalist" shipowners. This new middle class was more prosperous than its grandfathers and able to support an organized armed infantry of its hoplite sons, each of whom had to provide his own costly arms and armor. In general, then, from 800 to 600 the standard of living was rising for the upper and new middle classes. Yet the mass of commoners, growing in population beyond the food resources of the rocky Greek soil, continued to live at subsistence levels that differed little from those of the tenth or ninth century. Details about how they managed are only a little more accessible than those about the daily lives of their betters. Some can be gleaned, however, from the poet Hesiod's advice not to marry before the age of thirty, and then to produce only one son, who will feed his father's house. The swelling numbers of the lower class were without a tradition of law to protect them from virtual economic enslavement. The lawgiver Solon accepted human inequality as consistent with justice. The lower classes were without a political voice to pressure landowners, and the famous concept of democracy was a long way off in the future. Aristotle in his *Constitution of Athens* says there was "civil strife" for a long time because the poor, their wives, and their children were peons of the rich with no political rights. Confused and intermittent solutions to the problem of how to administer for the commonalty are recorded throughout the length of the period. None, however, was as successful as colonization. It was the political safety valve for governors and a promise of Utopia to the impoverished masses.

3

A quite different trace of Homer's own era is in the poet's biased treatment of Phoenicians. At his most flattering Homer calls them rascals, pirates, and thieves from whom no good can be expected. If through the oral tradition his audience had inherited any attitude at all toward the Phoenicians, it might have been a somewhat hostile one; they therefore had an appropriate groundwork on which to build fresh hostilities. We know that the history of Greek and Phoenician relations dates to the Bronze Age and we are therefore faced once again with a need to differentiate between Mycenaean reminiscences and information about Homer's own day. As is so often the case, however, reliable information is full of discontinuity; apparent certainties may be only approximations. It seems clear, nonetheless, that all through the Late Helladic period Phoenicia was an important power and the commercial rival of Mycenae. For centuries Phoenicians had been the point of contact between the eastern lands, familiar to us from the Bible, and the Aegean civilizations. Of their ships, their customs, and culture, relatively little is known. A good deal about where they went on their wide-ranging commercial travels, however, is known. There is little reason to believe they went to western Italy or Spain in the Bronze Age, since the single most important commodity was metal and Phoenicia (Ugarit in particular) seems to have had a virtual monopoly on a good deal of it. Ugarit controlled Cyprus' rich supply of copper ore. Tin and copper reached that city as well as other Phoenician ports by caravan routes from Anatolia, Mesopotamia, and Arabia. Gold and ivory, too, made their way to Phoenicia from Syria, on whose shores Solomon later maintained a fleet for the purpose of transporting the precious ore. Although Hittite records mention Achaean ships going directly to Syria (famous for its craftsmen in gold and ivory), such voyages probably predated the fourteenth century. For, so long as Mycenae had strong interests in Ugarit, her interest in ports farther south was secondary. In any case, goods from the south were brought up to the Phoenician outpost that became a distribution center for the products of many nations. The focus of all trade out of Ugarit was ancient Asia, the land that enriched both Crete and Mycenae. The Phoenician depot boasted a library of texts in a variety of languages from Semitic to Mycenaean, testifying that she was a crossroad of the known worlds. Crete would have brought oil to offer for Phoenician metals; Mycenae exported wine and perishables (to judge from the vast number of stirrup vases found in Phoenicia that would not have been shipped empty). On the return journey, Mycenaean coffers would have held metals, purple dye, perfumes, gums, and incense. Some Mycenaean traders were probably permanent residents in their quarter of Ugarit—a situation likely to have caused some social unease. A greater amount of hostility was doubtless generated when, in the thirteenth century, Phoenicians moved in on trading posts and watering places that weakening Mycenae could no longer control.

The barbarism in the following period of the sea raids (see Chapter VIII) is captured in the tales exchanged by Odysseus and his old swineherd, Eumaeus. Disguised as a beggar in Eumaeus' poor hut, Odysseus tells a long and inventive lie about his identity (he was born a Cretan) and his fortunes (dangerous but profitable at the expense of the slower-witted Egyptians). With the Egyptians he spent seven years, he says, but in the course of the eighth, he "fell in with a rascally Phoenician, a thieving knave who had already done a deal of mischief in the world." Odysseus is prevailed upon by this "specious rogue" to go to Phoenicia, where he is put aboard a ship bound for Libya, there to be sold as a slave. The swineherd is sympathetic but not too surprised, for his own experiences have confirmed him in expecting ill of the Phoenicians. His father ruled the island of "Surie," and as a child his household "was visited by a party of those notorious Phoenician sailors, greedy rogues, with a whole cargo of gewgaws in their black ship." One of the women in the house was seduced and then inveigled by the sailors to steal some of the house's treasures, including the young Eumaeus. He, after further mistreatment by them, was sold first as a slave in Sidon. Later, a Phoenician skipper brought him to Ithaca and resold him to Odysseus' father, Laertes.

The island "Surie" is probably Syria, for any region reached by sea might be referred to as an island until the hinterland was explored. Perhaps there is a fragment of a Bronze Age tale in Eumaeus' story, revived centuries later when the Greeks founded a port on the Orontes River. In ancient days the river was navigable up to Antioch, and Sabouni (modern Al Mina) was a settlement on the river that a Mycenaean would have visited when passing to or from Ugarit. The international city was an ideal place for a Phoenician to kidnap a Greek child.

It would be too much to expect that stage villains like these Phoenicians could actually have been responsible for the wide-

spread devastations at the close of the Mycenaean period. But the
two stories, much abbreviated here, give a grim picture of what life
may have been like in the period of the sea raids. Although Homer
knows little about Phoenicia, he refers to the country when he has
Menelaos visit with the king of the Sidonians. The latter is the
Greek rendering of the name the Phoenicians called themselves,
and it is found in the Old Testament. After the rise of Tyre, its king
added King of Sidonia to his titles, thereby claiming overlordship
of all Phoenicia. Or Sidonian in Homer may be a trace of Bronze
Age nomenclature used in the days when Mycenaeans from Ugarit
visited the Phoenician coast. The history of Ugarit itself, again like
that of most of the Aegean, came to an end at the close of the
Bronze Age and the city had no revival. The lines of trade—north
and south with Egypt and Asia, and east and west from Greece to
Asia—no longer intersected at Ugarit. Although the Phoenicians
continued to trade after the collapse of the Mycenaean world—had
even taken advantage of the power vacuum to occupy coastal sites
on Cyprus and open new exchanges with Cilicia and Armenia—their commercial contact with Greece was broken.

Early in the eighth century Phoenicia was once again
preeminent on the seas. Their chief city was Tyre, the reputed
founder of early colonies at Utica, Gades, and Carthage. But the
range of Phoenician relations with Greeks, like the Greeks' knowledge of them, was sketchy and filled with misinformation. Some
tension may have developed between the two powers as a result of
Greek expansionist policies. Their ancient role as intermediaries
between the East and the Aegean had declined, and now Greeks
were in direct contact with Cyprus and Syria. In the western
Mediterranean, Phoenicians had camps on Sicily and Sardinia
from the first half of the eighth century, well before the Greek
reawakening. To get to them, they must have had watering places
on Greek lands, and these might well have become trading depots.
The port of Phoinikous on the island of Kythera, famous for its
shrine to Aphrodite Ourania, was probably one such place. Twice,
Homer gives the epithet Ourania to Aphrodite, so he has heard
about, maybe even seen the Phoenician settlement. Odysseus himself talks briefly to a Phoenician skipper whose ship lies in another
Phoinikous, on Crete. That would have been a logical port of call
for Phoenicians en route to Carthage. These clues, together with a
scanty number of Phoenician objects dating to this period found in
Greece, suggest there was regular contact between the two countries. The first reappearance on Greek sites of gold and ivory that

increased in volume over the next two hundred years is a more positive indication that commercial relations were flourishing. At this date the sole supplier of ivory was Africa, controlled by Phoenician cities.

By the middle of the eighth century Phoenician journeys to the west coincided with Greek explorations in the same directions, and relations became definitely strained. Yet, in view of what seems to have been continuing and lucrative commercial relations during most of this three-hundred-year period, it is curious that mention of the Phoenicians in the *Odyssey* is unfailingly couched in terms of dislike and distrust. Perhaps, then, the hero's scorn of Phoenicians is emphasized by the poet for the benefit of his seventh-century listeners. Tension between the two powers reached a high in the seventh century, when Greeks ousted the Phoenicians from their encampments on the coast of Sicily. Nevertheless, at some times and under some circumstances relations between the two must have been more friendly than hostile, for early in the eighth century the Greeks adopted the Phoenician alphabet. Probably the point of contact between the two peoples was Cyprus, as it had been, differently, in the past. By some curious accident—nationalism?—the Cypriots kept their clumsy syllabary, at least for the language of officialdom, long after Phoenicians had given their efficient system to most of the reawakening Aegean. It was the final contribution of a people who had once controlled the economic life of the area.

4

In spite of all that has been said thus far about commercial voyaging, the image of travel projected by the poem has more to do with social and political behavior than with materialistic concerns, although the three are interrelated. Throughout, Odysseus shows that mixture of fear and familiarity that typifies the attitude of the period toward the seas. His emotions, moreover, match those of his hosts, who greet him with a paradoxical combination of xenophobia and courtesy. The stranger must always reassure a suspicious host about his impeccable lineage, a regular excuse for Odysseus' famous lies, before he is welcomed with the costly gifts that make bonds between aristocratic families. The Greek word for visitor is *xenos,* roughly translatable as "guest-friend." Yet the same word also means foreigner, stranger, and occasionally host, a confusion that aptly describes the ambivalent attitude of men separated from each other by the hostile seas.

Homer probably reflects Mycenaean custom very closely. In that dangerous age a network of great families, bound by a code of kinship and hospitality, made individual travel possible. If a visitor was unconnected with his host, was a shipwreck, an exile, or an alien, he became a suppliant. On entering a household he embraced the knees of the master and sat in the ashes of the hearth, much as Odysseus does at Phaeacia. The nobleman was obliged by Zeus, the protector of beggars and strangers, to offer minimal hospitality in the form of refreshment and courtesy. When, for example, the chief suitor Antinous strikes the beggar Odysseus, he is chided severely.

> Antinous, you did wrong to strike the wretched vagabond. You're a doomed man if he turns out to be some god ... the gods do disguise themselves as strangers from abroad and wander round our towns in every kind of shape to see whether people are behaving themselves or getting out of hand.
>
> [Book XVII: 486-7]

After the foreigner had identified himself, he was given a gift commensurate with his social rank. Odysseus probably expects a gift of metal from Polyphemus, for he opens their dialogue with a plea for traditional hospitality. He does not ask for refreshment first, having just fed amply on the island goats. The Cyclops, however, not a bit torn between the antithetic needs for wariness and generosity, answers dryly, "I shall devour you last among your crew; that shall be my gift of hospitality." Doubtless his Classical reputation for savagery owes as much to his refusal to be a proper host as it does to his propensity to make a dinner of his guests.

A guest in the house of a family friend would be performing a diplomatic function, tightening the kinship obligations imposed on him by their code. He would give as well as receive a gift matched in value, and behave in a manner to reflect credit on his tribe. Such a visit would be governed by reciprocity, the principle underlying all the gift-giving in the epic poems. Ultimately, reciprocity was the ideal that characterized Bronze Age trading. Probably the more apt term is barter. For whereas trade was motivated by an interest in profits, exchanges between leaders were a matter of mutual benefit to equals. Outright gains, on the other hand, were associated with warfare and piracy, of which the most famous examples occur during the course of the Trojan War. Booty was divided among a raiding party according to strict and hierarchical rules, ceremoniously observed.

The measure of a gift's value was cattle. Metals were measured in talents; but originally a talent was a weight of metal equivalent to the value of an ox. Trade in slaves existed in Mycenaean times—we have already met it as a Phoenician sideline in Eumaeus' story. More usual gifts, however, were hides, cattle, bronze, and other metals, often cast in the forms of caldrons, tripods, and armor. These especially added to the treasures of the house's storeroom, the index of the family's wealth and strength. Odysseus' first action on his return to Ithaca is to visit his storeroom.

As soon as the *Odyssey* is looked at as a travel tale, the question of its realism becomes acute. The poet's audience was Greek, and Greeks from time immemorial are associated with the sea. Would they not have asked, Where is Polyphemus' cave? To them the sea was not a fairyland, no matter how they might have reacted to single adventures of the hero. They would have wanted just the kind of detail about the settings of these many stories that the poet gives them. From a literary point of view it would not much matter whether his minute specifications were right or wrong. "Scheria is west of . . . and two days' journey from . . ." is the sort of statement that makes a place real, even if it is not. To us, however, a question like, Where is Ogyia (Calypso's island)? is intriguing, not because we accept the poem as fiction, but because Homer has helped to reconstruct so much ancient history. For reasons like these, finding the *Odyssey* landscapes has tantalized the ingenuity of geographers, archaeologists, and laymen alike. Even when there is general agreement about the identity of one locale, it is likely to dislocate the entire scheme of another theorist. Scylla and Charybdis are commonly thought to be personifications of navigational hazards in the Strait of Messina. Yet there is still a body of opinion saying that the Greeks did not venture into the western Mediterranean until c. 650, one hundred years later than the most likely date of the poem—which is about a wanderer some six hundred years earlier! Scheria, Homer's name for the isle of the Phaeacians, has been identified since ancient times with Corcyra. These people were great seafarers, very wealthy, and as highly civilized as the Achaeans, Odysseus' people. Yet the route Odysseus would have had to follow to reach Corcyra from Calypso's Ogyia (Malta? the Balearics?) contradicts what is known from sailors' manuals and modern navigational charts about patterns of wind and current. A modern Greek shipping line offers a cruise purporting to follow Odysseus' route from Troy to Ithaca, never touching the north coast of Africa, where one geographer locates the land of the Cyclopes. Scoffing at reconstructions of what is known about routes both ancient and Archaic, a Chicago lawyer insists that Odysseus went out through the Strait of Gibraltar to America, tarrying on the Azores with Calypso for seven years, and then coping with Scylla and Charybdis in Nova Scotia's Bay of Fundy! The disposition of the early Greek colonists to identify Homeric sites with lands they visited only further confused an already heady subject. Thus the promontory of the Sirens, the home of Circe, and the entrance to Hades all were reported to be on the west coast of Italy. Early Greek historians as avid as Herodotus and as scientific as Thucydides could only collect and perpetuate these and other conflicting geographies.

The most conservative reconstructions of Odysseus' journeys trace a line south from Troy and west along the coast of Asia Minor and Africa, avoiding the sandy shallows at the Nile Delta. Odysseus then would have continued west to Gibraltar, the mythic gateway to Hades thought by ancients to be at the outer edge of the great river Ocean encircling the world. The current would have taken Odysseus back along the southern edge of Spain, across to the western coasts of Sicily and Italy, then through the Strait of Messina and across the Adriatic. In these open waters, close to the Ionian islands and home, Odysseus would have been blown south and east toward Cyprus, another possible location of the Phaeacians. King Alkinoos' ship then presumably took Odysseus back in a northwesterly direction, around the tip of the Peloponnesian mainland to just within sight of Ithaca. Here his crew, resentful and curious over the heaped treasures aboard, chose the moment of Odysseus' only sleep at sea to open the sacks of Aeolos' four winds given him by Alkinoos. No one has tried to chart these unloosed storms which forced Odysseus to retrace his steps between Phaeacia and Ithaca. (See Map 6.)

In general, this theory is plausible and accords with Homer's references to travel times between landfalls, to topography, and to the position of named stars and constellations. The speculations of early geographers, the fancy of Homer's readers, comments by historians in the Classical period, and travel tales true and false of the Aegean peoples are nevertheless more conclusive than modern scientists have been about the *Odyssey* settings. They put Homer's text to proofs that poetry cannot always sustain. For even when a general course like the one just outlined gains acceptance, individual localities on its route may be uncertain. How, after all, does one identify the precise harbor of "shining calm" in which "no wave ever billowed, either great or small," surrounded by headlands of "towering rock"? One specialist finds it at the southernmost tip of Corsica; another on a promontory in Spain.

In our own century excavators have tried, mostly in vain, to find signs of Odysseus' visits at every conceivable and some quite inconceivable sites. The most interesting evidence is where we expect to find it: in Ithaca. Because of an inexplicable twist of Homer's tongue, controversy about whether modern Ithaca is Odysseus' home will never be resolved. Odysseus tells King Alkinoos that his home is one of four islands.

> There is a mountain there . . . Neriton . . . and there is Doulichion and Same, wooded Zakynthos, but my island lies low and away last of all on the water toward the dark, with the rest below facing east and sunshine, a rugged place, but a good nurse of men. . . .
>
> [Book IX: 24–7]

On every map past and present Ithaca nestles in the northeastern arm of her neighbor island, Kephallenia, and both are north of Zakynthos, a total of three islands. It would be tedious to recapitulate the innumerable quarrels of scholars over interpreting the passage. The historian Strabo recognizes the difficulty in the lines and offers some ingenious comments of his own. The key number he slides over by rewriting Homer as follows:

> I dwell in Ithaca, the far seen island. In it is a mountain called Neriton, thickly wooded and outstanding; and round about lie many islands very close to one another, Dulichion the western hump of Cephallenia [which Strabo says may have been cut off from the mainland at one time] and Same and wooded Zacynthus. . . .

This and two other brief references to Ithaca are all the *Odyssey* offers. The first comes when Telemachus refuses Nestor's preferred gift of horses because his country is "too wooded and rocky for driving horses." The other comes when Athena, teasing Odysseus for not recognizing his own land when he washes ashore, tells him, "It is rugged and unfit for driving horses." Yet, she goes on, "it grows abundant corn and wine . . . and has excellent pasturage for goats and cattle."

As guides to topography, these references are scarcely adequate. Yet a visitor's observations would confirm Homer's. The Ionian islands are the uppermost segments of a range of submerged limestone mountains. Two protruding peaks—neither of them now named Neriton—are connected by a neck of land to comprise Ithaca. In the north and south of the island, there are two plains of arable pastureland; but the remainder of the island, with little pasture and few streams, can produce only olives. Its geography, then, suggests that the concern of Ithacans was not agriculture but seafaring, for its inner position among the other islands makes it a safe coasting route for north–south runs. Probably barter with its neighbor Kephallenia provided Ithaca with fruits, grains, and wines. A bit to the north and east is Leucas, separated from the mainland by a narrow channel which silts up regularly. It is this nominal "island" that may have made up Homer's fourth, if we assume that a hypothetical separation of lands existed in ancient times. (See Map 7.)

If we look not at what the characters say but at what they do, a different set of clues to Ithaca's location emerge. The Phaeacians put Odysseus ashore at the "harbor of Phorcys," distinguished by a high, rugged promontory on either side, and by a large cave nearby sacred to the nymphs of the wellsprings. In the cave, the text says, are "mixing bowls and handled jars all of stone" and "stone looms," very long, on which the nymphs work. Furthermore, at its southern opening—it has two—is an eternal spring. It is in this cave that Odysseus hides the thirteen caldrons, fine garments, and other precious gifts heaped on him at his parting by Queen Arete. When they are described in plainer language, the stone bowls and looms resemble stalactite formations that dot the limestone countryside. These are particularly abundant near the mountain-girt Gulf of Nolo, whose conformation is like enough to the *Odyssey*'s Phorcys for a number of scholars to have identified the two. Only one cave on the entire island, Marmarospilia, has two entrances that fit Odysseus' description: one to the north, the other just a hole in the roof of the southern end that "only the gods could have used" for an entrance. Marmarospilia, moreover, is a short walk inland from the harbor.

When Odysseus sets out from the cave to find his old swineherd Eumaeus, he takes a rocky lane over hills and through woods till he discovers the pig farm "by the rock Korax, above the Spring Arethusa." Various place names in the district of Ergiros recall that pig keeping was carried on in the neighborhood. The spot itself is in

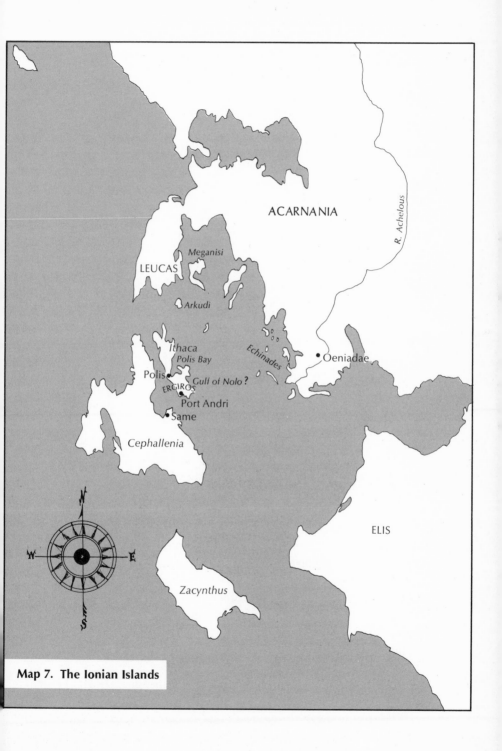

ACARNANIA

R. Achelous

Meganisi

LEUCAS

Arkudi

Ithaca
Polis Bay

Echinades

Oeniadae

Polis

ERGIROS   Gulf of Nolo?

Port Andri

Same

Cephallenia

ELIS

Zacynthus

Map 7. The Ionian Islands

the southeast of Ithaca on the edge of a plateau. Here, one visitor reports, is an impressive sheer cliff, below which a spring discharges its waters down a steep gully to the sea. Some short distance to the south lies Port Andri, the most southerly point on the island, where Telemachus must have landed his craft on his return from Pylos. The poet says these places—Eumaeus' hut and the port—were a half-day's journey from Odysseus' town. Now one other piece of information must be added to this deductive geography. Penelope's suitors, plotting to capture and kill Telemachus, lie in wait for his ship on a small offshore island opposite "a bay." The only bay a half-day north of Eumaeus' hut and Port Andri, and opposite a natural island ambush, is Polis. For all these interlocking reasons, Odysseus' home must have been a short distance inland from Polis' harbor.

On the northwestern coast of the island at Polis Bay, a cave shrine of the nymphs was discovered in 1868 by a local landowner. In it he found a bronze spear and sword, an inscribed flute, some coins portraying Odysseus as a local hero, and a stone slab with an inscription to Athena. For some inexplicable reason visitors, from Schliemann, who bought the items listed above, on down to scholars in the 1920's, failed to appreciate the possible importance of the site. The floor of the cave has been inundated regularly by the sea, higher now than in ancient times, and the roof has collapsed. But in 1930 excavation uncovered a stratified deposit of pottery and offerings to the shrine ranging from the Bronze Age to the first century A.D. These were the first vestiges of the Mycenaeans on Ithaca. Inscriptions on the shards showed that from the first the cave was sacred to the nymphs; another fragment reading, "A votive offering to Odysseus," is incontestable proof that the cave was further associated with him. At a very early stratum, possibly late thirteenth century, there is a bit of pavement, suggesting the importance of the shrine. Apparently it was visited often and was well kept. No find there was as remarkable as the twelve bronze tripod caldrons of very beautiful workmanship, dated to the ninth and eighth centuries. The gifts cannot show that the shrine was dedicated to a "real" Odysseus shortly after his death. It may well be, however, that the shrine helped to inspire the poet's description of the nymphs' cave in the *Odyssey*. Whoever brought the twelve caldrons to the cave knew that Alkinoos and each of his eleven chieftains gave Odysseus a great tripod and caldron.

The existence of the cave at Polis, of course, does not prove the existence of Odysseus' palace. It does prove, however, that Ithaca was intimately associated with Odysseus, and that he is linked firmly to the Bronze Age instead of to Homer's. That fact has implications which the poem sometimes ignores. Travel routes, the means and purposes of travel, the attitudes toward it, and the people engaged in it differed in the Bronze Age and in the Archaic period, when Homer writes. Place names changed; societies disappeared and new ones were born in the course of the 1800-year span between these periods; the poet's allusions, therefore, sometimes refer to Heroic times and occasions and sometimes to his own. At other times references are ambiguous because the two time periods are fused. One such allusion occurs during Athena's visit to the young Telemachus. The disguised goddess declares herself to be a Taphian engaged in the traffic of iron and copper. In the Bronze Age iron was a precious metal; it did not come into general use before c. 950. Here anachronism is apparent only because of the mention of iron. Distinguishing between the two time periods has become more difficult for Homeric scholars recently because Minoan, Mycenaean, and Phoenician artefacts, coins, and copper ingots have been found at sites once thought to have been known only since the Archaic Age. These finds indicate that men of the Archaic period unwittingly retraced the sea-lanes traveled by their centuries-dead ancestors. Not always, of course. Historians generalize that the western limit of the Bronze Age world was the western tip of Ithaca. Yet there is good reason to believe that the Mycenaeans reached western Italy and Sicily and perhaps traded for tin in southern Spain, where art shows the influence of the Mycenaeans. Often enough, therefore, the *Odyssey's* charts read like a palimpsest—here a loop westward made by sailors in Homer's time and beneath it a curve mapped by the Achaeans or Phoenicians.

XI

Odysseus, The Last Mycenaean

Mycenaeans, as we have seen, were engaged in a flourishing and extensive trade all over the eastern Mediterranean from 1600 to 1200 B.C. They established trading colonies on Rhodes and Cyprus, probably in the period of their greatest expansion early in the fourteenth century. They carried on complex trading and raiding relationships with Crete; and they became a powerful factor in the operation of the city of Ugarit. It seems anomalous, then, that travel on the open sea was yet full of perils and for the most part limited to organized voyages to known ports of call. Individual wanderers like Odysseus were very much an exception, and the poem's descriptions capture this uniqueness while projecting the terrors of hostile waters. Odysseus hugs the shorelines whenever he can; he calculates his evening's landfall with care. The nature of his experiences, however, does not speak for individual travel of other sorts during the Bronze Age. Noblemen had a variety of reasons for making journeys, many of them linked to tribal affairs. Autolycus, Odysseus' grandfather, pays a family visit when his grandson is born and receives the honor of naming the infant. When a boy Odysseus returns the visit and collects the gifts promised him. As a young prince he is sent as an envoy to Messenia by his father and the elders of Ithaca to demand reparation for the theft of three hundred sheep. Odysseus the wanderer journeys to Dodona to consult the oracular oak of Zeus about how to behave on his return home. And long before we meet Odysseus, his son, Telemachus, undertakes a visit to the Trojan heroes Nestor and Menelaos for news of his father. With a ship full of men and the disguised Athena as elder companion, the boy sets out on his first voyage away from Penelope and Ithaca.

For two and one-half books, the poet sings of the young man's alternating wonder and awkwardness in the presence of both the elder statesmen. Telemachus arrives first at "sandy Pylos" during the festival in honor of Poseidon. Nestor, his court, and his followers are on the beach preparing the ritual sacrifice of a bull. They welcome the young stranger and entertain him at their feast. In the evening he returns with them to the palace some distance away. Libations are poured; Telemachus is given rest, an elaborate bath, and a guided tour of the grounds. The following day he identifies himself to Nestor, and they exchange many formal courtesies before the boy is given gifts and sent on to the next leg of his journey. The entire visit is elaborated in charming details that have little to do either with Odysseus' wanderings for nine years or with his eventual homecoming. Why then, we might ask, is this visit made so important a part of the poem? And why, for that matter, does Telemachus see Nestor at all, since the aging, garrulous leader has no information about Odysseus?

Until recently the answers most often suggested were purely literary. Telemachus' journey was originally part of another epic in the Trojan cycle telling about the return of other great kings from Troy. Including it in the *Odyssey* was a poetic strategy to sharpen the contrast with Odysseus' nine-year-long effort to achieve his homecoming. Another suggestion saw the journey as the poet's way to emphasize the theme of courtesy. In that view the *Odyssey* is at least in part a worldly how-to book. It tells of what goes on in great houses and how one is to behave in them. It elaborates the religious importance of hospitality on the part of the host and the reciprocal obligations of the guest. Telemachus, the unsophisticated boy from the sheepherding land of Ithaca, has everything to learn from a social tour of foreign capitals. He needs not only advice about how to handle his first ship's command but also a guide experienced in good manners. Carrying this line of thinking further, still other critics saw Telemachus' quest as a parallel to that of Odysseus. Father and son both have to strengthen themselves for the final battle to rid Ithaca of Penelope's grasping suitors. Telemachus' assertion of his independence and his acquisition of the social arts expected of a prince are thus a complement to Odysseus' ordeal on the open sea, to test a man's physical and mental endurance. Explanations like these seem to be attempts to unify the various strands of myth, folklore, and custom in the epic as we have it.

To historians, however, the view that the episode is about the worldly education of a princeling has other implications. Courtesies like those the poet describes suggest a level of civilization far higher than any known to the poet or his audience in the eighth century, the date normally given to Homer. Details that an ordinary reader would probably overlook might to the historian be valuable clues to Bronze Age realities. It might even be that Homer, or some earlier epic singer, deliberately included Telemachus' story in order to describe a lost culture. For example, during the festival, Nestor commands that the horns of the sacrificial bull be gilded. Surely this implies that there is available a metals workshop and sufficient gold. Later, when Telemachus suggests he will sleep on his ship with his men, Nestor laughingly protests that he has many fine blankets to make sleep soft. Do blankets indicate a flourishing trade with sheep-rearing lands? Or again, what distant or remote splendors are hinted at in the passage that occurs at the end of the beach party?

> Then Nestor of Gerenia led them all,
> his sons and sons-in-law, to his great house;
> and in they went to the famous hall of Nestor,
> taking their seats on thrones and easy chairs,
> while the old man mixed water in a wine bowl
> with sweet red wine, mellowed eleven years
> before his housekeeper uncapped the jar.
>
> [Book III: 386–392]

Nestor pours a libation and prays. Then, the passage continues,

> ... all the company went to their quarters,
> and Nestor of Gerenia showed Telemakhos
> under the echoing eastern entrance hall
> to a fine bed near the bed of Peisistratos,
> captain of spearmen, his unmarried son.
> Then he lay down in his own inner chamber
> where his dear faithful wife had smoothed his bed.
>
> [Book III:395–403]

What is a "great house"? Why is Nestor's hall famous? Thrones and easy chairs are not the furnishings of even aristocratic families in the eighth century, nor is there usually sufficient wine for large amounts to be kept mellowing eleven years. How can all this company be bedded in comfort? Nestor's eldest son, Peisistratos, is "captain of spearmen." Does that imply a standing army organized in functional units like infantry, cavalry, and so on? Finally, where is this legendary place?

Some of these questions may have been in the minds of C. W. Blegen and his associates on April 4, 1939, when they mounted a steep hill in Messenia commanding a magnificent view of the Bay of Navarino. A year earlier, their discovery of several royal tombs in the area had led them to surmise the existence of a royal residence nearby. Now they stood looking at two masses of hard, concretelike debris projecting from the olive grove occupying the hill called Epano Englianos. They decided to excavate and on the very first trial dig uncovered stone walls, fragments of frescoes, stucco floors, five tablets inscribed in a strange pictorial language, and Mycenaean pottery—all of which confirmed their deductions that the hill covered a sizable and important site.

World War II and its complicated political aftermath came between that first day of discovery and any opportunity for methodical work. The long-delayed excavation finally got under way in 1952 and continued year by year until 1961, when Blegen announced his findings. Slow and patient clearing of thirty-one centuries' worth of vegetation and overgrowth revealed a huge structure with forty-nine rooms in the central section of its main floor, and more on what was an upper story. The entire foundation and those of several outlying buildings showed unmistakable signs of having been razed by fire. Calcinated remains of flooring, charred bits of wall and wall fresco were painstakingly cleaned under conditions of mounting excitement as pieces of this enormous puzzle began to fit together. Carbon-14 dating put the date of the destruction at about 1200 B.C. According to Blegen and other scholars—and the point is still controversial—this meant that the structure fell one generation after the violent destruction of Troy VIIa, that brought the legendary war to a close. It was, then, within the realm of possibility that a connection could be drawn between Pylos, the Pylians talked about in the *Iliad,* and this palace. Its location in the westernmost part of the Peloponnese fitted Homer's geographical references to Nestor's kingdom. Moreover, its dominating position on the high plateau implied the authority of its owner at least over the lower town on its northwest, southwest, and southeast slopes. The palace buildings themselves attested to royal magnificence of a settled and permanent nature. As room after room was cleared, it became obvious that this was the establishment of a wealthy and important king. Blegen was convinced he had found Nestor's palace at Pylos.

It was a spacious palace of conspicuous luxury. All the important rooms were lavishly and colorfully decorated with figures of gods and animals in fresco. (See Illus. 49.) In one panel a long-robed figure (Apollo? Orpheus?) sits on a mountaintop playing his lyre. From the remains of other panels we see that griffins, lions, bears, and horses once paraded around plaster walls in larger-than-life size, evoking the wonder of lands distant from Pylos and arduous to reach.

The experience of Telemachus' visit can be recreated by walking through the apartments of state at the core of this pretentious Mycenaean structure. Like the great hall at Mycenae, the one at Pylos was used for dining, conducting state business, and receiving guests. Telemachus would have moved through the great length of the central complex by first approaching the entranceway, or propylon, at its southeast end (see Illus. 51, Rooms 1–2). Next on his progress was the central court (Room 3), paved with stucco and open to the sky. Passing through a portico (Room 4) which had two large columns supporting the start of the roof, and through the doorway to the vestibule (Room 5), from which lateral doorways gave access to the upper story, he would finally have reached the entrance to the throne room (Room 6). This was some 43 feet long and 37 feet wide, and it had four fluted wooden columns ranged around a magnificent central hearth extremely well preserved. The hearth was edged with a flame pattern and had painted spirals running horizontally around its raised rim. Overhead, a small round opening in the roof provided ventilation. But it is probable that there was also a clerestory for light and air around the room at the gallery level. The floor was laid out in a checkerboard of brightly painted abstract designs. A large semi-realistic octopus was painted directly in front of a rectangular recess that must have held a built-in throne. This square, on which the king must have gazed, is presumed to have had some symbolic significance. A stone lion and griffin stood at either side of the throne, and more were painted on the walls, whose decoration included processions, duels, and sieges.

The galleried upper story, eight steps to which are still preserved, seems to have been living quarters for women, since combs and cosmetic boxes found in the central court must have fallen

49. Reconstruction of the Horse Frieze at Pylos.

from above. The queen, however, had her own grand apartments (Rooms 46–53). Directly underneath the second-story balconies were many pantries stocked and ready to serve the central megaron. And not far from the main court, off a little to the right, was a finely fitted-out bathroom (Room 43) making it clear to us that Telemachus' bath was an important and true detail of the famous Greek hospitality. A large tub rested on a base broad enough for a bath attendant to stand on. (See Illus. 50.) Unlike the many clay tubs in Crete, or the one at Mycenae, this one seems to have had no connection with burial rituals and is therefore firmly identified as a bathtub rather than a larnax. The placement of its painted decoration of leaves and spirals on the inside surfaces further distinguishes the tub at Pylos from others whose outer sides carried painted funerary motifs. Large jars, presumably for·the water that was poured over the bather, stood in one corner of the room. A small chest—for toiletries?—occupied another corner. In the tub itself was found a small cuplike vessel, either to hold the oils that Homer says anointed Telemachus before he was "dressed like a god," or to contain the wine the bather drank to enhance his already pleasant experience.

Nestor's palace was well equipped for royal banquets. Beside the front door was a small service room (Room 60) stocked with eight hundred pottery jars for wine and water ready to greet guests. Next to the throne room, a large set of storerooms (Rooms 18–21) similarly was found to contain large wine jars set to cool before serving to the dignitaries and petitioners awaiting audience with the king. And the large wine magazine at the northern corner of the grounds (Rooms 104–105), also overfilled with pottery, makes it clear that the service rooms within the building complex were easily resupplied and in constant use. In all, over eight thousand jars and vessels of many shapes, sizes, and styles were found at Pylos, each adding testimony to the enormous quantities of oil, water, wine, grain, and other commodities brought, exchanged, stored, and consumed at the establishment. None of these vessels, however, quite matches Homer's description of the "beautifully wrought cup" that old Nestor brought with him from home to Troy.

> It was set with golden nails, the eared handles upon it were four, and on either side there were fashioned two doves of gold, feeding, and there were double bases beneath it. Another man with great effort could lift it full from the table, but Nestor, aged as he was, lifted it without strain.   [*Iliad*, Book XI: 633–6]

50. The bathtub at Pylos.

A dove cup found in one of Mycenae's shaft graves is one of two that have been identified with excitement as the original golden vessel. The second, a delightful token of the respect that later ages accorded to Homer's heroes, bears the inscription, "I am the cup of Nestor." The urge to link these cups to Nestor illustrates our wish to make Homerica genuinely Mycenaean. Nevertheless, the word that Homer translates as "cup" was probably something like a soup tureen, *depas,* in the Bronze Age. One such *depas* listed on a Pylos Linear B tablet is, like Nestor's, large, with "four ears." And many household pots found in Crete had false bottoms, the probable

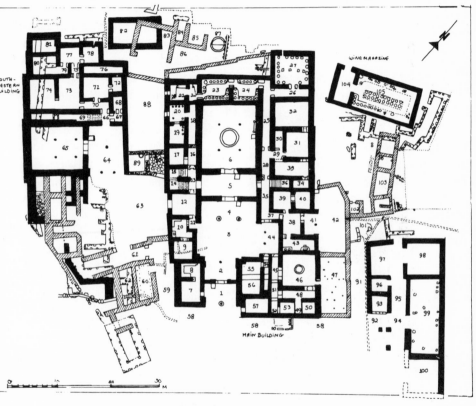

51. THE PALACE OF NESTOR
KEY PLAN

1-2 Propylon	29 Lobby	63 Court
3 Court	36 Northeast Stairway	64 Entrance Hall
4 Portico	37 Corridor	65 Hall
5 Vestibule	38 Lobby	66 Lobby
6 Throne Room	41 Northeast Gateway	67, 68 Pantries
7, 8 Archives Rooms	42 Court	69 Stairway
9 Pantry	43 Bathroom	70 Corridor
10 Waiting Room	44 Northeast Stoa	75, 79 Lobbies
11 Lobby	45, 51, 52 Southeast	76 Light-well
12 Possible Southwest	Corridor	88 Court
Entrance	46 Queen's Hall	91 Open Ramp
13 Corridor	47 Court	92 Court
14-15 Southwest Stairway	48, 49 Corridors	93 Shrine
18, 19, 20, 21, 22 Pantries	54 Southeast Stairway	94 Colonnade
23, 24, 32 Oil Magazines	58 Court	95 Corridor
25, 28, 35 Northeast Corridor	59 Open Ramp	101 Street
26 Corridor	60 Pantry	102 Reservoir
27 North Magazine	61 Corridor	104-105 Wine Magazine

Numbers on the plan not mentioned in the above list designate rooms and areas whose specific use has not been determined.

meaning of Homer's reference to "double bases" beneath the vessel.

Of all the finds at Pylos none was so overwhelmingly significant as the more than one thousand clay tablets, fortuitously baked into permanence by the final blaze, heaped in what is now called the archives room. When Blegen first looked at them, he recognized a resemblance to the writing on the tablets found a generation earlier by Evans at Knossos. In the interval, Linear B tablets had turned up in relatively small quantities at Mycenae, Thebes, and other sites. Not until the hoard at Pylos, however, were there a sufficient number of them for decipherment to progress systematically. Everything about the story of the tablets and their brilliant decoding by Michael Ventris was revolutionary to old conceptions about the ancient Greeks and fascinating to all who did not expect miracles of science, history, or fortune. First, here was undeniable proof that Minoans and mainland Greeks used the same ideogram language (see Chapter VI). The amazing uniformity of the scripts at Knossos and Pylos was only a little less startling than the fact that there was writing at all on mainland pre-Classical Greece, so long thought to have been illiterate. To the contrary, the tablets proved to be the work of rigidly trained scribes—one class in a highly diversified society of specialists which these records revealed.

What emerged as Ventris' deciphering progressed was a Bronze Age world whose complexity archaeologists had only guessed at. Here was the picture of a comprehensive bureaucracy, elaborately organized and minutely administered. The monarchy's unquenchable thirst for information was evident in these probing lists of the affairs of people in every level of society, from the highest officers of state down to the slave of the manual worker. Officialdom had the power to demand and the duty to record infinite detail about men, women, and children. What are the wheat and fig rations for thirty-seven female bath attendants and twenty-eight children at Pylos? How many nurses are employed in a particular Cretan village? (Two.) Where might one find a pair of brassbound chariot wheels (labeled "useless")? How many slaves has Korudallos (an unidentified male) and what are they doing? Who is watching over the cattle of Thalamatas? These and countless other seemingly small questions like them can be answered from the tablets—not that we are sure why they should be asked.

More apparently significant business is just as carefully listed. One tablet tells of the presence at Pylos of at least one Cypriot trader: "a man from Cyprus," recalling a similar reference to one "Maron of Cyprus" on the Knossos Linear B tablets. As a whole the tablets show that every sort of industrial manufacture, material, agricultural produce and livestock, all kinds of holdings of all kinds of lands, the administration of religious festivals, the movements of troops and the manning of ships—all are subject to a vast officialdom. Eighteen places are each obliged to make contributions to Pylos of six commodities—bronze, wool, wine, barley, and so on in a fixed schedule of assessment. Something of the Pylian bookkeeping system can be gleaned from tablet Un 1322, on which payments to a netmaker and a weaver are made in wheat and figs. Another entry equates an amount of wheat with an unspecified number of garments. Here is the first record of an exchange of commodities. Perhaps the number of garments was not specified because there was a standard payment per garment which would have allowed officials to calculate the number. Since the person from whom the garment is received is not named, the point of view is that of the official in charge of the granary: he records the circumstances under which grain is dispensed. The record of goods received in the exchange would have been the province of another official, and therefore would have been shown on another tablet.

Several particularly intriguing tablets conjure an image of the Pylian soldier. His armor was identical to that of his kinsman at Knossos: a two-piece coat of mail with plates *(o-pa-wo-ta)* sewn on in five rows, and a helmet with four plates and two cheekpieces. The equipment invites comparison with the well-known finds of Mycenaean armor at Dendra. Five rows of plates are composed of twenty larger and ten smaller bronze segments to form the coat. The shoulders were protected by two curving plates which seem to correspond to descriptions in Homer. Three horizontal strips of bronze in front and three more behind complete the corselet. The Dendra helmet, like the Pylian Linear B one, has four bronze plates and two cheekpieces, but it corresponds more closely to Homeric descriptions in its addition of protective boars' tusks. The Dendra armor was simply attached to a leather jerkin and is dated by the ceramics in the tombs to c. 1450–1400. Later, Pylian corselets required a somewhat higher degree of technical skill, for they do not seem to have been structured over basic leather undergarments.

All this information is clearly not of equal importance. The equipment of soldiery and the number of pottery jars available for oil must have had markedly different significance, a point about which more will be said. Still, the ultimate purpose of the archives is conjectural. The tablets represent a part only of the records for a single year. Yet the fact that they preserve thousands of transactions in hundreds of places implies that Pylos was the monarchic seat of a powerful government which administered several smaller kingdoms. To a modern consciousness—accustomed to the privileged inquisitiveness of tax offices, the personnel files of large corporations, the multiple-copy forms for driver's licenses, charge accounts, and passports—a many-headed bureaucracy at work is not a wonder but the sign of a normal way of life. To marvel at Pylos we need to remind ourselves not only that in Egypt an equally great storage government was flourishing, but also that after 1200 B.C. most of the Aegean reverted to a level of civilization economically poorer and politically simpler than the one at Pylos.

Evidence that the palace at Englianos was Nestor's is strong. In its general characteristics, its size, contour, decor, and function, the palace, including its most recently uncovered outer walls, gate, and the lower town, is the only such complex structure in the whole of the western Peloponnesos. Historians could hardly be convinced that Homer's "sandy Pylos" and Blegen's Englianos were one and the same merely because Homer calls Nestor "Lord of the Western Approaches."

It is known, however, that Nestor's ancestors, the Neleid family, were the only dynasty in the Peloponnesos politically and economically on equal terms with the lords of Mycenae, Tiryns, and Sparta—all of whom sent divisions of men and supplies to the Trojan War. There is, moreover, a long and complex mythological tradition about the Pylians that derives in part from a lost epic that Homer seems to have known. To judge from the fragmented references to it that he incorporated into his epic poem *Nekyia* and into the *Iliad,* the Pylian epos was more historical in character than mythological, concerned with the dispersion of Minyans from Boeotia, first to the southwest Peloponnese and later to Ionia. The sense of both the tradition taken as a whole and Homer's references to it is that the Minyans brought a Mycenaean civilization to Messenia. Whether Neleus, Nestor's father, was himself a Minyan is not clear. In one passage he is said to have set out from Boeotia to conquer or acquire by some other means the settlement he found at Pylos. This he razed before rebuilding his own dynastic seat. Here tradition matches fact. According to findings at the deepest layer of excavation, a settlement earlier than Nestor's was demolished by burning before a new citadel in a new architectural style was built on the hilltop. The *Nekyia* simply says that Neleus, king of Pylos, married Chloris, the youngest daughter of the Minyan king of Orchomenos. Strabo, the Roman historian, thinks that the River Minyeios in the district of Pylos, mentioned in the *Iliad,* took its name from the Minyans who came along with the royal bride.

The later history of the family is clearer. Neleus was succeeded by his son Nestor, who ruled for at least three generations before being succeeded first by his nephew, and then by other Neleids through another three generations before Pylos was invaded and captured by the Dorians. More evidence can be pieced together in detective-story fashion from information on the Linear B tablets. The name Pylos appears on more than fifty tablets in contexts that can sensibly refer only to the palace at Englianos. Still more startling is the fact that two towns named in the *Iliad* correspond to two recorded on the tablets. As already pointed out, these government records show that Pylos exercised authority over two groups of subordinate kingships or dependencies. One group is comprised of nine communities, always listed in a fixed order; the other, of seven communities, also listed in fixed order. Both the groupings and the numbers nine and seven tally with the information about Nestor in the *Iliad.* In the Catalog of Ships that each king has contributed to the wars, King Nestor is said to rule nine towns. When Agamemnon and Achilles quarrel, the commander-in-chief offers the hero a group of seven towns, situated on the Gulf of Messenia, as a peace bond. Presumably Nestor agrees to the gift of some of his lands as an inducement to the sulking hero to rejoin the wars.

The tablets thus show nothing to contradict Homer's picture of Nestor as the ruler of a populous and powerful state to which other states owe some sort of allegiance. One scholar, for example, estimates the number of people at Pylos itself as 347 women, 240 girls, 159 boys. (Curiously enough, men are not numbered, perhaps because only dependents were of concern.) In such a context the thirty-seven "bath pourers" listed on the Pylos tablets were understandable, and Telemachus' bath was truly an epic event. As for other men and women mentioned on the tablets, they may be allies, captives, or refugees, but their very presence in such numbers only strengthens the evidence for a connection between Englianos and Homer. So do the pottery styles, so important to archaeologists for dating their finds. At Englianos, no pottery has been found with designs known to have been current after 1200 B.C. It can hardly be mere coincidence that the dates approximated for the pottery, the carbon-14 dating results, and the information on the tablets all

agree so well with the Greek literary tradition. Numerous smaller
Mycenaean settlements have been discovered throughout the
whole of the Pylian region, but nowhere has a palace been found
that vies with the one at Englianos.

Once the full complexity and splendor of Nestor's Pylos is
understood, several other details of the Telemachus story fall into
place. Small wonder that the young prince, reared in mountainous
country and ignorant of the great world, needs an older companion
as a guide. That detail is merely an ancient equivalent of any
modern tale about a country boy introduced to salon society.
Telemachus needs instruction in how to address his host, the elder
statesman and confidant of Agamemnon and a king for three
generations over all of Messenia. Noble blood is no substitute for
practice in courtly manners. We can also guess at why Homer has
Telemachus arrive during the ritual festival honoring Poseidon,
strange timing since Odysseus is in disfavor with Poseidon. Would
a son in search of his father be successful in a place that worships
his father's enemy? The Linear B tablets confirm that Poseidon was
one of the two chief divinities at Pylos; therefore the poet, in spite
of literary continuity, may be reflecting an outstanding tradition of
the place he is telling about—a tradition his audience may well have
known from other tales about the Pylians.

It may have been equally well-known to them that Messenia
was rich in horses, for that is true of other plain land in Greece. The
parting gift to Telemachus of a chariot and relays of horses for the
next leg of his journey to Sparta may therefore shed light on
Homer's repeated association of Nestor with horses—"Nestor,
breaker of horses" and "Nestor, the Gerenian horseman." And
finally, it is from a "sheer city" that Telemachus takes his leave, and
one perched on a hilltop matches Homer's descriptive image:

> ... they winged their way unreluctant into the plain and left
> behind the sheer city of Pylos.

Telemachus' visit must have taken place sometime shortly
before 1200, after Nestor returned from Troy, but before Odysseus
found his way to Ithaca. Nothing in the poem betrays that Pylos
was under any threat of danger, or that business and housekeeping
at the palace were operating in other than a usual fashion. In that
same year, nevertheless, Pylos was razed by invaders that Professor
Blegen identified as Dorians. Death came swiftly to the Pylians at a
moment when they were engaged in the routine tasks of everyday

life. How is it that, elsewhere on the mainland, rumblings of danger had been heard for fifty years and were being answered by the construction of fortifications? Was Pylos alone unprepared for the attack that took her life? Was her lack of fortifications of any sort a matter of heedlessness? of overconfidence? In short, what happened at Pylos?

It first must be said that there is not a single trace anywhere in Greece of the Dorians. Never during an assault did they lose an iron sword that might have been found among the charred ruins of a Mycenaean citadel and used to testify, Here was a Dorian. They exist only on the authority of the Classical historians Herodotus and Thucydides, who claim that a people ruder and more primitive than the Achaeans spilled into Greece eighty years after the fall of Troy (traditionally dated to 1184). Archaeologists know that they used a cist-tomb form of burial, and that they used iron weapons. These two features mark a passage southward through central Greece, appearing first in Epirus or western Thessaly and later stretching from northwestern Greece across the Corinthian Gulf and into the western Peloponnese. On their route these "Dorians," or new Greeks, destroyed all the Bronze Age kingdoms except Athens, a point of Athenian pride; occupied most of the Peloponnese, Rhodes, and most of Crete; and introduced a Doric dialect of Greek. As a result, Greeks of the Achaean stock migrated to the coast of Asia Minor and to islands on the fringes of the Aegean basin, where the Ionian dialect continued into the Classical period. Many modern scholars have found no reason to doubt the general accuracy of this account, although nearly all its details are missing. Some suggest that humble people of Dorian stock may have been moving southward into the Peloponnese and mingling with Achaeans of the lower classes for years before their warrior class launched their attacks. Others go further and posit small groups of Dorians taking up residence on landfalls outlying the Peloponnesos during the second half of the thirteenth century, and then taking advantage of the peninsula itself when it was weakened by the removal of most of its weapon-bearing manpower to Troy. There is no hard evidence of these theories either way, and they are, in any case, only tangential to the circumstances at Pylos.

A few years ago Professor L. B. Palmer remarked that "a sense of emergency pervades the whole Pylian Linear B archive." The handwritings of forty scribes have been distinguished in the Pylian tablets. Of these only eight seem to have been responsible for most of the tablets, leaving open the probability that the others also functioned in other capacities: a steward, for instance, might have taken the animal census; an oil merchant might have weighed and checked deliveries of oil. Tax accountants, stationed in the archive room, would also have been transcribing the clay tablets into permanent records. Given all this activity, and given the passion for record keeping that the Pylos bureaucracy betrays, one thousand tablets is a small output for forty scribes unless the tablets cover only a very short period of time. If that is the case, the "emergency" that Professor Palmer detects was perhaps weeks away. And, if his interpretations of the tablets is accepted, Pylos did have some warning of impending trouble. What seem to be military plans described in the tablets are a cornerstone in his deductions. Nowhere in the over three thousand tablets at Knossos, another unfortified city, is there any mention of military activity; therefore it may have been unusual to describe the deployment of soldiers, the position of guard stations, and the like. (See Illus. 52.)

An important set of tablets suggesting preparations to defend the city is headed, "How the watchers are guarding the coastal regions." Each coast-watching unit is distinguished by the name of its commander, probably a local nobleman. After his name follows a place name, presumed to be the place where his unit was stationed. A list of officers (?) follows, and then numbers of men, thus giving the precise manpower strength of the units (roughly one hundred each). Each unit also had attached to it someone called a companion. Like the commander, the companion was a nobleman, so presumably owned a chariot. It would be logical to assume that his function with the unit was to relay messages to headquarters. One of the great noblemen named on the tablets is Echelawon, who was posted with the *lawagetas,* or leader of the host, at a place called *A-pe-e-ke*. This spot on the Messenian Gulf may therefore have been the general headquarters.

52. Linear B tablet at Knossos listing military equipment.

In another set of tablets "rowers" are listed "going to Pleuron" and other locations. Forty is the usual number of rowers in one group, suggesting that this is the usual complement of seamen for one ship. Were these, as one opinion has it, merchant vessels converted by need into warships? So few place names of the Mycenaean period have survived that it is difficult to locate the fleet by the place names given. But Nestor's "nine towns" and "seven towns" are so regularly inscribed in an unvarying order that it has been possible to reconstruct a hypothetical geography. The coast-watching infantry seems to have been stationed at the north and south ends of the Pylian coast. None seems to have been sent to the center of the coastline, but this is where places like Pleuron have conjecturally been located. The tablets contain no reference to a standing army or a reserve of troops at the ready. But since the time covered by the tablet record may have been very brief, an army may have been organized and positioned sometime before the record begins.

Professor Palmer's impression from other, somewhat more confused, tablets is that logistical support had been arranged for the Pylian forces. It would seem that musters of bronze workers, bakers, and other craftsmen were being sent to southern Messenia, where the rowers were concentrated. The bronzesmiths, we note, would have been invaluable in their function as armorers. To this point Joseph Alsop, in his book *From the Silent Earth,* makes a persuasive contribution. He notices that the most impressive evidence of invasion preparation at Pylos comes from the decipherments of Ventris and Chadwick and has to do with collections and allocations of bronze. Scrap or ingot bronze was gathered from local officials with the title of *ko-re-te* (mayor?) in all the Pylian administrative districts. The tablets also record issues of bronze to bronzesmiths all over Pylos. On these are given a place name, the name of the smith who received the allocation, and its quantity. Below are also listed names of "smiths having no allocation." Alsop surmises that the object of listing those to whom no bronze was given was to have ready a register of unemployed workers to be put to work when more bronze was available. The quantities of bronze allocated during the brief period of the tablets' record must be a significant feature of the situation at Pylos during its last days. Over a ton, or 1046 kilograms, of bronze was collected from the district officials, and of that more than four-fifths was allocated to 193 smiths. In a period when bronze was a semiprecious metal, these were considerable quantities. The two amounts of bronze most commonly allocated to smiths were 1.5 kilograms, enough to make one thousand small Mycenaean arrowheads, and 5 kilograms, enough for fourteen Mycenaean swords. The total allocation of bronze would have been sufficient to produce 534,000 arrowheads or 23,000 swords—a large number indeed when it is remembered that the numbers of men in the coast-watching units totaled about one thousand.

It was not only the military tablets that impressed Professor Palmer as bearing a sense of emergency. Many tablets concern the movement of women and children to safe places, either within Pylos itself or to a place called Leuktron, perhaps the kingdom's secondary administrative center. Rations are shown to have been issued to these people whom another scholar calls "fugitives." On one tablet of this group ninety women and children are assigned to be "grain pourers," interpreted to mean bread makers substituting for the regular bakers called up to military service. Another tablet shows that fourteen slaves from the kingdom's chief sanctuary at Pakijana, together with the sanctuary's "sacred gold," had been removed to the palace, an extraordinary action which suggests they had been shifted for safekeeping. And a still further series of tablets tells of the collection from many villages of a commodity at first thought to have been flax and later identified as linseed. That each coast-watching unit received amounts of the linseed proportional to its strength in manpower was a puzzling fact until it was recalled that linseed was used as an iron-rich ration by the later Greeks during later wars. So even this seemingly unrelated detail contributes to a picture of Pylos preparing for invasion. Lastly, there is one tablet among those published by Ventris and Chadwick that rings an ironic note. It lists the "masons going to build" at Pylos and three other places, and the rations issued to them sufficient to last twenty days. Is this the hint of an effort to construct fortification walls—too small an effort and far too late? Was there some last-minute warning to the Pylians that destruction would come not from the sea, where they were organized and strong, but from the land, where they were confident and unprotected? In any case, the daily round of life went on without panic up to the city's very final moments.

2

Nestor prepares Telemachus for his visit to Menelaos by telling the tale of their joint return from Troy. They left the destroyed city together, he says, "with friendly thoughts toward each other" and reached holy Sounion on the cape of Athens. There Menelaos' steersman was killed by the "painless arrows of Apollo"(?), and so the hero had to halt his journey to bury the dead man and give him due rites. Nestor proceeded to Pylos on his own without difficulty; but Menelaos' ships were now set upon by storms. His fleet was cut in two parts, and those ships that remained to him were blown to Crete. From there he crossed to Egypt, Nestor says, where he stayed for eight years. Menelaos himself tells the rest of his story to Telemachus when the young prince has been welcomed in Sparta. No details of the long sojourn in Egypt are offered, but the duration of his stay suggests that the hero made the country a tolerable temporary home. (Perhaps Euripides found in this passage the idea for his proposal that the enigmatic Helen was already there, waiting for her husband, when he arrived. She was innocent, he says in his play *Helen,* of having dallied with Paris at Troy. The Trojan Helen was a charming figment, a decoy placed there by the clever Aphrodite to keep Paris amused while she protected the wifely reputation of the true Helen!) Menelaos must have had ships and money at his disposal (his war booty?) for he made trips to Libya, Cyprus, and Phoenicia, in each of which places he was entertained hospitably. Eventually he made his way to Pharos, where the Old Man of the Sea, Proteus, told him of the fates of Agamemnon and Odysseus. Menelaos then returned to Egypt, raised a cenotaph to his brother, and proceeded onward to his home in Sparta without further delay.

Relative to the homecomings of the other heroes, that of Menelaos is peaceful and somewhat romantic. Although eight years elapse between the war's end and his return to Sparta, the interval does not seem to have been hazardous. Nor is he greeted by disasters at home. Homer's picture of Menelaos and Helen at home is rich, quiet, and wholly domestic. There are no clues to the source of Sparta's power, and no hint of the role it plays in the declining fortunes of the Peloponnesos in the twelfth century. Unfortunately, archaeology has nothing to add to Homer's information. Neither tombs nor citadels that might suggest a link to Menelaos' story have ever been found in Sparta. Instead, artefacts, pottery, and the prevalence of the Doric dialect testify that Menelaos' city became the greatest of the Dorian states. How the transition occurred, however, is a mystery.

Equally mysterious is the truth about Menelaos' stay in Egypt, for it raises the issue of Mycenaean-Egyptian relations at the turn of the thirteenth century. Homer's references to Egypt, Libya, Cyprus, and Phoenicia as places where the hero was welcomed imply there was a similar degree of Mycenaean familiarity with each place. Yet about Libya in the Bronze Age all is hypothesis. Some of the Minoan racial stock may have originated there, as we saw in Chapter I, and for centuries its geographical location directly south of Crete seemed to prevent the Mycenaeans from engaging with the country directly. Of the flourishing Mycenaean community of En-komi on Cyprus and of that island's importance as a source of copper, Menelaos' tale seems to be unaware. So, too, the mere mention of Phoenicia contributes not at all to our store of information about the country's ambiguous relations with the Myce-naeans. The imprecision in these three references would seem to prove that Homer is simply inserting into his narrative names of places that came down through the tradition because they were once famous and had by his time become exotic. Yet Egypt is a different case. Greek myth is filled with references to Egypt and places that may be Egyptian. So strong is the folk memory of a time when Greece and Egypt were in close contact that Herodotus traveled there seeking out resemblances between Egyptian and Greek custom in order to prove that the older culture was the parent of his own. Nor is there any lack of hard evidence to prove that the two cultures were acquainted, as scattered allusions to the fact in this text show. There are numerous Mycenaean artefacts in Egypt and vice versa, but whether the contact they imply was direct or through a middleman is not at all clear. Whether, moreover, the two countries were in contact at all at the turn of the thirteenth century, when Menelaos would have been visiting, is very conjectural.

In the sixteenth century, Egyptian segmented beads of faience made a chain stretching northward into central and western Europe, passing through Mycenae as the central link. The beads probably were being retraded for other commodities on this long route, or perhaps were used as a form of currency. Several of the shaft graves of Mycenae (see Chapter V) contained rare and beautiful Egyptian wares. They may, however, have been acquired in any number of ways, including trade, although their rarity mitigates against that. There is pottery evidence in Syria and Palestine indicating that Mycenaeans and Egyptians were trading during the fifteenth century; yet again, the evidence does not tell whether this contact was direct or indirect. A Hurrite cylinder seal from the hinterland of northern Syria, for instance, is very similar to one at Argos, but it may have made most of its journey to the mainland in the pocket of a Minoan sailor. The bulk of Nubian gold reaching Mediterranean shores in the Bronze Age doubtless passed through Egyptian hands. But like fine linen, a product of Egypt from time immemorial, it reached the Greeks through Phoenician markets. The very word for the Greek garment made of Egyptian linen—chiton—has Semitic associations, a reminder that the seafarers with virtual monopoly on commerce in the ancient world were not Greek but Phoenician. A considerable quantity of pottery of Rhodian and Cypriot types dating to c. 1400 suggests the possibility that the Mycenaeans had established a small commercial settlement at Tel el Amarna. Mycenaean pottery from other provinces also appears at other Egyptian sites, suggesting continuing and fruitful exchange. Then these traces of Mycenaean penetration into Egypt ended with the death of Tutankhamen c. 1340. Not one piece of pottery is referrable to a date thereafter, and conversely by the thirteenth century Egyptian objects all but ceased to appear on the mainland. There is a tantalizing hint that the Libyan king Mer'eye may have used groups of Mycenaeans as allies or as mercenaries in an expedition of Sea Peoples against the Delta Egyptians in about 1225. This was the moment when Menelaos and Odysseus, too, were supposed to have visited Egypt, although there is no hint that either of them served as mercenaries. Even though ancient alliances were in flux all over the Aegean (see Chapter V), it is not likely that whole Mycenaean colonies or cities would have taken part as Sea Peoples in the march against Egypt through Syria and Phoenicia that was stopped by Rameses III, for they still had vital interests in the Levant.

To summarize, then, Mycenaeans may have been engaged in some degree of trade with Egypt until about 1400. After about 1340, contact between the two countries diminished, and there followed a period where relations between the two nations may have deteriorated to outright hostility. Finally, in post-Mycenaean days, there was an absolute severance of their relations. In the *Odyssey*, Egypt is a name only a little more familiar than Phoenicia. Homer's ignorance of the place is evident in the trouble Menelaos has in reaching Proteus' home on Pharos, only a day's sail away from the

Egyptian coast. The only Egyptian town mentioned is Thebes, and that was not reopened to the Greeks until the seventh century. Perhaps its name survived because visitors in its great days came from the Aegean and the Levant and spread its fame.

3

The Ithaca to which Telemachus returned differed markedly from both Pylos and Sparta. Nestor administered properties and people engaged in every manner of occupation necessary to sustain a diversified and affluent kingdom. His palace architecture was a late development of Mycenaean styles, in contrast in every way to the more brutal splendor of Mycenae and Tiryns. By the time Nestor's family built Pylos, a culture that was class-conscious and bureaucratic, peaceful and commercially oriented, had evolved out of the simpler warlike aristocracies of the eastern Mycenaean centers. Odysseus' kingdom, in the far west, was more primitive than Nestor's and more land-oriented than the eastern ones. His holdings on the island of Ithaca and nearby Epirus supported a population that was mainly pastoral or engaged in home industries like tanning, pottery making, and spinning.

Even seafaring was either a prerogative of the wealthy or a communal undertaking. When, for example, Telemachus decides to set out on the search for news of his father, an assembly of Ithacan elders is called upon to equip him with a ship and twenty crewmen. Telemachus' status as a dependent of Odysseus' household, and the enmity of Penelope's powerful suitors, may be why the assembly refuses his request. Athena circumvents the assembly decision by borrowing a vessel for him from the shipowner Noemon, and she herself recruits a crew. Noemon is then careful to apologize to the suitors, protesting that he could not refuse so great a young nobleman. The sense of the incident seems to indicate that ships belonged to the man who could afford to build them. If the assembly so judged, however, the owner was obliged to place his ship at the disposal of the tribe, who then supplied him with a crew. Since the aristocratic owner was also, necessarily, an important member of the tribal assembly, his vote in council was doubly powerful. Whether this system of republicanism among the elite was common to other Mycenaean kingdoms is not known. The incident may be truer of custom in Homer's day than in Mycenaean times. Or again, there may be some confusion in the incident of practices from both times.

In spite of their modesty compared to Pylos, Odysseus' properties are extensive enough to have excited the envy of one hundred suitors for Penelope's hand in marriage. An estimate of this wealth can be gleaned from a conversation between the hero, disguised as a beggar, and his old swineherd, Eumaeus. The old man is bewailing the depredations to the master's herds made by the ill-bred suitors. "My lord," he says, "was enormously wealthy; there wasn't a lord on the black continent or in Ithaca itself to touch him. . . . [He had] on the mainland, twelve herds of cattle, as many flocks of sheep, as many droves of pigs, and as many scattered herds of goats, all tended by hired labour or his own herdsmen; while here in Ithaca eleven herds of goats graze. . . ." Eumaeus, chief of the swineherds, also looks after "twelve of swine." What all this amounts to is about thirty thousand head of animals, at a low figure. One could be rich on much less.

Land was the sign and legal token of status and position in the state. Maintaining property from generation to generation involved anxieties and stratagems on the part of fathers and sons. Old Laertes, Odysseus' father, bought up the property of a relative in financial straits; he also encroached on the fallow lands that were common property of the state; and then he enlarged his domain farther by asserting squatter's rights. The disguised Odysseus, telling an inventive life story to Eumaeus, advises that another way to hold onto inherited lands is to limit the number of legitimate births in a family. Sons of concubines, he says, receive only a house and a small plot. Is there an echo here of the problem of over-population in the Archaic Age? In no period, of course, does the acquisitive nature lack resources for accumulating wealth. The great gift exchanges between Mycenaeans were certainly one. A wife like Penelope with independent possessions was another. And movable possessions in metals and jewels were the other measure of riches. At Ithaca the king's storeroom holds "stocks of bronze, of gold and of wrought iron." It is also an arsenal filled with reserves of weapons and armor, and a place for treasured articles like Odysseus' incurved bow and quiver full of deadly arrows.

From the extent of the lands owned in the family's name, one might imagine a more lavish family seat than is likely to have been the case. Homeric scholars hypothesize that Ithaca's central town was very like the small town of Chios, founded in the eighth century and lasting to the end of the seventh. About fifty small houses were grouped around an acropolis containing a large house and a separate temple to Athena. The total number of people living in the town unit and subsisting on its produce would have been about 250. From the language of one of the suitor's insults, we know that Odysseus' house is just above a small town surrounded by farmland. The suitor says that he would offer the vagabond (Odysseus in disguise) good farm work at a proper wage were he not sure that begging in the streets of the lower town was preferable. The population figures at Chios are probably lower than those at Odysseus' town. Eurycleia, Odysseus' nurse and housekeeper, calls upon some fifty workers and servants to ready the great house for a coming holiday. Several girls are to "sweep and sprinkle" the floors; others spread purple coverings on the chairs; more wash the wine bowls and the "best two-handled cups." Twenty others go off to draw water from a well, while some menservants chop wood for the fire. Other women under Eurycleia's eye would be grinding corn and getting meals ready. Such a number of servants is disproportionate to a town population of about 250, and is indeed far in excess of that maintained by any princely household in Greece after the Mycenaean Age. Like all the heroes, Odysseus adds to the peoples in this city whenever he returns from a war. Homer names captive women from the eastern Aegean—Lesbos, Tenedos, and Skyros—and Linear B tablets at Pylos prove that the heroic practice was a reality.

From the other details in the poem, it seems that Odysseus' house can only be Mycenaean in plan and scale. Its large megaron and porch, its great pillars to support the roof, its central hearth, its side doors and passageways all correspond to features at other Mycenaean palaces. A close parallel between Odysseus' house and one within the citadel at Mycenae has been remarked by A. J. B. Wace. The House of Columnus he excavated had a stairway leading from the megaron to an upper story and an inner room, very like Penelope's "gay apartment" situated on a gallery above the megaron. Other rooms, in both the real and fictional houses, are grouped around the central court. A special feature of Odysseus' house may be a particular Mycenaean reminiscence, preserved in the vocabulary of oral poetry, and that is the small door opening out of the back of the megaron into the storerooms. Odysseus' servant Melanthius uses this door to bring weapons secretly into the megaron to father and son. Probably Melanthius is unnoticed by the suitors trapped in the megaron because lighting is poor. Even with braziers stationed at intervals around the hall and a fire in the central hearth, the walls would be cast in darkness. And smoke. Although typically there is an opening in the roof above the hearth, Homer does not mention it. Years of smoke and neglect have badly tarnished Odysseus' armor, hanging on the megaron walls since his departure. When laying his plot for revenge, he has to include instructions to Telemachus to clean the armor.

Life in the household centered around the megaron, just as it did at Pylos. And again as at Pylos, pantries for wine jars and cooking utensils would have been located convenient to the hall. Furnishings were simple, the bulk of them being long wooden tables, benches, and stools. Several passages, however, reveal a taste for luxury quite at variance with the predominantly plain style. Penelope's "throne," a raised armchair with a high back, is the work of a particular craftsman named Icmalius. Its overlay of ivory and silver and its attached footrest so that the queen may mount in dignified fashion distinguish it from other, plainer chairs ranged around the walls. More ivory forms the handle of the copper key to the king's storeroom—as though the implement symbolizes the value of the goods it locks up. In sharp contrast, the door to the storeroom itself is described as a massive affair of wood, attached to doorposts by an intricate arrangement of leather thongs. There is a similar contrast between sturdiness and opulence in Odysseus' design of his marriage bed. He smoothed the stump of an olive tree so that it might serve as a pedestal, that was then secured firmly to the floor. Over that were stretched wooden stays through which strips of leather were webbed. On top was placed a stuffed mattress, dyed an expensive purple. The bedposts of the complex fixture were encrusted with gold, silver, and ivory, complementing the elaborate bedcoverings of embroidered fleece and wool.

These touches, like the gilt on a brown panel painting, hint at the Mycenaean fondness for ornamentation that the Linear B tablets confirm. When the poet heaps praise on the physical beauty of his favorite characters, it is in formulaic phrasings. Odysseus has "great thighs"; Penelope has "large white hands"; both are "godlike" in stature. Robes are "gleaming" or "fine-spun." But attention to jewels and precious objects is less common and more specific. One of the suitors, for instance, drinks from a "golden cup" as befits his princely rank, a reminder that a nobleman would have carried so precious an object with him as part of his equipage. Or, Homer makes a point of noting that Odysseus went off to Troy wearing a magnificent purple cape. It was fastened by a minutely worked golden buckle with a double pin representing a dog holding a spotted fawn between its two front paws. It is fair to infer from such isolated references to personal display that neither the lavishness of Pylos nor the conspicuous gold of Phaeacia is commonplace in Ithaca. Penelope, for instance, in a speech that tells us much about courtship customs, chastises the suitors for failing to bring their own cattle and sheep to make a banquet for her, and especially for neglecting to "give her valuable presents." They immediately comply with the following rich gifts (and a cautionary reminder that, nevertheless, they are not leaving her hall until she makes her choice of marriage partner).

> They brought a long embroidered robe of the most beautiful material on which were fixed a dozen golden brooches, each fitted with a curved sheath for the pin . . . a golden chain of exquisite workmanship strung with amber beads that gleamed like the sun . . . a pair of earrings, each a thing of lambent beauty with its cluster of three drops . . . [and a] necklace which was a lovely piece of jewellery too.   [Book XVIII: 294-297]

Many Homeric details relating to Penelope's suitors are unique illustrations of social custom. A wealthy father's decision to marry off his daughter when she is about sixteen is followed by invitations to potential bridegrooms to visit. Their competition for her hand begins with an appraisal of their gifts of food for the household and personal objects for the girl. Like Hippodameia's suitors in the Pelops myth (Chapter V), they enter into athletic contests that test their strength and skill. Perhaps only in later ages did they also compete in song, dance, and speechmaking. When the father has chosen the future husband, the latter offers more substantial presents like metalware and jewels and the father gives a dowry, returnable in the event of repudiation. It is probably with this rich exchange in mind that Penelope's suitors ask Telemachus to send her back to her father, Icarius. The actual transfer of presents was the solemn ritual which sealed the marriage agreement. The bride was then conveyed by chariot from her father's house to her husband's. There were feasts and festivities at each place and in the evening a torchlight procession.

The Heroic Age was monogamous. In noble families the marriage contract had all the solemnity of a treaty between friendly but prudent states. The wife was guaranteed her own apartments in the husband's manor and, as head of the household, enjoyed a position of dignity and authority. Queen Arete is the perfect example of the honored wife to the ideal husband. Theoretically, the man was master: he could punish the wife if she compromised the interests of his house, or even kill her if she committed adultery. But he would consider twice before taking any action at all against his wife, for she remained under the protection of her paternal family, whose vengeance for any wrong done to her was bloody and mandatory. If the *Odyssey* is to be believed, infidelities of the husband were a somewhat different matter. Penelope listens mutely to the long tale of her husband's romantic adventures, told without a trace of awkwardness. Not that there is in any of them a threat to Penelope's position. Odysseus' mother, however, was not nearly so docile. Old Laertes was very fond of Eurycleia. He had paid a high price for her (twenty oxen) and was pleased that she came from a family of freemen. But he never dared to lie with her for he dreaded the scenes his wife would make. It may be that concubinage was a matter of family policy when there were no male heirs. After her sensational liaison with Paris, the gods decreed that the beautiful Helen would be forever sterile. With Helen's acceptance, therefore, Menelaos gets a son on a slave woman. It is this son, Megapenthes, who is being married when Telemachus arrives at Sparta to inquire after his father. Helen herself is presiding regally over the festivities.

It is unlikely that Penelope could have taught the girls in her household the mythic art of magic weaving. She was responsible, however, for passing on to them an everyday skill at spinning and needlework. No other woman's work was as important or as highly prized, and all Homer's women, nymphs, gods, witches, and wives excel at it. Helen is followed into Sparta's great hall by maidens carrying her exquisite silver workbox on an embroidered pillow. These girls, like those under Penelope's guidance, would observe their mistress's deftness and simultaneously learn a lesson in deportment. Indeed, such education that young women had—in spinning, singing, and housekeeping—it was a wife's task to give. In managing the slaves and servants, a wife had the assistance of her nurse-stewardess indoors, and a steward like Eumaeus on the lands. His supervision also extended over the animal butchers and the cooks.

Albeit against her will, Penelope sets the athletic competitions that will decide her new marriage partner. There is high excitement throughout this public festival, but Homer's particular attention is given to the contest of the bow. The game is one Odysseus played as a young man, and all the equipment has been stored away against such time as he may wish to play again. Twelve double axheads are set in a trench and so aligned that the center of the aperture in each is two or three inches from the ground, all the apertures directly behind one another. The trick is to pass an arrow through the entire file, one which requires a sure eye and a very steady hand. Since, according to the poet, the contestant kneels or sits in order to take aim, the axes must have a span of about four feet and be extremely heavy. Their further description makes them sound very like axes familiar from depictions at Knossos, and perhaps Odysseus acquired them during a raiding party. Their place of origin, nevertheless, is probably Lydia for, unlike Cretan axes, these have recurved edges that nearly meet to form a circle. Many golden miniatures of such axes have been found in Anatolia in contexts that suggest that the game itself originated there. Did the Mycenaean Odysseus learn about the game from a visiting Anatolian, or while he or his ancestors were visiting Anatolia? Or is this minute detail a hint of Homer's own Ionian background? The axes are utterly foreign to the suitors, and so is Odysseus' bow. But then, Homer's description of how the bow is used makes it confusing to us. The suitors treat it unsuccessfully like a European or Asiatic bow, strung from an erect stance and shot from the shoulder. It may have been a Scythian or Anatolian model, for Odysseus remains seated, passing the bow under one knee and allowing the other end to rest on his thigh. If, as the poet says, the bow is solid horn and eight feet long, it would have been too inflexible and too unmanageable for such treatment. Whatever its composition, it seems to be a reflex bow, strung by bending it in the opposite direction. Decoration on a draughts box from Enkomi shows an archer using Odysseus' method of bending the bow into a hoop while in a seated position. It is valuable evidence that the reflex bow was known in Mycenaean times.

The house beggar, who has earned his right to enter the competition by charming Penelope, shoots his first arrow through all the axheads. He then tears off his disguise and becomes the principal actor in the drama of reprisal that the poem has been moving toward. Telemachus, forewarned, is ready with his weapons; stewards, whose loyalty Odysseus has tested and whose armed help has been sworn, move forward into the hall. Odysseus, now an executioner, puts his first arrow of battle through the breast of the chief suitor, Antinous, and begins a massacre.

Odysseus is responsible for administering his own justice, not as a private avenger but as tribal leader and king. His slaughter of the suitors and of the slave girls who slept with them is an exercise of his political protectorship of the clan, the authority for which derives from the rule of primogeniture. Old Laertes, his father, has abdicated his office to Odysseus—we are never told why—and withdrawn to a small plot of property some distance from the court. Infirmity, or some physical defect, might have made him incapable of conducting *his* hereditary duties. We know he is innocent of any major crime, one reason for exile, for he retains the respect of the clan and merely withdraws from family business. There is a clue to how tribal wars began in the fact that Odysseus fully expects the suitors' tribes to retaliate. Since he has raised no army of kinfolk, he has to consider where to find a temporary refuge. In typical Mycenaean fashion he is less concerned about how to replenish his depleted stores of goods. He tells Penelope later that he will pillage some weaker local tribes until his wealth is restored to its former worth.

The king was also judge over crimes committed inside his clan. In most cases a father himself punished the offenses of his daughters, young boys, and servants with expulsion or, in extreme cases, death. Odysseus acts in this double legal capacity when he has the servant girls hanged, as much for sexual misconduct as for flouting Penelope's authority. Retributive justice of a similarly primitive sort is exacted by Orestes. He wins glory as the new head of his clan by killing his mother, Clytemestra, for her murder of Agamemnon. In practice, the father and judge was unwilling to shed the blood of the clan members, preferring a sentence in severe cases of exile from the state—a pitiable enough condition—or of exile from the immediate environs in milder cases. Such a condemned man would live isolated in a distant corner of the domain, wholly dependent on charity.

The judge, rather than the father, intervened in cases involving free adult males. Attempted murder, quarrels between sons of different mothers, promiscuity between men and female servants were all offenses most often brought before him. The duty of mutual generosity makes one scholar suppose that theft was unknown. The legal preference for isolation over bloodshed can hardly be attributed to delicacy about violence in these Mycenaean warlords. It was more than likely motivated by economics: strong males were valuable assets. Nor is squeamishness in the poet's character. Here, for instance, is his description of Antinous' death.

Odysseus shot his bolt and struck [Antinous] in the throat. The
point passed clean through the soft flesh of his neck. Dropping the
cup as he was hit, he lurched over to one side. His life-blood
gushed from his nostrils in a turbid jet. His foot lashed out and
kicked the table from him; the food was scattered on the ground,
and his bread and meat were smeared with gore.

[Book XXII: 10–40]

In addition to these considerable powers, the king was the
tribe's religious leader, accountable for honoring the cult of his
ancestors and on occasions for offering sacrifice to the deities. In his
own court Nestor officiates at one such ceremony in honor of
Athena during Telemachus' visit. He provides the best bull from his
herd and has its horns gilded by the master smith. Then he assigns
to each of his sons several duties. Two lead the animal by the horns;
one holds a basket of barley and a jar of libations; another handles
the sacrificial ax; another opens the bull's throat; a sixth gathers the
blood in receptacles reserved for this purpose. The animal is cut up
according to ritual: it is held in position with long, five-pronged
forks and roasted on an altar. Nestor, in the interim, distributes
lustral water and barley, throws some hair from the beast's head
into the fire, and supervises the roasting of choice offerings—the
thighs wrapped in fat. His final act is to pour a libation of dark
wine.

A modern reader might cringe at Odysseus' slaughter of the
suitors because legal or formal justifications beg the question of the
act's morality. To the Mycenaean warrior aristocracy there was no
concept of moral justice antecedent to and abstract from actions:
what they did was right because they did it, just as what a god wills
is so because he wills it. The humanized gods of the epics fight
alongside heroes and display characters as capricious and willful as
those of men. Yet they are as immune from judgment as are heroes,
and there are no restrictions on the behavior of either. What
deference Odysseus pays to Zeus or Athena or Poseidon is from
simple respect for their greater powers, not from fear of punishment for wrongdoing. Homer's irresponsible aristocrats are full of
zest for the physical life—for food, drink, love, and war. Their
prowess brings them enjoyment as well as wealth and fame. Custom alone decrees what forms their appreciation of this robust life
may take, just as custom establishes the behavior appropriate to
each station in life, whether that of a god at the top of the class
system or a peasant at its base.

Yet to the extent that Homer accurately reflects Mycenaean

behavior one can deduce that they were not without an ethical code. This enormous freedom of gods and heroes did not justify pettiness or behavior that belittled their status. Cruelty and a quick temper are not unseemly; but bad manners or crude speech to a weaker man certainly is. Antinous' insults to the "beggar" Odysseus are an important illustration. In such a universe self-consciousness of one's position in relation to other men is the nearest equivalent to an internalized moral force. For, of course, no act or its consequence is internalized by any of these mythic-heroic people. There is no idea of personality or character, in our understanding of these terms, and a notion of soul takes form only in relation to death. Instead, the unexplainable, be it a flash of intuition, a thunderclap on a day of clear skies, or a dream, is attributed to some feature of the physical world—sometimes one which still retains its link, formed long ago, to the figure of a god. Odysseus' acts often show this combination of pragmatism and piety. He consults the oracular oak tree at Dodona about how to present himself at his homecoming. Nonetheless, he spends days thinking out his own revenge and fretting over what bloody retaliation from the suitors' people he may expect as a result. Then he prays to Zeus for a sign that all will go well. The god obliges with a well-timed thunderbolt, for which the hero gives appropriate thanks.

As we have already discovered, the veneration the Mycenaean paid to his god, and in what form, and why, is a subject about which little can be taken as certain. Homer's anthropomorphic gods have already lost most of the elements of animism and theriomorphism they probably had in the Bronze Age. Athena, the *Odyssey*'s principal deity, is a literal and rational character whose divinity consists chiefly in her ability to materialize instantly in a variety of disguises. She brings courage to Telemachus simply by the fact of her presence; she brings comfort to Penelope when her sister dies by sending a dream figure to stand at the head of Penelope's bed. There is no doubt, however, that Athena is a genuine Mycenaean goddess and the patron of Minoan and Mycenaean princes. In some opinion, she was pre-Greek—an avatar of the Mountain Mother goddess found in Crete and the East. She is more generally accepted as having been a household benefactress to both men and women. Hence her puzzling association with the arts of spinning and weaving on one hand and warlike skills on the other. To the Classical Greeks, she retained only her martial aspect, acquired by life among the Mycenaean warlords. (See Illus. 53.)

It was not until the 1930's that Athena's Mycenaean connec-

tion was well established. When the Swedish-American Oscar
Broneer found that Athena's traditional home on the Acropolis of
Athens was built over ancient Mycenaean walls, her antiquity was
proved. She took up residence at the citadel of a Mycenaean prince
in Athens at about the same time that Pylos, Mycenae, Tiryns, and
Gla built temples to her at their own fortresses. About her still
earlier animistic features, evidence is sketchy. There is no Greek
etymology for her name. It seems, however, that the Acropolis was
originally called Athene, a place name comparable with the pre-
Greek Mykene (for Mycene). Athene was the singular form, eventually replaced by the plural Athenai, just as Mykene came to be
replaced by Mykenai. The goddess was named Athene like the rock
of the Acropolis because at the outset she *was* the rock, a Mountain
Mother of the usual Anatolian sort. Scholars explain that any
life—animal or vegetable—linked to a god's dwelling place would
be venerated as a divine manifestation of his fertility. The olive, the
snake, and the owl, all creatures of the Acropolis, therefore became
sacred to Athena.

Athena's later adoption by the Mycenaeans would account for
her acquisition of new arts (spinning and weaving) and for her
place among the Olympians as a daughter of Zeus. As for her
transformation from mother to perpetual virgin who turns away

53. Athena in costume that reflects
her twin peaceful and martial aspects.

from marriage, the invading Greeks may have had a maiden goddess, a martial Valkyrie type, with a name something like Pallas ("girl"). One of Athena's constant epithets, Pallas Athena, would then be an equivalent of her other titles meaning "maiden," Kore and Parthenos. Although one cannot dogmatize about the continuity of the gods from earliest to Classical times, syncretism in the life history of other gods makes it likely that Athena is yet another such syncretized figure.

4

From the *Odyssey*'s first verses, Penelope's suitors are presented as a grave threat to Odysseus' house. Attempts to discover the precise nature of that threat, however, lead one into generalizations about depredations to Odysseus' estate and boorish behavior that make the suitors resemble folklore daemons like Polyphemus more than quasi-historical personages or figures in heroic myth. Antinous, the principal suitor, has harassed the family for twenty years, a period of time that is too long to be other than a folktale exaggeration of number, very like the profusion of eager bridegrooms. Their scandalous breaches of the rules of hospitality—depleting the livestock, insulting the servants, seducing the slave girls—are equally appropriate to the poem's folkloristic strain. And where else but in folktale would twenty years of adversity be concluded by the cast of a single, and special, arrow?

Yet such folklore detail does not obscure a kernel of realism in the pattern of events at Ithaca, or the circumstances in which they take on life. The excesses of the princely suitors offer a hearthside perspective on the time of troubles in the late days of the Bronze Age, much as Eumaeus' life story gives a fictional view of the days of the sea raids. For Odysseus' saga, like Agamemnon's, ends in an atmosphere of tension caused by a struggle between kings and noblemen for local power. In the Agamemnon story, the throne is usurped by a prince who has not gone off to Troy. In mythic terms, Aegisthus' seizure of the crown is the fateful working out of the curse on the house of Atreus. And so, too, is Orestes' retaliation and overthrow of his uncle. In the context of twelfth-century history, the pattern seems anything but mythical. The city does not live for long after Orestes' ascendancy: his son Tisamenos is the last of the royal

Mycenaeans. The situation in Ithaca is similar. Men without title to
rule take advantage of a power vacuum created by the absence of
the king and his army. Other leaderless cities, too, must have been
an easy prey to foreign princes, raiders, and pirates. Kinship relations, so fundamental to political stability during the Bronze Age,
break down and new alliances form and re-form. Aegisthus joins
with Clytemestra; one hundred suitors aspire to join with Penelope.
In Ithaca as in Mycenae the sons of the Trojan heroes graduate
rapidly into their majorities out of a need to protect their pat-
rimonies. Neither Telemachus nor Orestes is yet capable of pitting
himself against the authority of men of his father's generation. Nor
have they recourse to aid from their tribes. Both the number of
Penelope's suitors and the duration of time that Ithaca tolerates
their unwelcome presence suggest that community machinery for
imposing sanctions has long since been weakened. Telemachus
summons a meeting of the Ithacan assembly to hear his complaints
against the rapacious suitors, yet that body of "kinsmen who hear
both sides" is incapable of assisting him. It is as though their power
to act has been paralyzed by the absence of the king, in whose
actual person reside the will and authority to define and enforce
law. The longed-for return of Odysseus, then, means the return of
the sole figure around whom retaliation can be organized, be it a
simple declaration of justice or an open exercise of force. His
standing among the nobility, his wealth, and his personal prowess;
his connections by marriage and other kinship alliances; the manpower in his command all will determine his capacity to overcome
his enemies. In epic fashion, Odysseus triumphs over the suitors
with only the help of his young son.

    Absentee kings who went off to serve in the Trojan War were
not the only cause for power vacuums and political realliances
during the period. Before Troy fell, a wave of dislocations on the
mainland was precipitated by the series of internecine wars
referred to in Chapter V. Mycenae's first destruction c. 1230 was
one result of the outbreak of violence; the burning of Tiryns was
another. Apparently, the cities recovered and began to shore up
their defenses with huge fortifications. But these first shocks to the
mainland's political stability initiated a chain of migrations that
were to increase as the century progressed, reaching climactic
proportions during the Dorian invasions. The number of landless
princes who survived these early local wars was swelled by the
numbers returning from Troy to find their castles threatened, so
that in the period immediately following Troy's fall rulerships of

several cities changed hands. There is no lack of mythic representation of the noble migrant driven from his city to settle or found a
new home. Philoktetes is expelled from his city of Meliboea in
Thessaly and eventually founds the city of Petelia (?) in southern
Italy. Demophon the Athenian leaves a new bride in Thrace, on the
pretext of visiting his mother in Athens (!), only to hazard his
fortunes in Cyprus. The great hero Diomedes, some say, is forced
from Argos and retires to Corinth. Then, discovering that his
grandfather needs help in quelling a rebellion, he sails with aid to
Aetolia. Still later he moves on to Italian Daunia, where he builds
the city of Brundisium.

The plight of these mobile princes must have demanded all
their resources of tact and force. When the Dorians expel the
Achaean princes from Argos and Sparta, they and their king
Tisamenos, Orestes' son, try to settle peacefully among the Ionians.
The latter, however, are frightened by the possibility that
Tisamenos' glorious ancestry will cast their own heroes into
shadow, and so they take up arms against the Achaeans. Tisamenos
falls in the course of battle, although the Achaeans triumph and
drive the Ionians from their homes. They in turn go to Attica, where
the Athenians receive them as fellow citizens. Perhaps Athenian
hospitality was in fact a clever strategy to increase their own
strength against the Dorians. The city's invulnerability to the new
Greeks was a source of pride out of which Athenians in historical
times made a good deal of political capital.

Penelope's many suitors might well have been royal exiles like
these, depicted in the *Odyssey* from the point of view of the Ithacans. To them the suitors would have been villains attempting to
wrest power from the island's older chiefs. For Ithaca, like Achaea
and Cyprus, did become an outpost of refuge for fleeing Mycenaeans. Unlike Mycenae or Pylos, Ithaca was untroubled by the
depredations of internal wars, Sea Peoples, or Dorians. While the
rest of the Peloponnesos was combatting shock waves of invasions
and dislocations, Ithaca remained a quiet backwater, an ideal
sanctuary for immigrants and survivors. Since Ithaca and its
neighbor island Kephallenia had been populated by a mixture of
non-Mycenaean peoples from Early Helladic times onward, the
new appearance of clearly identifiable Mycenaean remains dating
to the years after 1300 argues all the more forcefully that the islands
played host to uprooted mainlanders. Instead of distributing
themselves among the scattered hamlets of Ithaca, the exiles established their own settlements at Polis and Aetos, where ar-

chaeology shows that occupation continued without interruption into historical times. The number of Mycenaean descendants was not great, but their instincts for survival were good. It may have been the sons of these exiles who, in a reverential gesture toward their own past, kept alive the memory of Odysseus at his famous cave shrine in Polis.

The general pattern of late Mycenaean migrations is traceable by etymology and literary references as well as by pottery. These indicate that there were two large group movements, one to Kephallenia and Ithaca, and another to Achaea; and smaller, more haphazard movements to peripheral islands and Cyprus. Achaea was already within the Mycenaean sphere and so more readily accessible than the remote coastal area of Ithaca. The mountains in the central Peloponnesos are one natural barrier to easy east–west passage, and encampments of hostile Greeks were another. Some colonizers doubtless took a sea route around the Peloponnese. The close resemblance between pottery designs at Athens, in the east, and Patras, nestled on the northwest coastline, speak strongly for such a solution to the geographical problem. About the Mycenaean settlement of Achaea, Pausanias is the chief source. He says that Mycenaeans (from Mycenae) were driven from the Argolid to Achaea. They spread themselves over the province in twelve cities, six of them known to Homer. Pausanias is also helpful in plotting the probable routes taken by the invaders. He records that when "three-eyed Oxylos" led his contingent of Dorians across the Corinthian Gulf and onto the Peloponnesos, he swerved through Arcadia into Elis instead of going by the coast road in order to avoid a battle. One can infer a great deal from this scanty information. Oxylos' maneuver implies the presence of a surviving Mycenaean kingdom in the area of Rhion strong enough to contest his passage. Elis is very likely to have joined its neighbors to the north in a last-stand alliance against Oxylos, so that he would have been wise to approach the Alpheios Valley from its back, instead of facing the combined Achaean forces along the shore. Professor Emily Vermeule, who worked extensively on the evidence for Mycenaean migrations in the Late Helladic period, agrees that this is more than mere conjecture. Pausanias' report of a Mycenaean inhabitation of Achaea not only is consistent with his later description of the route chosen by Oxylos, but is confirmed by the abundant Mycenaean pottery remains in Achaea dating to immediately after the Trojan War—that is, before the sack of Pylos in 1200 and after the burning of Mycenae. According to one traditional story, when Oxylos needed a Greek from pre-Dorian days to help him consolidate his kingdom, he was told to seek out a descendant of Mycenae. He found him in a great grandson of Orestes who was still at Helice in Achaea. A rough genealogical calculation places him in the period between 1060 and 1025, just when the Mycenaean style of pottery at Achaea was fading out. These last Mycenaean potters do not seem to have died violently. A dwindling of contact with all outsiders resulted in lower and lower levels of energy and resources. Fear of the sea, or of those now in control of the sea, forced them to eke out an ever more sparse living from their land until they perished from simple starvation.

Mycenaean refugees on Cyprus fared better. They moved into settlements like Enkomi that had been flourishing since their establishment c. 1450. Mycenaean kinsmen from Rhodes were there to greet them, for in about 1225, the period of the Trojan War, the number of mainland Mycenaeans on Cyprus seems to have diminished while the numbers from Rhodes increased. Copper was so vital a material in the Bronze Age that the island continued to be economically prosperous in spite of shifts in population and political complexion. In 1200, for instance, the Sea Peoples used Cyprus to consolidate their forces before advancing against Egypt in the famous battle with Ramses III (1190) that reversed their record of triumphs. Apparently, some Sea Peoples remained on the island, intermarrying with the native inhabitants and becoming Cypriots. With the arrival of mainland Greek refugees, the island assumed something of an international character, with enclaves of different Aegean races dotted over its length and breadth. Geologists speculate that sometime around 1150, when the Dorians were strengthening their hold on the Peloponnesos, a massive change in the climate brought a more North Atlantic type of weather to the Mediterranean. Thereafter, Enkomi was a regular victim of heavy flooding, perhaps a factor in the desertion of this important city by 1050.

Apart from Homer's mention of Alasia (Cyprus), the island had little share in the mythic tradition of the Age of Heroes. Yet Cyprus, more than other outposts of the declining Mycenaean civilization like Ithaca, consciously allied itself with the Bronze Age past. Tombs dating to the eighth and seventh centuries reveal that horse sacrifices were still being offered for important people. Indeed, there were more horses sacrificed on Cyprus during the proto-Geometric, Geometric and Archaic periods than there were anywhere at the height of the Mycenaean ascendancy. At Salamis, the dromos of one tomb contained the bones of two horses lying head to head, buried with the pole of a hearse or chariot in the eighth century. The ceremonial character of the burial and the horses' postures are reminiscent of the well-known horse burial at Marathon (see Illus. 13). Early in the seventh century, the tomb was used again for a king (?) with whom were interred six horses, yoked in pairs, the bronze or ivory blinkers and frontlets from their original harnesses still in place. Such evidence makes it tempting to suppose a continuity of Mycenaean custom being practiced by Mycenaean descendants, rather than by other, racially alien Cypriots who had adopted some Mycenaean forms.

One point in the foregoing summary may in time come to earn more serious consideration than it has received to date. If the weather change that occurred in the eleventh century can be shown to have affected population shifts and densities throughout the area of the southern Mediterranean, present theories about why and how the Mycenaean world collapsed may have to be revised. It is curious, for instance, that many mainland centers *not* destroyed were yet abandoned by the Mycenaeans and not reoccupied by the Doria. Areas in the path of their invasion, like Lakonia, became fully occupied, while centers nearby, already built up and fortified, were ignored and eventually forgotten. What happened to all the people is equally mystifying. Population figures, as we have already discovered, were generally high from about 1300 to 1190, and not all men either emigrated or died. Some Mycenaeans, probably those at the lowest economic level, must have remained on their lands, eventually to have been absorbed into the new Greek culture. One has in mind here peoples living in the hamlets that were grouped around the major citadels. Certainly their life-styles changed dramatically. The introduction of Dorian iron, combined with the cessation of trade in copper and tin, meant the obsolescence of bronze and craftsmen in bronze. The absence of interest in or need for other commercial shipping meant a corresponding decline in the employment of sailors, shipwrights, sailmakers, carpenters, and like workers. In short, Mycenaeans of the artisan class would have become dependent on a limited, land-based economy, poorer and less diversified than that of the Bronze Age. Agricultural workers, presumably, would have suffered the least change in their life patterns, performing the same farming labors for different masters. But if, as the final assumption in this hypothetical picture would have it, the crop and cattle yield remained nearly constant, many mainlanders would have survived the transition from

Mycenaean to Dorian rule tolerably well. There were no palaces, no commerce, no art, no luxury goods—in brief, no evidence of high civilization; but there would have been adequate resources to sustain a fair-sized agriculturally oriented population. Yet, from all the existing evidence it would seem that the post-Mycenaean era experienced an immediate drop in living standards, not directly attributable to the effects of either the destruction of key sites or the influx of new peoples. If, however, the climate in the late twelfth and early eleventh centuries did become cooler and wetter, so that farming habits and crops typical to the Aegean were no longer viable or productive, a massive change from prosperity to poverty would have been inevitable.

Climatologists have long maintained that atmospheric changes bringing extensive periods of drought were responsible for converting the once Fertile Crescent into patches of arid desert. That change, they claim, resulted ultimately in the decline of the great Babylonian civilizations and the gradual depopulation of the Bible lands. Political historians account for the rise and fall of these nations differently; and social historians have still other theories. Studies in the relationship of climate to population, difficult enough in contemporary contexts, are overwhelmingly so in retrospective ones. It is possible to imagine, for instance, that a reduced food supply presented the late Mycenaeans with a choice of emigration or starvation, and that both occurred. Perhaps, too, lands once farmed by Mycenaeans were no longer put to the plow by the new mixed population either because of a reduced yield or because crops planted by Dorians, accustomed to an Atlantic climate, were unsuited to the new mountainous terrain. That is to say, even given the new, favorable climate, new crops failed and Dorians, too, faced starvation for different reasons. It might even have been the new Atlantic-type weather that made the Aegean a natural area for Dorian expansion. Or, finally, all hypothetical reasons for the collapse of Mycenaean civilization may have been coincidentally and simultaneously true: the climate changed; the Dorians arrived; Mycenaeans abandoned their cities; and life continued—poorer, darker, unrelieved by heroes.

Appendix I

Chronology

B.C.	CRETE	TROAD	MAINLAND	B.C.	
3000			**LERNA I**	3000	NEOLITHIC
2900				2900	
2800	Early Minoan I		**LERNA II**	2800	
2700				2700	
2600		**TROY I**		2600	
2500			Early Helladic I	2500	
2400	Early Minoan II	**TROY II**		2400	
2300	Early Minoan III		Early Helladic II **LERNA III**	2300	
2200		**TROY III AND IV**	**ARRIVAL OF THE GREEKS**	2200	
2100	Middle Minoan I		Early Helladic III **LERNA IV**	2100	
2000	**FIRST PALACES AT KNOSSOS AND MALLIA**	**TROY V**	**LERNA V**	2000	
1900				1900	
1800	Middle Minoan II	**TROY VI**		1800	
1700	Middle Minoan III		Middle Helladic	1700	BRONZE AGE
1600	**SECOND PALACES AT KNOSSOS AND MALLIA**		**GRAVE CIRCLE B (c. 1650)**	1600	
1500	Late Minoan I **ARRIVAL OF THE GREEKS (c.1450)**		Late Helladic I **GRAVE CIRCLE A (1500)**	1500	
1400	Late Minoan II		Late Helladic II	1400	
1300	Late Minoan III	**TROY VII A AND B**	Late Helladic III	1300	
1200	**FALL OF KNOSSOS**	**FALL OF TROY (1220-1200)**	**DESTRUCTION OF PYLOS (1190-1120)**	1200	
1100			**FINAL DESTRUCTION OF MYCENAE (1150-1120)**	1100	GEOMETRIC
1000				1000	
900	Sub Minoan			900	
800				800	ARCHAIC

Appendix II

The Parian Chronicle

The Greeks of the pre-Classical age were as interested in their history as we are, and they faced the problem of prehistory by compiling annals, the records of current "authorities," catalogs of discoveries, handbooks of travelers, and, of course, myths. Their chronological scheme was based on heroic genealogies made by calculating backward from some one fixed date, like that of a particular king's reign. One such famous record, incised on a slab of Parian marble and thus known as the Parian Chronicle, has a history as fabulous as that it compiles. The monument seems to have been vandalized and sold to a traveling English physician in the time of Charles I. When it arrived in London in 1627, it was placed in Arundel House in the Strand. Fortunately, it was there studied and its text published by a distinguished scholar of antiquities. During the English Civil War the marble was cut in two; the upper half was used to repair a fireplace (!) and has not been heard of since.

The original Greek document is flawed by many gaps in the text. The words in brackets are those restored from the context or from odd letters that can be read. Dotted lines indicate passages that could not be so restored. The entire inscription retrieved from scholars' notes appears below.* An asterisk before the entry indicates that reference to it has been made in this text.

	TEXT	DATE
		B.C.

I ... [name of compiler lost] ... inscribed this record of (former times) from Cecrops the first king of Athens to the archonships of ... in Paros and Diognetos at Athens.   264/3

* 1 Since Cecrops was king at Athens and the country previously called Acticê after Actaios the autochthon received the name of Cecropia.

                           1318 years   = 1582

2 Since Deucalion was king in Leucoreia by Parnassos, in the reign of Cecrops at Athens,

                           1310 years   = 1574

3 Since Ares and Poseidon came to judgment at Athens on account of Halirrhothios son of Poseidon, and the place of judgment received the name of Areiopagos, in the reign of Cranaos at Athens,

                           1268 years   = 1532

4 Since the flood occurred in the time of Deucalion, and Deucalion fled from the waters from Leucoreia to Athens . . . and founded the temple of Olympian Zeus and offered the sacrifice for safety, in the reign of Cranaos at Athens,

                           1265 years   = 1529

5 Since Amphictyon son of Deucalion was king at Thermopylai and brought together the people who dwelt around the sanctuary, and gave their names to the Amphictyons and to Pylaia where the Am-

---

* Reprinted by permission from John Forsdyke's *Greece Before Homer* (London: MacDonald & Co., 1957), pages 52–66. Spellings of names and places conform to his translation.

phictyons still sacrifice. in the reign of Amphictyon
at Athens,

$$\text{1258 years} \quad = 1522$$

6 Since Hellen son of Deucalion was king of Phthiotis
and the people previously called Greeks were
named Hellenes and the Games . . . ., in the reign of
Amphictyon at Athens,

$$\text{1257 years} \quad = 1521$$

* 7 Since Cadmos son of Agenor came to Thebes . . .
and built the Cadmeia, in the reign of Amphictyon
at Athens,

$$\text{1255 years} \quad = 1519$$

* 8 Since (Cilix and Phoinix sons of Agenor) were kings
in (Cilicia and) Phoenicia, in the reign of Amphictyon at Athens,

$$\text{1252 years} \quad = 1516$$

* 9 Since a ship . . . sailed from Egypt to Greece and
was called a pentecontor, and the daughters of
Danaos . . . and Helicê and Archedicê were selected
from the rest by lot . . . and offered sacrifice on the
shore at Lindos in Rhodes during the voyage, in the
reign of (Erichthonios at Athens),

$$\text{1247 years} \quad = 1511$$

10 Since Erichthonios harnessed a chariot at the first
celebration of the Panathenaic Festival, and instituted the Games, and gave the Athenians their
name, and . . . of the Mother (of the gods) was
revealed in Cybela, and the Phrygian Hyagnis invented flutes . . . and first played the mode that is
called Phrygian and other music of the Mother,
Dionysos, Pan, and the . . ., in the reign of
Erichthonios who harnessed the chariot at Athens,

$$\text{1242 years} \quad = 1506$$

* 11 Since (the first) Minos (was king in Crete and)
founded . . ., and iron-working was invented in

Ida, the inventors being the Idaian Dactyls Celmios
and . . . , in the reign of Pandion at Athens,

$$(\quad \text{years}) = 1462-$$
$$1423$$

12 Since Demeter came to Athens and (instituted)
harvest, and (the first Proerosia was performed by
instruction of) Triptolemos son of Celeos and
Neaira, in the reign of Erichtheus at Athens,

$$1146 \text{ years} = 1410$$

13 Since Triptolemos . . . sowed in the place called
Rharia at Eleusis, in the reign of Erichtheus at
Athens,

$$1145 \text{ years} = 1409$$

14 (Since . . .) produced his own poetry, the Rape of
Corê and Demeter's Quest, and the . . . of those who
received the harvest, in the reign of Erichtheus at
Athens,

$$1135 \text{ years} = 1399$$

15 (Since . . .) produced the Mysteries at Eleusis and
published the poems of . . . Mousaios, in the reign
of Erichtheus son of Pandion at Athens,

$$(\quad \text{years}) = 1398-$$
$$1373$$

16 Since purification was first instituted . . . , in the
reign of Pandion son of Cecrops at Athens,

$$1062 \text{ years} = 1326$$

17 Since the gymnastic (contest) at Eleusis, . . . the
Lycaia in Arcadia was established and . . . of
Lycaon were given . . . to the Hellenes, in the reign
of Pandion son of Cecrops at Athens,

$$(\quad \text{years}) = 1325-$$
$$1308$$

* 18 Since ... Heracles ..., in the reign of Aigeus at
     Athens,

                                   (years) = 1307-
                                                    1296

  19 Since harvests (failed) at Athens and Apollo di-
      rected the Athenians who consulted the oracle to
      make (amends) ... which Minos should demand, in
      the reign of Aigeus at Athens,

                                   1031 years = 1295

* 20 Since Theseus ... became king at Athens and
      brought the twelve townships together and gave
      them (one) constitution and the democracy, and ...
      founded the Isthmian Games after killing Sinis,

                                   995 years = 1259

  21 Since the Amazons (invaded Attica), in the reign of
      Theseus at Athens,

                                   992 years = 1256

  22 Since the Argives with Adrastos (attacked Thebes)
      and founded the Games at (Nemea) ..., in the
      reign of Theseus at Athens,

                                   987 years = 1251

* 23 Since the Hellenes made the expedition to Troy in
      the thirteenth year of the reign of Menestheus at
      Athens,

                                   954 years = 1218

* 24 Since Troy fell in the (twenty-)second year of the
      reign of Menestheus at Athens, on the seventh day
      from the end of the month Thargelion,

                                   945 years = 1209

* 25 Since Orestes ... (and Erigonê) daughter of
      Aigisthos (came to judgment) at the Areiopagos (on
      account of Aigisthos and Clytaimnestra) and

Orestes won the suit . . . in the reign of Demophon at Athens,

$$9(44) \text{ years} \quad = 1208$$

26 Since Teucros founded (Salamis) in Cyprus, in the reign of Demophon at Athens,

$$938 \text{ years} \quad = 1202$$

27 Since Neleus founded (Miletos and all the rest of Ionia), Ephesos, Erythrai, Clazomenai . . . Colophon, Myous . . . Samos . . . , and the Panionia was established, in the reign of (Medon) at Athens,

$$(82)3 \text{ years} \quad = 1087$$

28 Since the poet Hesiod (lived), in the reign of . . . at Athens,

$$67(3) \text{ years} \quad = 937$$

* 29 Since the poet Homer lived, in the reign of Diognetos at Athens,

$$643 \text{ years} \quad = 907$$

30 Since Pheidon of Argos established (weights and measures) and coined silver in Aigina, being eleventh in descent from Heracles, in the reign of Pherecles at Athens,

$$631 \text{ years} \quad = 895$$

Select Bibliography

The bare titles of the books and articles that follow cannot convey my debts to several special studies on which I have drawn freely. Sometimes, rather than distort a subtlety or risk a misunderstanding, I have paraphrased an important point. This was the case in two or three instances with my use of Professor Emily Vermeule's immensely valuable book *Greece in the Bronze Age*. On other occasions I have adapted a summary or a chart that presented information I wanted to establish. So, for example, the estimated chronology on page 201 of Chapter VIII abbreviates a fuller one by Professor George Mylonas in his *Mycenae and the Mycenaean Age*. And so, too, the Blegen-Palmer reconstruction of the probable sequence of events at Knossos was published also in Joseph Alsop's fine book, *From the Silent Earth*. Since we have dispensed with most footnotes in order to simplify the text, I acknowledge gratefully my long list of such borrowings here instead. I refer the reader to Professor Anne Ward's scholarly and readable volume *The Quest For Theseus* to supplement my brief account of that hero's adventures in Chapter VI, and refer him also to J. G. Frazer's translation of and commentary on Pausanias' *Description of Greece* for many useful annotations. After sifting through many editions of Greek myths, I most often returned to the monumental collection

by Robert Graves for its fullness of detail and richness of interpretation. Very often the shape and style of his narratives influenced my own retellings of the myths.

A Land Called Crete (A symposium in memory of Harriet Boyd
    Hawes, 1871-1945). Northampton, Massachusetts, 1967.
Aeschylus, *Agamemnon; The Libation Bearers; The Eumenides,*
    trans. and ed. David Grene and Richmond Lattimore. New
    York, 1962.
Alexiou, Stylianos, Guanella, Hanni, and Platon, Nicholas, *Ancient
    Crete.* New York and Washington, 1968.
Alsop, Joseph, *From the Silent Earth: A Report on the Greek Bronze
    Age.* New York, 1962.
Angel, J. Lawrence, *The People,* Vol. II, *Lerna: A Preclassical Site
    in the Argolid.* Washington, 1971.
Apollonius Rhodius, *The Argonautica,* trans. R. C. Seaton. London
    and New York, 1912.
Astour, Michael, *Hellenosemitica.* Leiden, 1967.
Bachofen, J. J., *Myth, Religion, and Mother Right,* trans. Ralph
    Manheim. Princeton, 1967.
Bacon, J. R., *Voyage of the Argonauts.* Methuen, 1925.
Balcer, Martin Jack, "The Mycenaean Dam at Tiryns." *American
    Journal of Archaeology,* Vol. 78, No. 2 (April, 1944).
Banti, Luisa, "Divinità femminili a Creta nel tardo Minoico III,"
    SMSR, Vol. XVII, Bologna, 1942.
Beye, Charles R., *The Iliad, The Odyssey and the Epic Tradition.*
    New York, 1966.
Blegen, Carl W., *Troy and the Trojans.* London, 1963.
―――― and Rawson, Marion, *The Palace of Nestor at Pylos in West-
    ern Messenia.* Cincinnati, 1966.
Boardman, John, *The Greeks Overseas.* England, 1964.
Bonfante, Giuliano, "Gil elementi illirici nella mitologia greca."
    Archivio Glottologico Italiano, LIII, Fasc 1-2. Florence, 1968.
Burn, A. R., *Minoans, Philistines and Greeks,* B.C. *1400-900.* Lon-
    don, 1968.
Carpenter, Rhys, *Folktale Fiction and Saga in the Homeric Epics.*
    Chicago and London, 1958.
Carson, L., *The Ancient Mariners: Seafarers and Sea-fighters of the
    Mediterranean in Ancient Times.* London, 1959.
Catling, H. W. and Millet, C., "A Study of the Inscribed Stirrup Jars
    from Thebes." *Archaeometry,* Vol. 8 (1965); Vol. 11 (1969).

Chadwick, John, *The Decipherment of Linear B.* Cambridge, 1958.

Desborough, V. R. d'A., *The Greek Dark Ages.* London, 1972.

———, *The Last Mycenaeans and their Successors.* Oxford, 1964.

Dodds, E. R., *The Greeks and the Irrational.* Berkeley, Los Angeles, and London, 1971.

Dumézil, Georges, *Le Problème des Centaures.* Paris, 1967.

Eliade, Mircea, *Myth and Reality.* New York, 1963.

Finley, M. I., *Early Greece: The Bronze and Archaic Ages.* London, 1970.

Forsdyke, John, *Greece Before Homer.* New York, 1957.

Frazer, Richard McIlwaine, *The Trojan Wars: the Chronicles of Dictys of Crete and Dares of the Phrygian.* Bloomington, Indiana, 1966.

Gordon, Cyrus, *Evidence for the Minoan Language.* Ventnor, New Jersey, 1966.

Graves, Robert, *The Greek Myths.* Harmondsworth, England, 1960.

———, *Hercules, My Shipmate.* New York, 1945.

Gurney, O. R., *The Hittites.* Baltimore and Middlesex, 1969.

Guthrie, W. K. C., *The Greeks and their Gods.* Boston, 1954.

Harrison, Jane, *Themis, A Study of the Social Origins of Greek Religions.* Cambridge, 1927.

Herodotus, *The Histories,* trans. Aubrey De Sélincourt. Harmondsworth, England, 1954.

Hesiod, *Theogony,* trans. Norman O. Brown. New York and Indianapolis, 1953.

Homer, *The Iliad,* trans. Richmond Lattimore. Chicago and London, 1951.

———, *The Odyssey,* trans. R. Fitzgerald. New York, 1961.

———, *The Odyssey,* trans. R. Lattimore. New York and London, 1965.

Hood, S., *The Minoans: The Story of Bronze Age Crete.* New York, 1970.

Hutchinson, R. W., *Prehistoric Crete.* Harmondsworth, England, 1962.

Hyde, W. W., *Ancient Greek Mariners.* New York, 1947.

James, E. O., *Prehistoric Religion.* London, 1957.

Jung, C. G., and Kerenyi, C., *Essays on a Science of Mythology.* Princeton, 1949.

Kirk, G. S., *Myth, Its Meanings and Functions in Ancient and Other Cultures.* Cambridge and Berkeley, 1970.

———, *Songs of Homer.* Cambridge, 1962.

Krappe, A. H., *The Science of Folklore.* New York, 1964.

Lawrence, A. W., *Greek Architecture,* 2d ed. *The Pelican History of Art.* Harmondsworth, England, and Baltimore, 1967.

Leaf, Walter, *Homer and History.* London, 1915.

Lorimer, H. L., *Homer and the Monuments.* London, 1950.

MacKendrick, Paul, *The Greek Stones Speak.* New York and Toronto, 1962.

Marinatos, Spyridon, *Crete and Mycenae.* New York, 1960.

Matz, F., *Minoan Civilization: Maturity and Zenith,* Vols. I–II, *Cambridge Ancient History,* rev. ed. 1923, 1931.

McDonald, Edward, and Rapp, George, *A Bronze Age Environment.* The Minnesota-Messenia Expedition. Minneapolis, 1972.

McDonald, William A., *Progress into the Past: Rediscovery of Mycenaean Civilisation.* New York, 1967.

Mertz, Henriette, *The Wine Dark Sea.* New York, 1970.

Michels, Joseph W., *Dating Methods in Archaeology.* New York, 1973.

Mylonas, George, *Eleusis and the Eleusinian Mysteries.* Princeton, 1961.

———, *Mycenae and the Mycenaean Age.* Princeton, 1966.

Nilsson, Martin P., *The Minoan-Mycenaean Religion,* 2d ed. New York, 1971.

———, *The Mycenaean Origins of Greek Mythology,* intro. and biblio. E. Vermeule, 2d ed. Berkeley, 1973.

Obregon, Mauricio, *Ulysses Airborne.* Library of Science Book Club, 1971.

Page, Denys, *History and the Homeric Iliad.* Berkeley, Los Angeles, and London, 1972.

———, *The Homeric Odyssey.* Oxford, 1955.

Palmer, L. R., *Mycenaeans and Minoans.* New York, 1962.

———, and Boardman, John, *On the Knossos Tablets.* Oxford, 1963.

Pausanius, *Description of Greece,* trans. and ed. J. G. Frazer. New York, 1965.

Pendlebury, J. D. S., *The Archaeology of Crete.* New York, 1965.

Platon, Nicholas, "Crete," *Archaeologia Mundi.* Cleveland and New York, 1966.

———, *Zakros: The Discovery of a Lost Palace of Ancient Crete.* New York, 1971.

Renfrew, Colin, *The Emergence of Civilization: The Cyclades and the Aegean in the Third Millennium.* London and New York, 1972.

―――, Cann, J. R., and Dixon, J. E., "Obsidian in the Aegean," *British School at Athens,* Vol. 60 (1965), pp. 225–247.

Rose, H. J., *A Handbook of Greek Mythology.* New York, 1959.

Schaeffer, C. F. A., *Stratigraphie Comparée.* London, 1948.

Schoo, Jan H., *Hercules' Labors: Fact or Fiction.* Chicago, 1969.

Spekke, Arnolds, *The Ancient Amber Routes and the Geographical Discovery of the Eastern Baltic.* Stockholm, 1957.

Spyropoulos, Theodore G., "Terracotta Sarcophagi." *Archaeology,* Vol. 25, No. 3 (June, 1972).

Stanford, W. B., *The Ulysses Theme.* Oxford, 1954.

Starr, Chester, *The Ancient Greeks.* London, 1971.

―――, *Early Man: Prehistory and the Civilisations of the Ancient Near East.* New York and Oxford, 1973.

―――, "The Myth of the Minoan Thalassokracy." *Historia,* 3 (1953), pp. 282ff.

Strabo, *The Geography,* trans. Horace Leonard Jones. London and New York, 1917–1933.

Symeonoglou, Saranlis, *Kadmeia I: Mycenaean Finds from Thebes, Greece; Excavation at 14 Oedipus St.* Goteborg, 1973.

Taylour, W. Lord, *The Mycenaeans.* London, 1961; Cambridge, 1964.

Thomson, George, *Studies in Ancient Greek Society: The Prehistoric Aegean.* London, 1949.

Tsountas, Chrestos, and Manatt, Irving, *The Mycenaean Age: A Study of the Monuments and Culture of Pre-Homeric Greece.* Chicago, 1964.

Ventris, M., and Chadwick, J., *Documents in Mycenaean Greek.* Cambridge, 1956.

Vermeule, Emily Townsend, *Greece in the Bronze Age.* Chicago and London, 1972.

―――, "The Mycenaeans in Achaia." *American Journal of Archaeology,* Vol. 64 (1960), pp. 1–21.

Von Bothmer, Dietrich, *Amazons in Greek Art.* Oxford, 1957.

Wace, A. J. B., *Mycenae: An Archaeological History and Guide.* Princeton, 1949.

―――, and Stubbings, F. H., eds., *A Companion to Homer.* London, 1962.

————, and Thompson, B., *Prehistoric Thessaly.* Cambridge, 1962.

Walpole, R., *Travels in Various Countries of the East.* London, 1820.

Ward, A. G., *The Quest for Theseus.* New York, 1970.

Webster, T. B. L., *From Mycenae to Homer.* New York, 1964.

Weinberg, Saul S., ed., *The Aegean and the Near East: Studies Presented to Hetty Goldman.* New York, 1956.

Willetts, R. F., *Cretan Cults and Festivals.* London, 1962.

Wunderlich, Hans Georg, "Das Geheimnis der Minoische Pälaste Alt-Kretas." *Naturwissenschaft und Medizin,* No. 36 (March, 1971).

Zafiropoulo, J., *Mead and Wine: A History of the Bronze Age in Greece.* London, 1966.

Index

Abas, 94
Abel, 164
Abraham, 246
Achaea, 314-315
Achaeans, 11, 52, 53, 72, 129, 133, 178-179, 181, 204, 230, 264, 273, 279, 293, 313
Achaiwa, 204
Achilles, 77, 92, 164, 175, 186, 190, 192, 203, 206, 219, 291
Acraephia, 215
Acrisius, 95, 96, 146, 163, 181
Acropolis, 131, 310
Adonis, 26, 257
Adrastus, 57
Aeaea, 241, 255
Aegean Bronze Age, 68
Aegeus, 119, 121, 134
Aegina, 126
Aegisthus, 92, 175, 186, 187, 198, 202, 311, 312
Aeolos, 215, 252, 274
Aerope, 162, 163
Aeschylus (525-456 B.C., Greek playwright), 92, 174, 175, 184, 187, 189, 196, 198, 199, 200, 230
Aetos, 313
Africa, 271, 274
Agamemnon, 5, 8, 10, 87, 91, 92, 94, 99, 129, 150, 167, 178-205, 291, 292, 297, 307, 311
Aganippe, 81
Age of Heroes, 2, 16, 18, 41

Agenor, 13, 30, 31, 32, 33, 50
Agora, 131
Agrigentum, 240
Ahhijawa, 204
Ahmosis, 30
Aia, 246
Aietes, King, 213, 233, 238-241, 245, 246, 247, 256
Aison, 215, 216
Aithiopis, 233
Aithon, 134
Aithra, 121
Ajax, 219
Ak-alan, 227
Akhatmilku, Queen, 185
Akhnaton, 96
Akrotiri, 126
Al Mina, 269
Alaca, 99
Alasia, 315
Alasians, 204
Alchemy, 221
Alexander, 234
Alkinoos, King, 170, 185, 260, 264, 265, 274, 275, 278
Almopians, 97
Alphabet, Phoenician, 44, 271
Alpheios (huntsman), 154
Alpheios (river), 153, 154, 160
Alpheios Valley, 314
Alsop, Joseph, 295
Altis, 108

331

Amarna Letters, 203
Amathus, 122
Amazons, 120, 134, 229, 232, 233-237
Amber, 212, 222, 224, 225-227, 231, 232
Amnissos, 23, 118
Amphiaraus, 152
Amphictyon, 50
Amphilochus, 203
Amphion, 56
Amphitryon, 109
Anatolia, 20, 21, 22, 23, 24, 31, 33, 50, 59, 61, 62, 64, 66, 67, 99, 115, 125, 203, 236
Anatolians, 6, 35, 50, 63, 65, 67, 72, 73, 233
Androgeus, 120
Andromeda, 91, 95, 97
Angel, Lawrence, 65-66, 101
Animal sacrifice, 48, 78-79, 111, 112, 137, 141, 190, 191, 213, 242-243, 281, 308, 315
Animism, 76, 82, 309
Anthropology, 10, 20, 21, 22, 24
Antigone, 56
Antinous, 272, 306, 307-308, 309, 311
Antiope, 56, 79
Ao-ka, 114
A-pe-e-ke, 294
Aphrodite, 55, 229, 239, 257, 270, 297; Temple of, 236
Aphrodite Ariadne, 122
Apoikia, 265
Apollo, 9, 38, 40, 54, 56, 177, 198, 203, 242, 284, 297
Apollodorus (c. 415 B.C., Athenian painter), 91, 95, 134
Apollonius Rhodius (3rd Cent. B.C., Alexandrian poet, librarian), 212, 222, 229, 231, 232, 238, 242
Apples, 160
Apsidal houses, 64
Apsyrtos, 240, 241, 245
Arcadia, 80, 154
Arcadians, 92
Aras Valley, 227-228
Archaeology, 4-5, 10, 11, 18, 22, 33, 34, 35, 41-42, 57, 59, 61, 77, 93, 110, 113, 129, 266
Archippe, 106
Architecture, Mycenaean, 208
Ares (god), 37, 38, 40, 41, 54, 55, 231 temple to, 79
Ares (island), 231
Arete, Queen, 259, 264, 276, 305
Arethusa, 154, 276
Argeiwa, 204
Argives, 96, 97, 98, 163, 204
Argo (Jason's ship), 217-222, 228-229, 231, 239, 241
dating problem, 219-220
Argolid, 92, 95, 146, 182
Argolis, 94, 95, 96
Argonautica, 212, 228
Argonauts, 57, 152, 206-247, 254
Argos, 46, 57, 78, 91, 92, 93, 95, 96, 97, 98, 105, 146, 228
Argus, 253
Ariadne, 120, 121, 122, 132, 133, 138

Arion, 80
Aristocracy, 267
Aristotle, 4, 267
Arkanes, 78, 79
Armenia, 227
Art, 5, 10, 25, 93, 102-103, 110, 152, 189, 236; Minoan, 104, 128-129; monumental, 73; relationship of European to Greek, 254; Vapheio, 115-117; votive, 60
Artemis, 56, 152, 175, 176, 194, 199, 242, 243, 244; Temple of, 176
Aryans, 65
Arzawa, 178
Asclepios, 245
Asherat, 28, 29, 30
Ashtoreth, 26, 256
Asklepiades, Publius, 110
Assuwas, League of, 178, 179
Assyrians, 205, 228, 236
Astarte, 26, 256
Atalanta, 152
Athena, 9, 32, 34, 36, 37, 41, 54-55, 147, 196, 198, 216, 239, 241, 249, 252, 253, 257, 259, 275, 278, 279, 281, 300, 301, 302, 308, 309-311
Athene, 310
Athenians, 119, 120, 121, 132, 133
Athens, 118-123, 131, 132, 133, 134, 152, 161, 162, 201, 293; Amazon attack on, 234
Atlas, 160, 161
Atreidai, 134
Atreus, 91, 99, 106, 146, 162-164, 167, 168, 169, 171, 174, 175, 177, 200, 201; House of, 215, 216, 311; Tomb of, 169; Treasury of, 161, 168-169, 170, 201
Attarissiyas, 177, 178
Attica, 123, 134, 182, 313
Attis, 26, 257
Augeias, 108, 148, 153, 155, 156; stables of, 148, 153, 154
Aulis, 174, 175, 176
Autolycus, 280
Axes, 306
Azerbaijan, 228
Azores, 274

Baal, 30
Babylonians, 72, 76, 246
Bachofen, J. J., 229n.
Balearics, 273
Balkans, 65, 67
Baluchistan, 70
Barter, 272, 276
Basileus, 114
Bear Cult, 253-254
Bellerophon, 9
Beycesultan, 23
Birds, 28, 231-232
Bistones, 76
Black Sea, 148, 212, 221, 222, 231; colonization of the, 212, 222
Blegen, C. W., 69, 129, 130, 131, 133, 134, 283-284, 288, 290, 292
Boeotia, 36, 37, 41, 45, 55, 157, 176, 182, 207, 208, 209, 213, 214, 215, 247, 290
Bogazkoy, 25, 72

Bonfante, Giuliano, 97
Book of Kikkuli, 72
Bosporus, 231, 232, 233
Bows, 305-306
Britomartis, 26, 242
Broneer, Oscar, 310
Bronze, 5, 67, 228, 295-296, 301, 316
Bronze Age, 5, 7, 9, 10, 11, 12, 18, 67, 68, 282
  Aegean, 68
Bronzesmiths, 295-296
Brundisium, 313
Buildings, 5, 24, 129, 141-145, 168-169
  Neolithic, 59, 60-61
Bulgarians, 99
Bull, 48, 60-61, 80, 135-141, 165
  bronze, 240
  Europa and the, 13-31
  fire-breathing, 238, 239
  sacrifice, 308
Burial customs, 22, 34, 59, 60, 64-65, 66,
  77-78, 86, 93, 99-101, 114-115, 188, 191,
  293
Burnaburiash II, King, 49
Buthoe, 54, 55
Byblos, 25

Cadmea, 37, 41, 42, 44, 48, 50
Cadmeans, 41
Cadmeioi, 30, 35, 50, 54
Cadmos, 10, 13, 25, 107, 155, 239, 240
  founds Thebes, 32-58
Cain, 164
Calydon, 152
Calypso, 249, 252, 258, 262, 273, 274
Canaan, 13, 30, 32, 50, 101
Carpathian Mountains, 217
Carthage, 32, 33, 270
Caskey, J., 78
Cassandra, 175, 183, 187
Castalian Spring, 36
Cattle, 273; cattle raising, 25, 165, 301
Cavalry, 267
Cecrops, 97, 132
Centaur (constellation), 83
Centaurs, 9, 74-77, 82-85, 120
Cerberus, 83, 148, 150
Chadwick, John, 197, 295, 296
Chalybians, 232
Chariots, 71, 72, 73, 74, 108, 110, 114, 117,
  210
Charvati, 91
Charybdis, 252, 261, 273, 274
Cheiron, 75, 83, 216, 245
Chem, 99
Chemmis, 97, 99
Chimera, 9
Chios, 301-302
Chloris, 291
Chronology, 318
Chrysothemis, 56
Cilicia, 32, 33, 203
Cilicians, 94
Cilix, 13, 32
Circe, 222, 239, 241, 245, 246, 252, 255, 256,
  257-258, 260, 261, 274
Cist-tomb form of burial, 293

City-states, 265
"Clashing rocks," 231
Clay, 47-48
Cleitarchos, 234
Clytemestra, 92, 175, 184, 187, 192, 200, 259,
  307, 312
Coins, 28, 49
Colchians, 4, 221
Colchicine, 238
Colchis, 213, 221, 222, 227-228, 238, 241, 246
Communion, 243
Comus, 258
Concubinage, 301, 305
Constitution of Athens (Aristotle), 267
Copais Lake, 157, 209-210
Copper, 5, 24, 47, 67, 126, 164, 264, 268, 315
Corcyra, 273
Corinth, 56, 181, 212, 213, 247
Cow, 32, 36, 37
Cremation, 34, 204
Creon, 52, 57
Crete, 5, 6, 12, 13, 14, 16, 17, 19, 20-31, 47,
  48, 50, 51, 63, 78, 79, 93, 94, 103-104,
  116-117, 118-145, 148, 268, 280, 297
  trade and, 24-25, 29, 48
Cult(s)
  bear, 253-254
  bull, 164-166
  fertility, 164, 216
  fusion of, 29-30
  goat, 164-166
  hero, 199
  Minoan, 31
  Mistress's, 242
  Mycenaean, 192-193, 198
  of Aphrodite, 229
  of the Great Mother, 26
  of Zagreus, 19
  of Zeus Laphystius, 214
Cumae, 266
Curtius, Ernest, 158
Customs
  matrilineal, 232-233
  matrilocal, 232-233
Cyanean Rocks, 231
Cybele, 26, 242, 256, 257
Cyclades, 21, 22, 93
Cycladic peoples, 6
Cyclopes, 95, 97, 153, 161, 252, 254, 260-264,
  266, 272, 274
Cyclops (Euripides), 263
Cylinder seals, 48-49
  Babylonian, 25
Cypriots, 122, 201, 203, 204, 252, 271, 315,
  316
Cyprus, 22, 48, 50, 77, 79, 122, 125, 126, 127,
  260, 264, 270, 271, 280, 297, 298, 314,
  315

Daedalus, 18, 118, 120, 139
Daemon, 38
Danaans, 94, 97, 98, 107, 203, 204
Danae, 91, 95, 96, 97
Danaoi, 96, 97, 98
Danaus, 94, 96, 104
Dardana, 203

Dardanelles, 213
Dares, 3
Dark Ages, 2, 265
Davis, Ellen N., 115n.
Deianeira, 74, 77
Delphic oracle, 32, 56, 109, 148, 199
Demeter, 26, 37, 54, 80, 81, 82, 83, 84, 196, 199
Democracy, 123, 267
Demophon, 313
Dendra, 9, 146, 289
Denyen, 203
Deucalion, 53, 134
Deucalion's flood, 4
Dictys, 3
Dimini, 61, 247
Diomedes, 76, 77, 182, 202, 203, 313
Dionysos, 56, 85, 122, 165
Disk, Phaistos, 23
Diuja, 196
Dodona, 281
Dorian invasions, 2, 55, 58, 92, 130, 201, 202, 230, 291, 292, 293, 312, 316-317
Dorians, 129, 130, 133, 152, 205, 230, 291, 292, 293, 313-317
Doulichion, 275
Dove, 231
Dragon, 39, 239-240
Dryopians, 97
Dumézil, Georges, 83, 84, 85

Ecarteurs, 137
Echelawon, 294
Echidna, 156
Eclecticism, 102
Eden, 161
Edonians, 32
Egypt, 21, 22, 23, 30, 94, 98, 124, 125, 127, 201, 203, 290, 297, 298-300, 315
Egyptians, 101, 115, 201, 203, 204, 221, 269
El, 28, 29, 30
Eleans, 108, 154
Electra, 187, 198
Eleusis, 83, 84, 85, 195, 202
Elis, 105, 107, 108, 109, 153, 154, 314
Elpenor, 192
Engineering, 152-160, 184-185
Enkomi, 126, 127, 298, 315
Epano Englianos, 283, 290, 291, 292
Ephesos, 204
Epigoni, War of, 52, 53, 57
Epigraphy, 10
Epirus, 300
Eratosthenes, 219
Ergiros, 276
Erinyes, 196
Eros, 238, 257
Eteocles, 45, 52, 56, 57
Eteo-Cretans, 129
Ethiopia, 99
Ethnography, 10, 20
Etruscans, 266
Etymology, 77
Euboean Channel, 210
Euippa, 77
Eumaeus, 269, 273, 276, 278, 301, 305, 311

Eumolpus, 83
Euneos, 230
Euripides (480?-406 B.C., Greek playwright), 148, 174, 246, 247, 263, 297
Europa, 9, 12, 32, 33, 35, 37, 50, 51, 53
rape of, 13-31
Eurycleia, 252, 302, 305
Eurystheus, 83, 91, 92, 146, 148, 149, 150, 159, 160, 161, 162
Eusebius, 219
Euxine, 227, 232, 234
Evans, Sir Arthur, 4, 6, 16, 17, 18, 23, 30, 44, 48, 103, 118, 119, 124, 126, 129, 130, 131, 132, 139, 141, 142, 143, 145, 288

Faience, 224, 298
Farming, 112, 208, 301, 316; Neolithic, 61, 62, 68
Feathers, bronzed, 231-232
Fertility cults, 216
Feudalism, 267
Fleece, golden, 213-245
Food and Agriculture Organization, 155
Forsdyke, John, 236n.
Frazer, James, 79, 158
Frescoes, 44, 283, 284
From the Silent Earth (Alsop), 295
Fruit, 160-161
Funeral rites, 99-100, 109, 188-192.
See also Burial customs
Furies, 196, 198, 200

Gades, 270
Gaea, 262
Galen, 226
Gamoroi, 266
Ganymede, 238
Gems, 49, 112, 115, 195, 224, 303-304;
workshops for, 44
Genealogies, 2, 3, 16, 17, 18, 20, 215; *see also* Appendix II
Genesis, 259
Giali, 217
Gibraltar, Strait of, 274
Gift-giving, 185-186
Gilgamesh, 161, 257-258
Gla, 67, 210
Glauce, 246, 247
Goat Pan, 162
Gold, 32, 48, 221-222, 227, 228, 268, 270, 299
Golden fleece, 213-245
Gorgon Medusa, 95, 96-97, 98
Gortyna, 28, 31, 129
Gournia, 127, 139, 141, 142
Graeae, 97
Grave circles, 93-94, 99-102
Graves, Robert, 41, 99, 163, 238
Graves, shaft, *see* Shaft graves; tholos, 114-115, 164, 168
Great Mother, 26-27, 31, 54, 84, 122, 193, 242, 256, 259
"Great year," 40
Gynocracy, 229, 230

Hades, 80, 81, 83, 84, 85, 148, 198, 249, 252, 254, 255, 257, 258, 259, 263, 274

Hagia Triada, 18, 142, 172
Hagia Triada Sarcophagus, 143
Hammurabi, 25
Harmonia, 37, 49, 52, 54, 55
Harpies, 32
Harrison, Jane, 40, 240
Hecataeus, 16
Hecate, 257
Hector, 5, 8, 175, 177, 190
Helen, 3, 79, 174, 259, 297, 305
Helice, 181
Helios, 252
Helius, 163, 240
Helle, 213, 215
Hellenes, 80
Hellespont, 213, 228
Hellotis, 26, 27, 28, 30, 31
Hequetai, 114
Hera, 9, 27, 160, 196, 199, 213, 216, 239, 241, 257
Heracleidae, 92, 162, 201
Heracles, 49, 74, 75, 76, 77, 82-85, 91, 92, 108, 109, 111, 120, 146-173, 177, 219, 229, 233
Heraeum, 95
Hermes, 84, 106, 162, 196, 255
Herodotus (484?-425? B.C., Greek historian), 16, 30, 97, 99, 154, 162, 214, 221, 228, 229, 234, 236, 245, 254, 274, 293, 298
Hesiod (8th Cent.? B.C., Greek poet), 9, 156, 233, 259, 267
Hesperides, 160
Hippaleus, 106
Hippasus, 106
Hippe, 81
Hippocrates, 226
Hippodameia, 75, 80, 105-106, 108, 109, 110, 162
Hippodrome, 108, 109
Hippokrene, 81
Hippolyte, 80
Hippolytus, 80
Hippothoe, 106
Hissarlik, 69
History, 93; cultural, 20; definition of, 1; distinguished from myth, 1-12
Hittites, 6, 64, 65, 72, 113, 125, 177-180, 201, 202, 203, 204, 268
Homer (800? B.C., Greek poet), 9, 11, 17, 41, 69, 72, 78, 79, 82, 91, 92, 95, 96, 113, 114, 119, 129, 130, 132, 133, 134, 150, 152, 157, 165, 169, 170, 174, 175, 177, 179, 186, 187, 188, 190, 191, 192, 196, 202, 204, 230, 232, 233, 248-279, 282, 283, 285-292, 297, 298, 299, 301-306, 308, 309, 314, 315. *See also Iliad; Odyssey*
Horon, 246
Horse, 64, 68-86, 106, 110, 116, 225, 227, 228, 233, 275, 292
Horus, 246
House of the Sphinxes, 167
House of Tiles, 64
Human sacrifice, 57, 77, 176, 190, 197, 203, 214, 240, 241, 243, 245, 246
  at Orchomenos, 212, 214

Hyginus, 105
Hyksos, 30, 31, 50, 94, 98
Hypachae, 33
Hypachaeans, 32, 33
Hypsipyle, Queen, 229

Ialysos, 34, 35, 50
Iasion, 245
Icarius, 304
Icmalius, 303
Idomeneus, 3, 17, 53, 129, 133, 134
Iliad, 58, 92, 99, 133, 150, 164, 174, 176, 177, 179-180, 182, 190, 191, 196, 230, 248, 259, 283, 286, 290
Ilios, 72
Illuyankas, 39
Illyria, 13, 54, 55
Illyrians, 4, 55, 92
Illyrius, 54
Immortality, 160-161
Inaras, 39
Incest, 105, 106, 163, 175
India, 64
Indo-European peoples, 64-66, 71-72, 113
Ino, 213
Iolas, 156, 160
Iolcus, 67, 203, 207, 213, 216, 217, 220, 222, 244, 247
Ionian islands, 63, 276
Ionians, 313
Iphigenia, 175, 176
Iphimedeia, 196
Iranians, 228
Iron, 232, 279
Iron Age, 212
Isaac, 246
Ischia, 266
Ishtar, 25, 26, 256, 257
Island of the Sun, 252
Italus, 4
Ithaca, 202, 248, 249, 250, 252, 253, 273, 274, 275, 276, 278, 279, 281, 300, 301, 304, 311, 312, 313, 314
Ithacans, 276
Ivory, 46, 47, 268, 270-271

Jack the Giant Killer, 161
Jason, 10, 79, 152, 155, 206-247, 254, 256
Jenghiz Khan, 234
Jewelry, 44, 48
Jocasta, 42, 52, 56
Joyce, James, 70
Juniper tree, 238

Kadesh, 203
Kalamata, 116
Kalchas, 175
Kassite dynasty, 48
Kassites, 72
Katabothrae, 209-210
Kea, 127
Keats, John, 81
Keos, 125, 127
Kephallenia, 275, 276, 313, 314
Kephisos River, 157, 158
Kerkyon, 120

Kidin Marduk, 49
Kingship, 12, 57, 61, 113-114, 163-164, 197,
  216-217, 221, 240
  symbol of, 244
Kladeos River, 154
Knossos, 6, 12, 14, 17, 18, 23, 24, 30, 44, 46,
  47, 48, 52, 53, 93, 103, 116, 175, 185, 196,
  197, 294
  excavations, 5, 6, 18
  fall of, 126
  Mycenaeans at, 118-145
Korax, 276
Kordudallos, 288
Kos, 230
Kretheus, King of Iolcus, 215, 216
Kronos, 108, 163, 263
Kulhai, 227, 228
Kuretes, 19, 242
Kurgan pit-grave people, 224-225
Kyan, 30
Kydonians, 129, 133
Kythera, 116, 126, 270

Labdakids, 57
Labdakos, 52, 57
Labyrinthos, 23
Ladon, 160
Lady of Wild Things, 242
Laertes, 269, 301, 305, 307
Laius, 52, 56, 57
Lake Copais, 157, 209-210
Lake Stymphalia, 158
Lakonia, 63, 115, 116, 122, 316
Lance, 40-41
Landes district, France, 137, 138
Language, 6, 23, 63; Cadmean, 44;
  Eteocretan, 23; hieroglyphic, 23;
  Luwian, 23; pre-Greek, 23. *See also* Lin-
  ear A script; Linear B script
Laomedon, 177
Laphria, Artemis, 243
Lapis lazuli, 44, 46, 48
Lapiths, 75
Larnakes, 137, 187-189, 192
Larymna, 210
Lascaux, cave paintings at, 70
Lawagetas, 113
Leaf, Walter, 180
Leda, 29
Lemnos, 228-230, 247
Lerna, 64-66, 67, 78, 86, 90, 156, 158
Lesbos, 230, 302
Leto, 56, 242
Leucas, 276
Leuktron, 296
Levant, 26, 125, 203
Libration Bearers, The, 230
Libya, 20, 22, 98, 297, 298
Libyans, 97, 98
Lindos Chronicle, 34
Linear A script, 6, 23, 44, 47, 127
Linear B script, 6-7, 8, 12, 45, 46, 47, 48, 82,
  113, 127, 128, 129, 130, 147, 171,
  172-173, 177, 196, 197, 288-296, 302,
  303
Linen, 299

Linseed, 296
Lion Gate (Mycenae), 166, 168, 201
Lions, 165, 256
Lithares, 60-61, 62, 80
Lotus Eaters, 252
Louis XIV, King (France), 234
Lucanians, 203
Lucian, 163
Lukka, 203
Luwians, 23
Lycia, 33, 34, 203
Lycians, 35, 203

Ma, 242
Macareus, 258
Macedonia, 63
Mackenzie, Duncan, 129
Magnesians, 217
Magritte, 135
Mallia, 14, 23, 24, 127, 139, 141, 142
Malta, 273
Marathon, 77, 78; battle of, 123
Mariadyne, 232
Marinatos, Spyridon, 99
Marmarospilia, 276
Marriage: goddess-hero, 257; sacred, 27, 31,
  257-262
Medea, 212, 213, 222, 237-247, 256
Megara, 120
Melanippe, 80
Melanthius, 302
Meleager, 152
Meliboea, 313
Melos, 125, 126, 217, 218
Menelaos, 3, 91, 174, 201, 259, 270, 297-299,
  305
Menoicus, 57
Menyeios River, 291
Mercury, 256
Mer'eye, King, 299
Merneptah, 204
Mesopotamia, 73, 94, 159
Mesopotamians, 72
Messenia, 63, 182, 186, 280, 283, 290, 292,
  295
Messina, Strait of, 273, 274
Metallurgy, 61, 67, 225
Metamorphoses, 13-31, 40, 54, 77
Midea, 92, 95, 146
Migrations, 6, 13-31, 33, 35, 68, 225, 265-266,
  314
Miletos, 125, 204
Mining, 221
Minoa, 18, 125
Minoans, 22, 29, 30, 31, 34, 48, 103, 129, 143
Minos, King, 14, 16-17, 18, 23, 31, 53, 118,
  119, 120, 121, 127, 130, 131, 132, 133
Minotaur, 118, 120, 122, 132, 133, 135, 139,
  140
Minyan ware, 207
Minyans, 147, 158, 206-247, 290-291
Minyas, 206, 208, 212; Treasury of, 208
Mitannians, 64, 65, 72, 125, 204
Moly flower, 256
Mongols, 234, 236
Moore, Marianne, 248

Mopsus, 203
Mother Earth, 38, 39, 68, 84
Mount Atlas, 160
Mount Dikte, 19
Mount Halus, 214
Mount Kithairon, 147
Mount Laphystion, 214
Mount Parnassos, 38
Mount Pelion, 215
Mount Sipylus, 105
Mountain Mother, 26
Muses, 54
Muthos, 11
Muwatallis, 203, 204
Mycenae, 5, 11, 52, 53, 67, 69, 86, 87, 90-117, 124, 126, 146-173, 268, 269; Agamemnon and, 174-205; destruction of, 201, 205; excavations, 5; Heracles and, 146-173; Lion Gate, 166, 168, 201
Mycenaeans, 6, 7, 8, 9, 11, 19, 30, 31, 34, 35, 37, 41, 48, 49, 51, 58, 87, 92, 98, 101, 103-104, 116, 117, 119, 124, 125, 126, 153, 154, 157, 180, 207, 224, 232, 278, 279, 280-318
    Knossos and, 118-145
Mylonas, George, 100, 101, 168
Myrtilus, 106, 110, 162
Myth: definition of, 1; distinguished from history, 1-12
Mythmaking, 1, 10, 14-17, 25, 31, 91-92, 107, 119, 131-135, 184, 246, 298

Nature Goddess, 26
Nauplia, 78
Nausikaa, Princess, 252, 258, 259
Naxos, 121, 122, 230
Near East, 22, 24, 25, 26, 64, 94, 96, 97, 101, 124, 185
Nekyia, 290, 291
Neleid family, 290-291
Neleus, 290, 291
Nemean Games, 92
Neolithic peoples, 59-61, 76, 217-218
Neoptolemus, 203
Nephele, 213, 215
Nereus, 160
Neriton, 275, 276
Nessos, 74, 75, 76, 77
Nestor, 3, 78, 113, 152, 182, 196, 202, 275, 281-292, 295, 297, 300, 308; Cup of, 93, 287
Nilsson, Martin, 8, 96, 193, 195
Nineveh, 236
Niobe, 56
Nirou Hani, 138
Noemon, 300
Nolo, Gulf of, 276
North Africa, 33
Nova Scotia Bay, 274
Nubia, 94
Nymphs, 9

Obsidian, 217-218
Odysseus, 9, 10, 54, 78, 133, 161, 182, 185, 192, 198, 202, 248-317

Odyssey, 134, 176, 192, 219, 248-279, 281, 299, 305, 309, 311, 313
Oedipus, 42, 45, 52, 56, 57, 58, 216
Oenomaus, 105-107, 108, 109, 110
Oenotrians, 4
Ogyia, 249, 273
Oil, 24, 46, 47
Old Testament, 270
Olympia, 108, 109, 110, 154, 191
Olympians, 54, 55, 196, 242
Olympic Games, 108-111
Omophagia, 163
Onagers, 71
Onga, 36
Onyx, 44, 48
Oracle, 56
    Delphic, 32, 56, 109, 148, 199
    Pythian, 108
Orchomenians, 202
Orchomenos, 41, 45, 67, 151, 207-210, 215, 247; dating problem, 207; human sacrifice at, 212, 214
Orestai, 92
Oresteia, 174
Orestes, 91, 92, 175, 189, 198, 199, 200, 201, 202, 307, 311, 312, 313, 315
Orontes River, 269
Orpheus, 243-244, 254, 284
Orphics, 244
Orphism, 212, 220, 243
Ourania, 270
Ovid, 154, 258
Oxylos, 314-315

Page, Denys, 177, 178, 179
Pakijana, 197, 296
Palestine, 236, 299
Pallas, 134
Palmer, L., 129, 131, 133, 134, 293-296
Pandora's box, 259
Parian Chronicle, 3, 17, 50, 51, 134, 234, 319-324
Paris, 3, 174, 175, 297, 305
Pasiphae, 118, 120, 121, 122
Pass of Kephalari, 210
Patrae, 243
Patroklos, 188, 190
Pausanias (c. A.D., 174, Lycian? traveler and geographer), 54, 91, 95, 105, 108-109, 110, 111, 134, 153, 154, 157, 158, 159, 169, 208, 209, 214, 242, 247, 314
Pegasus, 80, 98
Peirithous, 75, 152
Peisistratos, 282, 283
Peisos, 109
Pelasgians, 129, 133, 206
Pelasgus, 206
Peleus, 152, 219
Pelias, King, 213, 215, 216, 217, 221, 244
Pelopia, 163, 175
Pelopids, 91, 92, 164
Peloponnesians, 109
Peloponnesos, 3, 92, 106, 107, 109, 110, 111, 148, 150, 154, 156, 167, 174, 206, 297
Pelops, 3, 87, 91, 92, 104-111, 155, 162, 165, 175, 191; tomb of, 111

Peneios, 153
Penelope, 248, 249, 252, 258-259, 278, 281,
    300, 302-307, 309, 311, 312, 313
Penthesileia, Queen, 233
Pentheus, 56
Perati, 204
Pere, 196
Pericles, 123
Perseia, 91
Perseids, 146
Persephone, 80, 83, 84, 254, 257
Perseus, 4, 91, 94-98, 99, 101, 104, 146, 155,
    201; Age of, 87-117
Petelia, 313
Phaeacia, 252, 260, 264, 272
Phaeacians, 248, 252, 259, 260, 264, 265, 273,
    274, 276
Phaistos, 14, 18, 23, 24, 129, 139, 141, 142
Phaistos disk, 23
Pharos, 297, 299
Pheneus, 158
Philistines, 204, 205
Philoktetes, 111, 203, 313
Philology, 93
Phineus, 13, 32, 231
Phlegon of Tralles, 109
Phoenicia, 19, 31, 32, 35, 268-270, 297, 298
Phoenicians, 6, 30, 33, 35, 37, 264, 268-271,
    279
Phoenix, 13, 32, 33
Phoibos, 200
Phoinikous, 270
Pholus, 74, 83, 84
Phorcys, 276
Phrixos, 212-216, 221, 245, 246
Phrixus, 79
Phrygia, 26, 236
Phylakopi, 125
Picasso, 135
Picus, 258
Pindar (518?-c. 438 B.C., Greek poet), 108,
    111, 240
Piracy, 229, 260, 272
Pisa, 105, 107, 108, 110
Pisans, 108, 109
Platanos, 25
Plato, 4, 243
Pleuron, 295
Pliny, 238
Plutarch (46?-c. A.D., 120, Greek biographer
    and essayist), 214, 234
Polis, 313, 314
Polis Bay, 278
Polybius, 163
Polydorus, 52
Polynices, 45, 52, 56, 57
Polyphemus, 4, 248, 249, 262, 263, 272, 273,
    311
Polytheism, 256
Pompeii, 82
Port Andri, 278
Poseidon, 32, 68, 81, 82, 83, 84, 98, 106, 119,
    120, 121, 123, 133, 177, 196, 249, 253,
    262, 263, 281, 292, 308
Priam, 177, 233
Proetus, 94-95, 146, 163, 181, 297, 299

Prokrustes, 120
Prosymna, 9, 192
Prussia, 94
Puga, Isle of, 231
Pulos, 281-296, 297, 300
Punics, 32
Pylos, 52, 53, 67, 82, 113, 126, 130, 143, 151,
    177, 185, 187, 188, 195, 196, 197, 202,
    209
Pythian Oracle, 108
Python, 38, 39, 40

Ram, 212, 213, 214, 221
Rameses II, 204
Rameses III, 96, 201, 203, 299, 315
Rana Ghundai, 70
Ras Shamra, 25n.
Regeneration, symbol of, 240, 241
Religion, 27, 31, 33, 40, 55, 60, 79, 82, 93, 98,
    164-165, 193, 195-196, 199;
    Minoan, 31; Mycenaean, 8
Renfrew, Colin, 67, 159
Republicanism, 300
Rhadamanthys, 31, 51, 53
Rhodes, 32, 34, 35, 48, 50, 125, 127, 179, 203,
    204, 280, 315
Rhodesians, 79
Rhodians, 34, 203
Rip Van Winkle, 253
Roads, 182-183

Sabouni, 269
Saffron, 238
Sagittarius, 76
Salamis, 315
Salmoxis, 254
Same, 275
Santorini, 126
Sardinia, 270
Sardinians, 203
Sarpedon, 14, 31, 53
Sartre, Jean-Paul, 97
Saturn, 258
Satyrs, 85
Saul, King, 246
Sauromatians, 233, 234
Scapegoat-sacrifice, 214
Scheria, 273
Schliemann, Heinrich, 4, 5, 7, 12, 41, 69, 70,
    87, 90, 93, 94, 101, 151, 207, 208, 225,
    278
Schoo, Jan, 156, 158
Scribonianus, Alytarches Flavius, 110
Sculiman, 49
Scylla, 252, 258, 261, 273, 274
Scythians, 233, 236-237
Sea Peoples, 201-205, 299, 315
Seals, 48-49, 50, 77; Babylonian, 25
Sealstones, 50
Seamanship, 218
Semites, 98
Serpents, 36-41, 49, 54
Shaft graves, 86, 90, 93, 94, 99, 100-104, 115
Shardana, 203
Shekelesh, 203, 204
Sicels, 266

Sicilians, 203, 266
Sicily, 18, 125, 270, 271
Sidon, 28
Sidonians, 270
Siduri, 257, 258
Silver, 227, 228
Silver Siege Rhyton, 93, 103, 170
Sinbad, 254
Sinope, 232
Sipha, 228
Skyros, 302
Slave trade, 273
Smiths, 208-209
Snakes, 40, 49, 160-161, 193-194, 240-241. *See also* Serpents
Solomon, 268
Solon, 267
Sophocles (c. 496-c. 406 B.C., Greek playwright), 56
Sounion, 81, 133, 297
Spartans, 79, 199
Spartoi, 36, 37, 40, 41, 57
Sphinx, 56
Spring of Ares, 36, 38
Stirrup jars, 44, 46, 47, 48, 50
Stone Age people, 60-61
Strabo (c. 63 B.C.-A.D. 21?, Greek geographer and historian), 109, 209, 221, 236, 275, 291
Stymphalia, Lake, 158
Suidas, 221
Sumeria, 26
Suppiluliumas II, 204
"Surie," 269
Swan, 29
Swine, 256, 258
Symplegades, 231
Syncretism, 27, 31
Syracuse, 154
Syria, 24, 30, 31, 64, 94, 204, 268, 269, 270, 299
Syrians, 125

Tammuz, 26, 257
Tanagra, 137
Tantalus, 105
Tartarus, 83, 262
Tauroi, 175
Tawagalawas Letter, 177
Taylour, William Lord, 193-196, 199-200
Tegeans, 199
Teiresias, 57, 203, 252, 258
Tel el Amarna, 299
Telamon, 219
Telemachus, 78, 248, 249, 259, 275, 278, 279, 281-282, 284, 285, 291, 292, 297, 300, 303-306, 308, 309, 312
Telephassa, 13, 32, 34, 35, 36
Temenos, 113
Tenedos, 302
Thales, 226
Thalestris, Queen, 234
Thasians, 33
Thasos, 32, 33, 35
Thasus, 13, 32
Thebans, 54, 55, 147

Thebes, 11, 13, 147, 202, 300; Cadmos founds, 32-58; dating problem, 42, 51; excavations, 41-42, 44; Seven against, 45, 52, 57; trade and, 46-48
Themiscyra, 233, 234
Thera, 32, 126, 132
Theriomorphism, 309
Thermopylae, 92
Theseus, 5, 80, 118-124, 132-138, 140, 145, 152, 161
Thespiae, 228
Thessalians, 68
Thessaly, 63, 68, 206, 207, 208, 209, 212, 213, 214, 215, 218, 220, 221
Tholos tombs, 114-115
Thrace, 35-36, 77, 148
Thracians, 35
Thucydides, 201, 274, 293
Thyestai, 92
Thyestes, 91, 99, 106, 162-164, 167, 171, 174, 175
Tiles, 24
Tin, 5, 67, 226, 268, 279
Tipha, 228
Tiryns, 67, 92, 95, 132, 146, 148-155, 157, 160, 161, 181-182, 187, 201, 202
Tisamenos, 92, 311, 313
Titans, 262-263
Tleptolemus, 203
Tools, 5, 60, 62, 66
Trade: Crete and, 24-25, 29, 48; Minyans and, 208-209, 217, 219; Mycenaean-Egyptian, 298-300; Phoenicians and, 33, 268; Thebes and, 46-47; three-way, 50
Tradition, 254, 255
Trebizond, 228
Trees, 161; sacred, 28
Trialeti, 227
Trianda, 125, 167
Troad, 180
Troezen, 119
Trojan Horse, 178
Trojan War, 2, 3, 17, 52, 53, 57, 58, 111, 129, 133, 134, 174, 175, 176-180, 273, 312, 315
Trojans, 58, 69, 72, 174, 204
Tros, 177
Troy, 5, 6, 8, 42, 54, 58, 67, 69-72, 74, 90, 111, 159, 174, 175, 179, 253; excavations, 4; fall of, 2, 3, 200, 201
Tsountas, Chrestos, 115, 247
Tutankhamen, 177, 299
Tuthalijas IV, King, 177, 178, 179
Tyndareos, 79
Typhon, 156
Tyre, 13, 28, 32, 33, 53, 270
Tyrians, 33

Ugarit, 25, 29, 30, 125, 186, 268, 269, 270, 280
Underworld, 241, 248, 254, 257
United Nations, 155
Uranus, 262
Urartians, 228
Urartu, 227-228

Utica, 270
Utu, 257

Vapheio, 115-116
Vapheio Cups, 115, 116, 135
Varia, 158
Vases, 24
Ventris, Michael, 6, 12, 45, 288, 295, 296
Vermeule, Emily, 102, 192, 314
Voyage of the Argonauts, 57

Wace, A. J. B., 164, 167, 168, 302
Wanax, 113, 114
Warfare, 103
Weapons, 5, 68, 93, 115, 186, 289, 294, 296, 301
Weaving, 305
William, Friar, 236

Willow tree, 31
Wine, 24, 46, 165, 286
Wolf, 254
Women, 258-260
Wunderlich, Hans Georg, 142-145

Zagreus, 19, 28, 31
Zakro, 47-48, 127, 141-142
Zakynthos, 275
Zeus, 9, 13-31, 51, 53, 56, 68, 79-81, 83, 91, 95, 96, 105, 108, 109, 110, 111, 120, 123, 149, 154, 159, 163, 164, 165, 195, 196, 213, 242, 249, 254, 257, 259, 261, 263, 272, 281, 308, 309, 310; Europa and, 13-31; Temple of, 110
Zeus Acraeus, 215
Zeus Laphystius, 214
Zu, 246

88066

DF
220
N45

NICHOLS, MARIANNE
    MAN, MYTH, AND MONUMENT.

DATE DUE
